HISTORIC PHOTOS OF
ST. PETERSBURG

TEXT AND CAPTIONS BY ANDREW N. EDEL

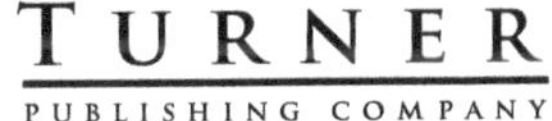

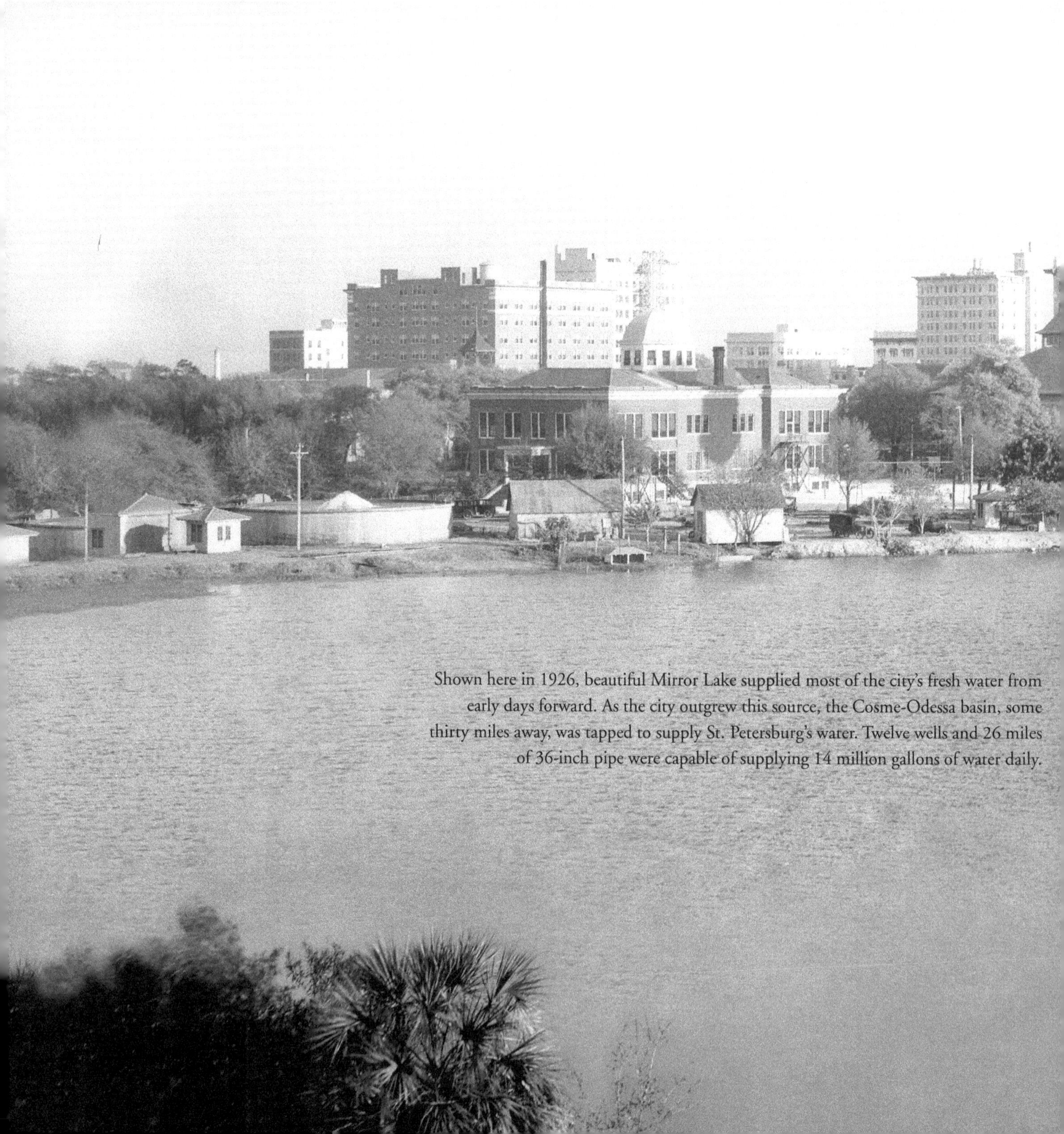

Shown here in 1926, beautiful Mirror Lake supplied most of the city's fresh water from early days forward. As the city outgrew this source, the Cosme-Odessa basin, some thirty miles away, was tapped to supply St. Petersburg's water. Twelve wells and 26 miles of 36-inch pipe were capable of supplying 14 million gallons of water daily.

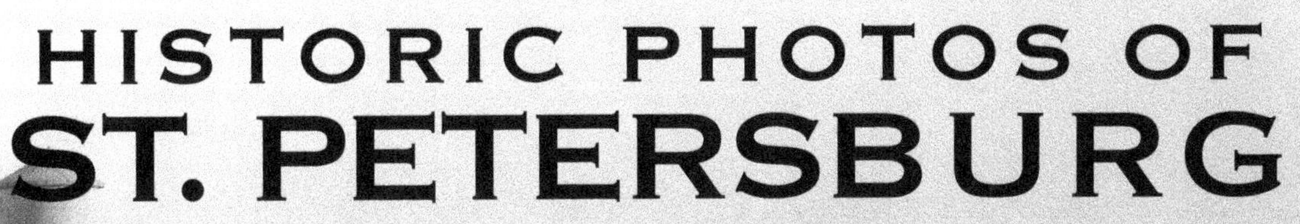

HISTORIC PHOTOS OF ST. PETERSBURG

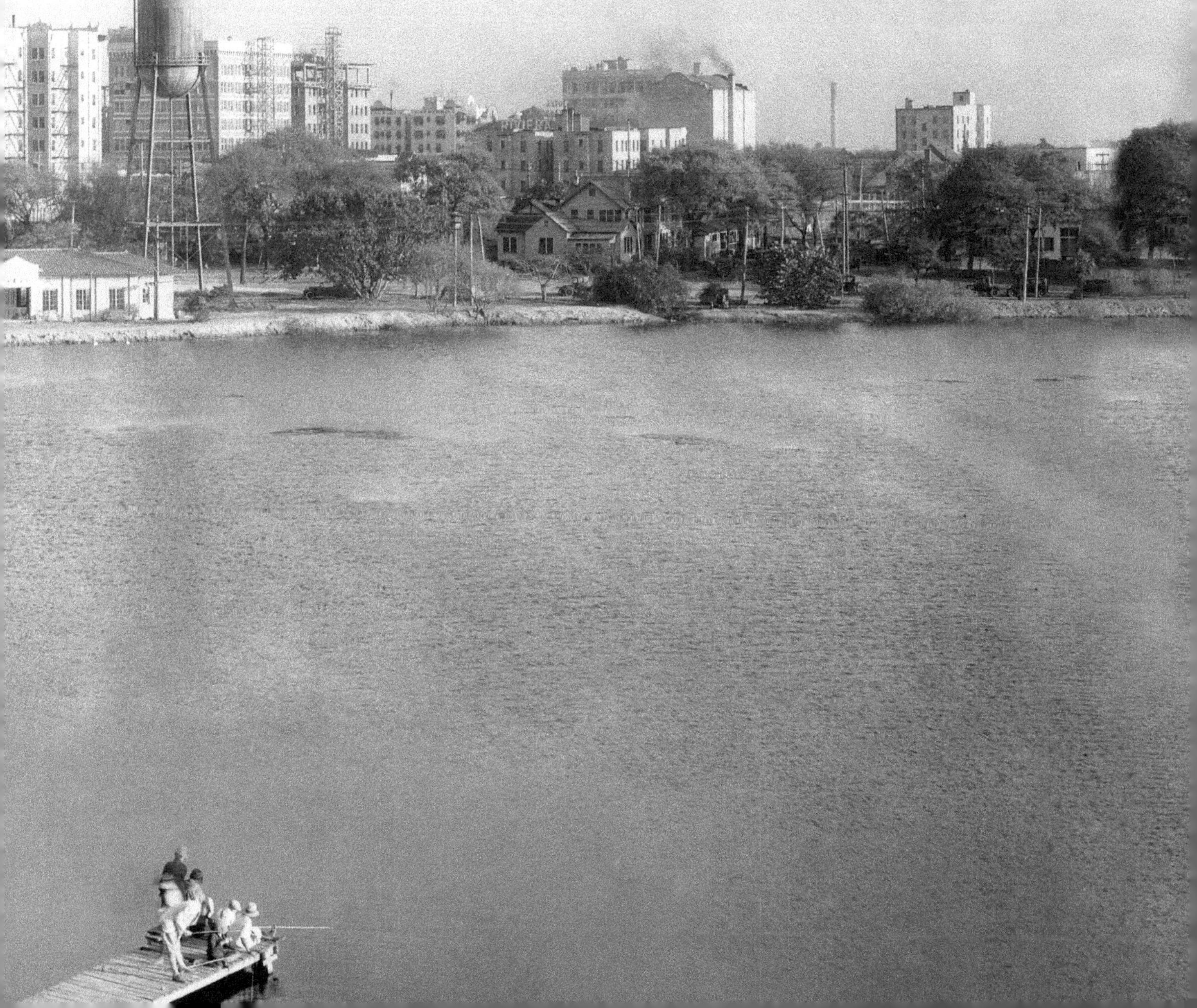

Turner Publishing Company
www.turnerpublishing.com

Historic Photos of St. Petersburg

Library of Congress Control Number: 2007938664

ISBN-13: 978-1-59652-423-1

Printed in the United States of America

ISBN 978-1-68336-999-8 (hc)

Contents

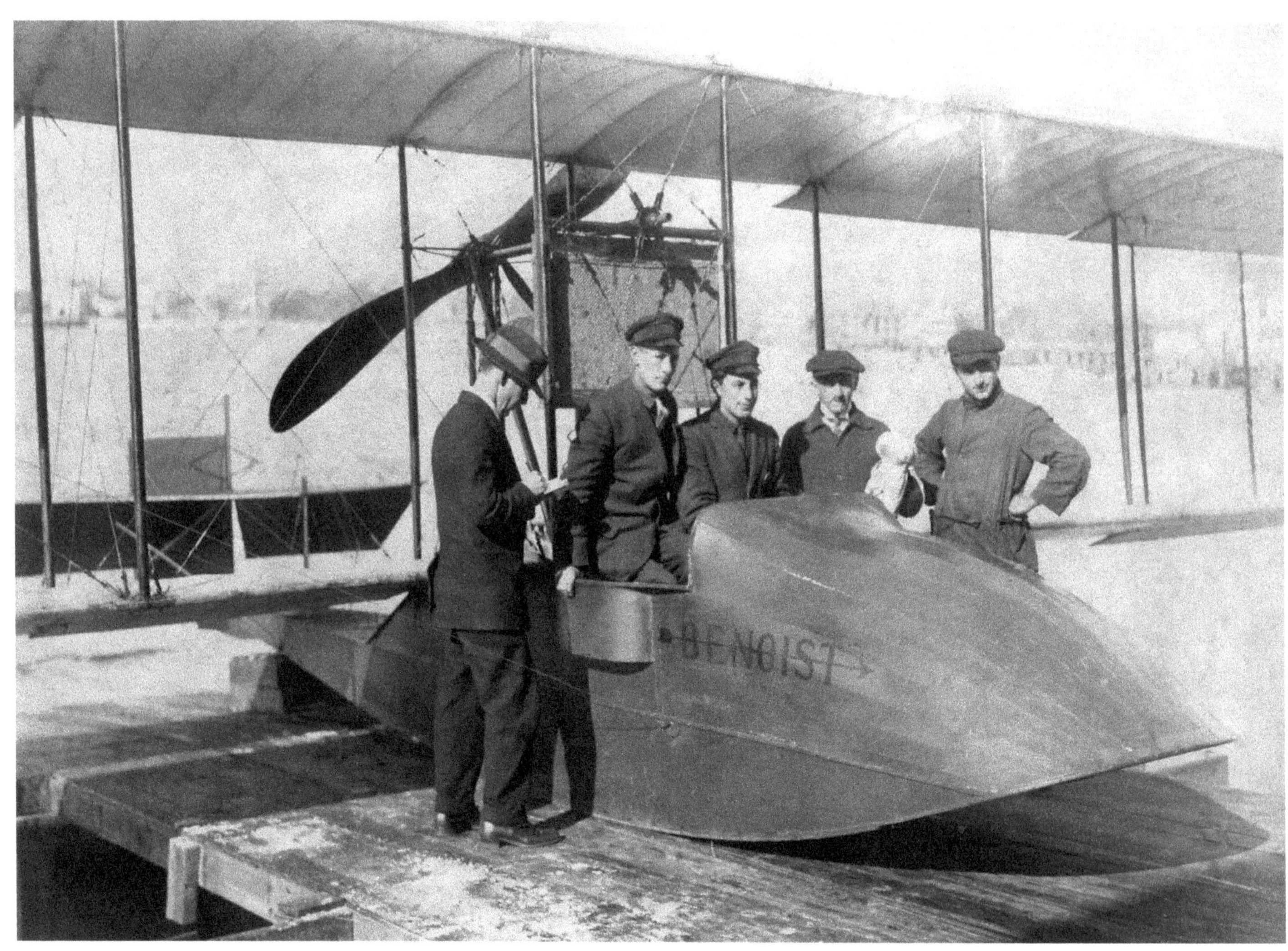

Tom Benoist's Type XIII flying boat merged the wings, tail, and engine of his Type XII airplane to a boat-hull style fuselage. Percy Fansler proposed to Benoist to use flying boats for an airline service between St. Petersburg and Tampa. Fansler arranged the financial support while Benoist built an improved flying boat, the larger Type XIV.

Acknowledgments

This volume, *Historic Photos of St. Petersburg,* is the result of the cooperation and efforts of many individuals and organizations. It is with great thanks that we acknowledge the valuable contribution of the following for their generous support:

Library of Congress
St. Petersburg Museum of History
State Archives of Florida

Preface

The photographic history of St. Petersburg is well documented thanks in large part to the founding of the St. Petersburg Historical Society in 1920. Numerous books with historic photographs of St. Petersburg have been published, thousands of area photographs are available online at the Florida Photographic Archives, and thousands of additional photographs are on websites. Why another book of historic photographs of St. Petersburg?

There are two compelling reasons. First, because of the sheer numbers of extant photographs, even those familiar with the city's history will likely find new images. Those unfamiliar with the city's past will get a fresh glimpse into the rich photographic history of the community. Second, in addition to its unique compilation of photographs, every book offers its own focus of interest and commentary on each photograph included. The focus of this volume is on the development of St. Petersburg through the drive, spirit, and optimism of its citizens, allowing the viewer to visually experience the continuity of St. Petersburg's past and present. As one of the nation's largest metropolitan areas, St. Petersburg is a growing and vibrant city still luring thousands of tourists annually. For all those newcomers and tourists wishing to discover more about St. Petersburg, the goal of this work is to provide some insight and perspective about its traditions, history, people, and culture.

The photographs are from the Florida Photographic Collection of the State Archives of Florida, the St. Petersburg Historical Society, and the Library of Congress.With the exception of cropping images where needed and touching up imperfections that have accrued over time, no other changes have been made. The caliber and clarity of many photographs are limited by the technology of the day and the ability of the photographer at the time they were made.

Individually, these photographs offer an unspoiled glimpse of another place and time along with informative text about specific elements, prompting the viewer to draw his own insights and interpretations. Arranged in chronological order, the individual photographs merge into a collective history of the various aspects of the community's challenges, growth, and development. This collection is organized into four broad periods of time, each with a summary providing a background of the period and historical context for the images. In each era the selection of photographs together with the captions and introduction provide a broad perspective on the development of St. Petersburg. Various aspects are traced from period to period focusing on the economy, civic improvements, education, state government, and social trends. The photographs for section One, "Sunrise," span the initial founding and growth of the town to 1918. Section Two, "Sunny Skies," covers the boom years and its tremendous impact on city development. Section Three, "Overcast," deals with the subsequent bust in 1926 and moves into the years of the Great Depression. The last section, "Clearing Skies," starts with World War II and chronicles the postwar boom up to the mid 1970s.

Throughout the years St. Petersburg has prospered in large part owing to its successful crafting of an image as a city of sunshine. Since its inception it has profited from nationwide publicity and promotions designed to attract tourists and new residents. The image portrayed is not imaginary—the city is justifiably proud of its natural beauty and climate, the hospitable and friendly residents, and its rich cultural resources—but the dream and the reality are not always synonymous. Like any American city, the city has faced its share of challenges—control of growth, public financing, the struggle for civil rights, environmental concerns. As a resort community, the city has also had to cope with a fluctuating economy. In Nathaniel Hawthorne's classic short story "The Great Stone Face," a young boy grows to emulate the positive personal characteristics that he has projected onto a local geological feature. Similarly, St. Petersburg has developed by trying to live up to its own image, trying to be the perfect city it has promoted. Perhaps it will always fall just short of the goal, but at the same time it will always aspire to be the "Sunshine City."

Commissioned in 1960 by MGM for the 1962 movie *Mutiny on the Bounty* with Marlon Brando, the *Bounty* was docked here from the 1960s through the mid 1980s. The oceangoing, 180-foot-long, 420-ton H.M.S. *Bounty* is a faithful re-creation of the original ship, constructed from drawings still on file in the British admiralty archives.

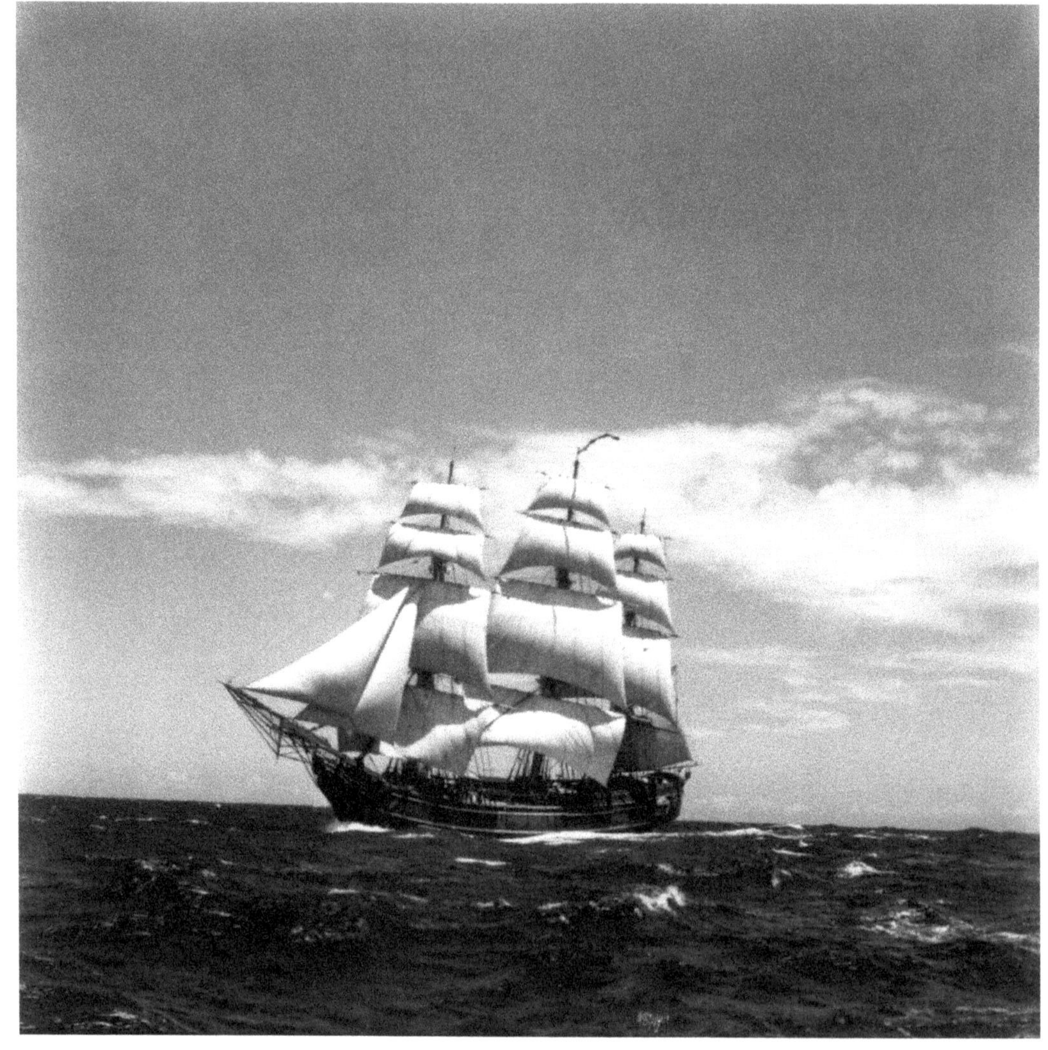

Sunrise: The Founding of the Sunshine City (1888–1918)

By the late nineteenth century the lower Pinellas peninsula was still undeveloped land, with a few pioneer inhabitants. There were no towns, no railroads, and no notable history except for the occasional explorers, Native Americans, or military unit generally moving through the area. This would change when a railroad looking for a town site, met someone with a town site looking for a railroad. Peter Demens' rickety Orange Belt Railway working its way from Lake Apopka needed a destination on the Gulf, and John C. Williams, after relocating to Florida with plans for founding a city, had lots of Tampa Bay property. The two met and a contract was signed. The railroad would receive half of a 500-acre town site, while the town would receive a wharf, hotel, and depot. The new town was named after Peter Demens' Russian hometown, St. Petersburg, and the hotel was named after Williams' hometown, Detroit. The railway workers soon completed a Russian-style train depot, a forty-room hotel large enough to house the entire town, and a huge wharf more than half a mile long to carry the railroad tracks to the steamers in the bay. The day the first train pulled into the fledgling town on June 8, 1888, the beginning of St. Petersburg was under way.

The little town faced the usual problems of new communities in America, with little law and less order. Livestock roamed the rough streets, sidewalks and utilities did not exist, and tension mounted between those who wanted to raise their glasses and those who wanted to raise a family. Eventually these problems were solved and the town started to grow, at first settled by railroad workers and a few shopkeepers. The community's main problem remained finding an economic base to ensure future development.

The answer was simple—the town would sell itself. Indeed, the town possessed a great climate in a beautiful outdoor setting, modern transportation linking it to large population centers, and lots of undeveloped real estate—everything needed for a perfect resort community. Frederick Davis, Edwin Tomlinson, and other civic leaders motivated the town to prepare itself as a winter resort through self-promotion and by building a modern infrastructure. Within twenty years the town had electricity, telephones, paved roads, new schools, modern utilities, and a trolley line. Mayor Lew Brown's nickname "Sunshine City" became the focus for advertising campaigns. As the railroad was absorbed by larger lines, it too was improved, enabling it to contribute its services to the town's growth. Steamers, like the *H. B. Plant* and the *Manatee,* connected the town to main ocean routes. The city even started the world's first commercial airport. The growing paused while the nation went to war in 1917-18, but afterward it was ready to resume. The little whistle-stop hamlet had grown, and fast—from 273 in the beginning to 14,000 by 1920—but the real growth was about to start.

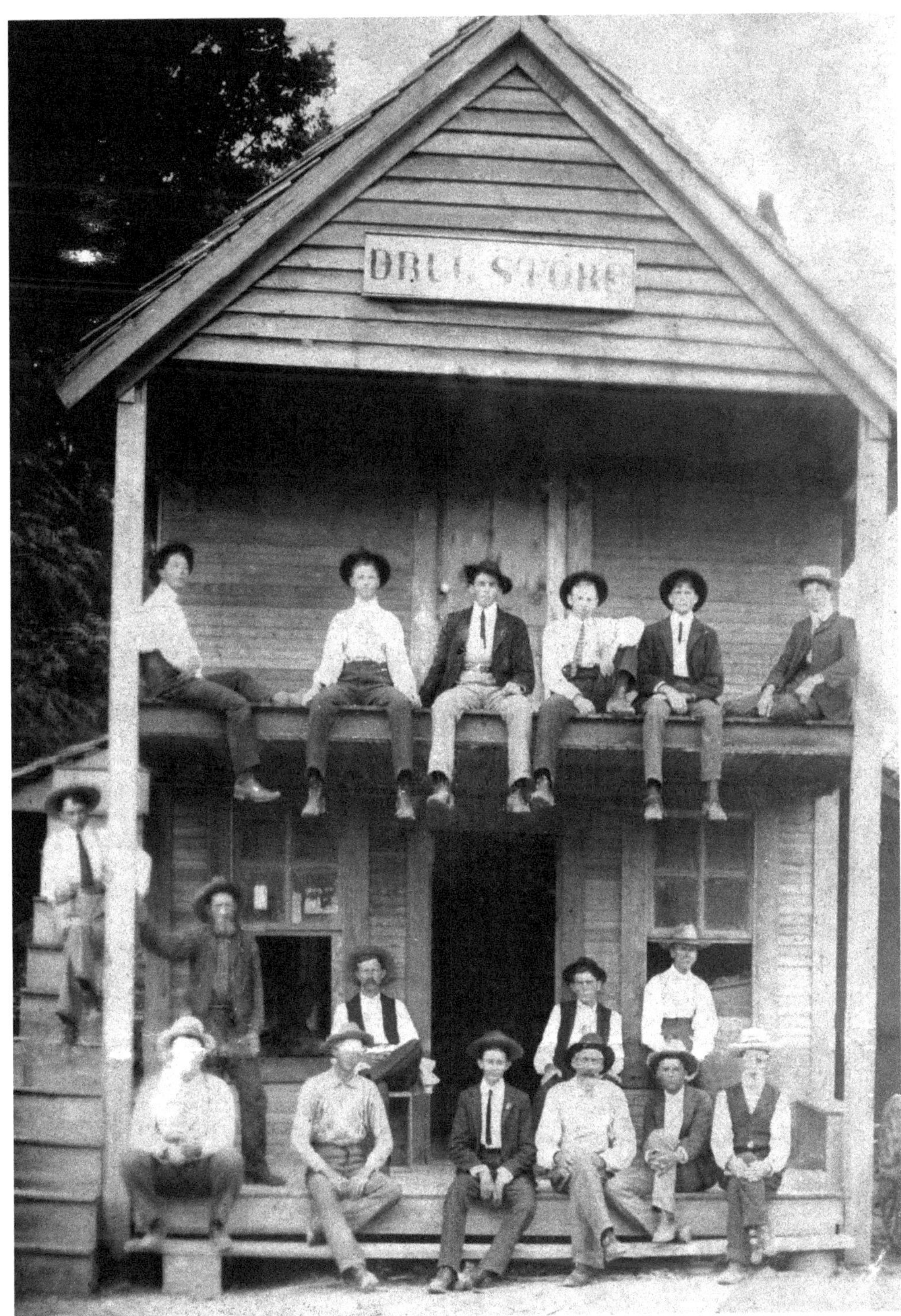

By 1885, the lower Pinellas peninsula remained sparsely settled, and various families owned and had tried unsuccessfully to develop land in what is now St. Petersburg. In 1880 there was one general store and one post office in the hamlet of Big Bayou, and this drugstore. The general store had only $200 worth of items—among them sugar, grits, tobacco, coffee, and flour.

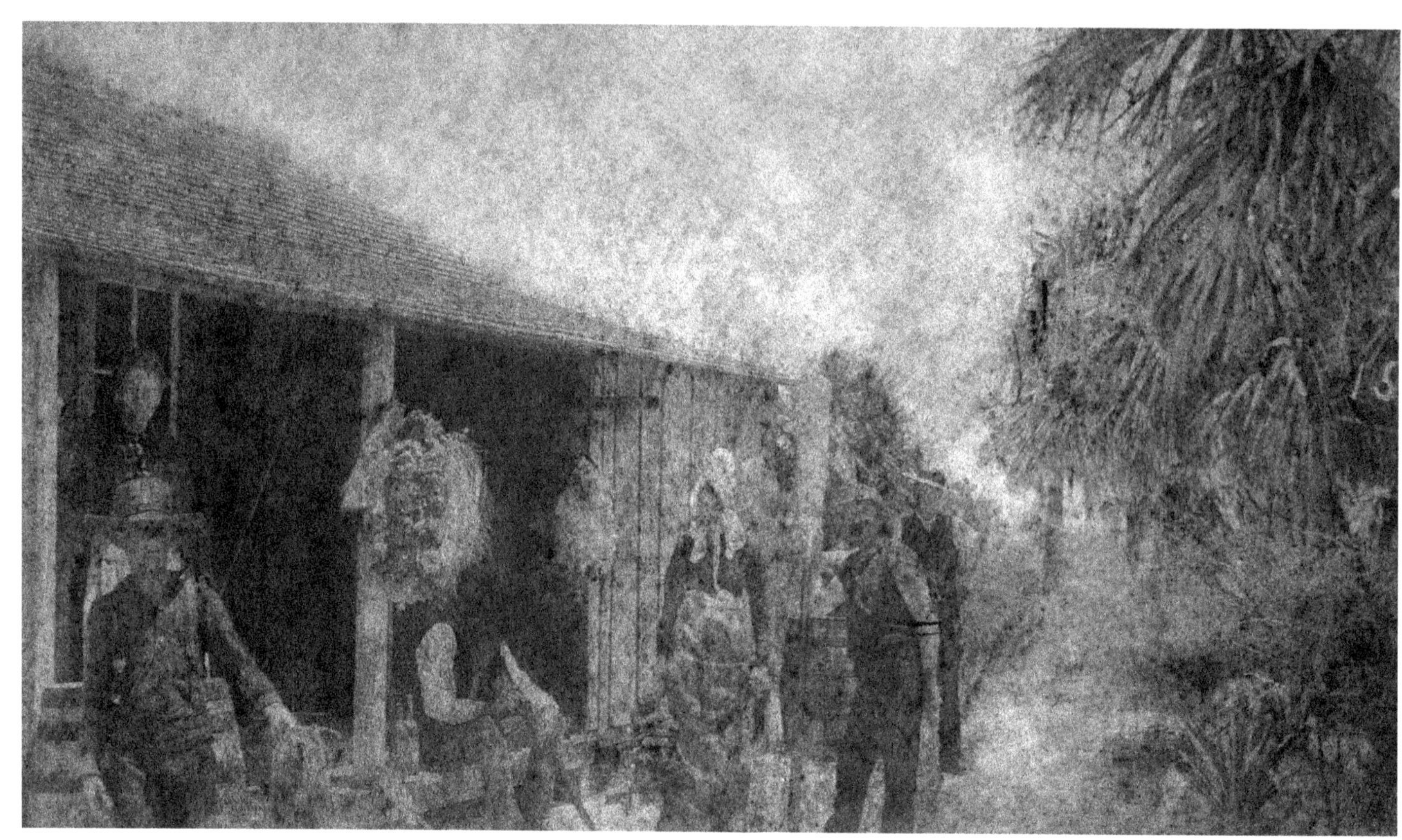

The first post office on the lower Pinellas peninsula was the home of one of the early pioneer families in the area. Established at Big Bayou in 1876, it was named "Pinellas." John A. Bethall served as postmaster for fourteen years, followed by his daughter Mary and then wife Sarah. John later wrote a history of Pinellas.

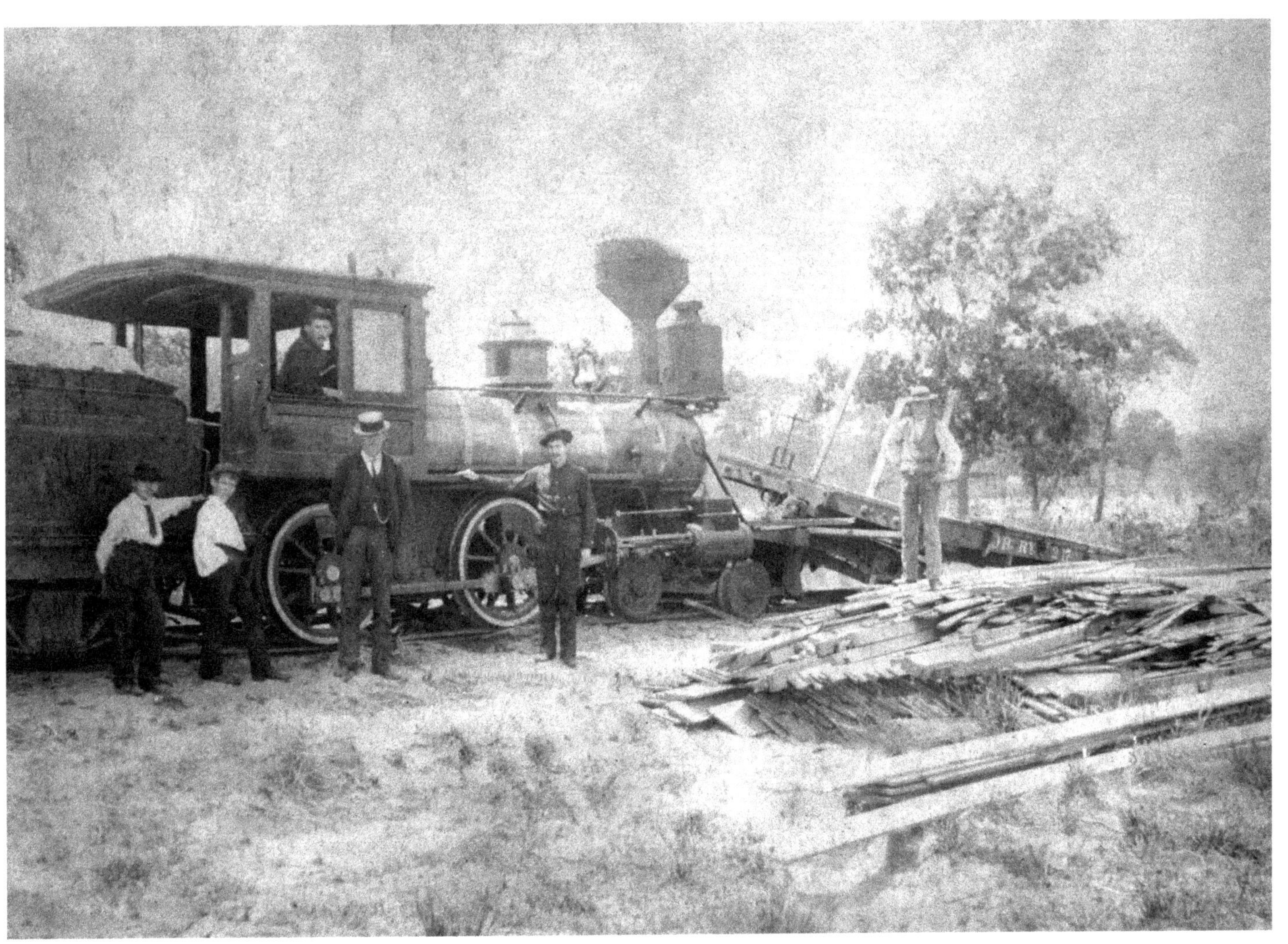

The derailment of the forward truck of an early steam engine and a flatcar prompts a photograph. In 1888 Peter Demens, alias Petrovitch A. Demenscheff, or "that redoubtable Russian hustler," extended the Orange Belt Railway to a point on the Pinellas Coast. A new town was founded at the terminus and named after Demens' birthplace of St. Petersburg, Russia.

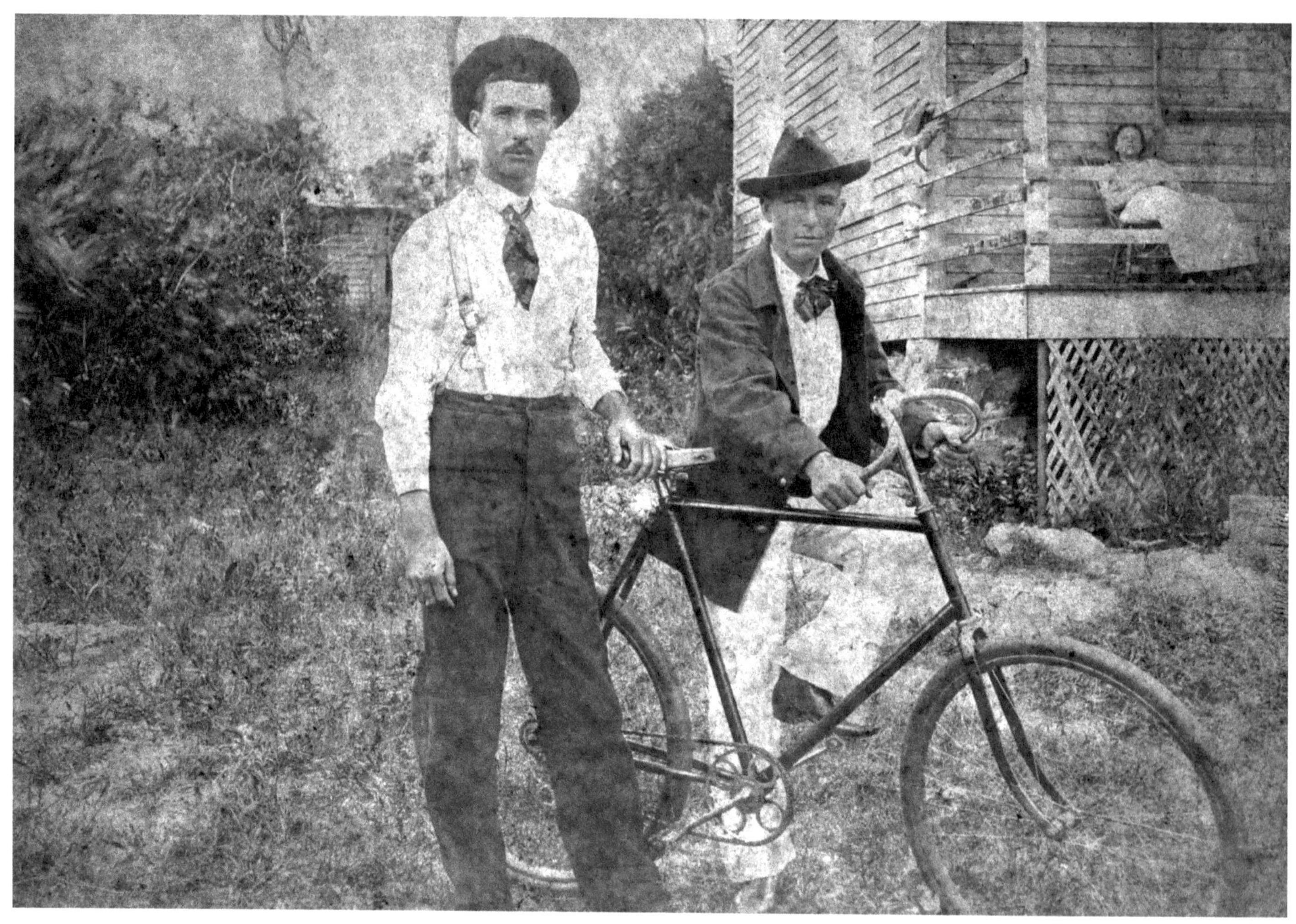

In the 1890s, a popular loop on the pebble phosphate streets wound through the business district around Reservoir (Mirror) Lake and back. Boys and young men on their bicycles competed along this "racetrack." In the evenings, it became a lover's lane as couples followed the same route in a horse and buggy.

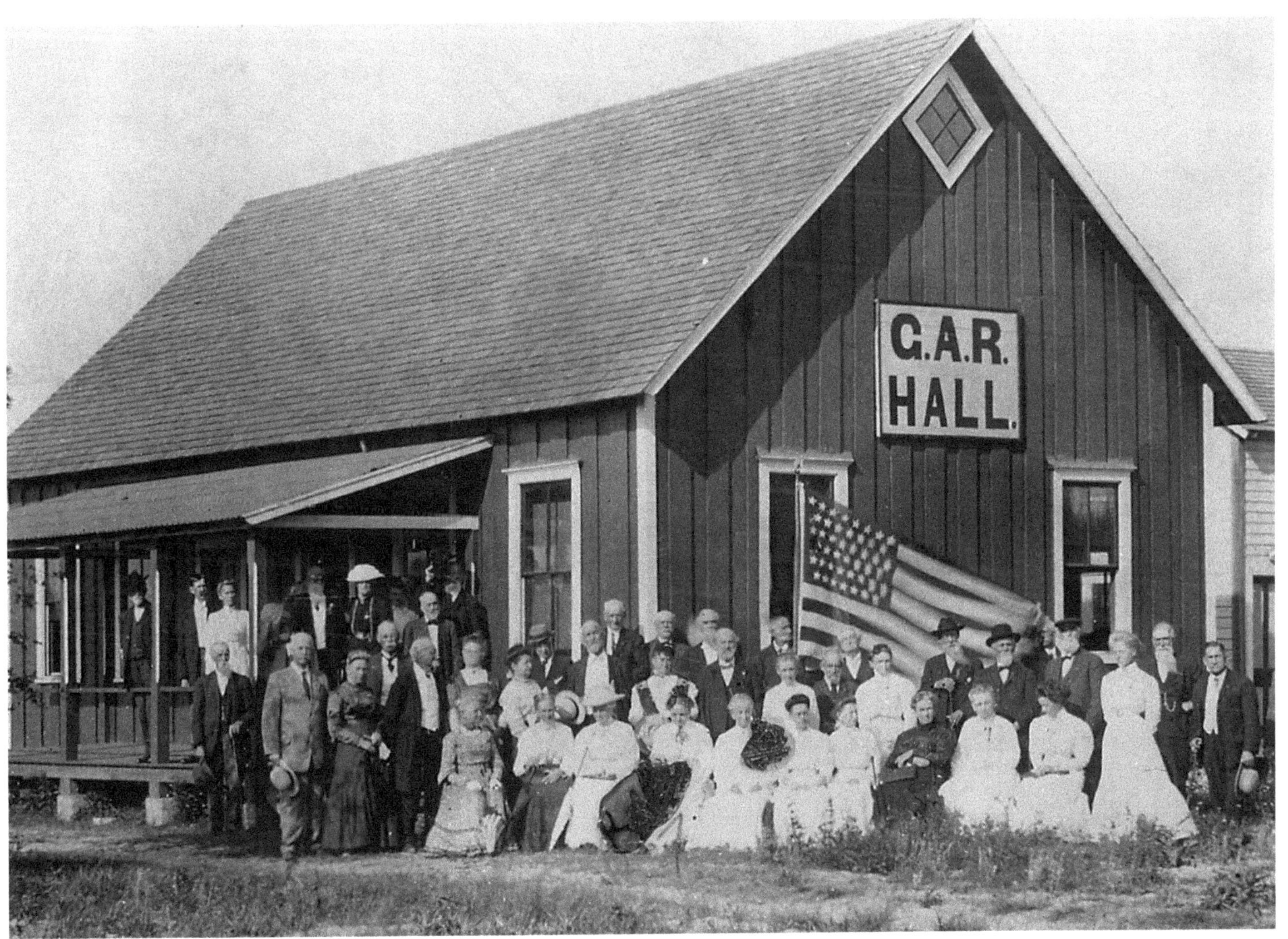

During the Victorian age, it was acceptable for women of poor families to work. Middle-class and upper-class women were expected to perform volunteer activities and church work. One of the first volunteer associations in the new town was the Women's Relief Corps of the Grand Army of the Republic.

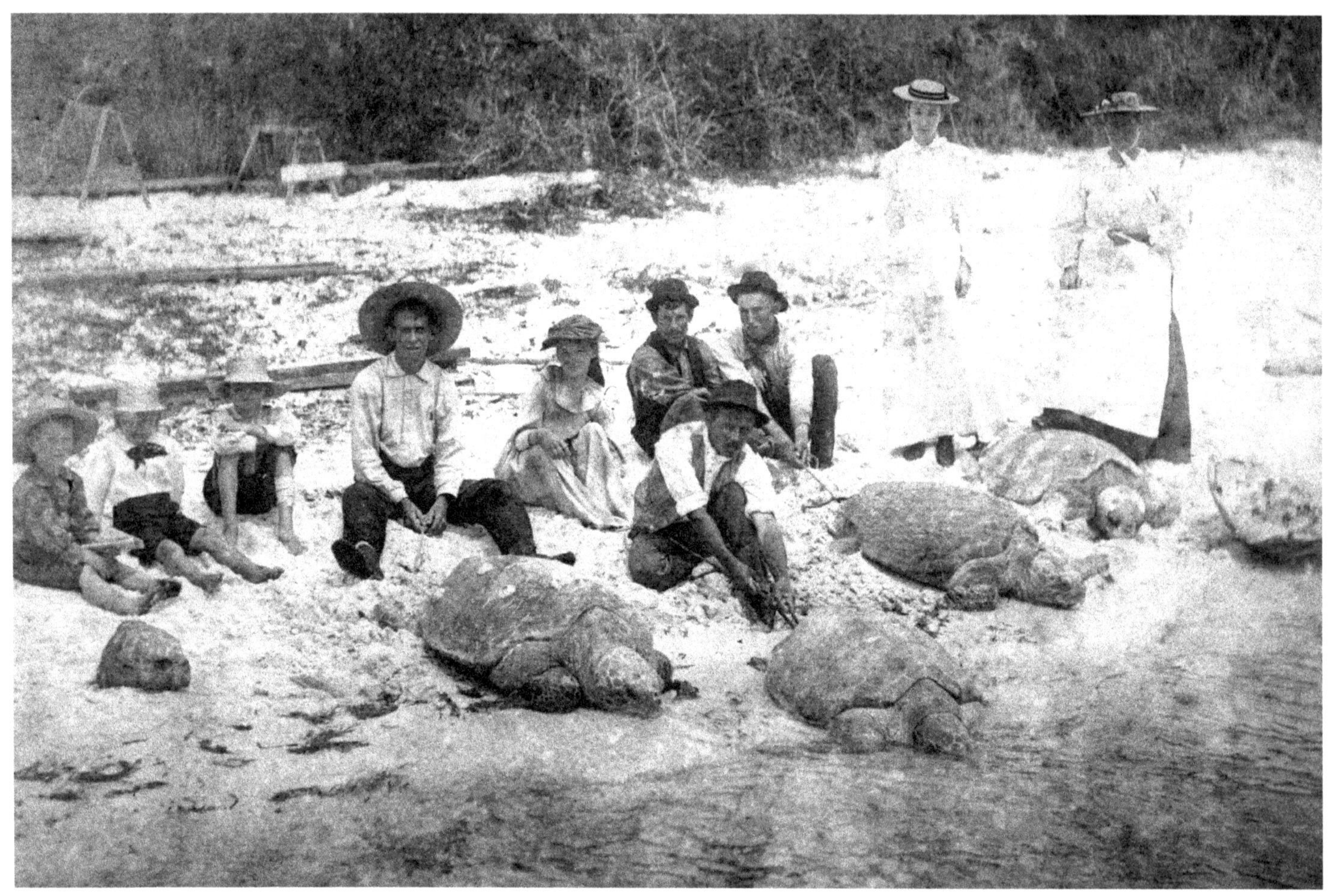

The Orange Belt Railway billed summer excursions to exotic "St. Petersburg-by-the-sea," and the young town gained fame as one of the state's first summer resorts. Tourists from the interior enjoyed the cooler peninsula weather and trips to the beach. Now a protected species, the loggerhead turtle was once highly prized for turtle soup.

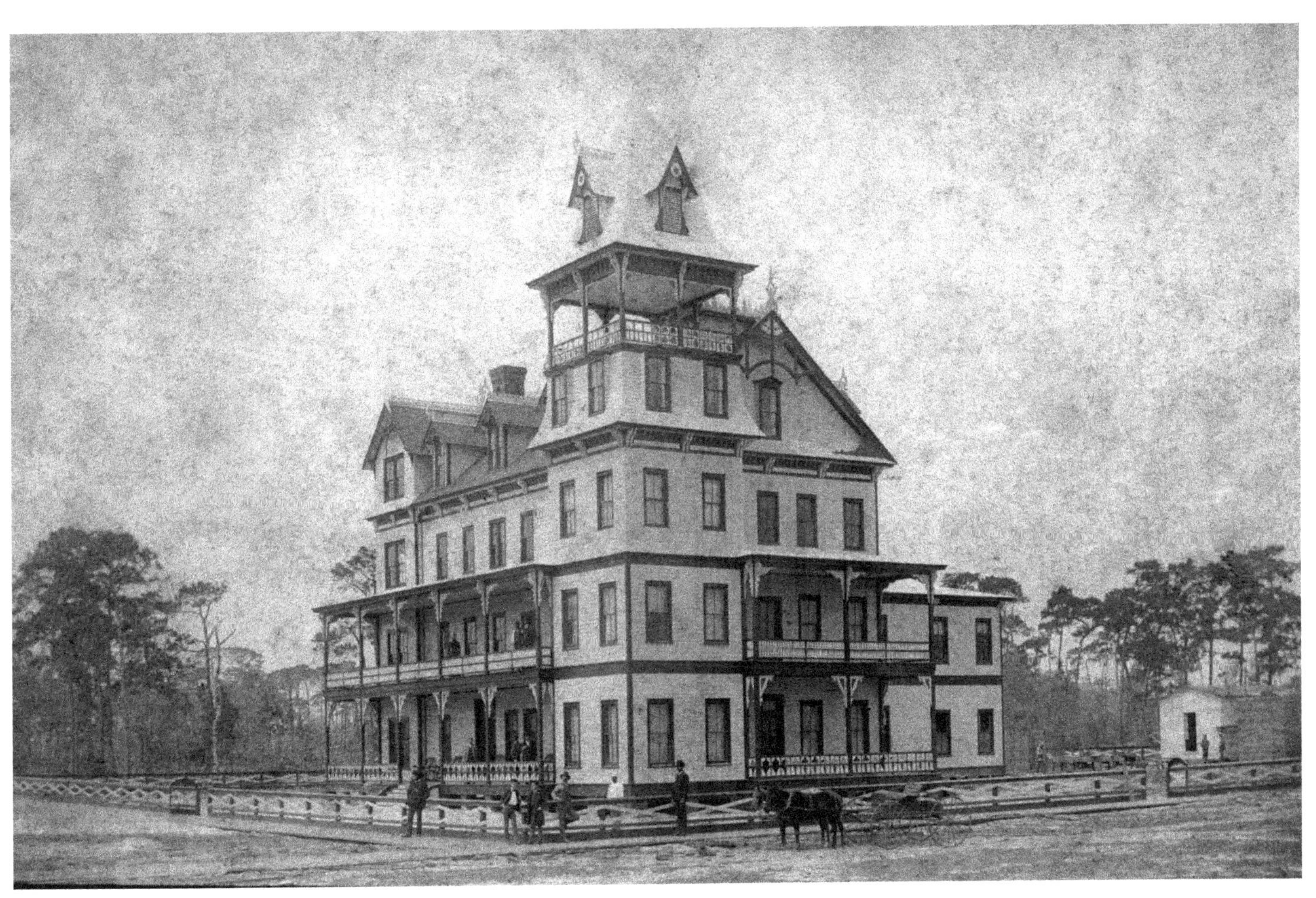

Imposing for a town of only fifty, the Detroit Hotel, named after the hometown of John Williams, was part of the original deal between Williams and Peter Demens that founded St. Petersburg. Built by the Orange Belt Railway, the three-and-a-half-story hotel boasted 40 rooms, a 70-foot tower, and striking views of the bay.

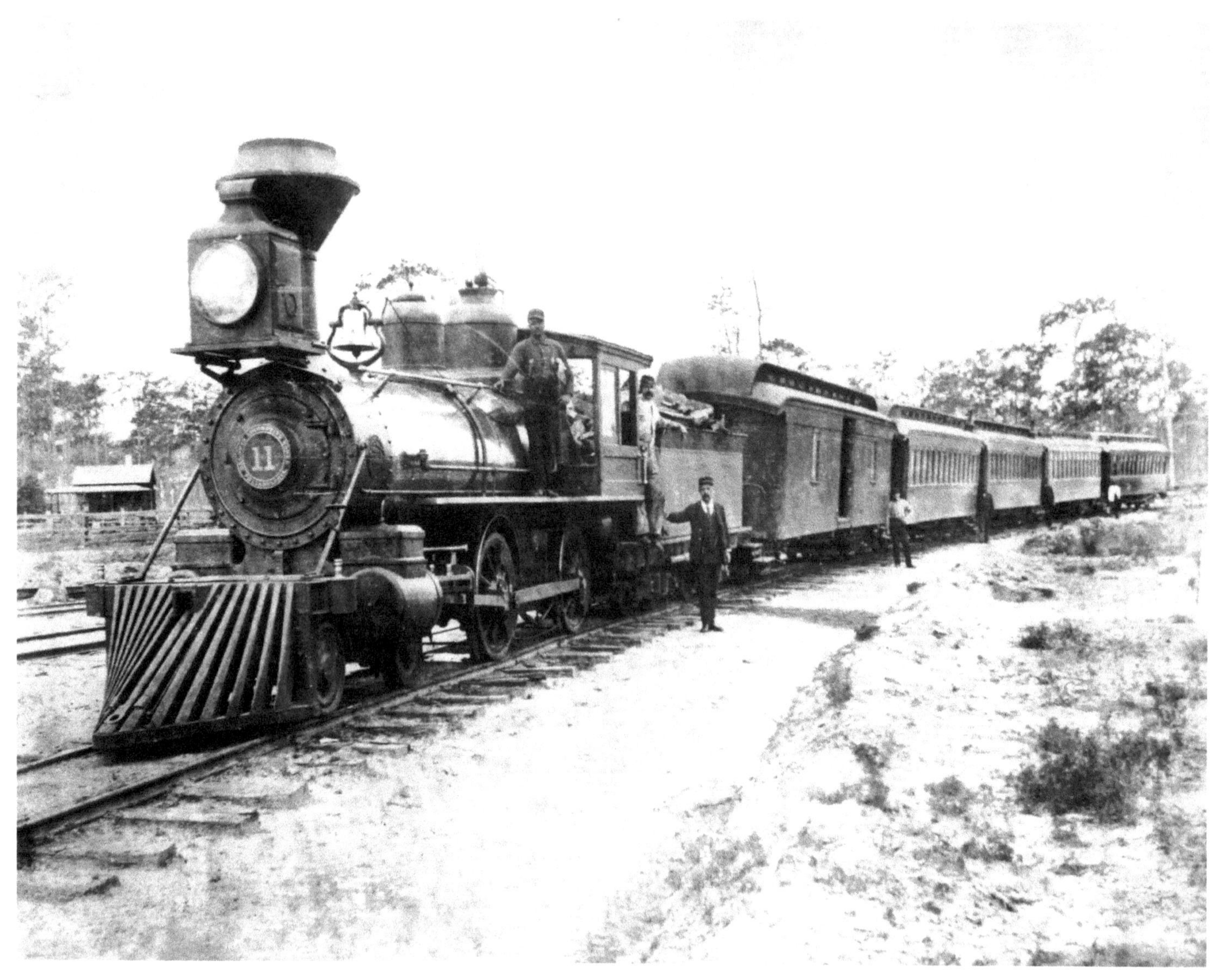

The crew poses with Engine no. 11 of the Sanford & St. Petersburg, part of the Plant line. Henry Plant, prominent Florida railroad owner, leased the financially troubled Orange Belt Railway in 1895. He renamed it and converted the narrow gauge to standard gauge in 1897, permitting an increase of rail traffic from the north.

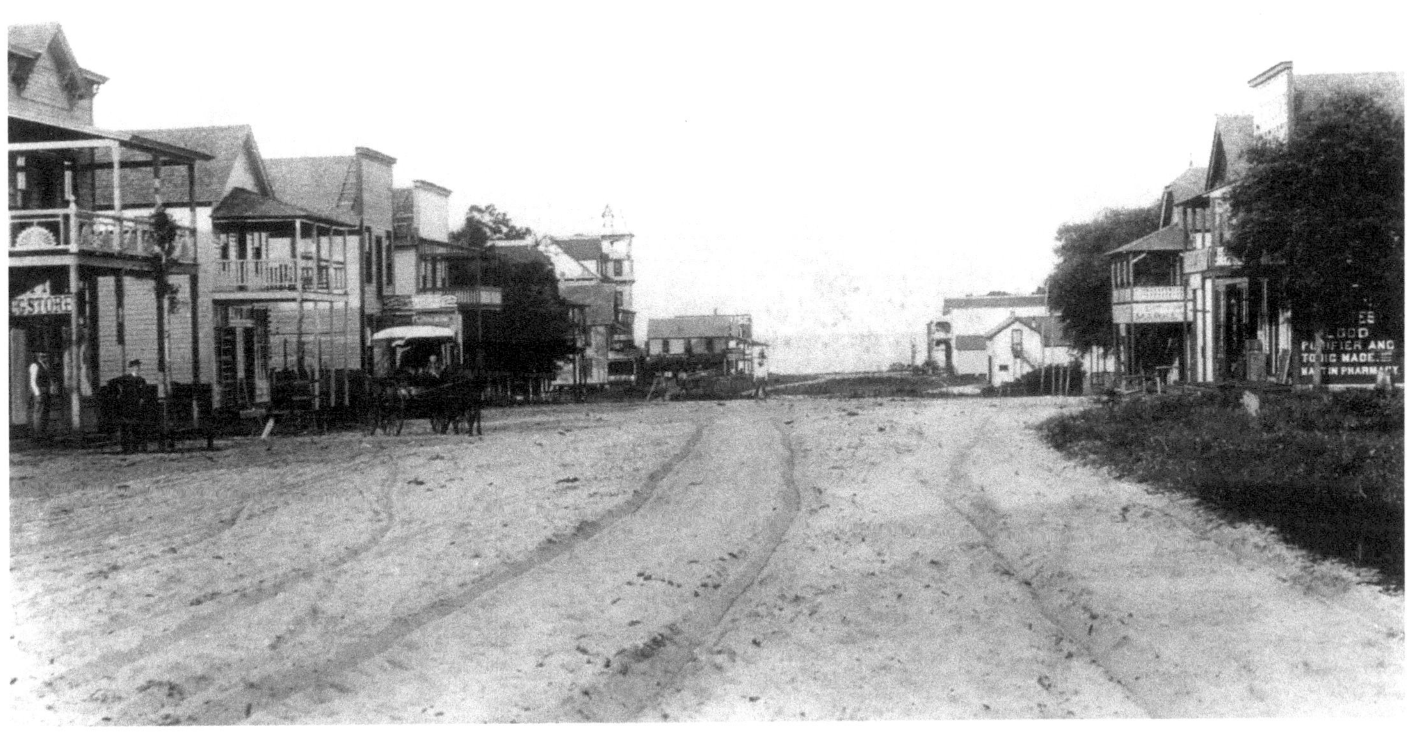

A view east down the 100-foot-wide Sixth Avenue (later renamed Central) in 1897. Like those of all new towns, the early streets were muddy, soggy, and almost impassable. Lacking city funds, St. Petersburg women took the initiative. Raising money through selling lemonade, ice cream, and sundries, they had sidewalks built.

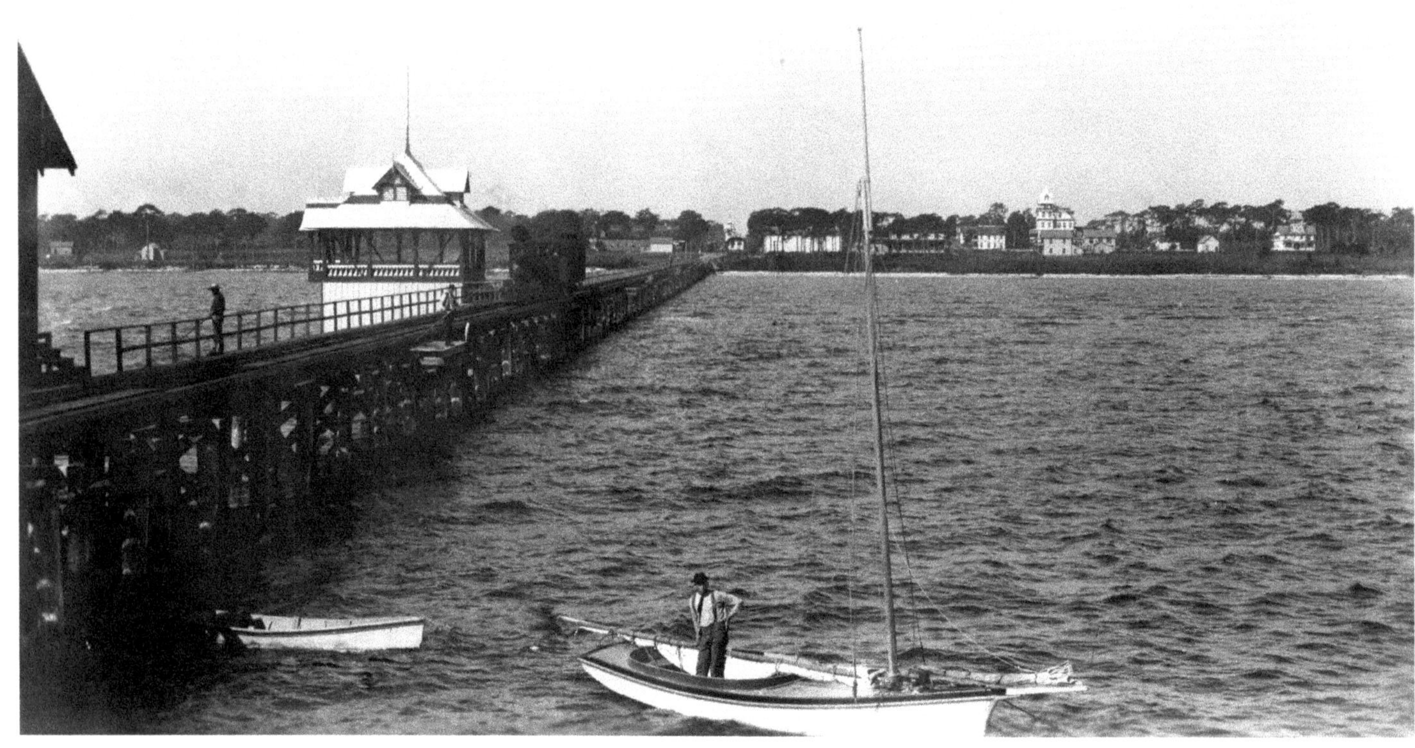

In an effort to attract tourists, the Orange Belt Railway constructed an ornate bathing pavilion on its pier in 1890. The pavilion had a toboggan slide and fresh water showers supplied by an artesian well. According to the *Times,* one feature of the bathhouse was "that you can get a fresh water bath after you take a dip in the briny blue." In this view, a steam engine approaches as fishermen at trackside try their luck.

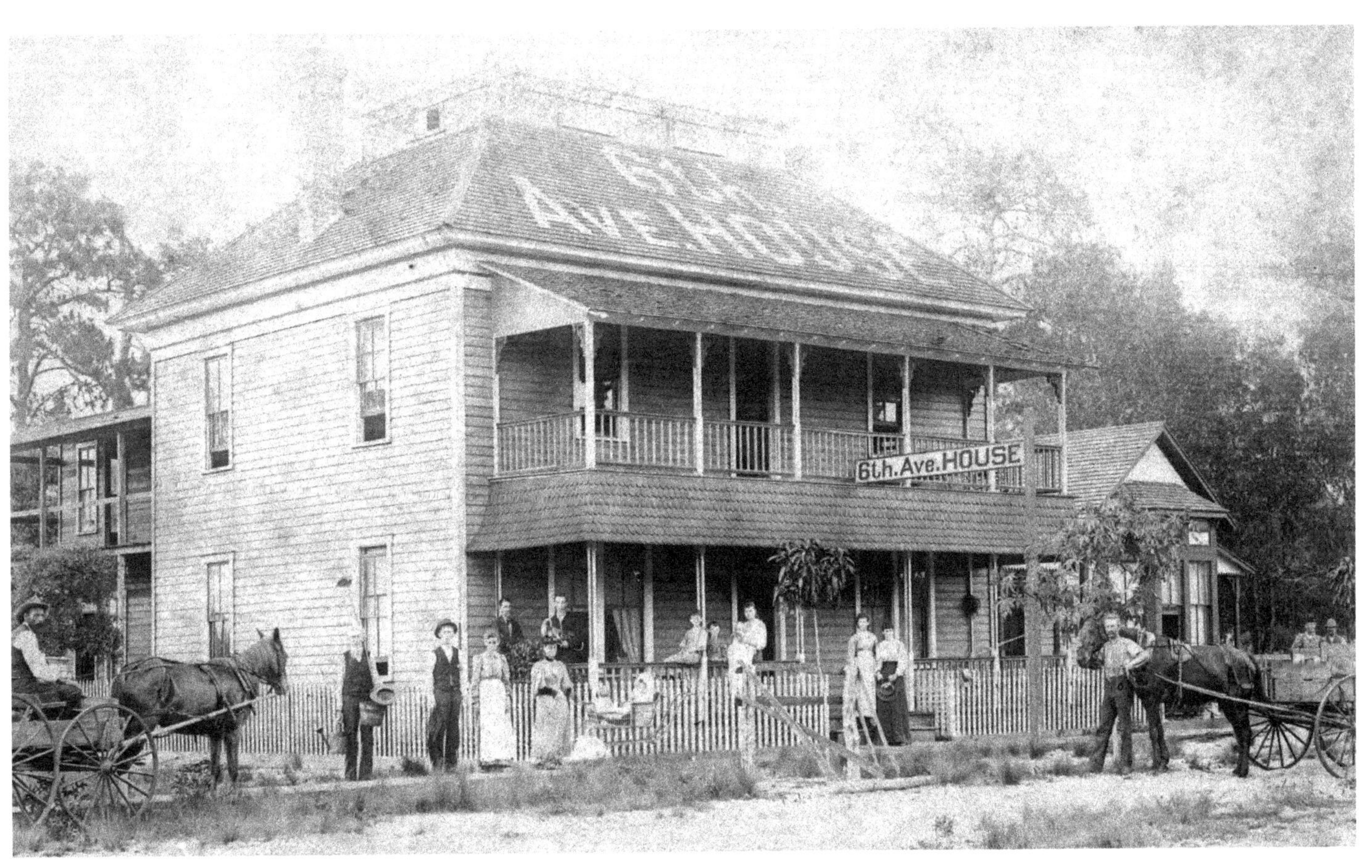

One of the first hotels in town, the popular Sixth Avenue House opened in 1893. George King bought it, remodeled it, and named it the Lakeview House. King advertised it in the *Strand Magazine* in England, stating that "we milk our own milk and lay our own eggs." King sold it in 1902 and it was renamed the Belmont.

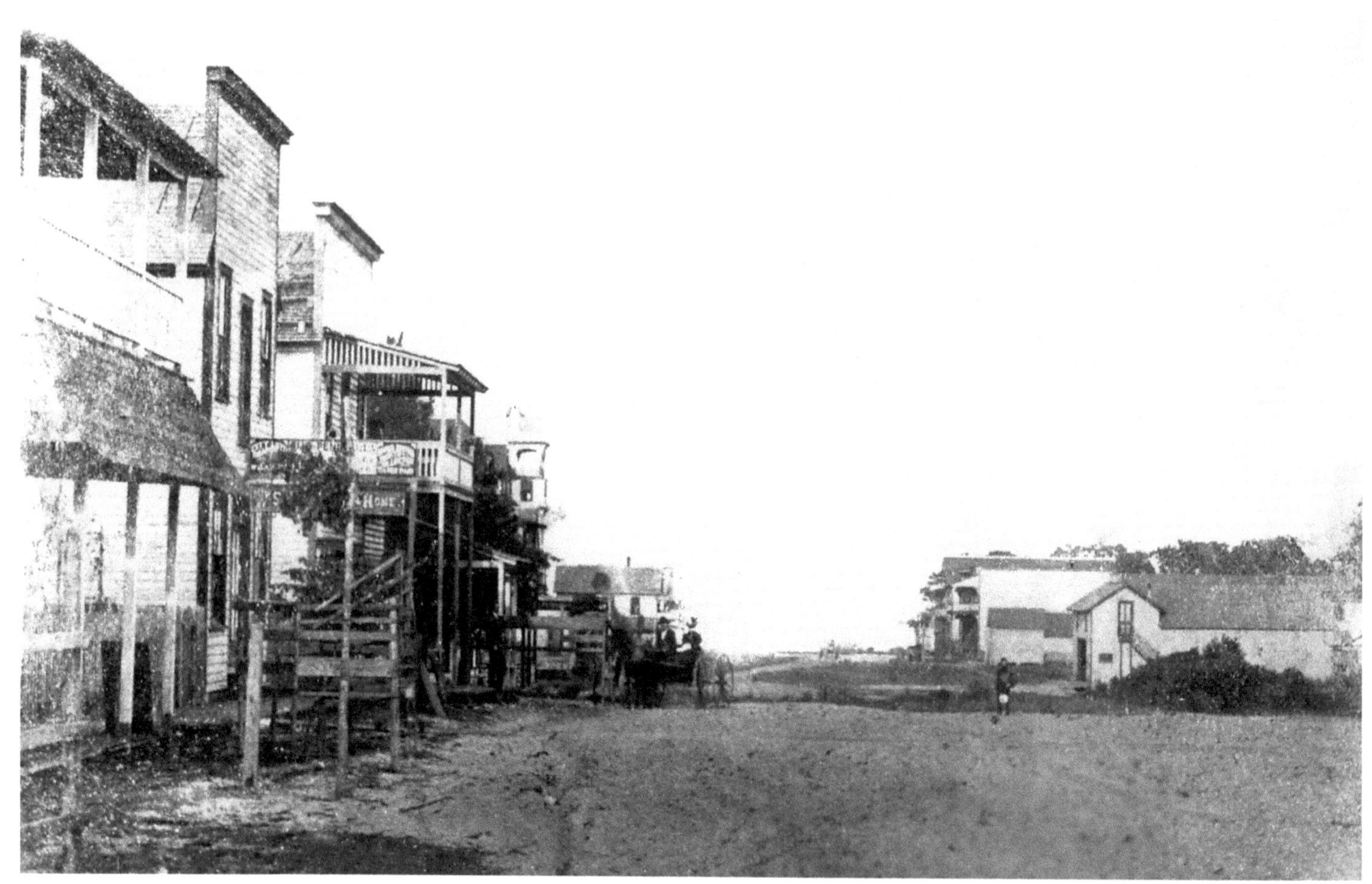

"The Swale," a large low area between Second and Third streets on Central Avenue, essentially became a pond after storms. The first sidewalks had to be raised over it. Borrowing money from the local bank, five city council members used the funds to have the Swale filled in 1894, permitting the east end of Central Avenue to prosper.

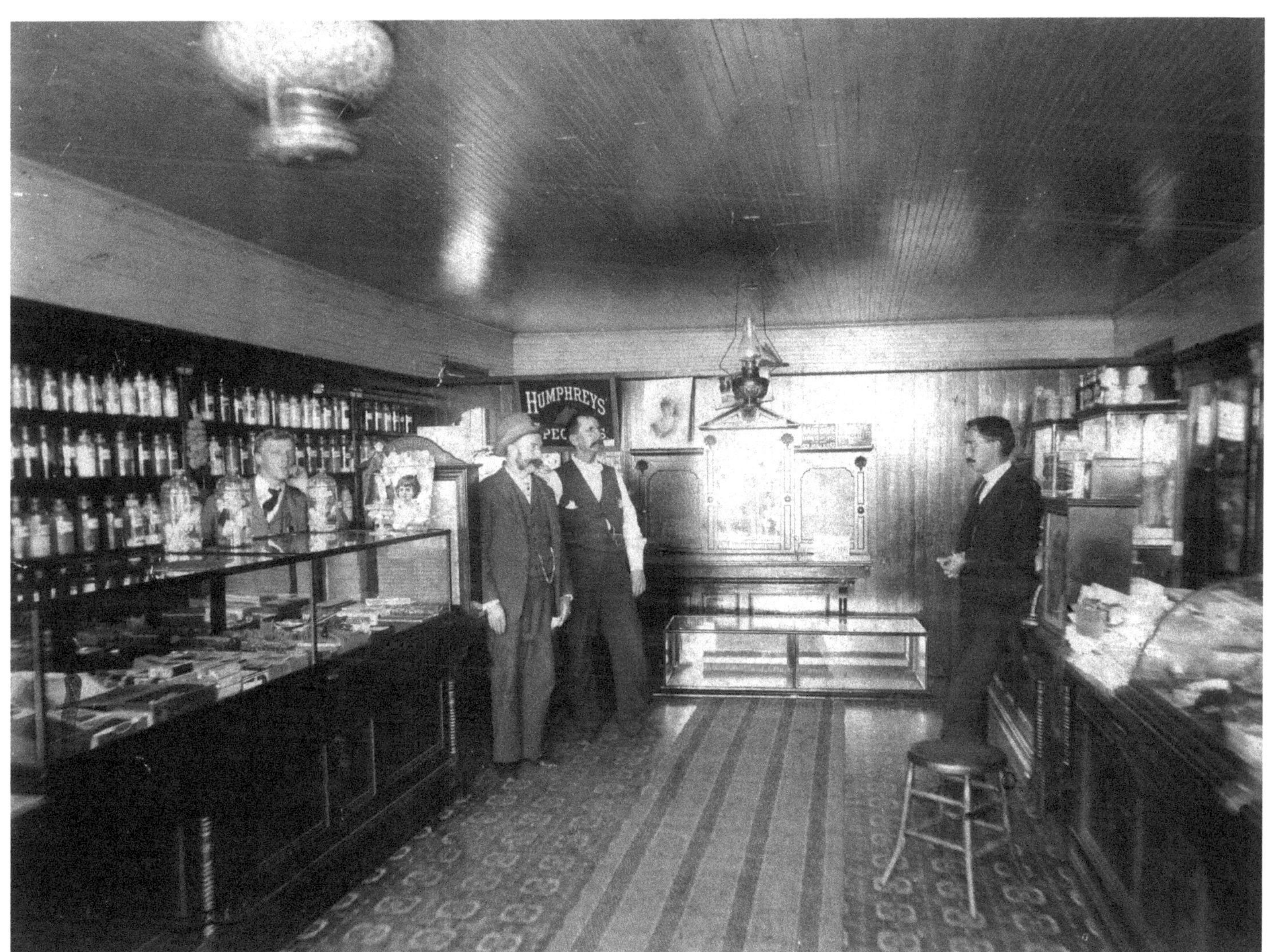

The interior of James G. Bradshaw's Drugstore around 1896. Bradshaw (third from left) served as the city's mayor from 1913 to 1916. The local paper boasted that the young town also had a bicycle shop, a steam laundry, two dairies, a small cigar factory, three general stores, two lawyers, and five doctors, but only one undertaker.

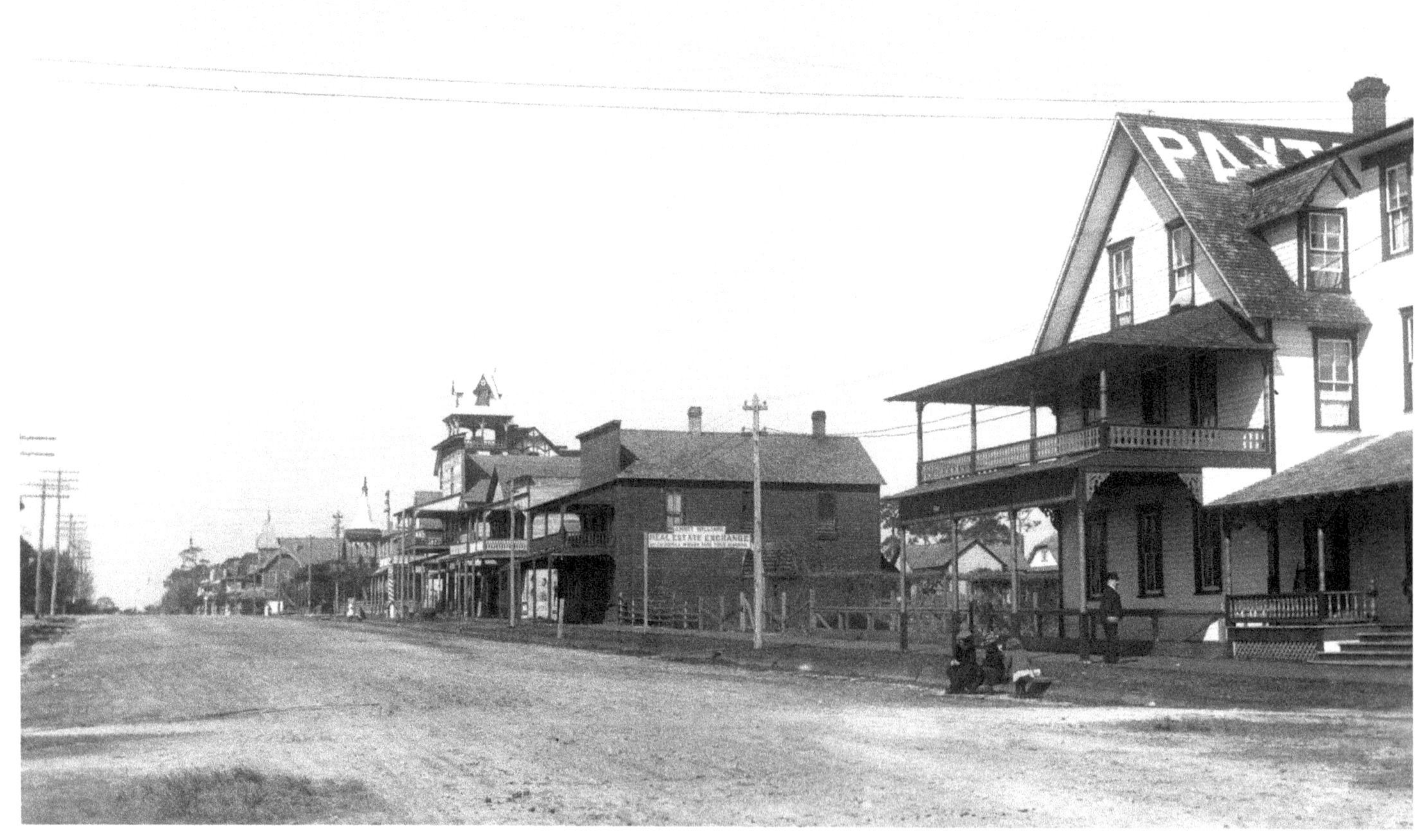

Wires along Central Avenue in 1900 attest to improving utility services. Arthur Norwood installed the first telephone in 1898, linking his two stores. A year later a small local system served 18 phones. The first utilities franchise was granted to Frank A. Davis, and his power plant started generating electricity in 1897.

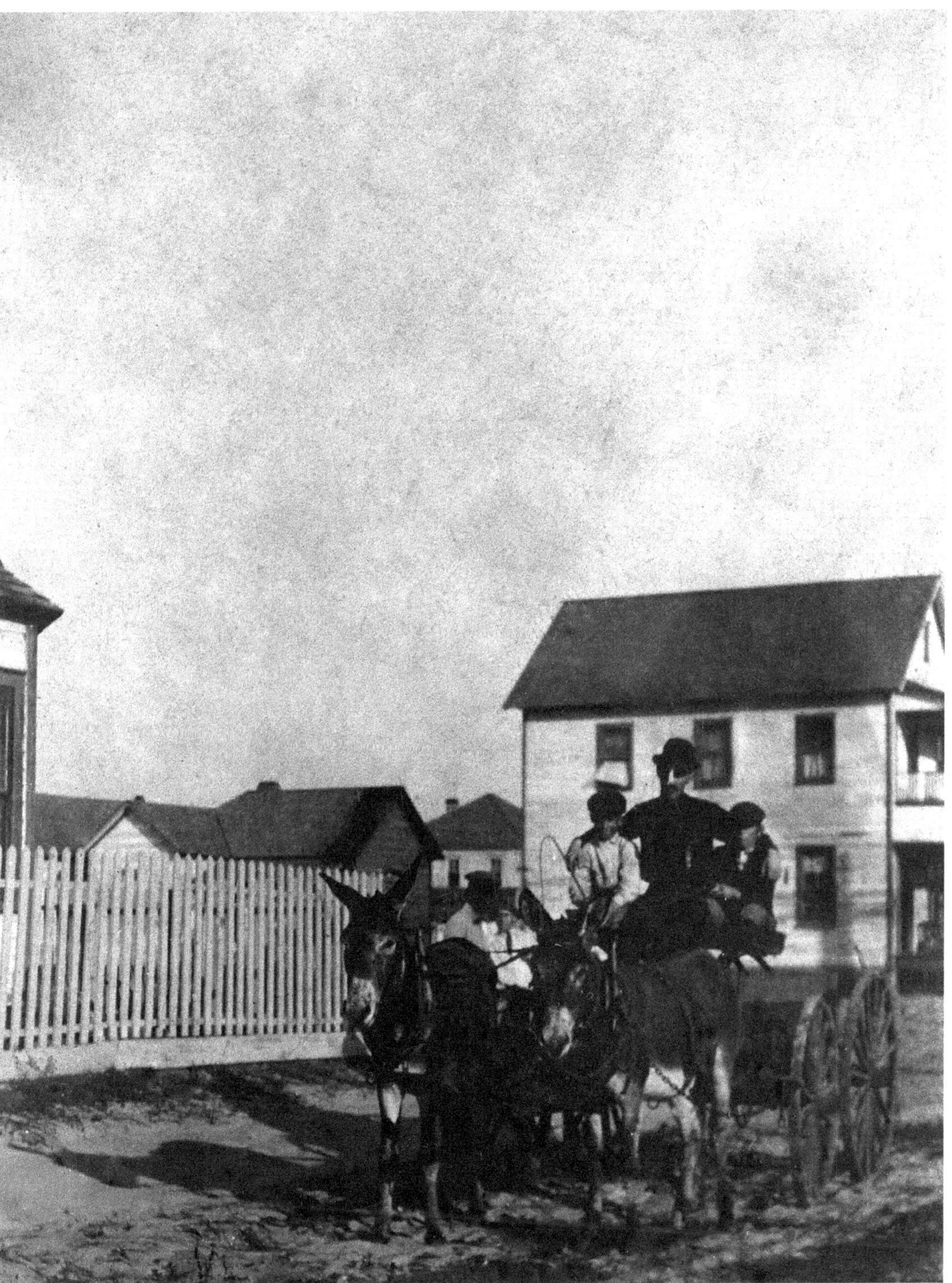

Hubert and Walter Coleman in a mule-drawn wagon. An early passenger in one such conveyance, pulled by a very slow mule, said of the mule, "When hit on the right side he made a graceful curve to the left and when hit on the left side the curve was reversed but in neither event was the speed perceptibly altered."

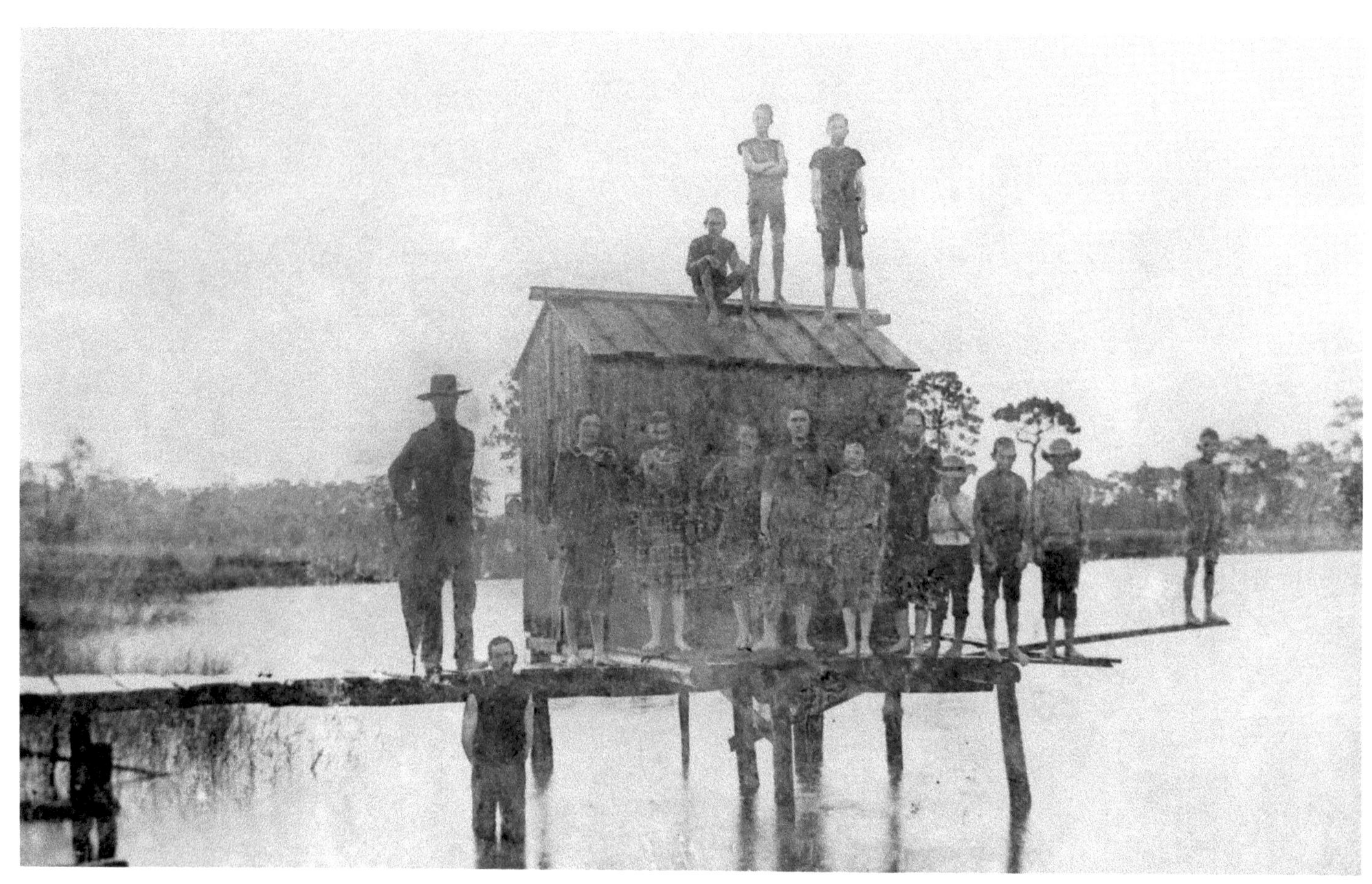

A group of young swimmers pose on a dock on Lake Weir around 1900. Named after the first settler H. A. Weir, who purchased forty acres around the lake in 1876, it was known as Lake Weir for years. Later it was called Reservoir Lake and was the source of water for the first town-owned waterworks in 1899. It was renamed Mirror Lake in 1915.

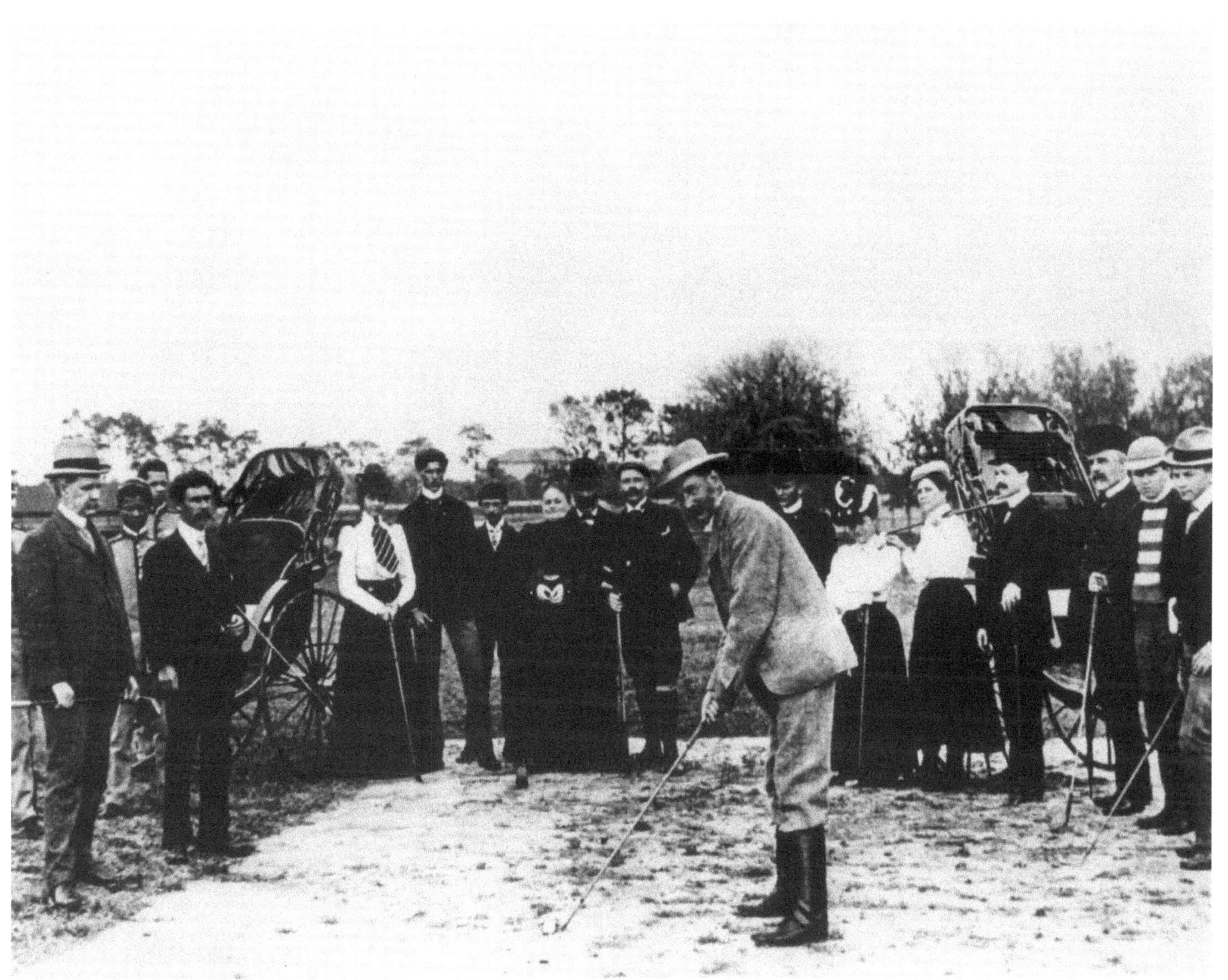

Frustrated by the high prices for waterfront land in St. Petersburg, Henry Plant changed his location for a grand hotel. The luxurious Belleview Hotel opened in Belleaire, south of Clearwater, in 1897. The Belleview's original nine-hole golf course had sand greens, but later added Florida's first grass greens.

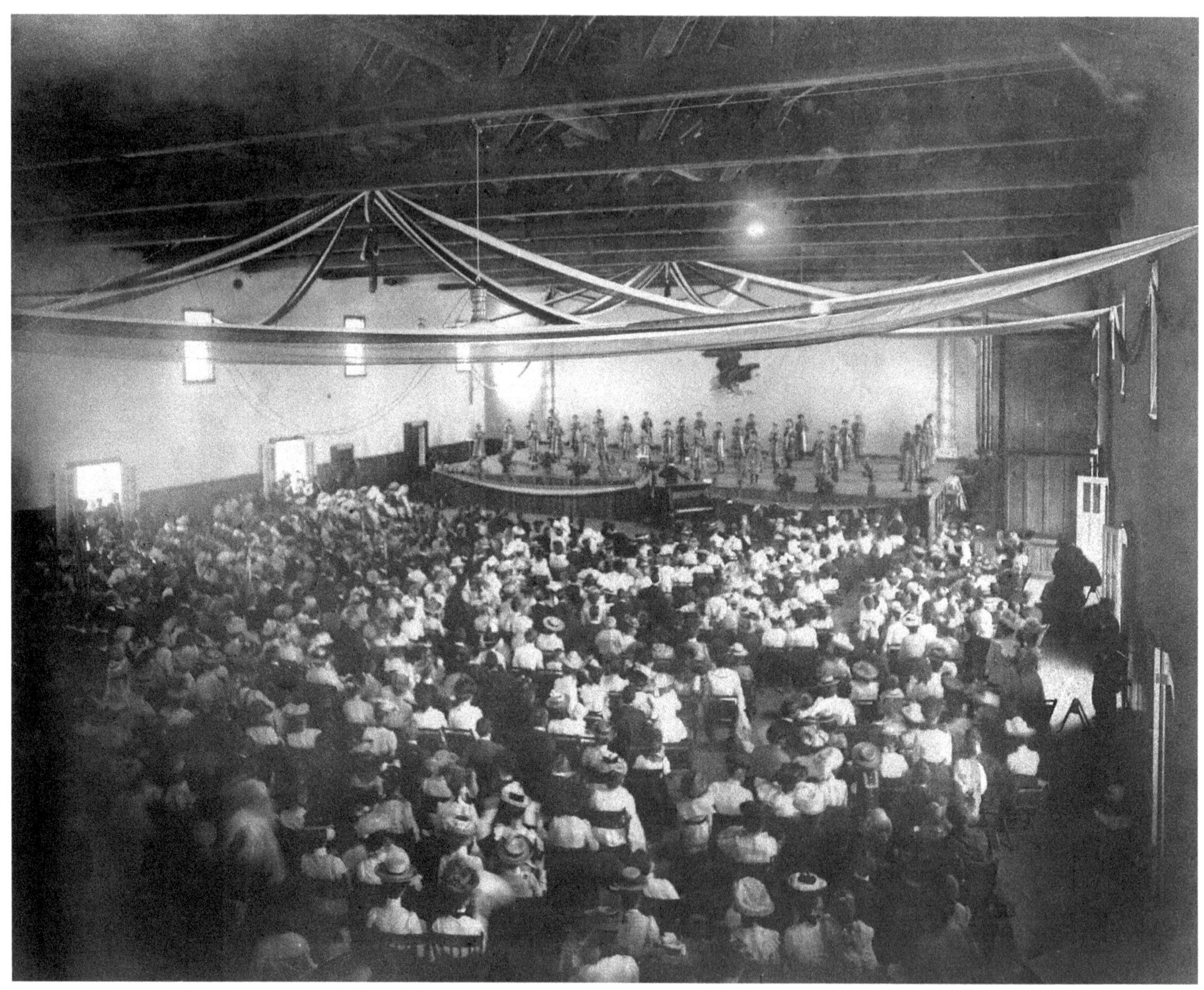

St. Petersburg schoolchildren celebrated Washington's Birthday, starting on February 22, 1896. Edwin H. Tomlinson's purchase of 250 silk flags for the first celebration helped ensure that it would become an annual winter event. A parade was followed by an indoor ceremony, performed by the schoolchildren.

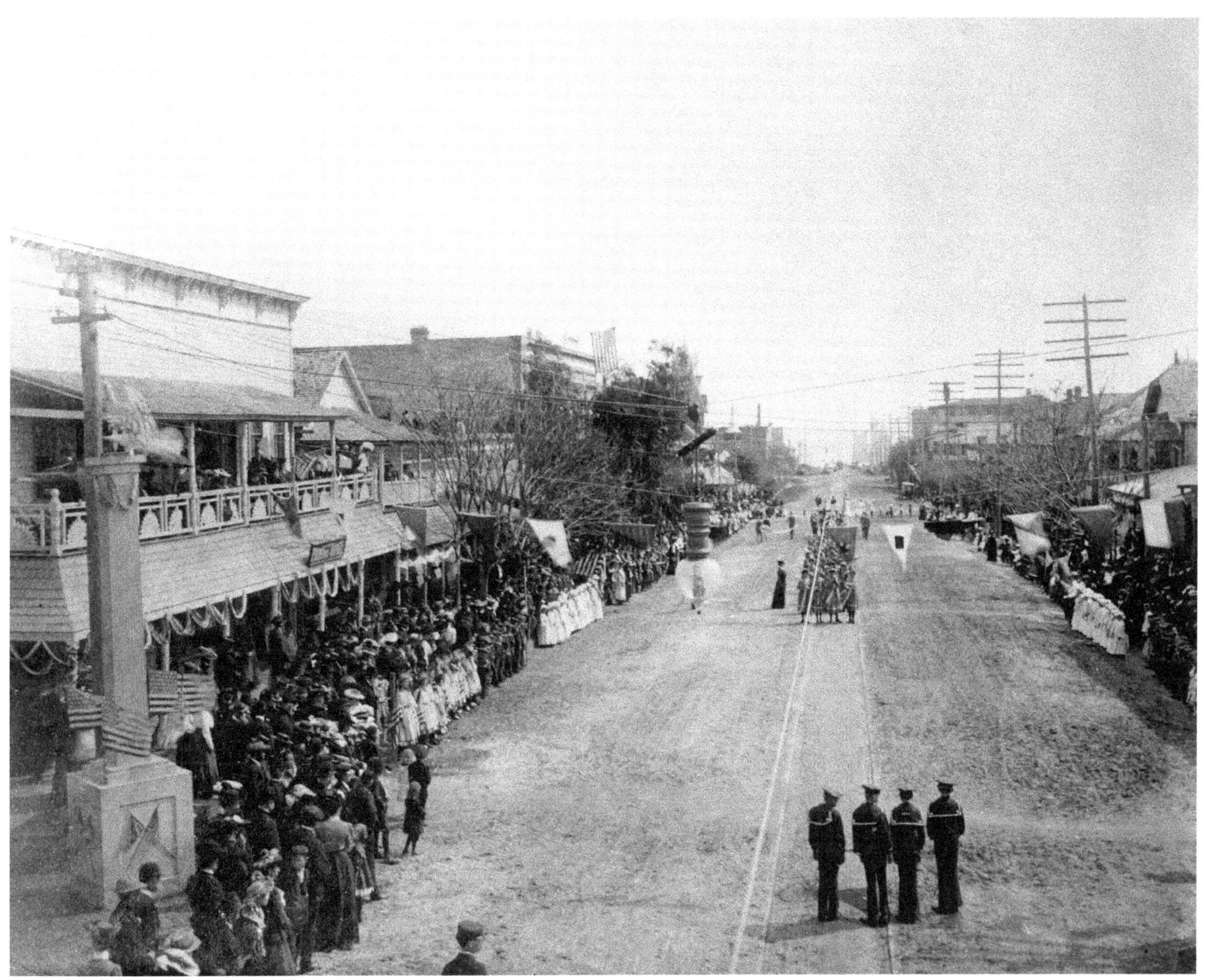

A midwinter fair association was formed in 1900, with 106 subscribers at $10 each. The fair opened in 1901 with a parade and a month-long exhibit. Its success prompted the construction of an auditorium, but the fairs failed a few years later. The auditorium was sold and each backer received $26 for his $10 investment.

Pass-A-Grille on Long Key was one of the earliest Gulf Island resorts. By 1900, regular excursions from St. Petersburg permitted visitors to enjoy picnics, shell hunting, fishing, and swimming on the Gulf. James H. Forquer, manager of the Detroit Hotel, built a floating hotel at Pass-A-Grille in 1895, but it lasted only a few years.

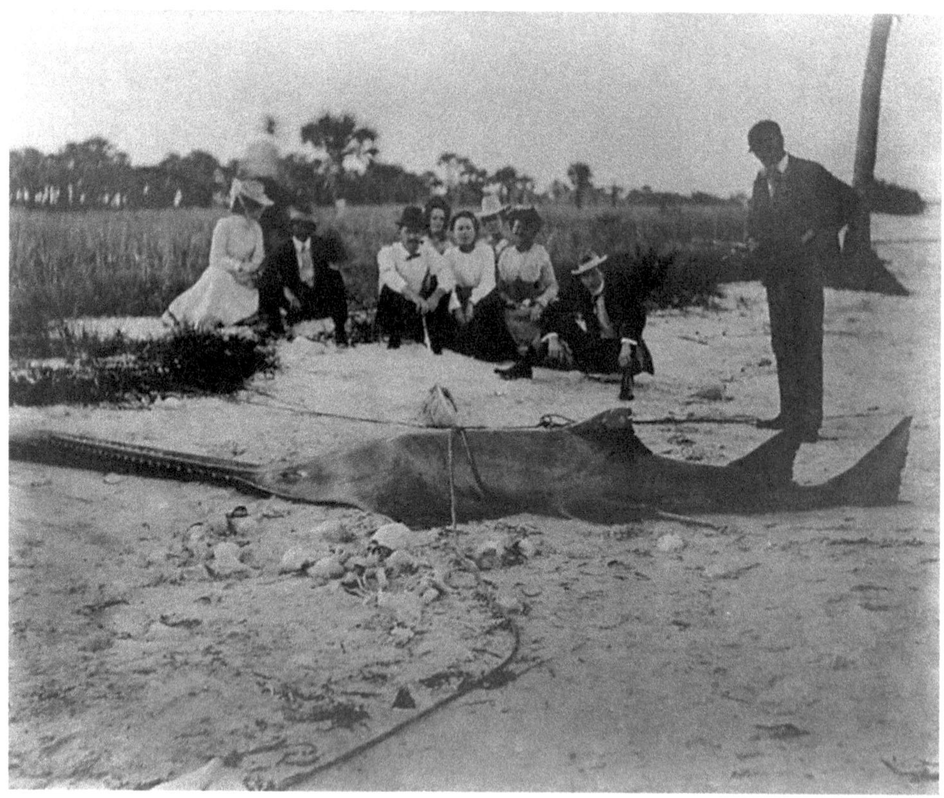

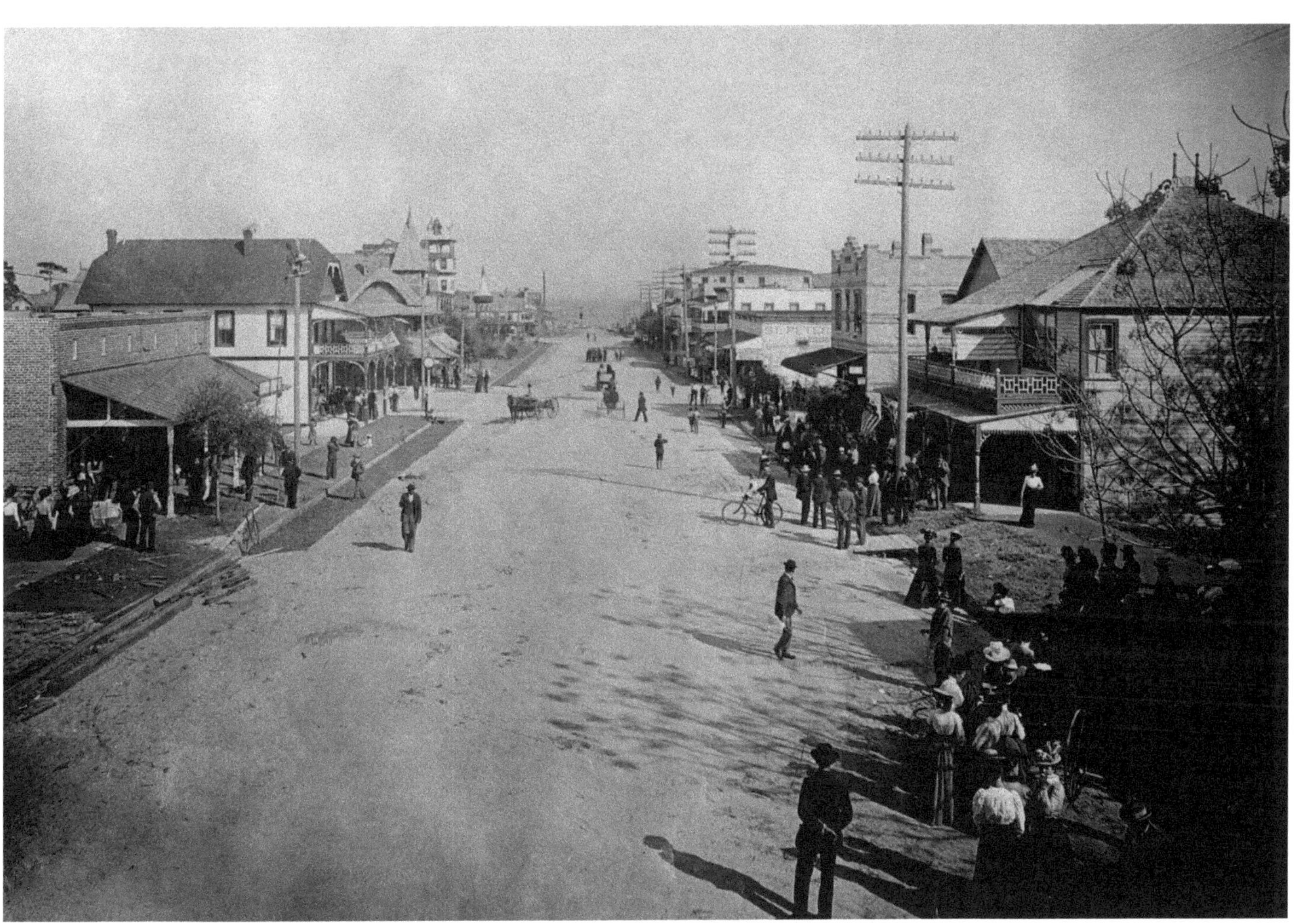

Crowds line the east end of Central Avenue in 1900. Noticeable civic improvements include clean streets, sidewalks, telephone lines, and well-kept buildings. The main business district since the town's beginning, from this area business steadily pushed west, finally crossing the "Fifth Street Barrier" about 1908.

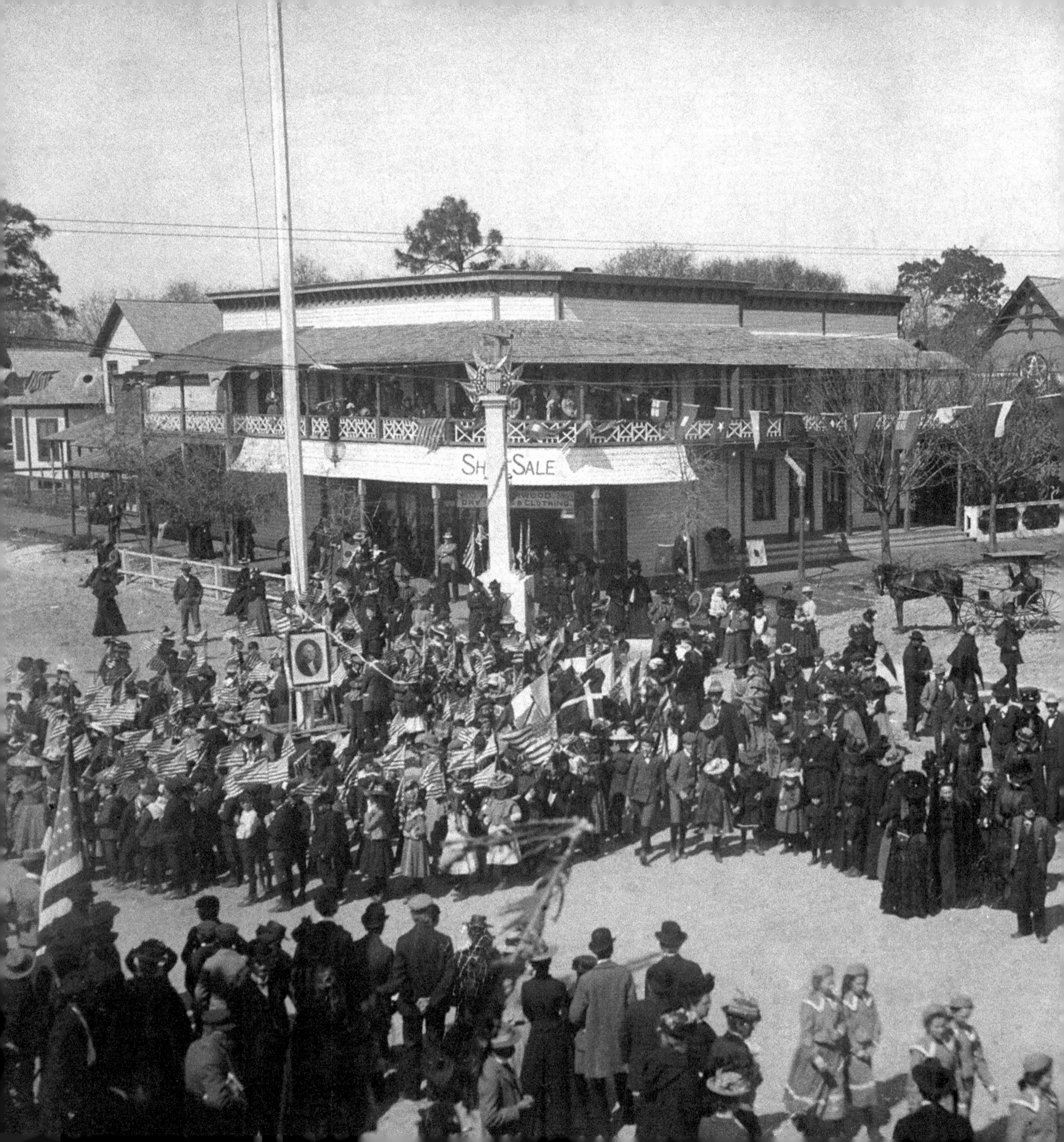
SH SALE
CLOTHING

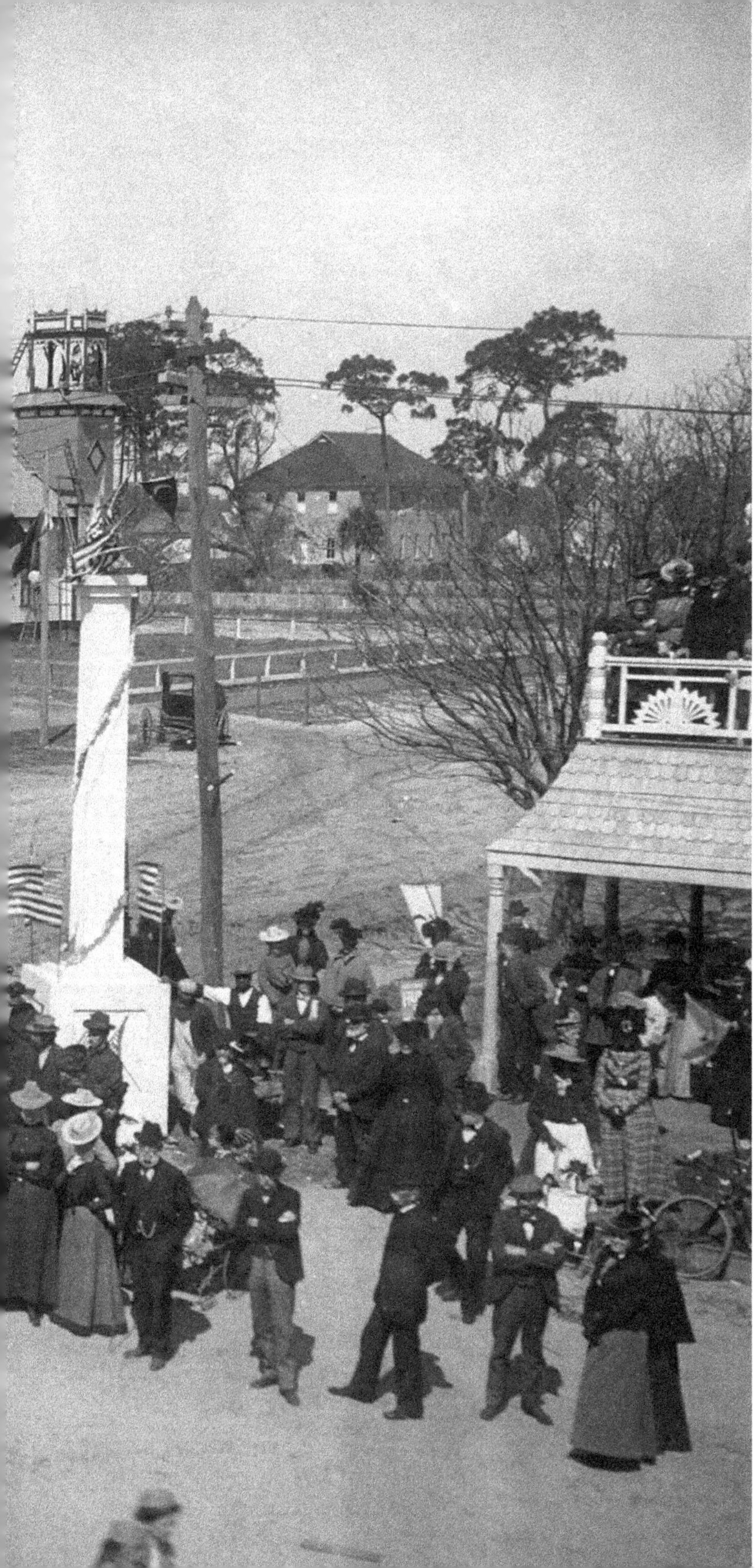

The school parade for Washington's Birthday Celebration passes the Durant block at the corner of Fourth Street and Central Avenue around 1901. Other activities included May pole parties, ceremonies, performances, and drill teams. The celebration was halted in 1914 because the school board felt that too much of the students' time centered on the activity.

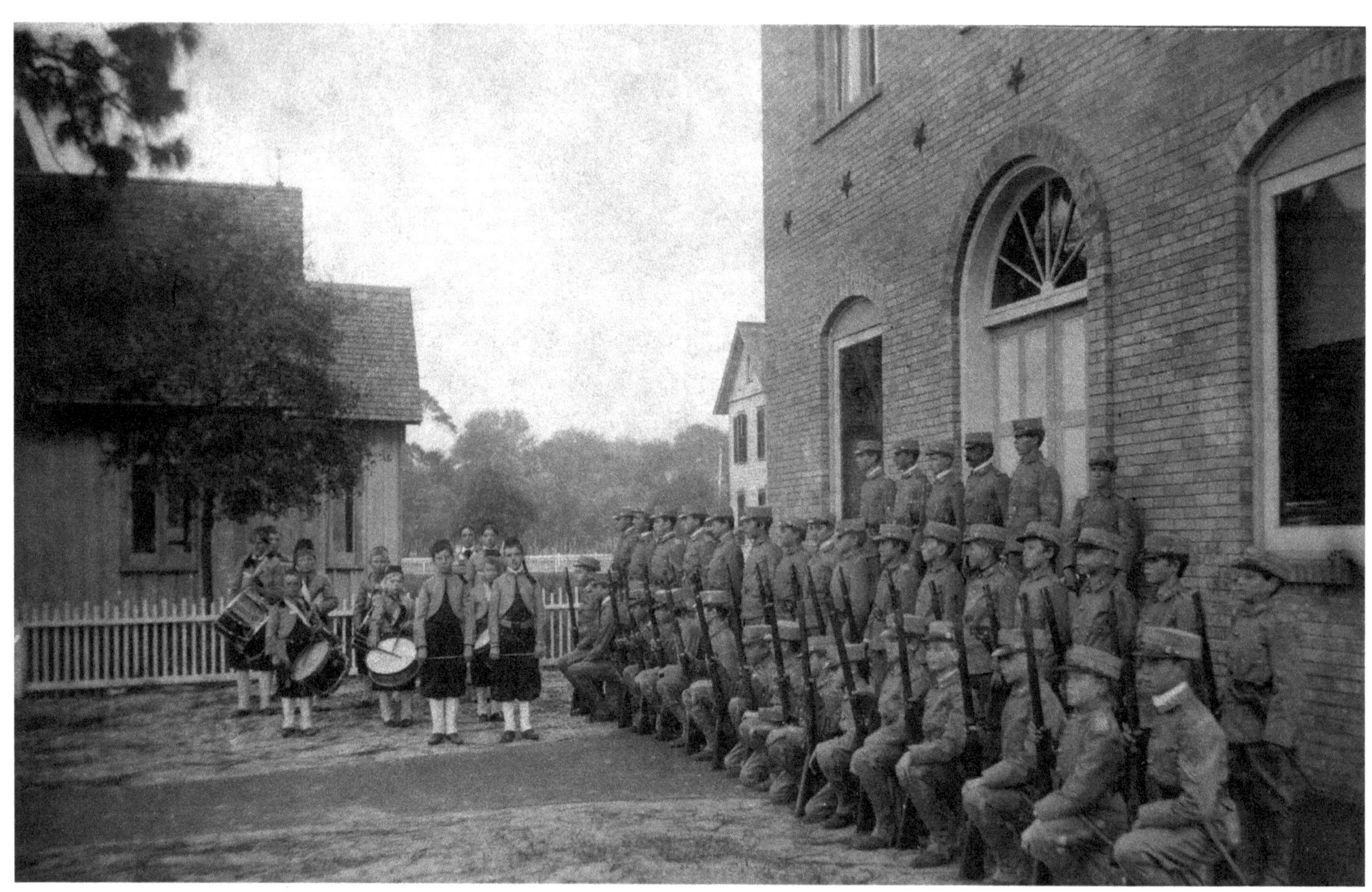

Zouave fife-and-drum and military cadets pose at the Manual Training School in 1902. One of the earliest school buildings in town, it was also used as a community center. The solidly constructed building with its one-foot-thick brick exterior walls was listed in the National Historic Register in 1999. It was still standing in 2007.

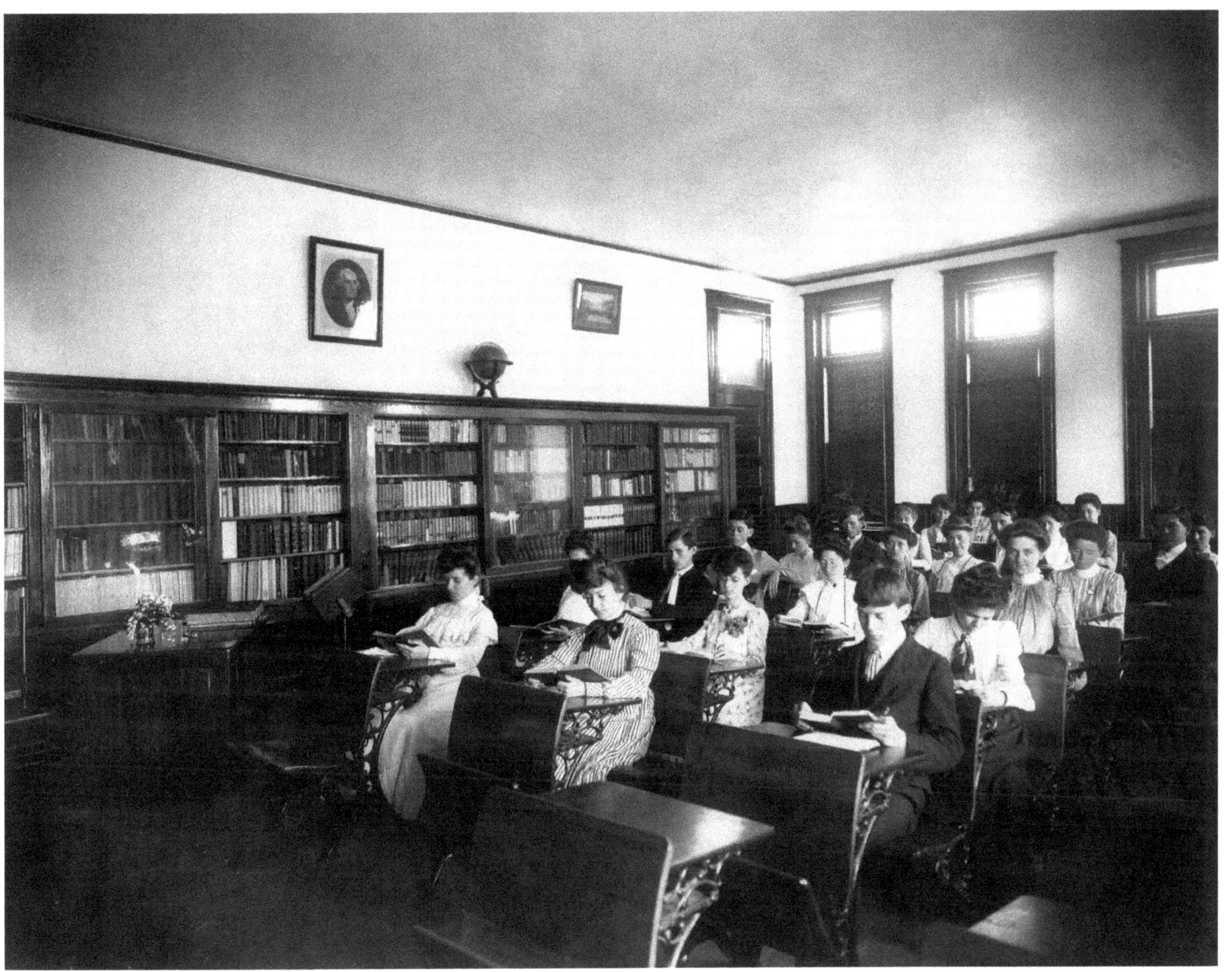

This 1902 classroom with its shiny new desks, bookcases with glass doors, teacher's desk with flowers, and well-dressed students may depict one of the first high school classes in the city. The St. Petersburg Normal and Industrial School opened in 1902 in a new brick building and was renamed St. Petersburg High School by 1904.

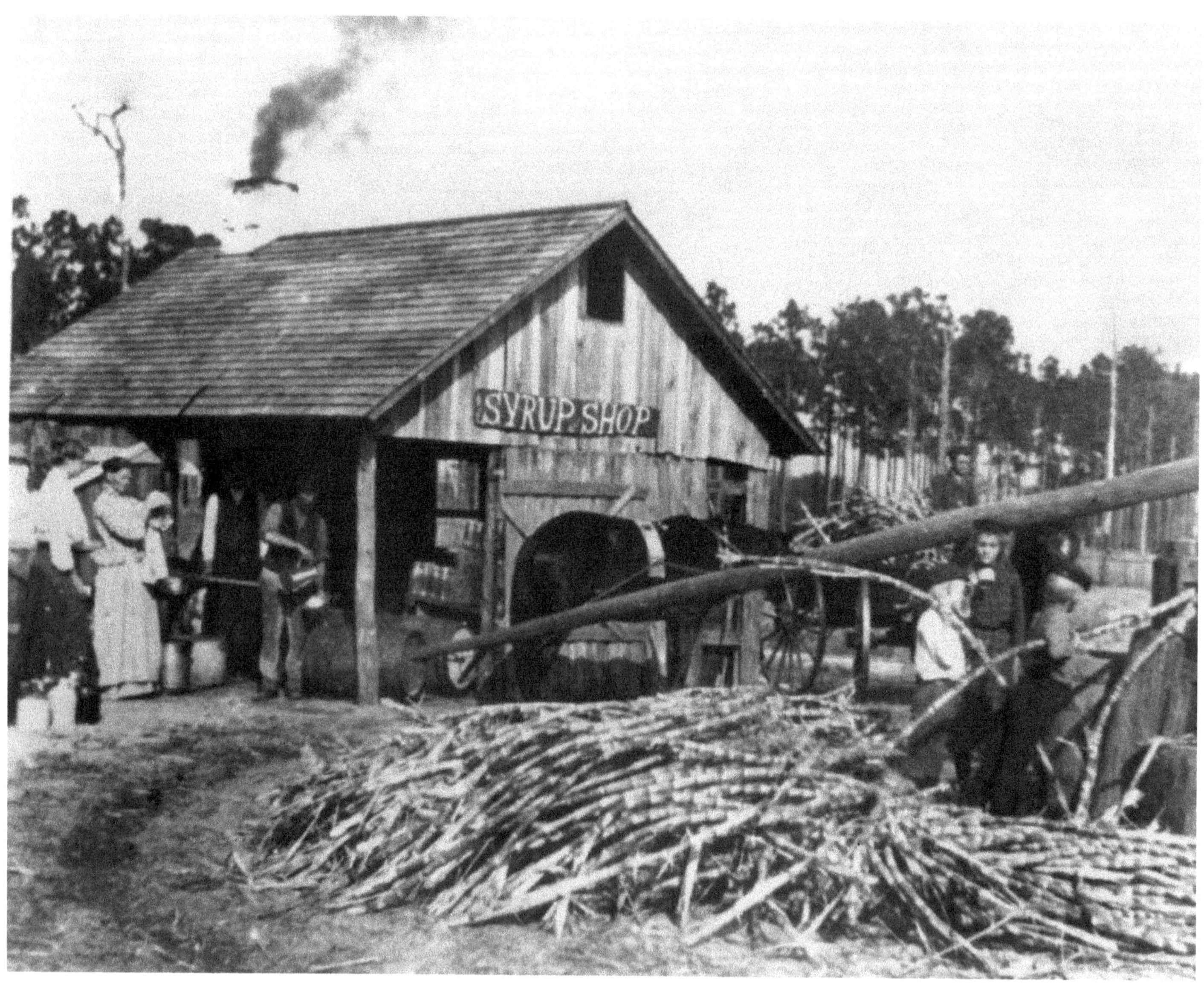

Before the era of railroads, sugar and other commercial crops were generally unprofitable on the lower Pinellas peninsula. Lack of access to markets and the semitropical environment's insects and weeds proved insurmountable. By 1903, better transportation and a growing local market made possible small operations like this syrup shop.

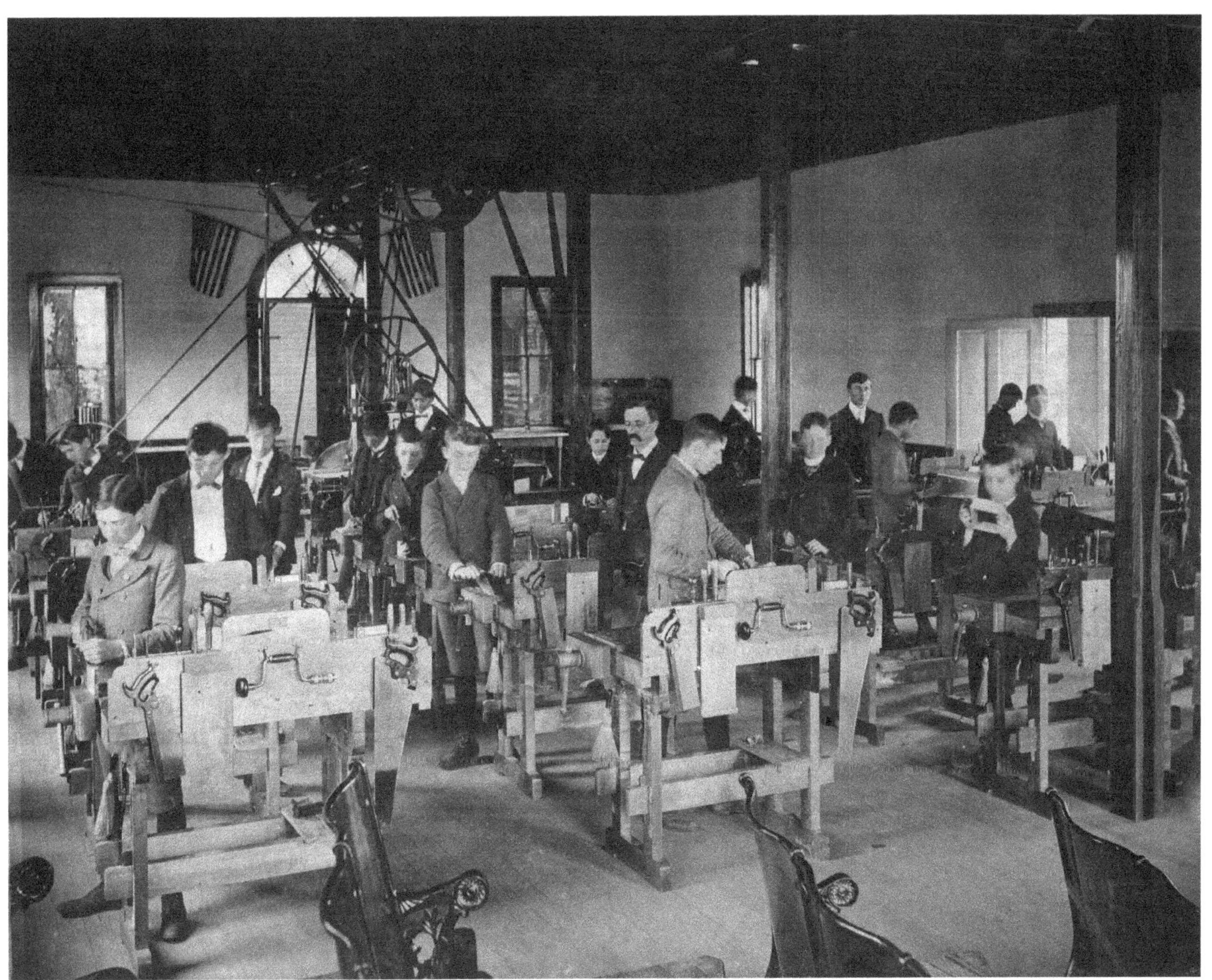

Students work on their projects at the Domestic Science and Manual Training School in 1903. Edwin H. Tomlinson provided $10,000 for the school, construction began in the spring of 1901, and it officially opened on December 29 of that year. The school provided valuable vocational training for youth, the first in Florida, until 1925.

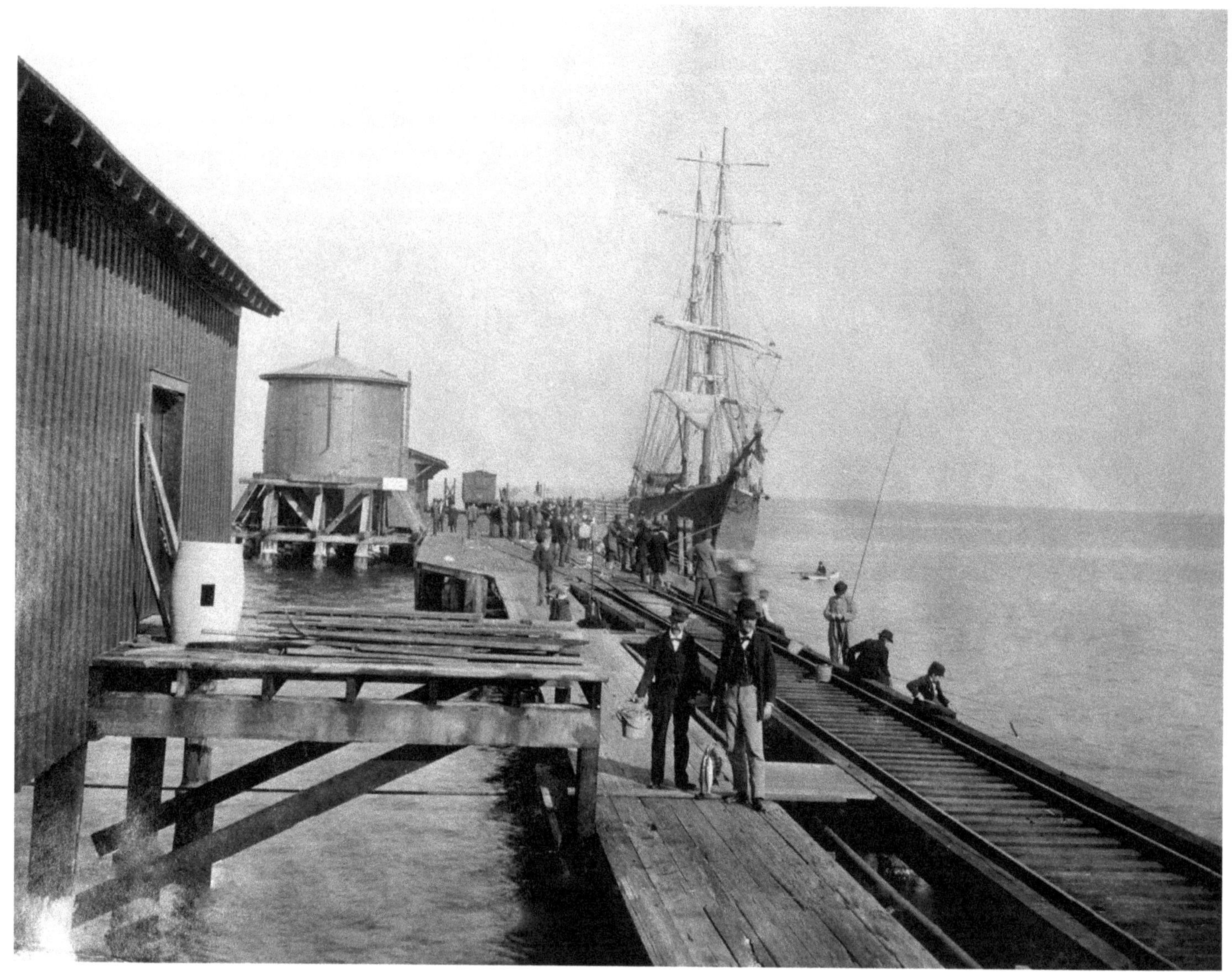

After acquiring the Orange Belt Railway and pier in 1895, Henry Plant charged a 25-dollar docking fee for independent boats. Control of the city's main pier gave Plant control over local commerce. Three years after Henry Plant's death in 1899, the railroad and pier became part of the Atlantic Coast Line.

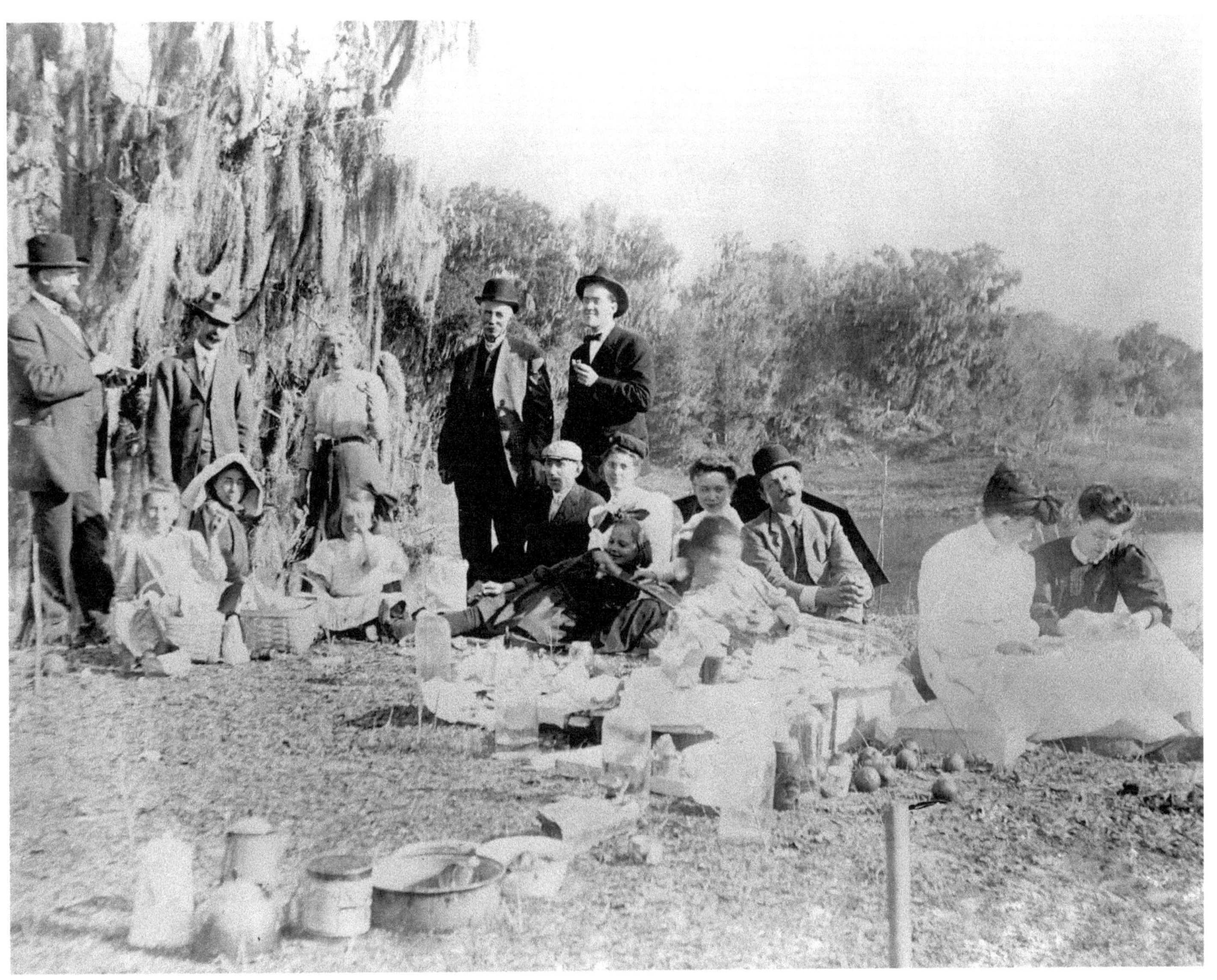

Effie Stone Rolfs, believed to be standing third from the left, with a party on picnic near St. Petersburg around 1910. Her husband, Dr. Peter Henry Rolfs, a prominent Florida botanist, served as director of the Florida Agricultural Experiment Station from 1906 until 1921, when he accepted an offer to found an agricultural college in Brazil.

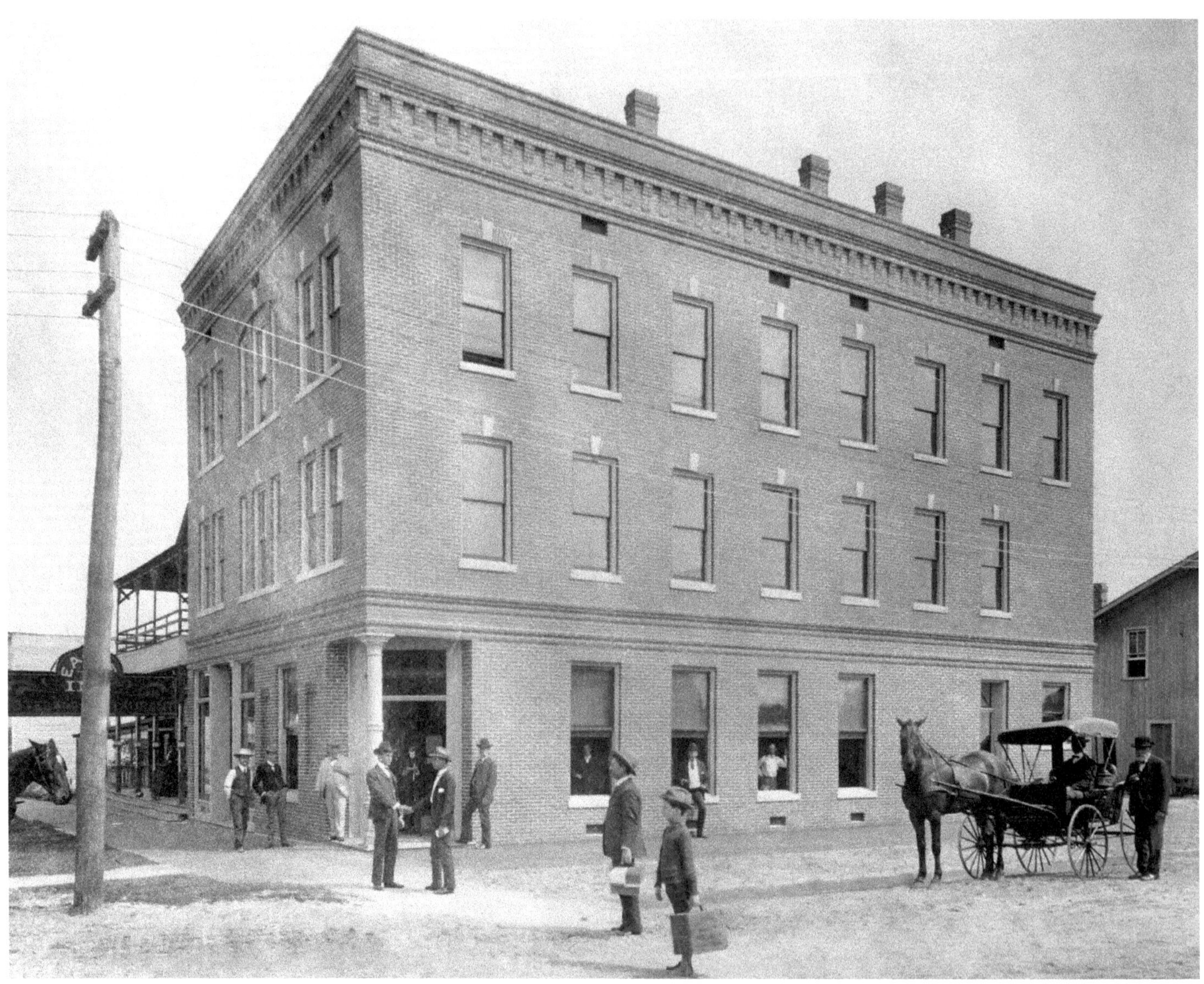

In 1902, the St. Petersburg State Bank closed its doors with $51,000 of local deposits, a large portion of the town's wealth. After years in court, the depositors received little of their money back. The new West Coast bank opened in this three-story brick building in 1903. Two years later it was renamed First National Bank.

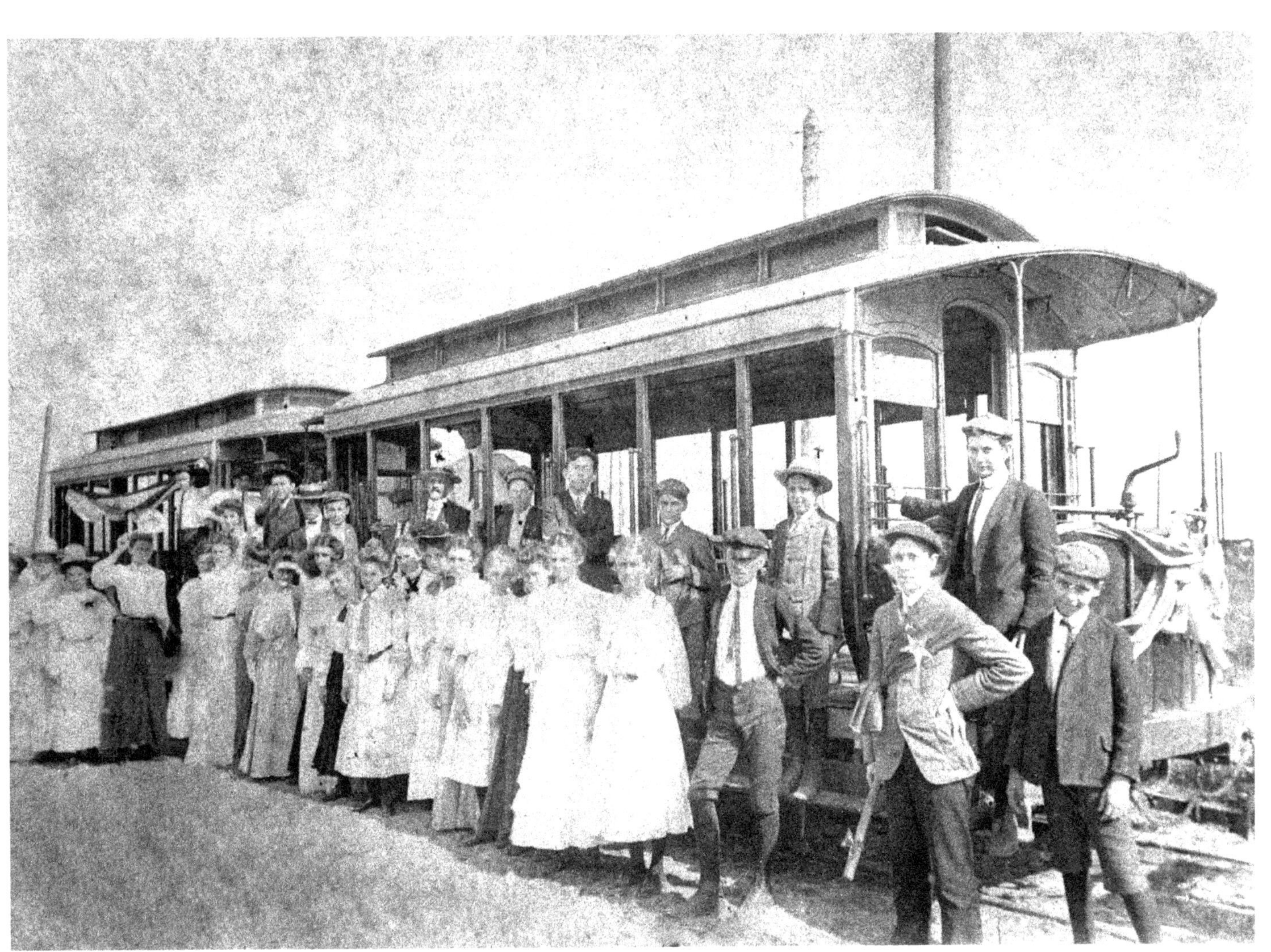

These grade-school students seem ready to ride the town's first trolley. Constructed by Frank A. Davis and operating by late 1904, its route traced Mirror Lake to Central Avenue, eventually extending to the Pass-A-Grille ferry. Davis, a Philadelphia publisher, played a leading role in the early development of St. Petersburg.

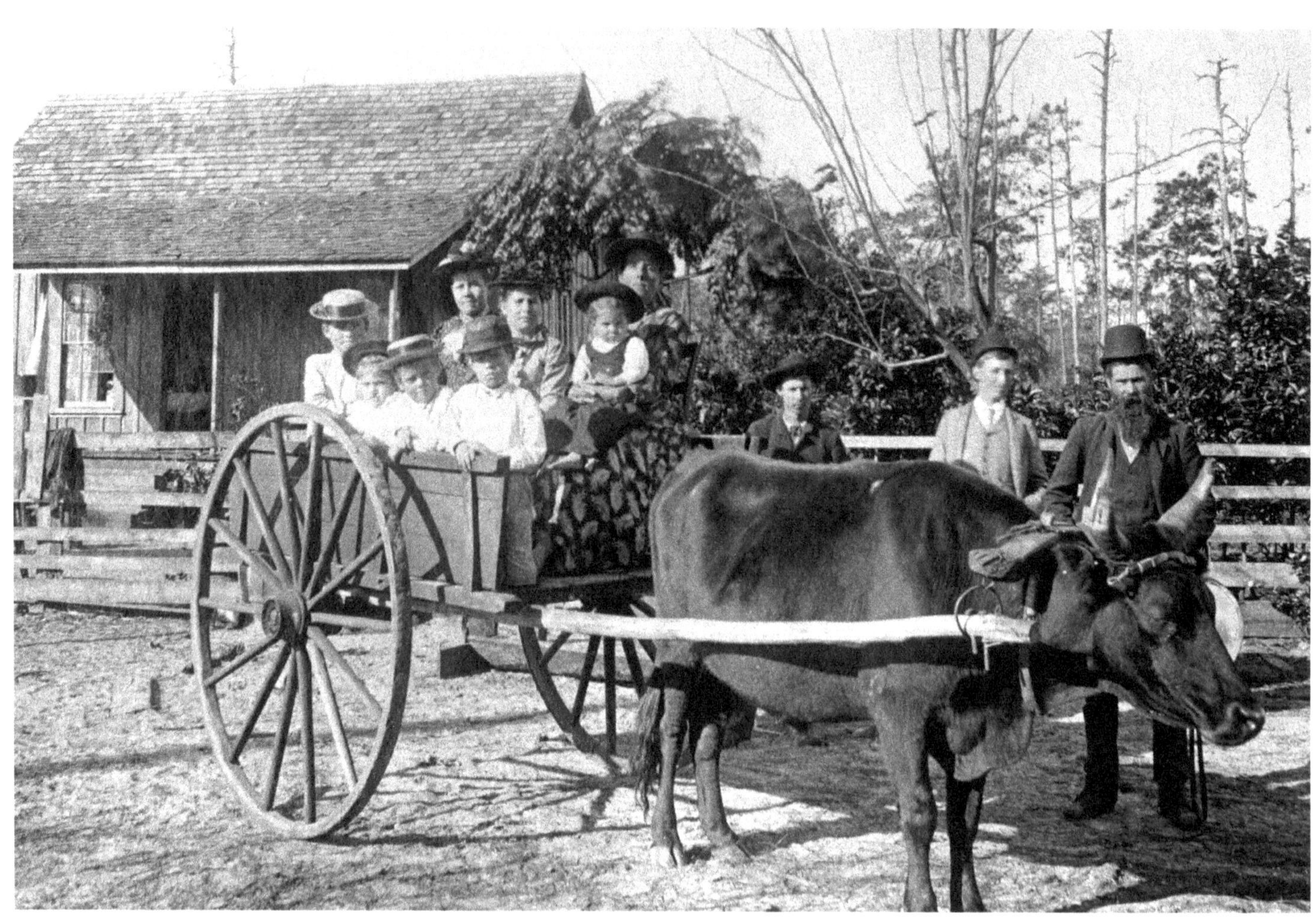

Dressed in their "Sunday Best," this party, traveling by ox-cart, is on the way to church. Around 1900 seven denominations had churches in St. Petersburg. Attempting to create a "good town," their combined influence had a significant effect on the community: no gambling joints, no red-light district, and a careful watch on saloons.

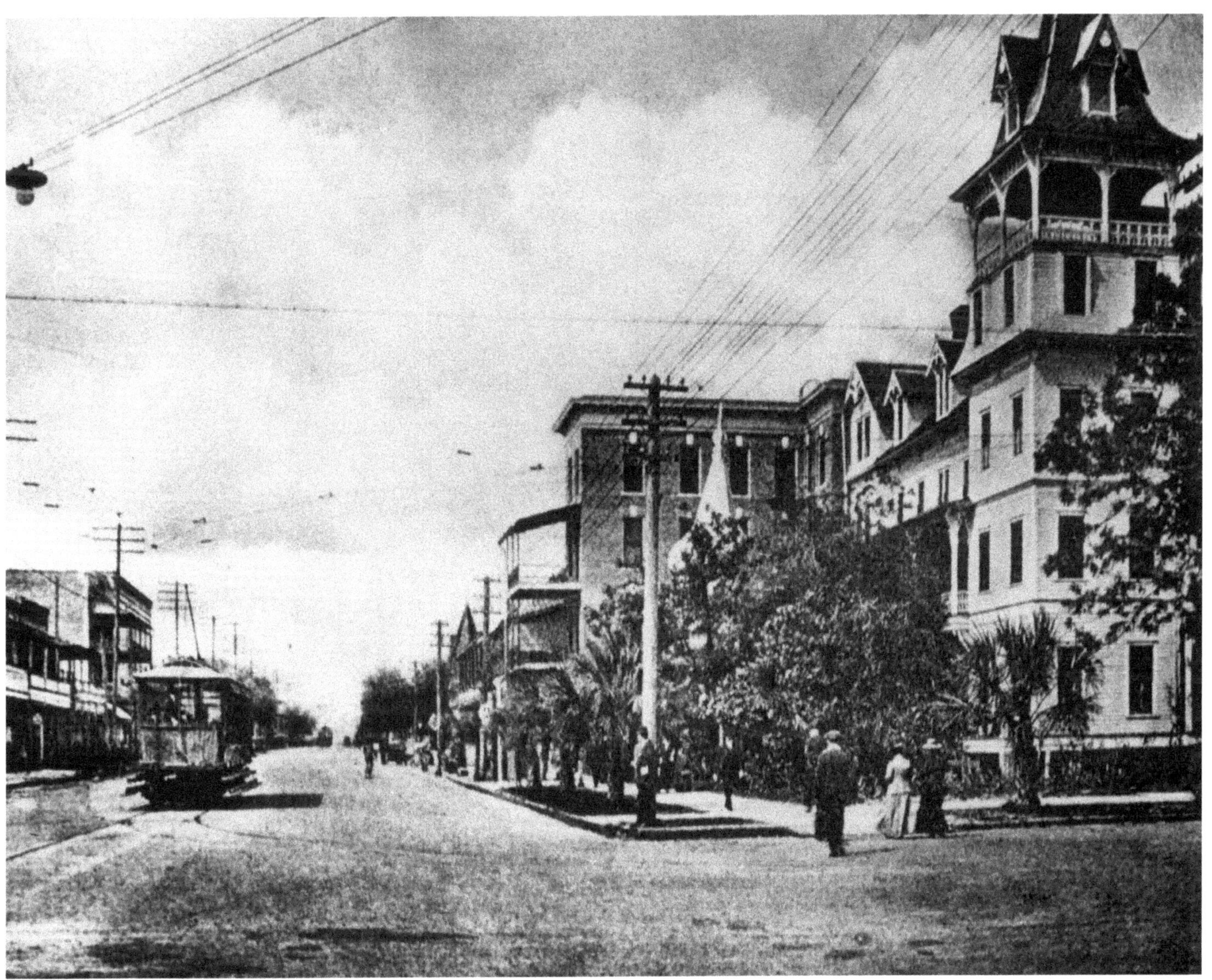

A trolley passes in front of the Detroit Hotel, with its minaret-topped gazebo just visible behind the trees. In 1901, a temperance group installed an $80 bronze fountain on one corner of the hotel grounds in an attempt to promote temperance. The fountain offered cold water, chilled by ice stored in the base of the fountain.

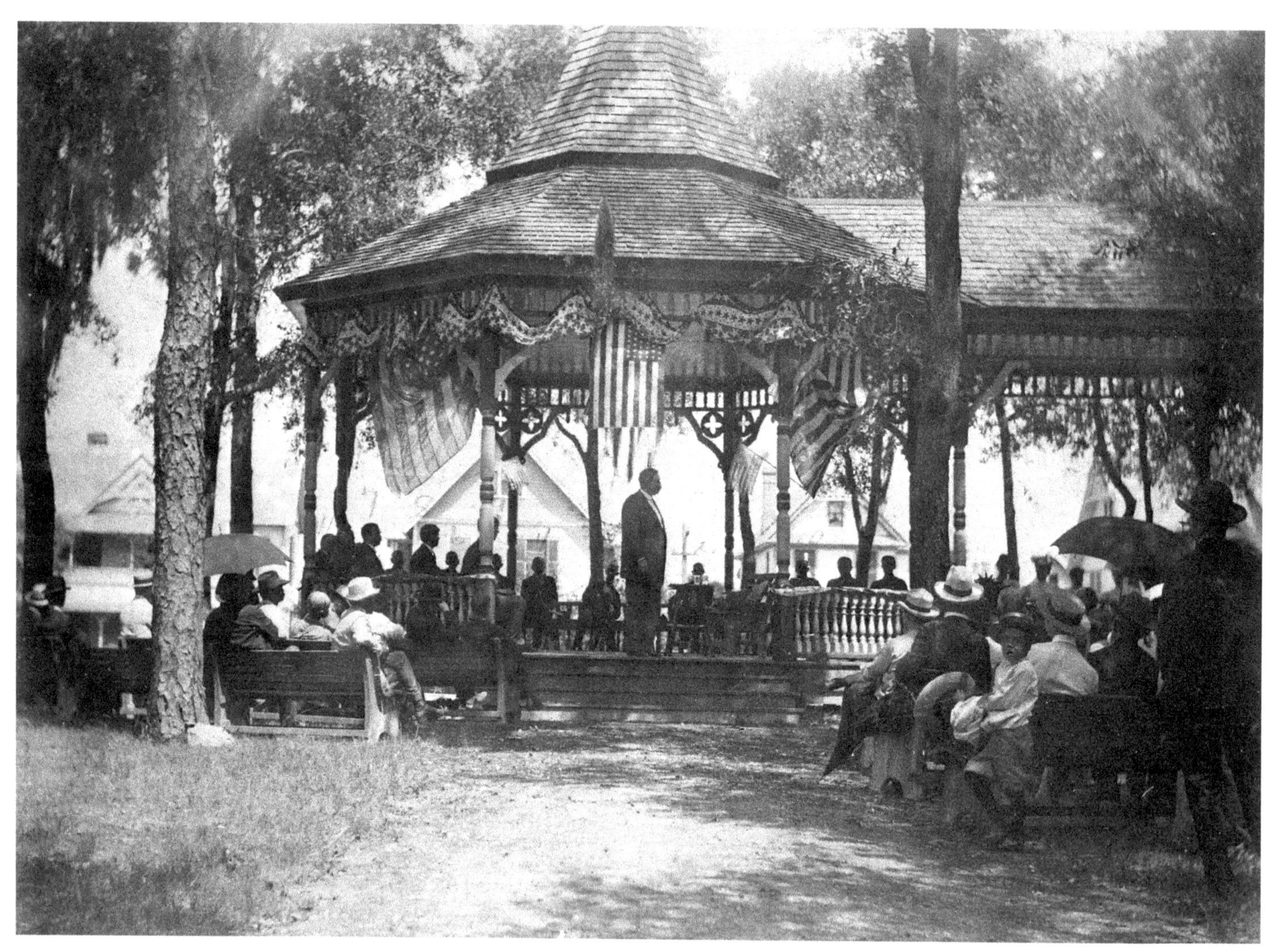

Napoleon Bonaparte Broward speaks at Williams Park on September 14, 1906. Although best-known for his Everglades drainage plan, Broward supported many reforms including better schools, a university system, good roads, prisons, a state library, and improved regulation of railroads and telegraph systems.

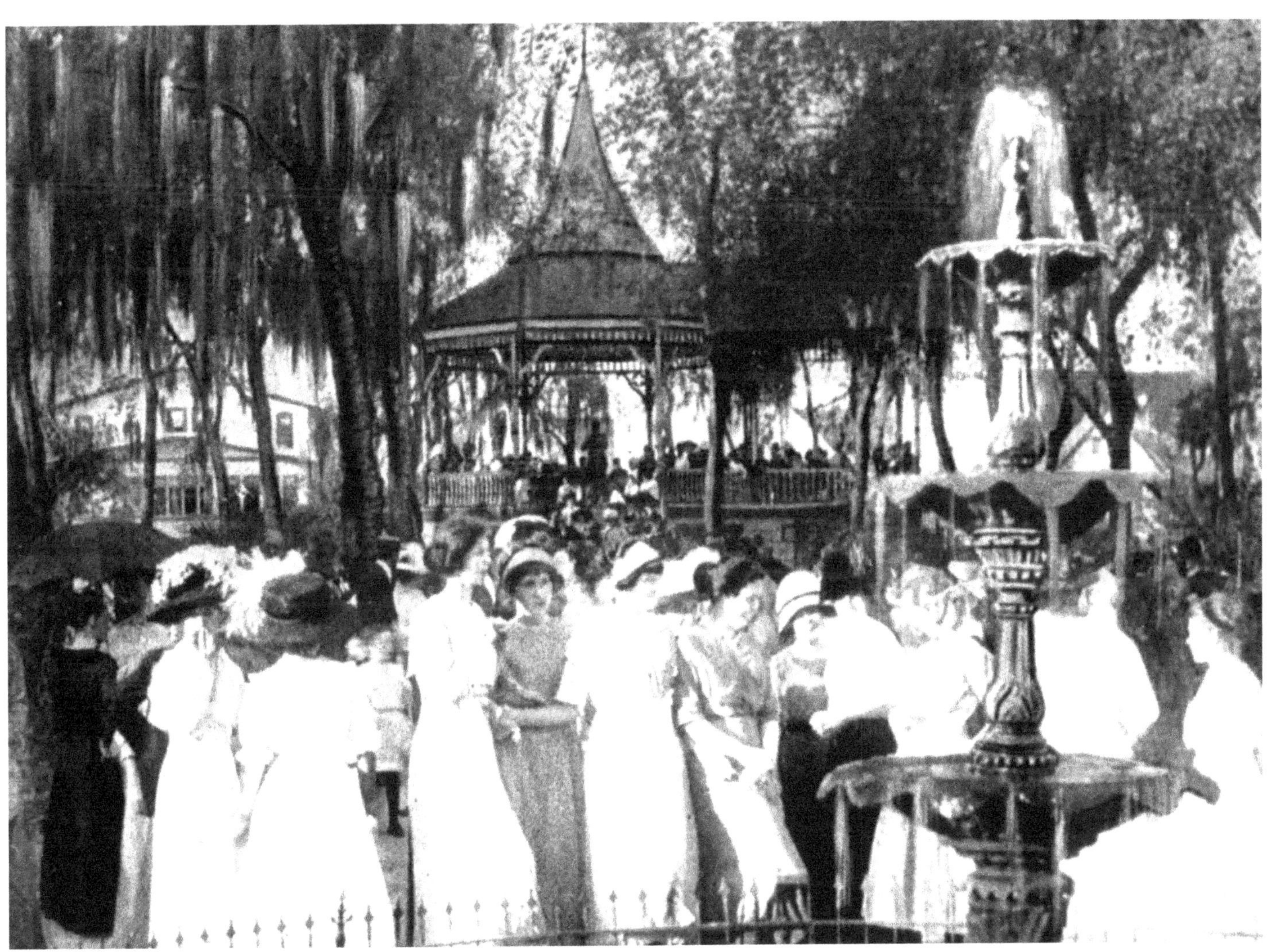

St. Petersburg women organized the Park Improvement Association in 1893 to clear Williams Park. On "Park Day" the ladies provided refreshments and gentlemen furnished the labor. The ladies saw the project through to completion, raising money for sidewalks and having a fence and a bandstand constructed.

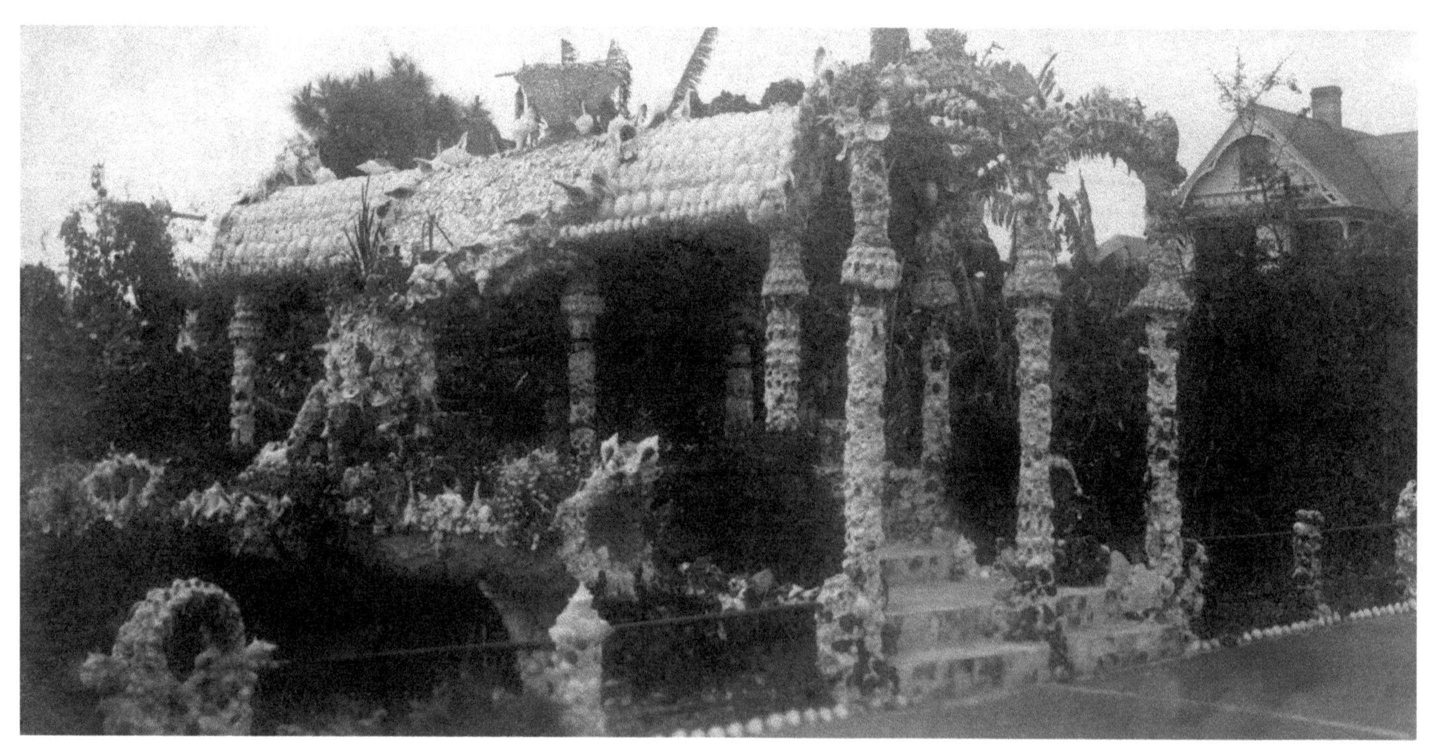

Collecting hundreds of thousands of sea shells from the Gulf Shore beaches, Owen Albright constructed an unusual shell fence at his home on First Street north of Second Avenue. The fence became one of the town's early tourist attractions, drawing visitors for more than twenty years until it was destroyed by the 1921 hurricane.

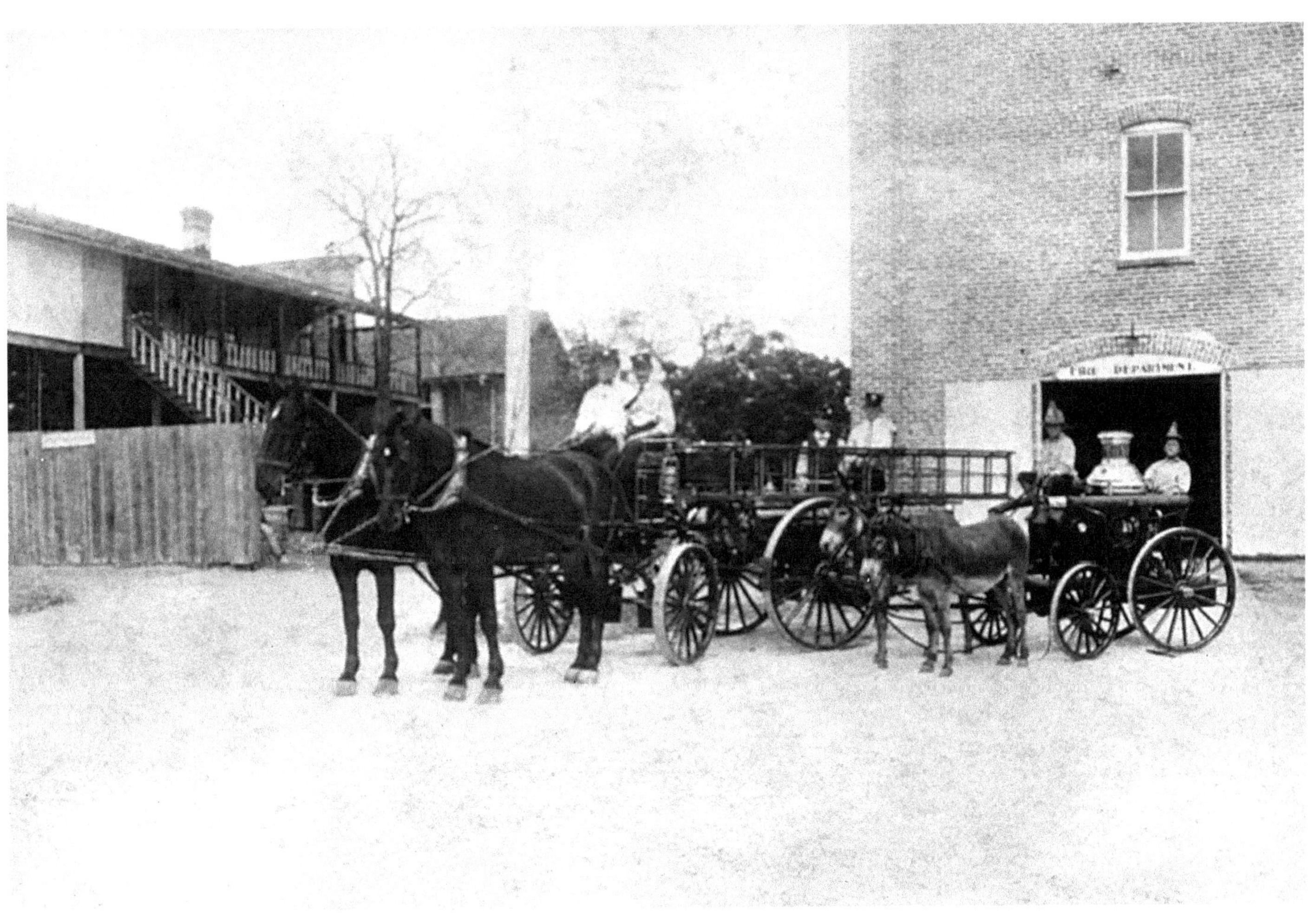

The fire department displays its new equipment, with Walter and Hubert Coleman in the mule-drawn pump wagon. In 1907, the Colonial Hotel was destroyed in a blaze that was seen for miles, but volunteer firemen safely evacuated the building. Shortly afterward, the first paid force was organized under Fire Chief George Anderson.

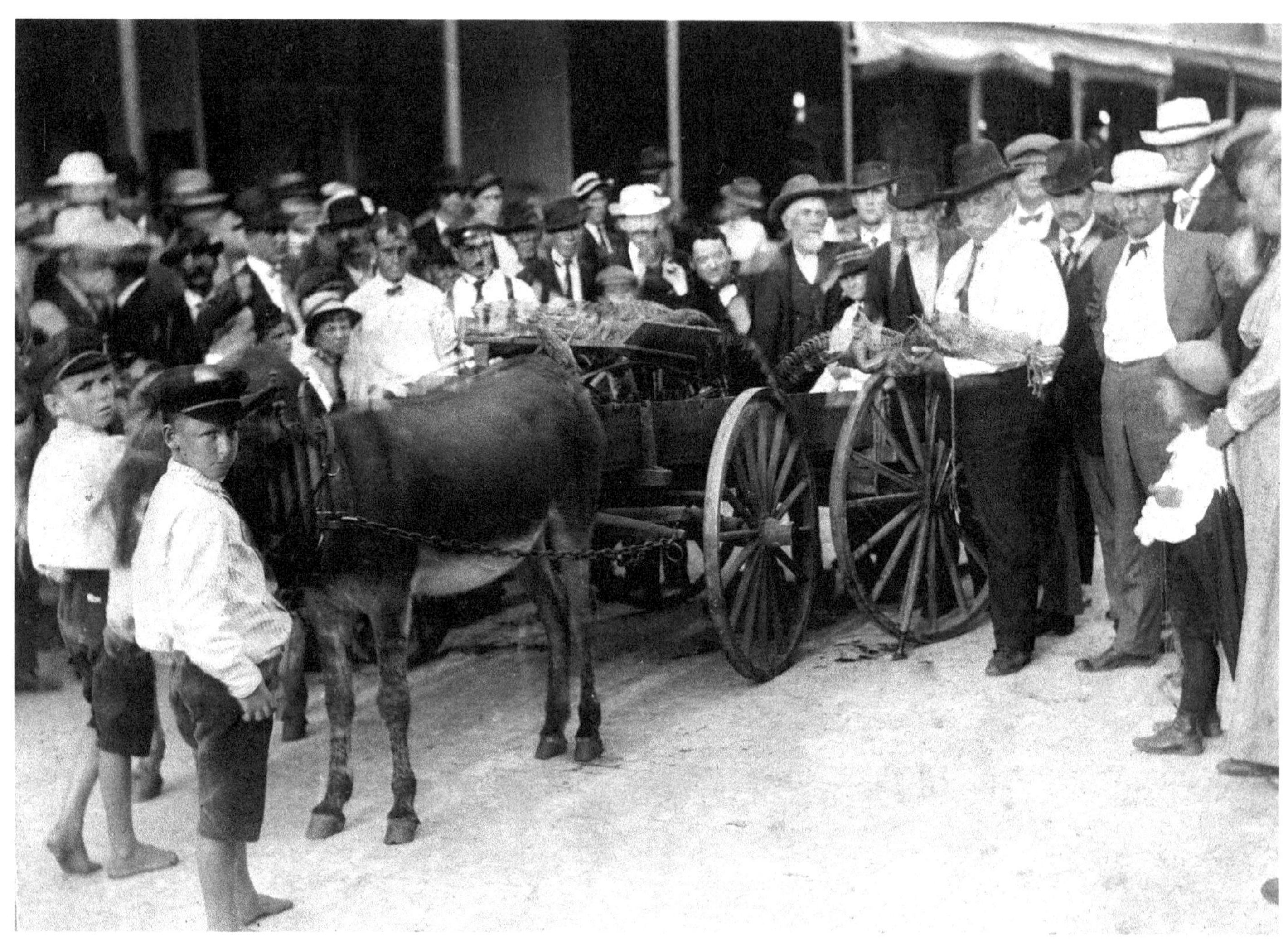

Young Hubert and Walter Coleman, again with a mule-drawn wagon, this time trying to cash in on the growing tourism boom. They would catch small alligators in Lake Maggiore and then transport them by wagon to downtown St. Petersburg, where for a nickel tourists could touch and hold them.

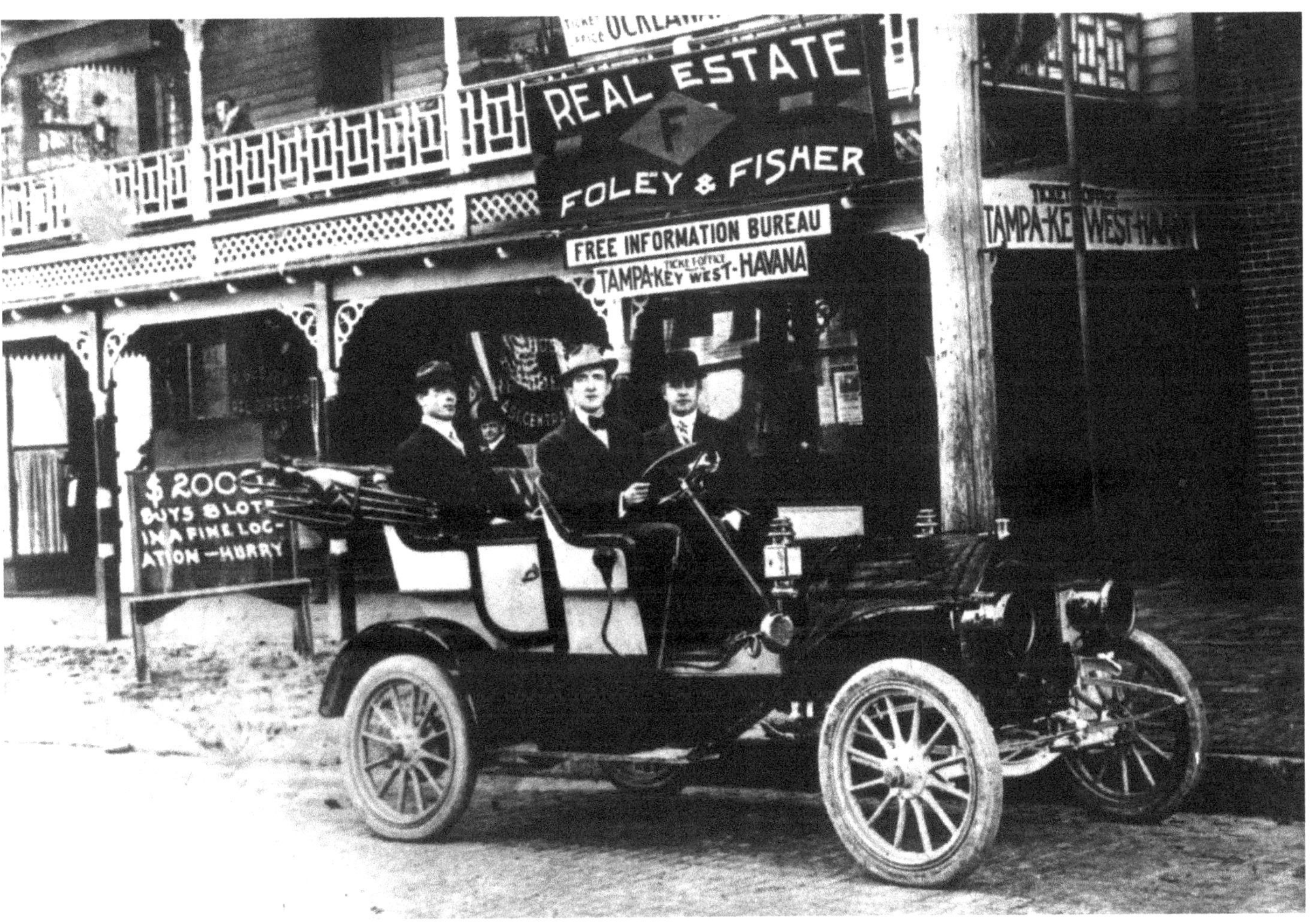

Offering a variety of "opportunities," the Foley and Fisher Real Estate office of 1908 promotes free tourist information, acts as travel agents, and advertises real estate lots. The sign behind the automobile announces, "$2000 buys 8 lots in a fine location—hurry." In 1905, Edwin Tomlinson, owner of the town's first automobile, occasionally drove along the new sidewalks when the city streets were impassable.

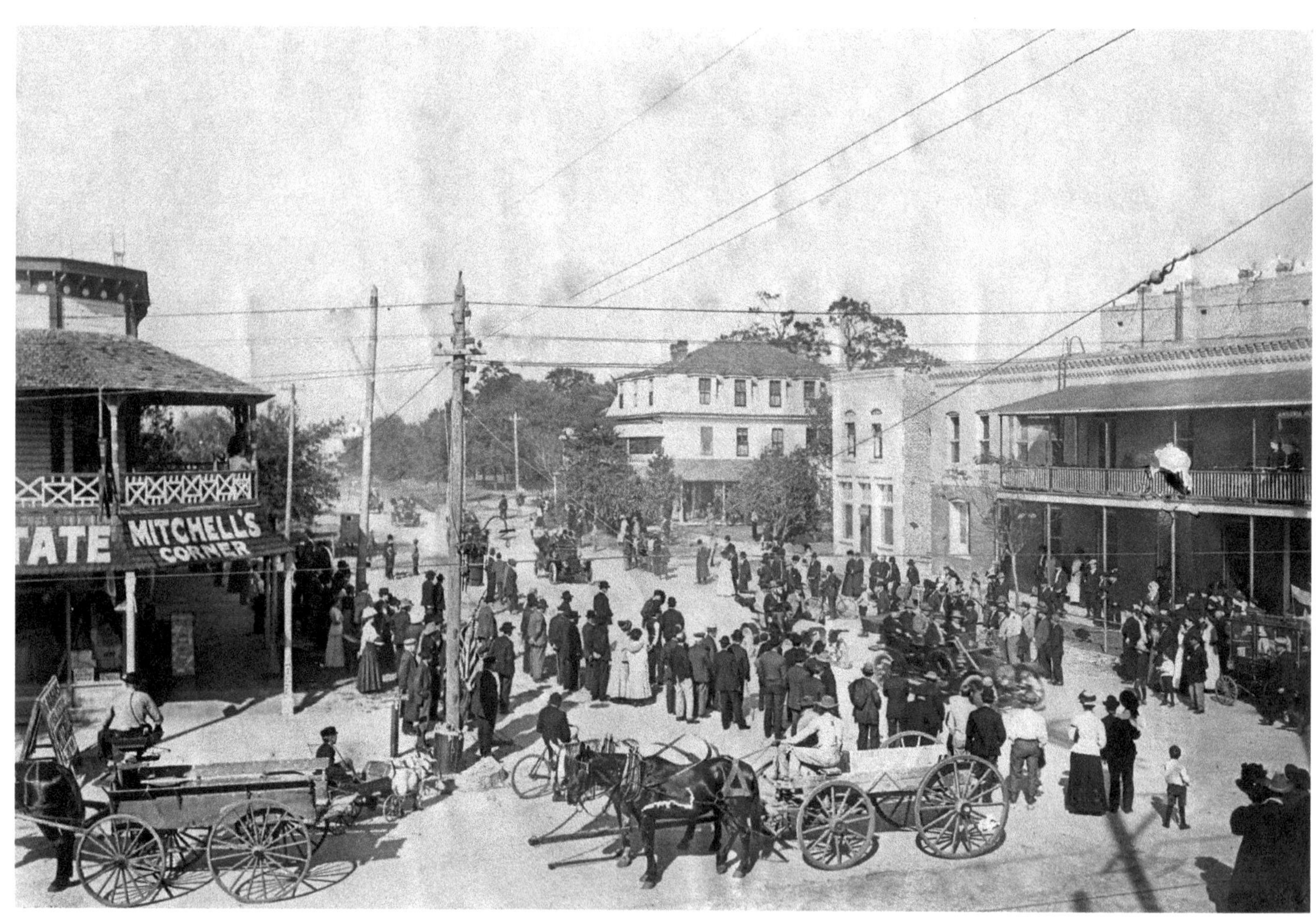

A crowd gathers to greet returning cross-country motorists. At far-right is Ed Tomlinson's original open-air post office. Mitchell's corner, at far-left, was built by Charles Durant in the early 1890s, then used as Arthur Norwood's department store. In the 1920s, it was the site of the towering Snell Arcade building.

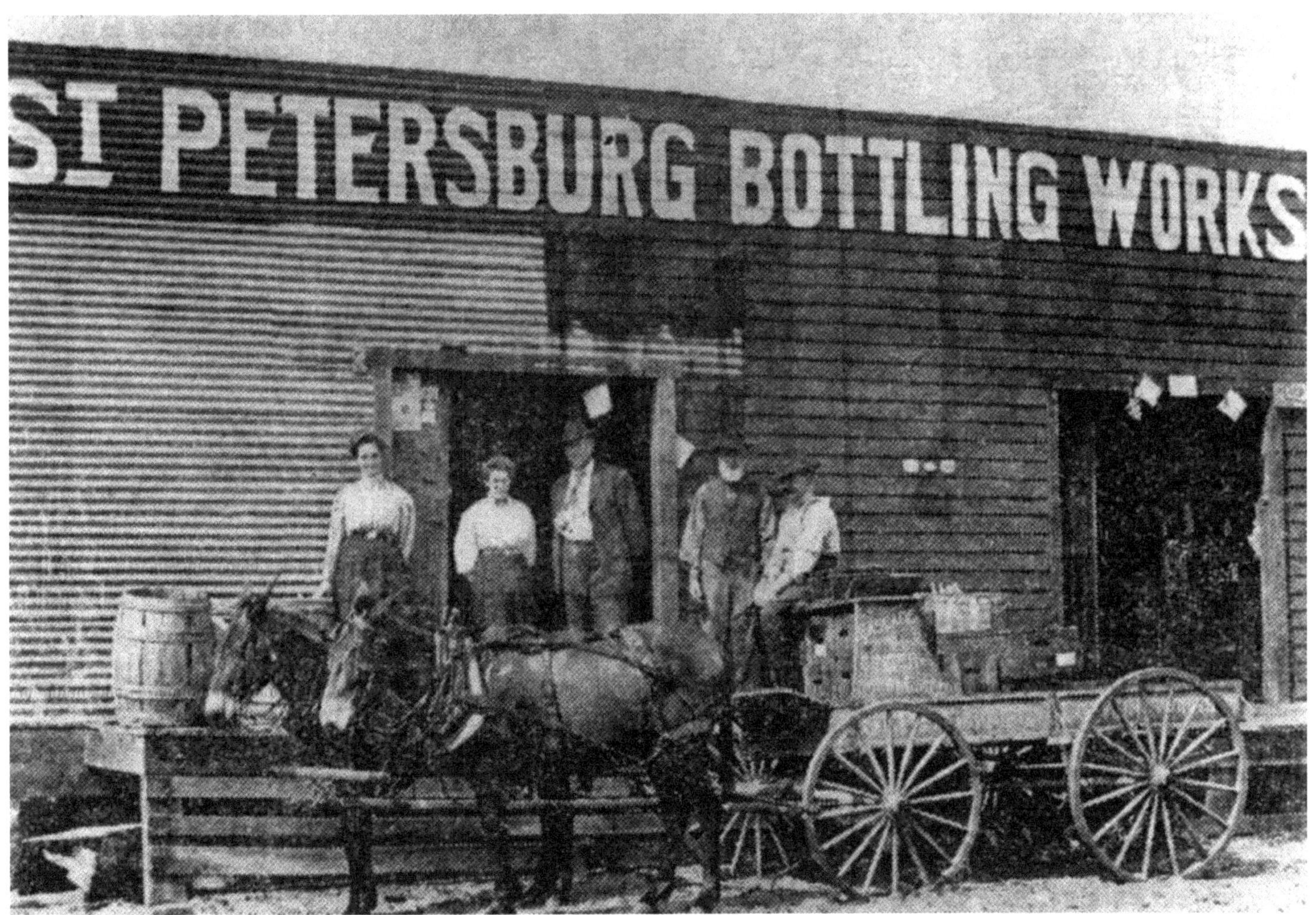

St. Petersburg experienced an economic boom starting in 1909 that lasted about five years. Spurred by a strong real estate market, the town enjoyed numerous new homes, businesses, and public works. Spending more in five years than in the previous years combined, the city improved streets, the water system, parks, sewers, and the waterfront.

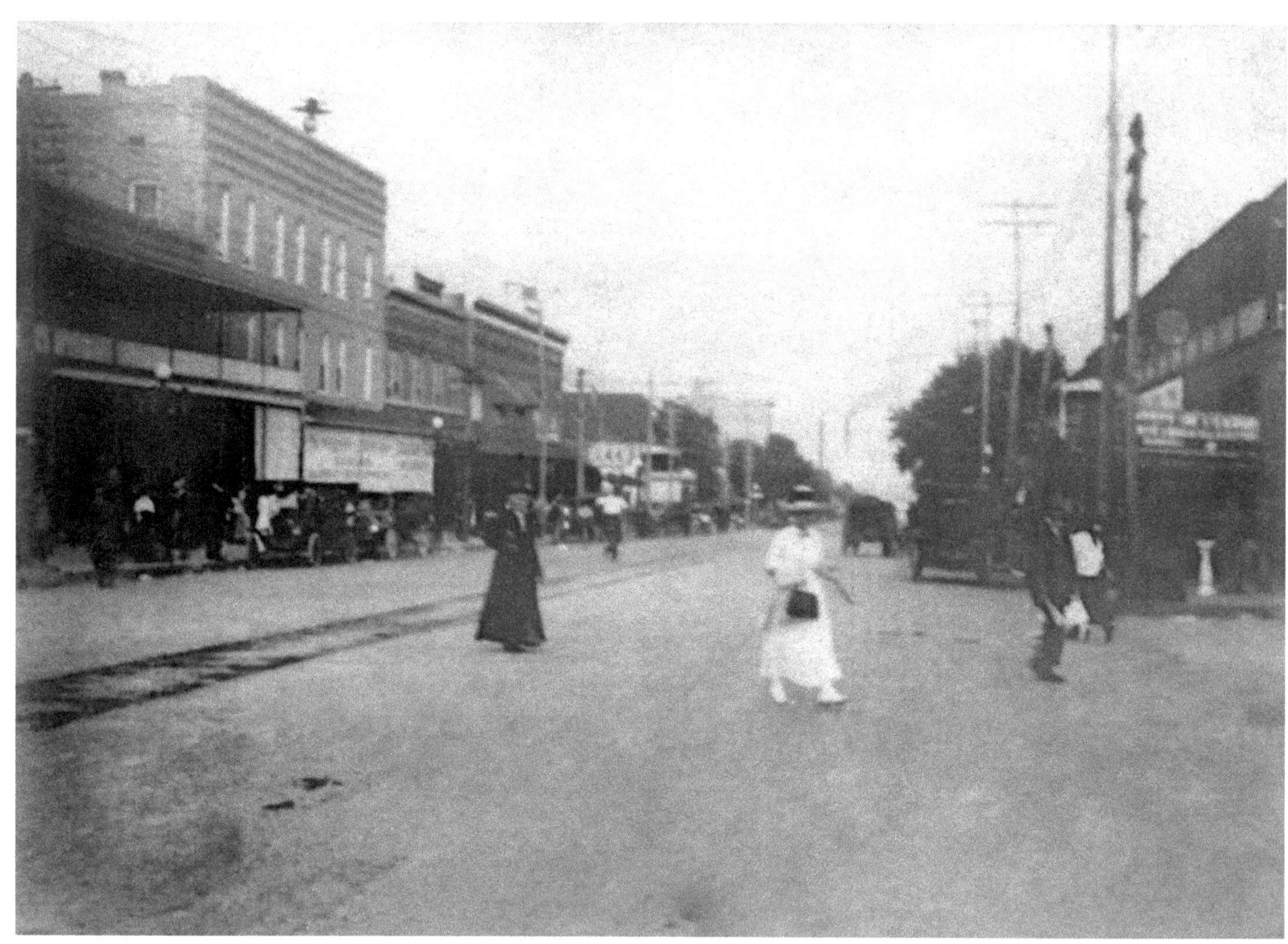

The town turned its attention to improving its roads, as seen here by the paved street and parked cars on Central Avenue in 1910. The $202,000 worth of improvements were needed—the first long-distance automobile tourist had arrived in 1906, overland travel to Tampa took days, and in 1908 there were only 22 automobiles owned by town residents.

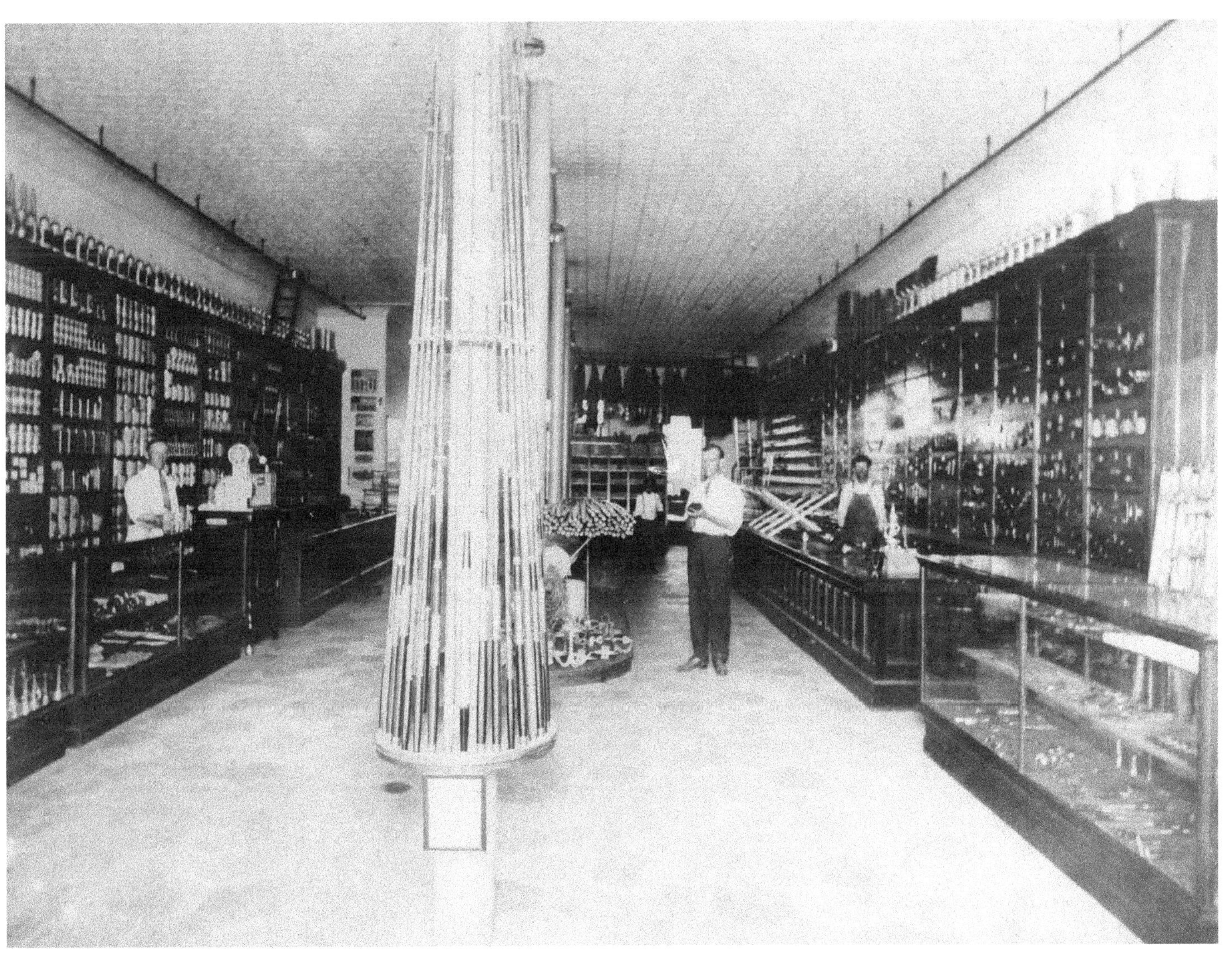

Tracy Lewis operated this Marine Supply store, shown here around 1910, out of his own two-story building at the corner of Central Avenue and 1st Street. The Lewis family was very active in the early development of St. Petersburg. Tracy's father, Fred Lewis, built the first house within the city limits, and his brother Edwin was a member of the city council.

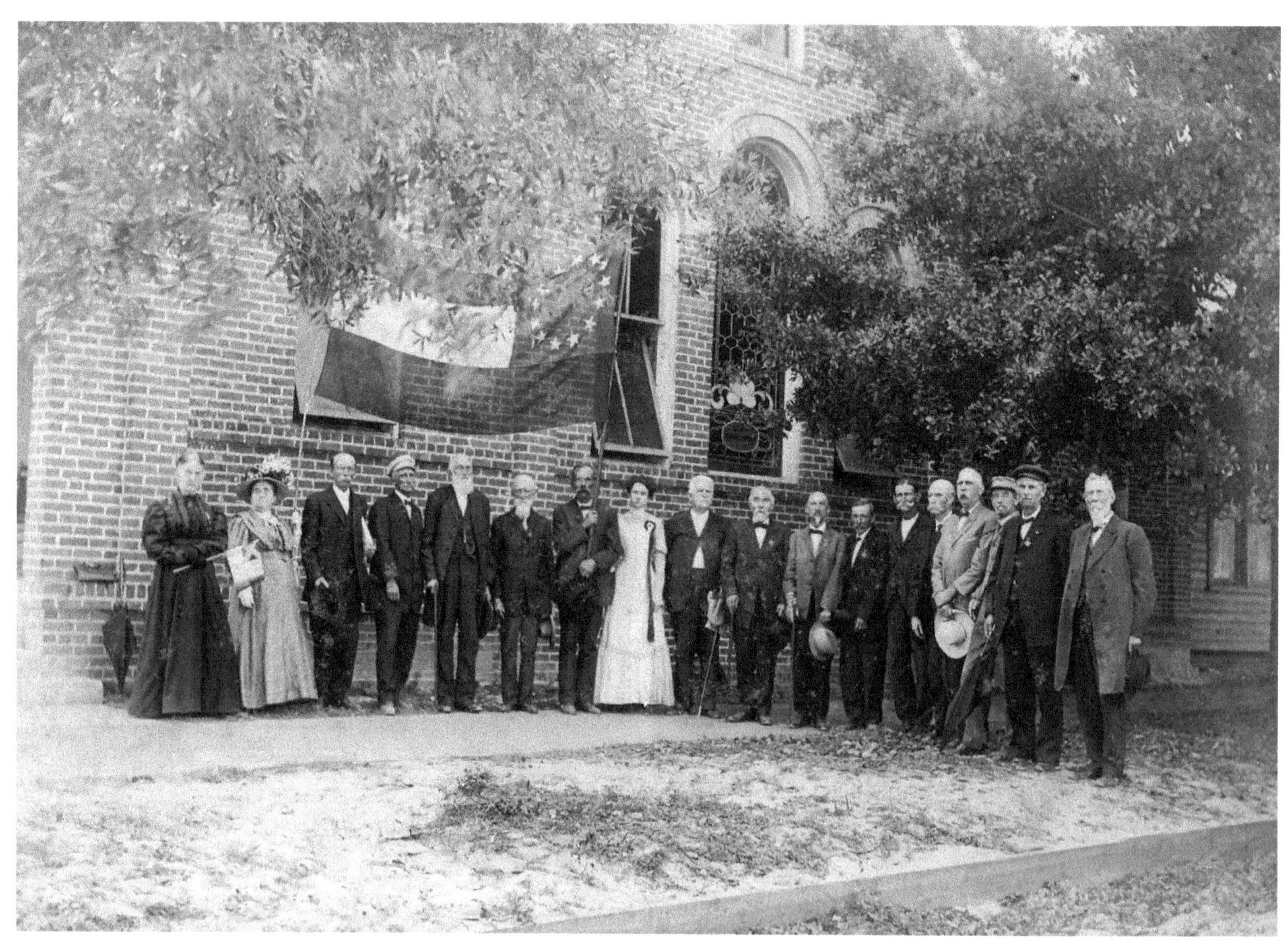

The local chapter of the United Confederate Veterans held monthly meetings at the Methodist Episcopal Church. In 1911, the Grand Army of the Republic objected to the Confederate flag in Washington's Birthday Parade. Some felt that only their age kept the two groups from fisticuffs and the disagreement was nicknamed the "Little Civil War."

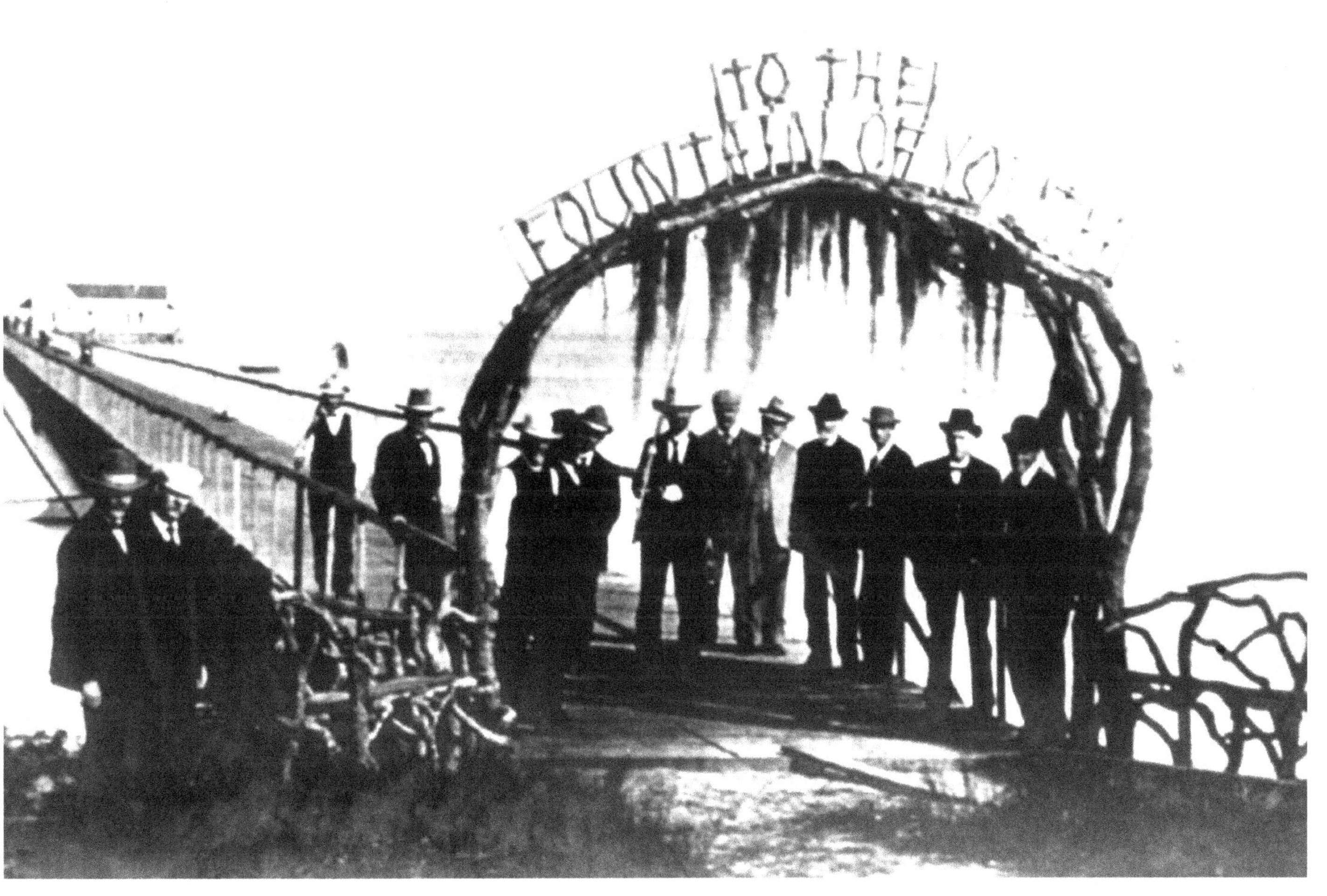

Adept at promoting the local community, Edwin Tomlinson created the "Fountain of Youth," a sulfuric artesian well located on the waterfront at Fourth Street South. Some townspeople noticed that Edwin's cottage at the end of the nearby "Fountain of Youth" pier was positioned just far enough to escape the odor of the sulfur well. This photograph of the attraction is from 1910.

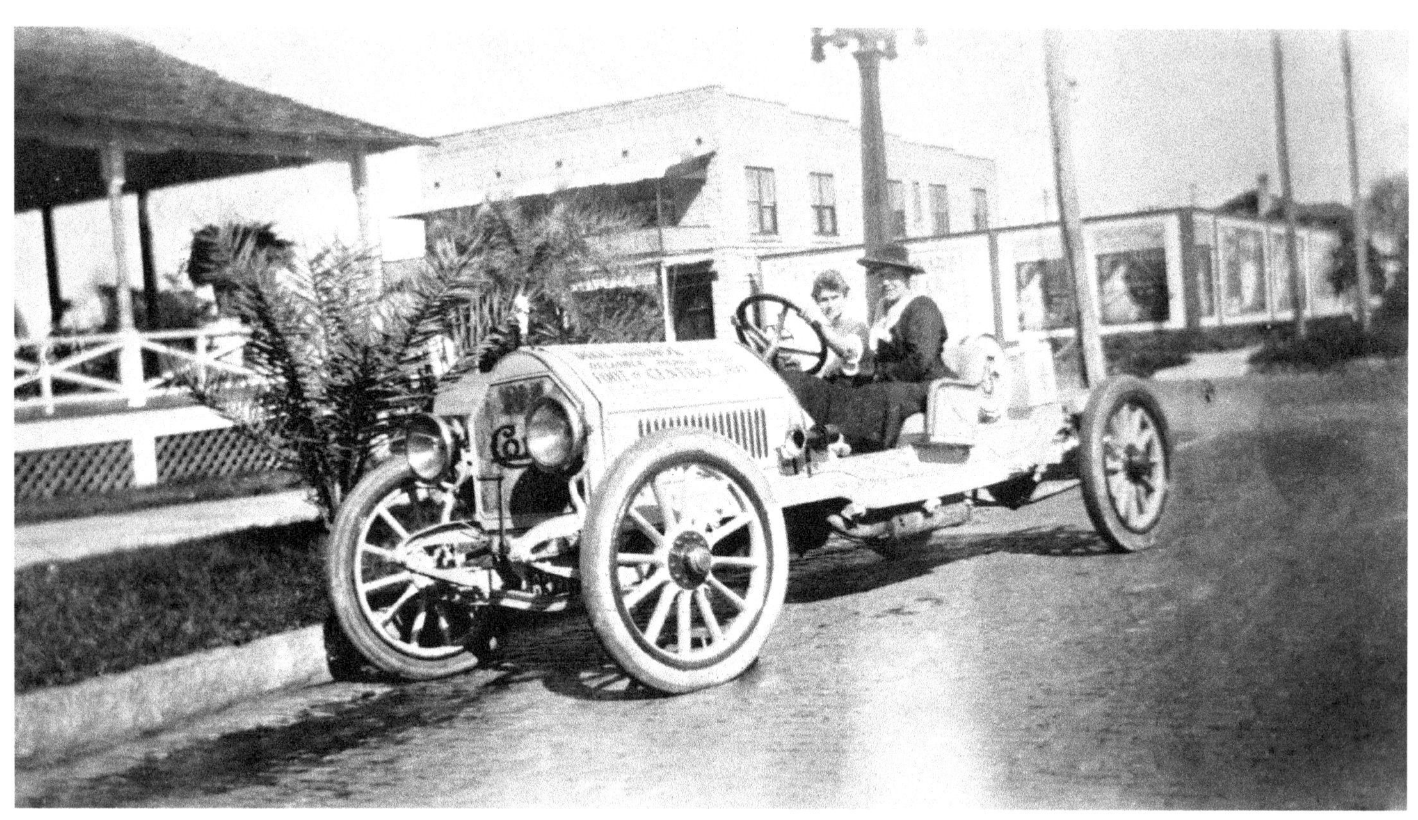

This early driver in St. Petersburg is visible evidence of the growing popularity of automobiles. This epoch saw the first garage, opened by Fred Ramm; the first filling station at Harrison Brothers hardware; and the first speeding ticket, a $100 fine to Mott Williams, for doing 18 miles an hour in a 10-mile-an-hour zone.

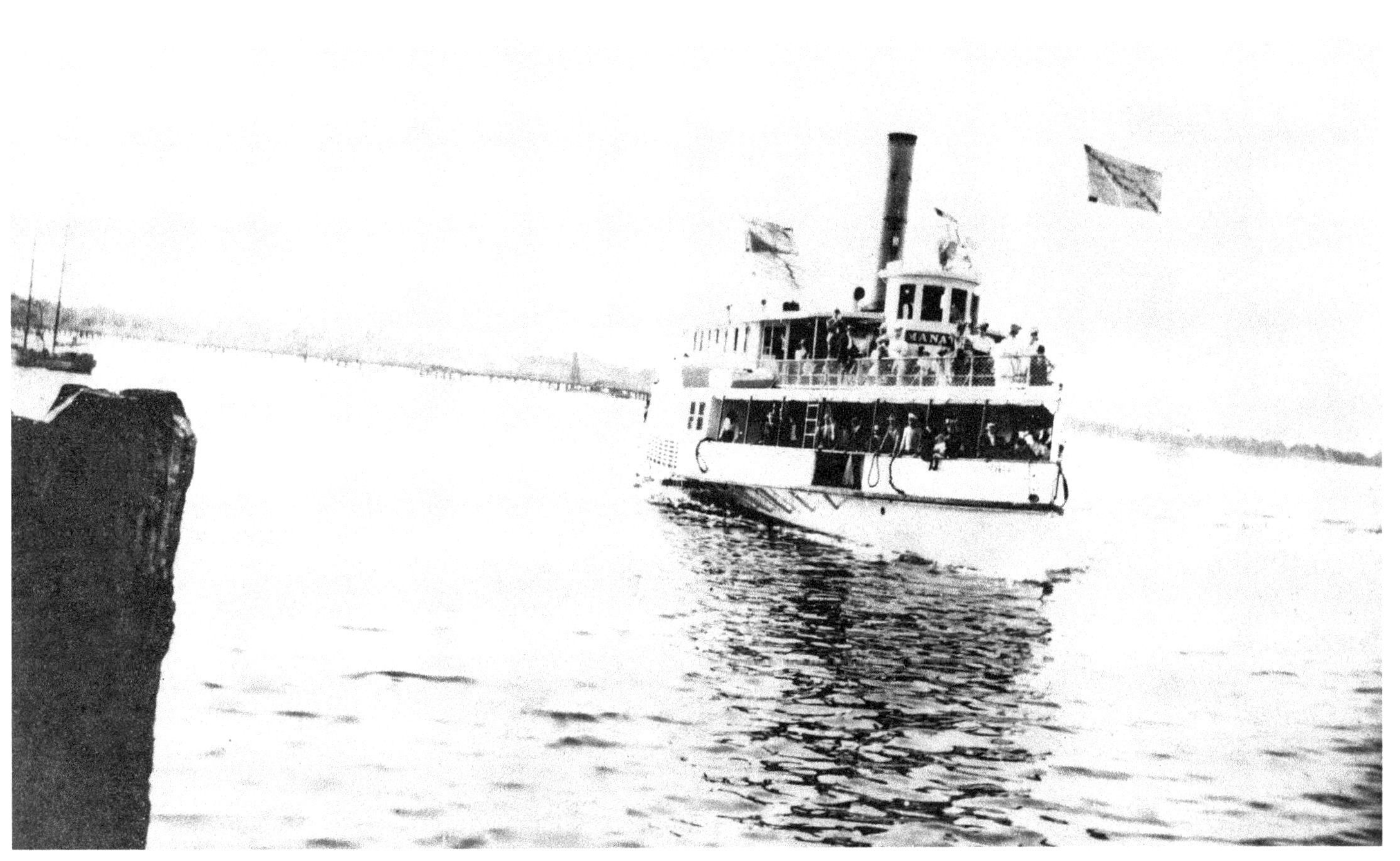

The Steamship *Manatee,* a regular sight on the St. Petersburg waterfront, arrives in town around 1910. Built in 1885, the 32-foot-wide, 125-foot-long steamer operated until 1928. The *Manatee* was part of the Favorite Line of steamers that operated between Tampa, St. Petersburg, Manatee River, Sarasota, and Ft. Myers.

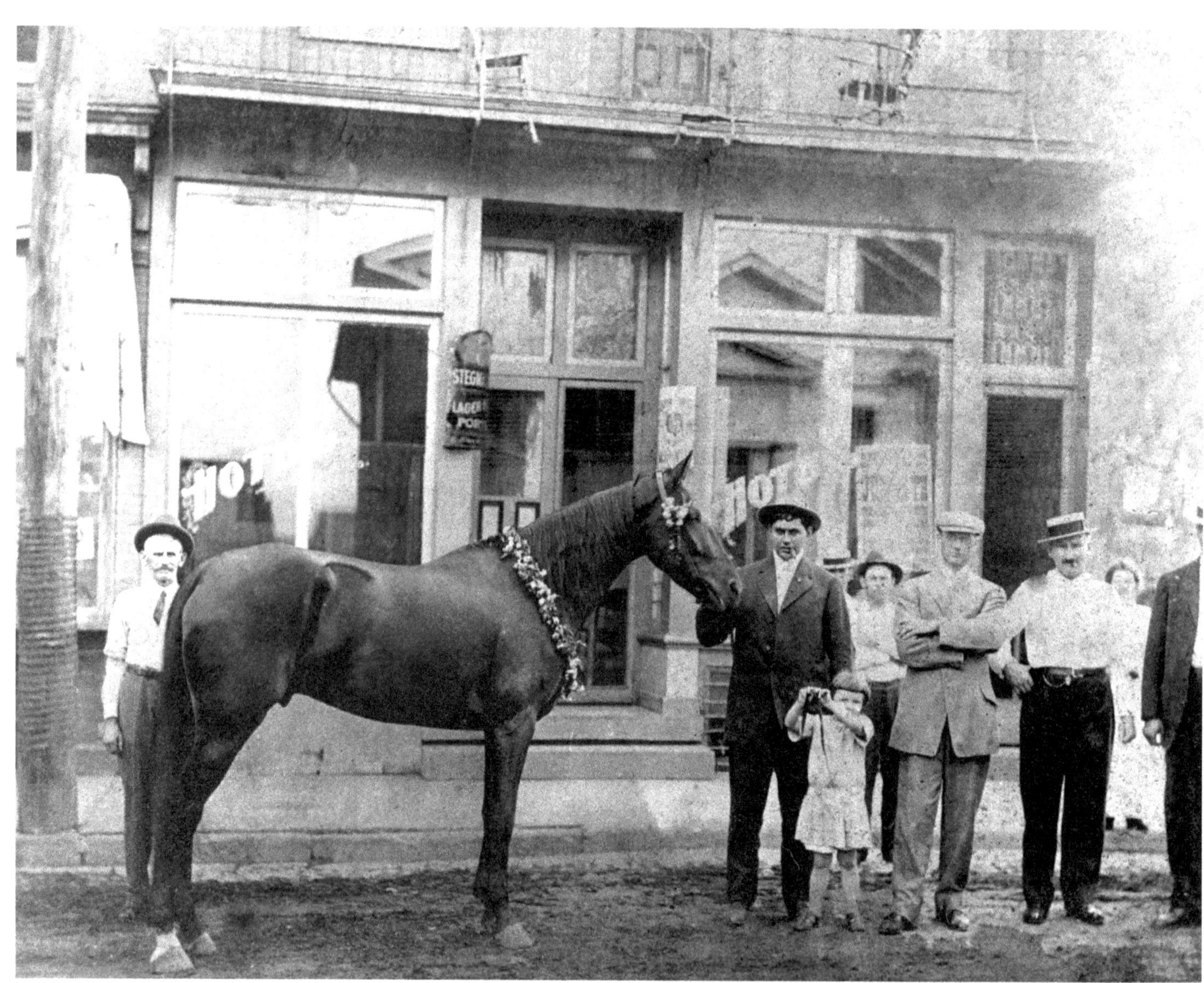

Although more and more automobiles were seen in St. Petersburg, horses were still very evident in town. Here local businessman Peter Sickler, at right in straw boater and white shirt, and Arthur Wiggins show off a beautiful horse. The decorations may be for a parade.

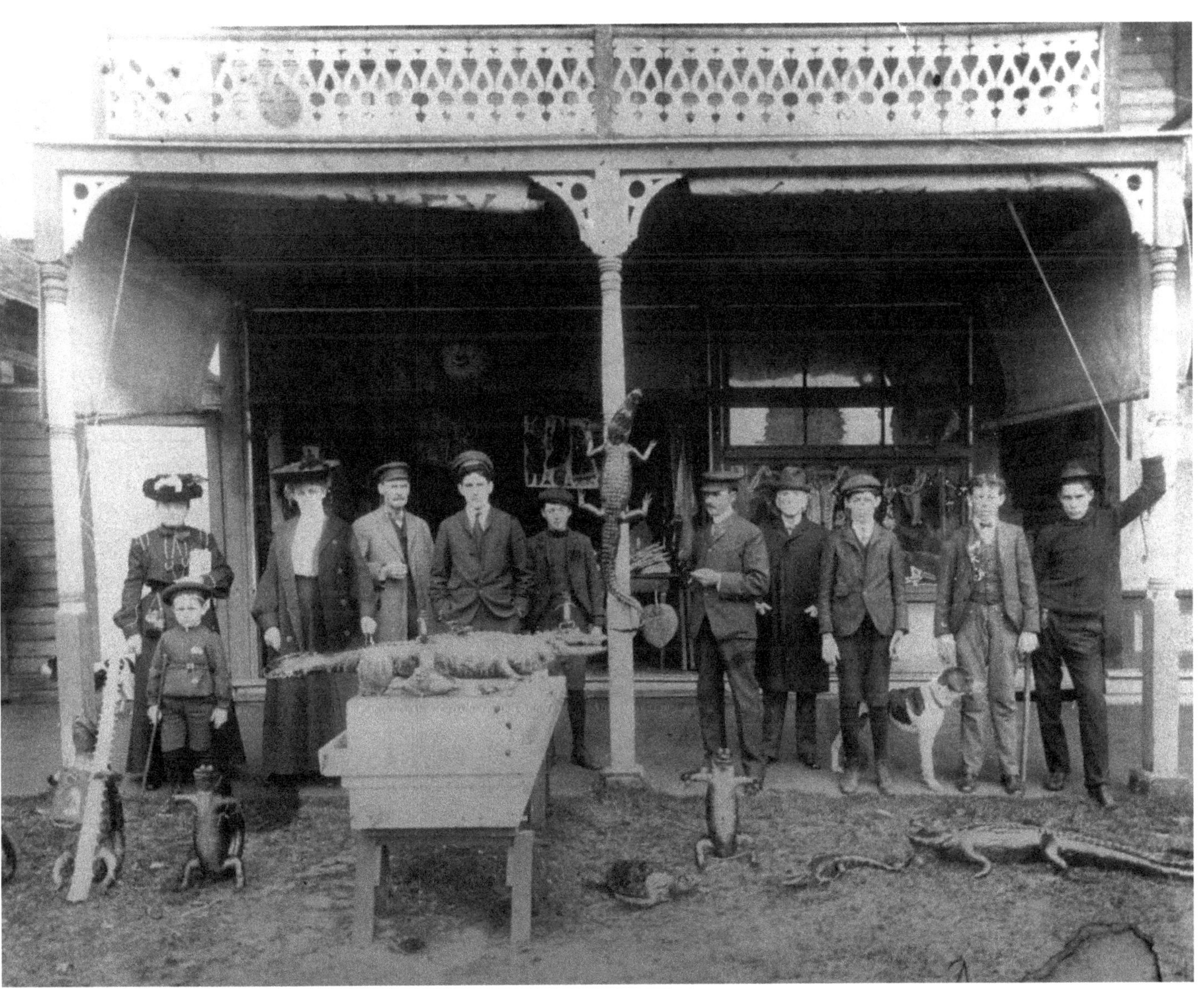

William "Alligator man" Carpenter, second from right, opened this gift shop next to his Royal Palm theater, the city's first. He often amazed tourists with live alligator shows. Four years later Carpenter took his alligator show on the road, touring the country with a six-foot alligator named Trouble and promoting St. Petersburg.

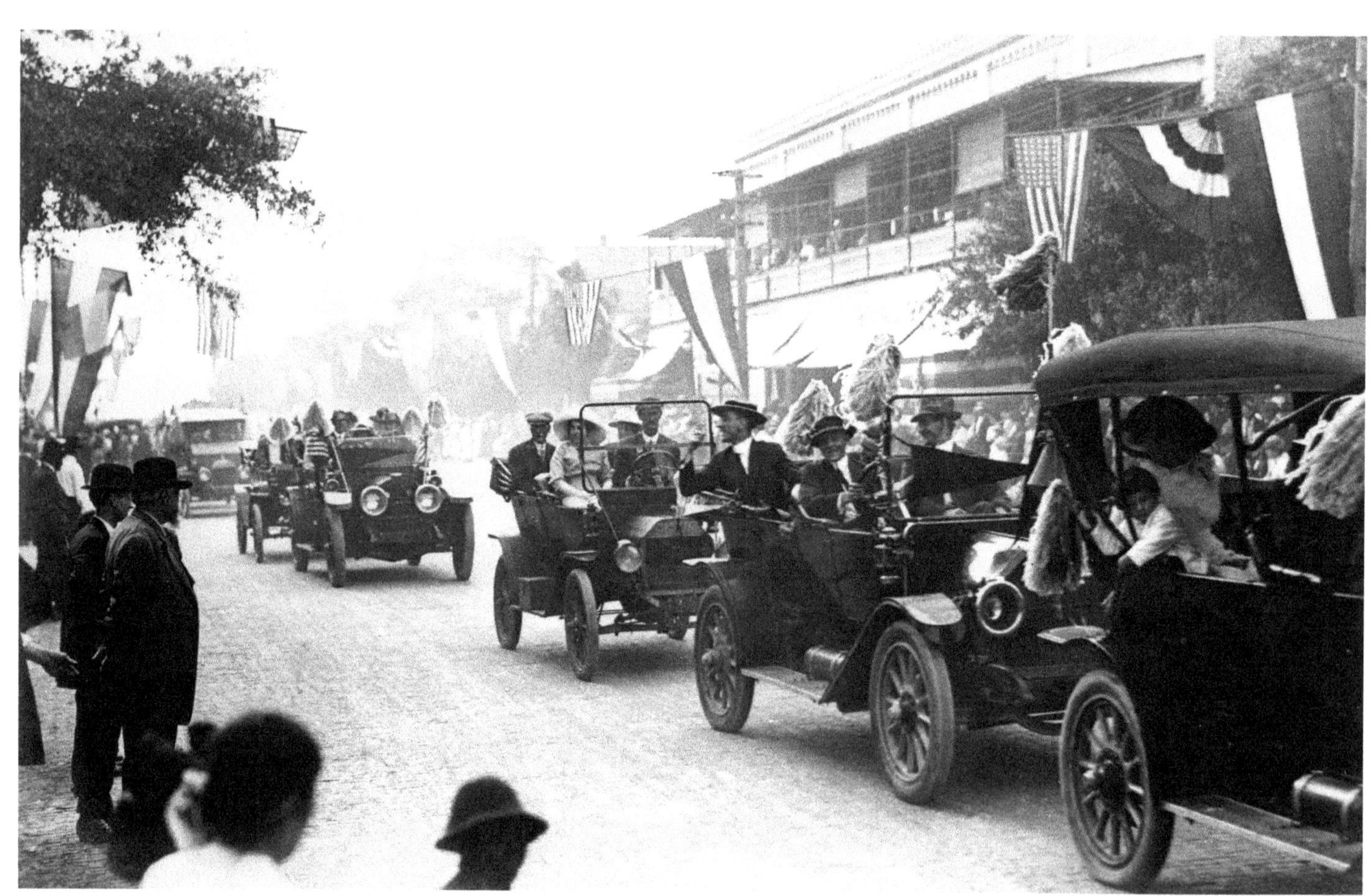

A 1912 publicity brochure declared, "St. Petersburg is an automobile town. The 100-foot wide streets paved with vitrified brick arouse the enthusiasm of visiting motorist." In the tract a visitor acclaimed, "The people are so energetic, sociable, friendly and free from snobbery and do so much for one's entertainment and amusement."

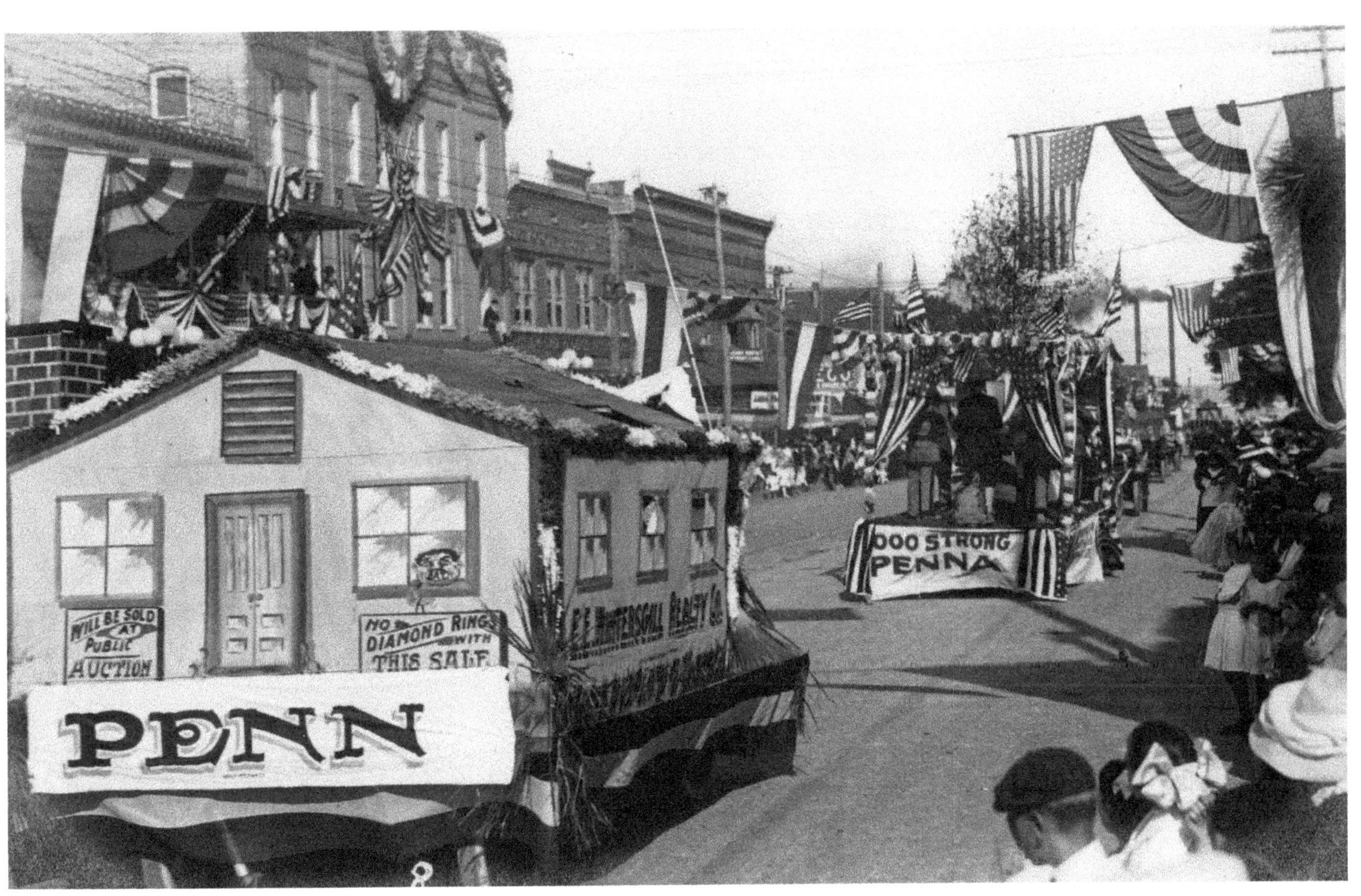

Between 1896 and 1914, St. Petersburg tried a variety of themes for various fairs, festivals, and celebrations, including Washington's Birthday celebrations, a midwinter fair, a Chautauqua assembly, the St. Petersburg Fair and Tourist Week, and a DeSoto celebration. The inaugural Festival of States parade was held in 1917.

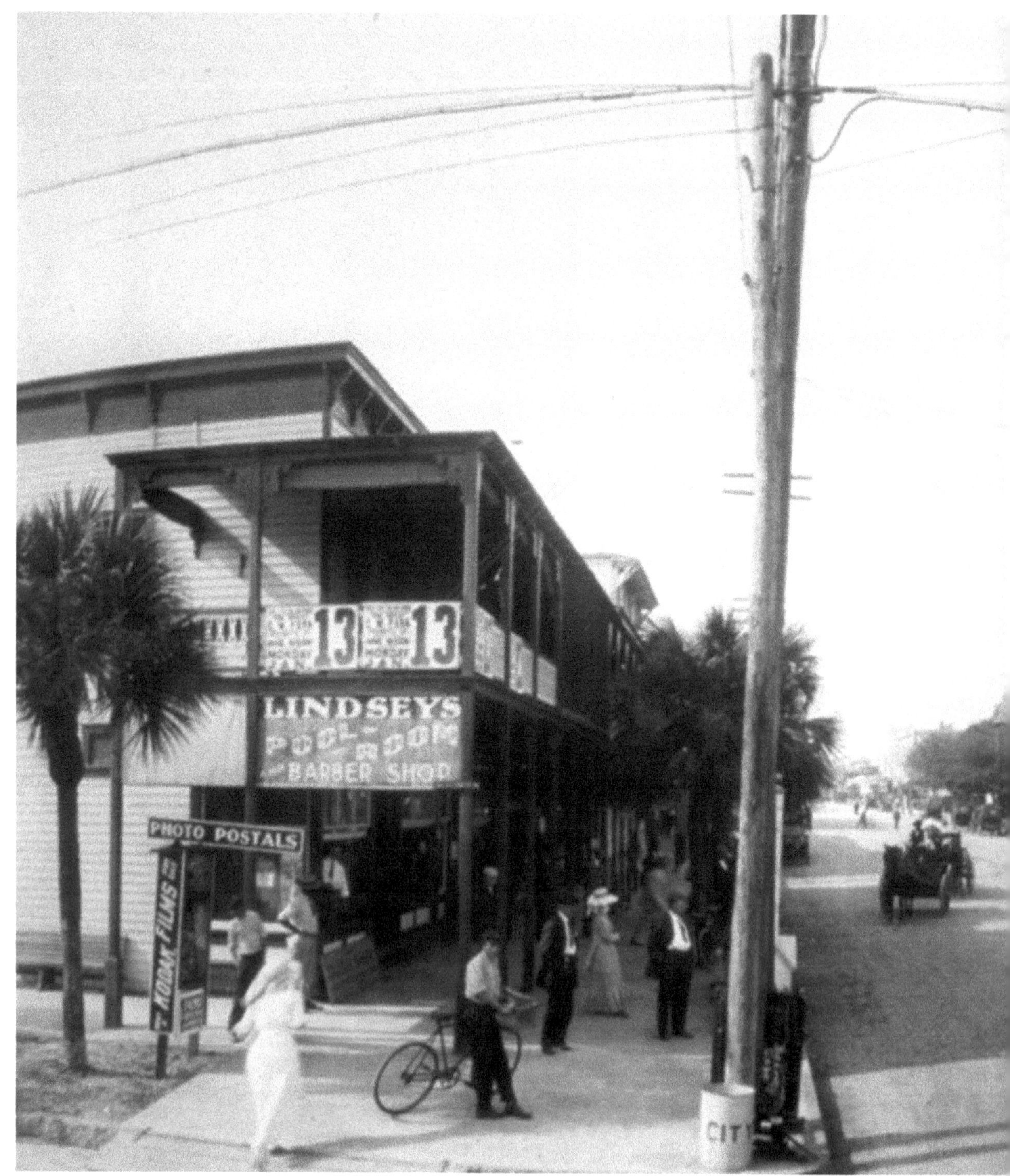

The stately Detroit Hotel dominates the corner of Central Avenue and Second Street. The 60-room brick addition was completed in 1914, bringing its room capacity to 100. W. S. Lindsey, owner of the pool room and barbershop across the street, became city police chief and county sheriff.

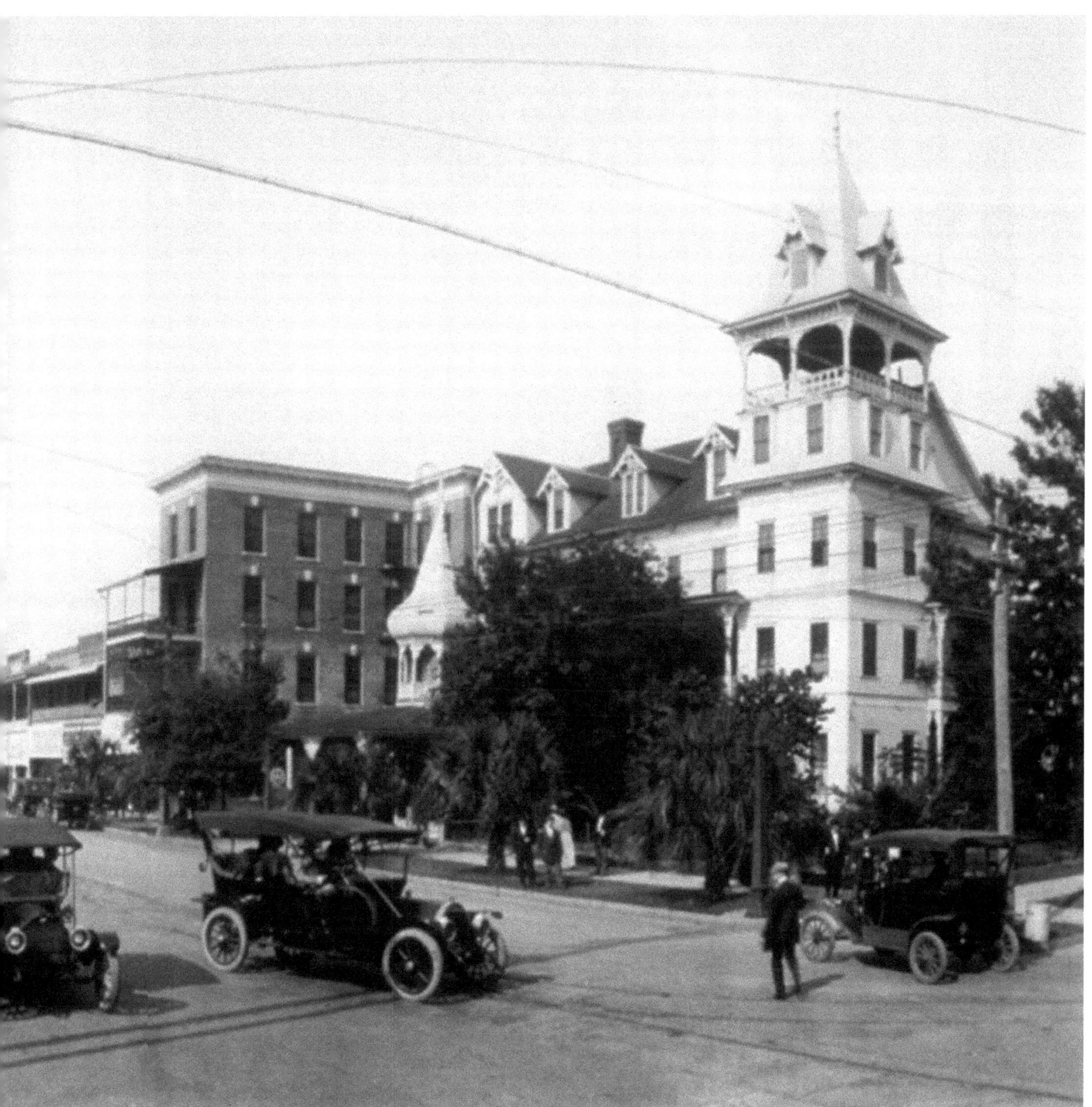

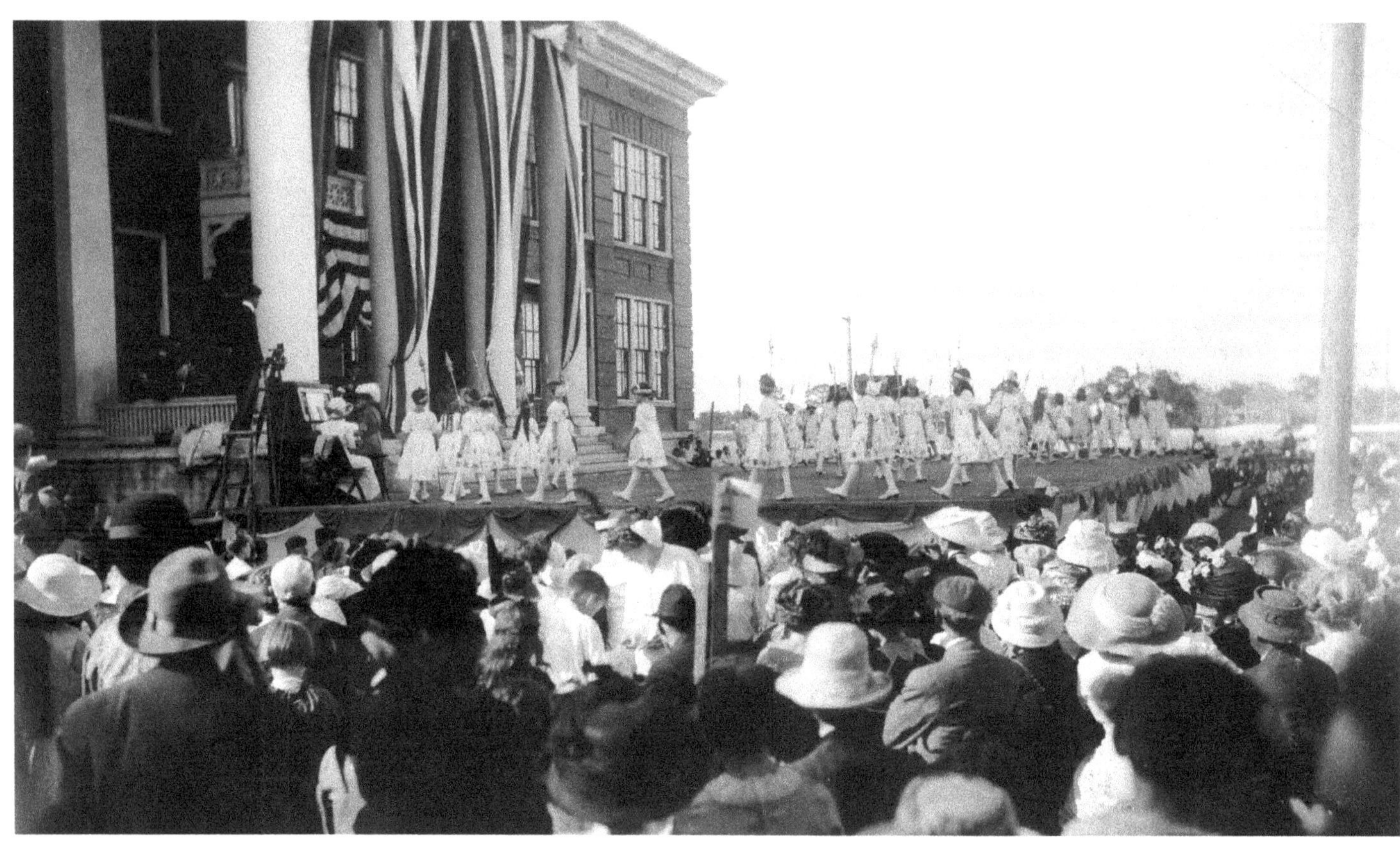

Students perform in front of the new St. Petersburg High School. Funded by the city in 1909, the school bond was struck down by the courts, since only counties not cities were then authorized to issue school bonds. The city transferred the bonds to local residents, who transferred them to Pinellas County after it was formed in 1911.

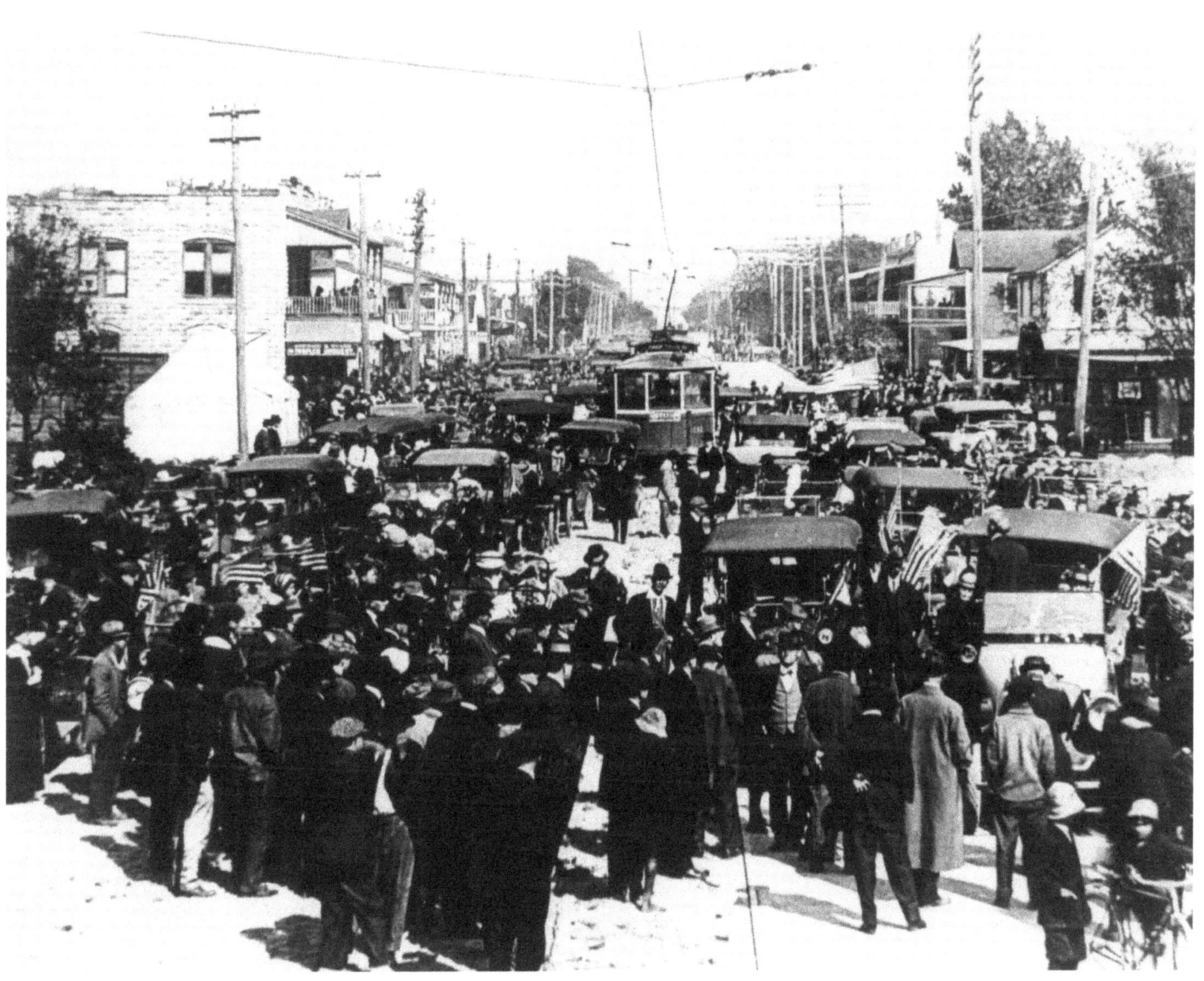

Streetcars, automobiles, pedestrians, and cyclists all crowd Central Avenue around 1913. As the population grew by more than ten thousand from 1910 to 1920, the streets became crowded and increasingly vital to the tourist industry. Accordingly, Central Avenue was paved with brick and officially reopened on March 23, 1914.

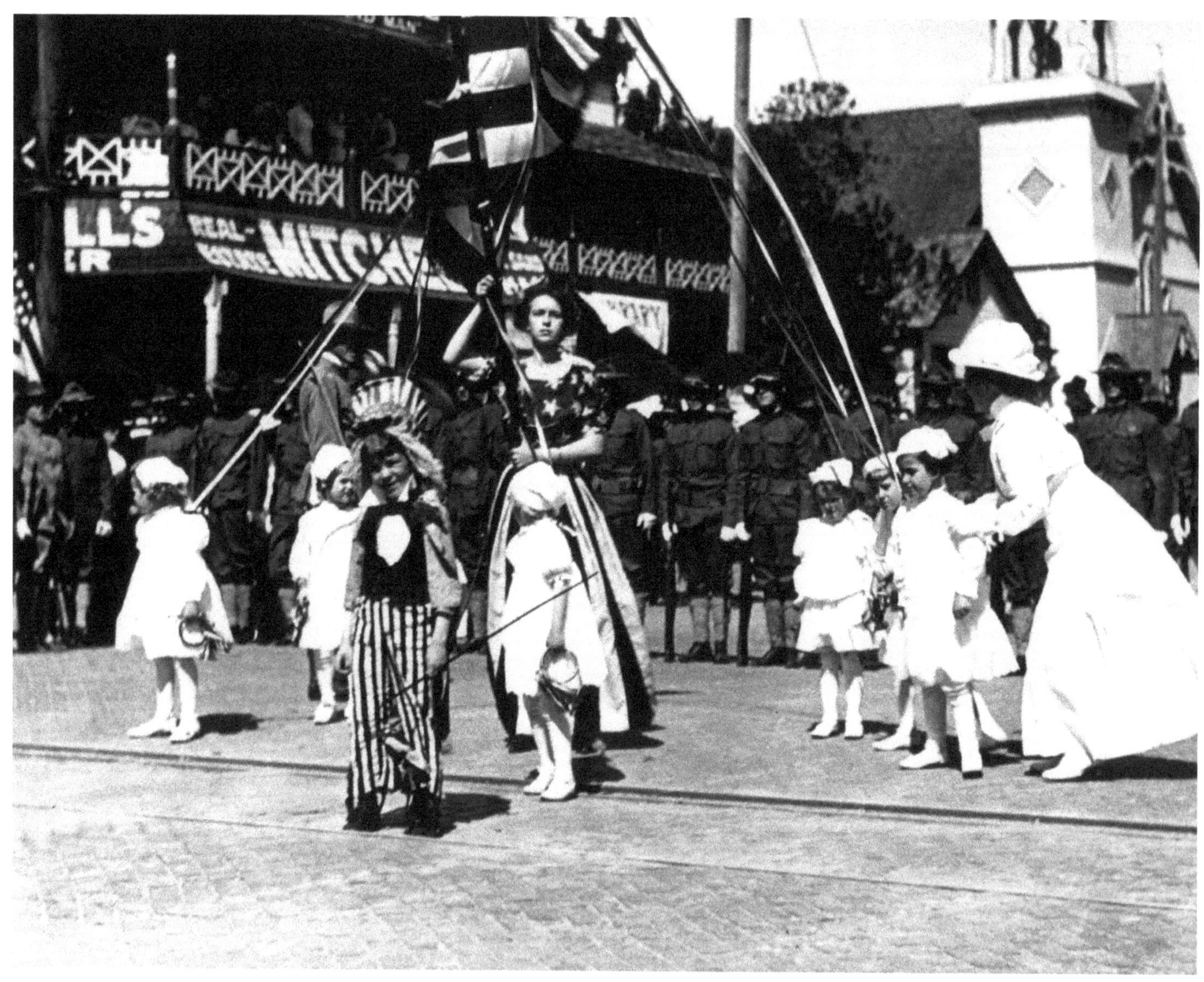

Marguerite Blocker is the flag bearer as this parade passes the First Congregational Church during the 1913 Fair and Tourist week. A 1912 promotional brochure described it as "a carnival time. Business is practically suspended . . . until the final day when the fair is closed by a grand parade of beautifully decorated autos and floats."

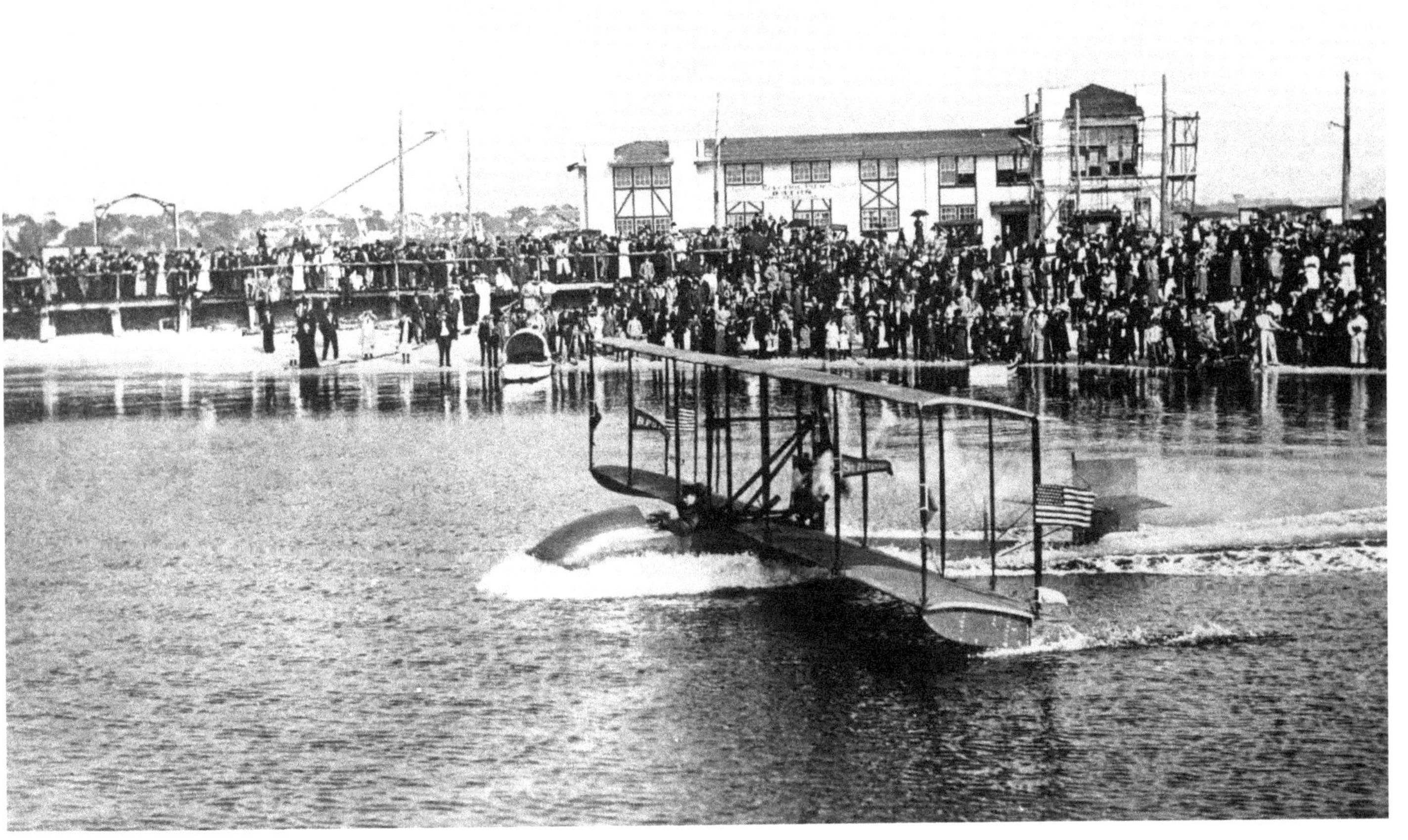

In this famous photograph from January 1, 1914, Tony Jannus pilots a Benoist Type XIV flying boat on the world's first regularly scheduled commercial airline flight. Former St. Petersburg mayor Abram Pheil won the auction to be the first passenger paying $400 for the 23-minute historic flight.

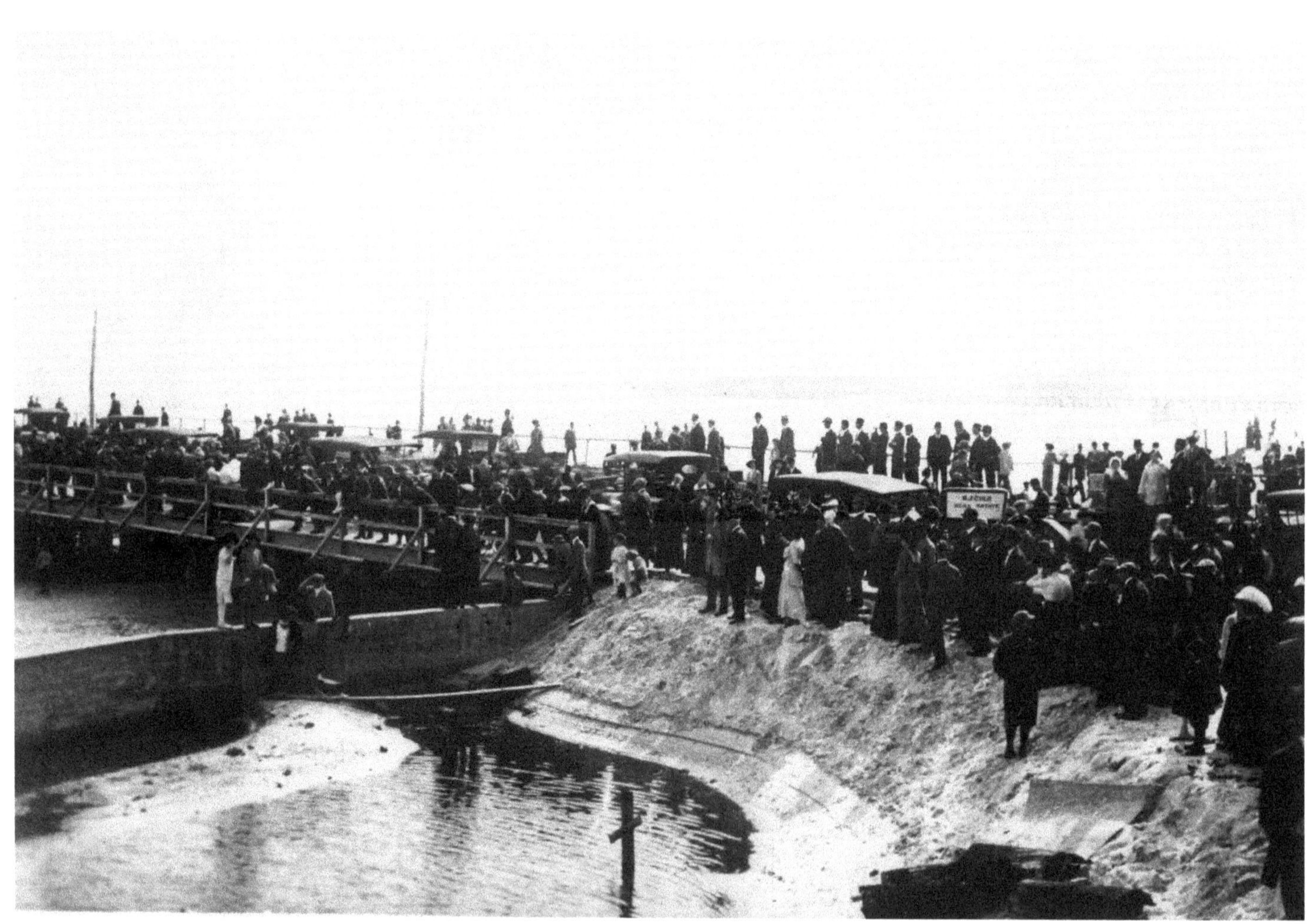

This crowd anxiously awaits the return of the Benoist flying boat on its inaugural flight. Employing two Type XIV flying boats, the airline flew service twice daily across Tampa Bay, charging five dollars for a one-way ticket. When it folded in May 1914, the airline had carried 1,204 passengers without a serious accident.

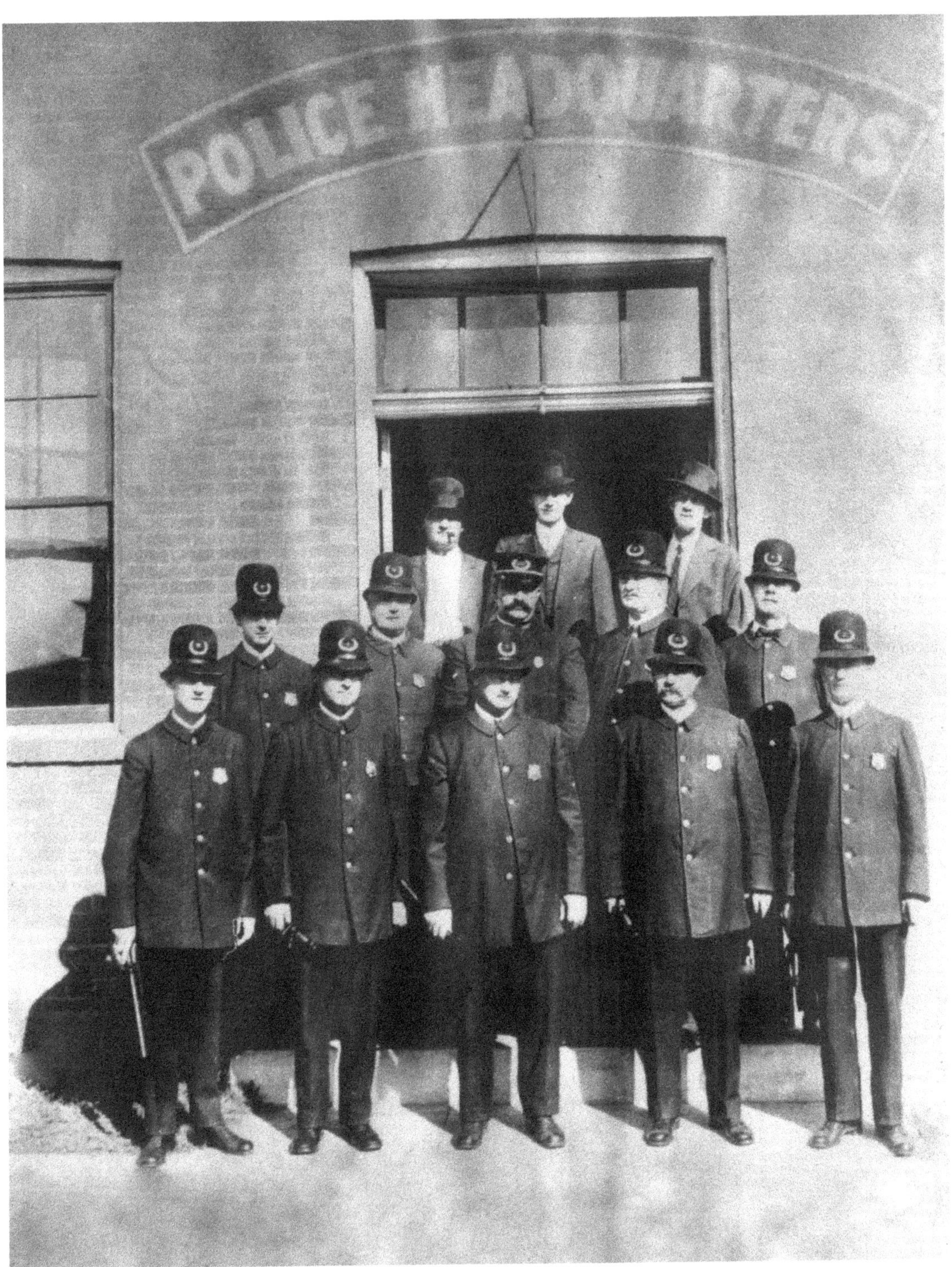

St. Petersburg Police Department officers in 1915 with three plainclothesmen in the back row. Police Chief A. J. Esters, second row center, served as chief from 1906 to 1921. In 1912, Chief Esters warned that any youth caught violating curfew would be paddled and turned over to their parents. It is unknown if the threat was carried out.

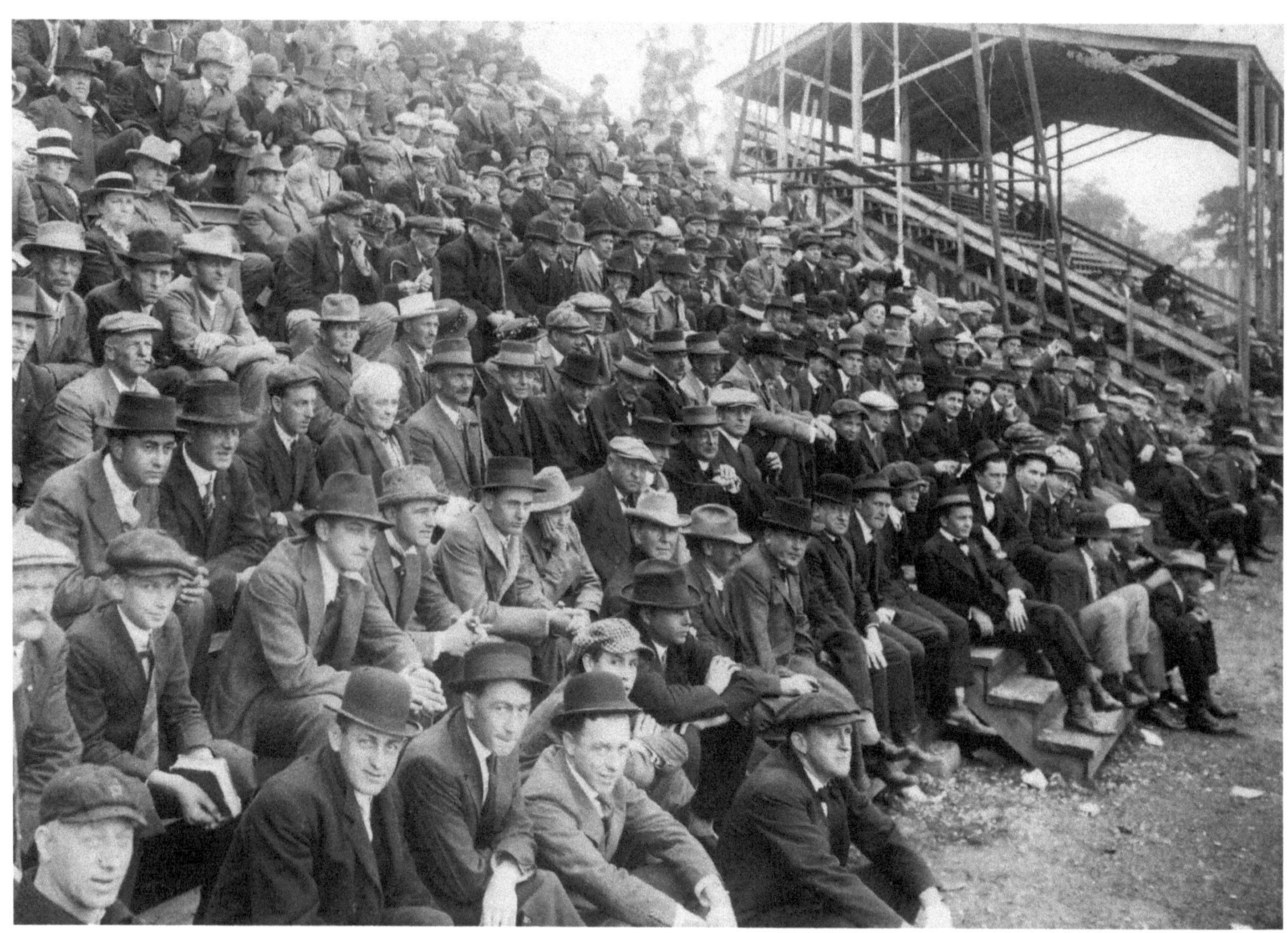

A crowd watches a Browns-Phillies baseball game in 1915. In the spring of 1914, the St. Louis Browns had trained in the area but did not return. Albert Lang then arranged to have the Philadelphia Phillies train in St. Petersburg, in the spring of 1915. The Phillies won the pennant that year and baseball remained in the fledgling city.

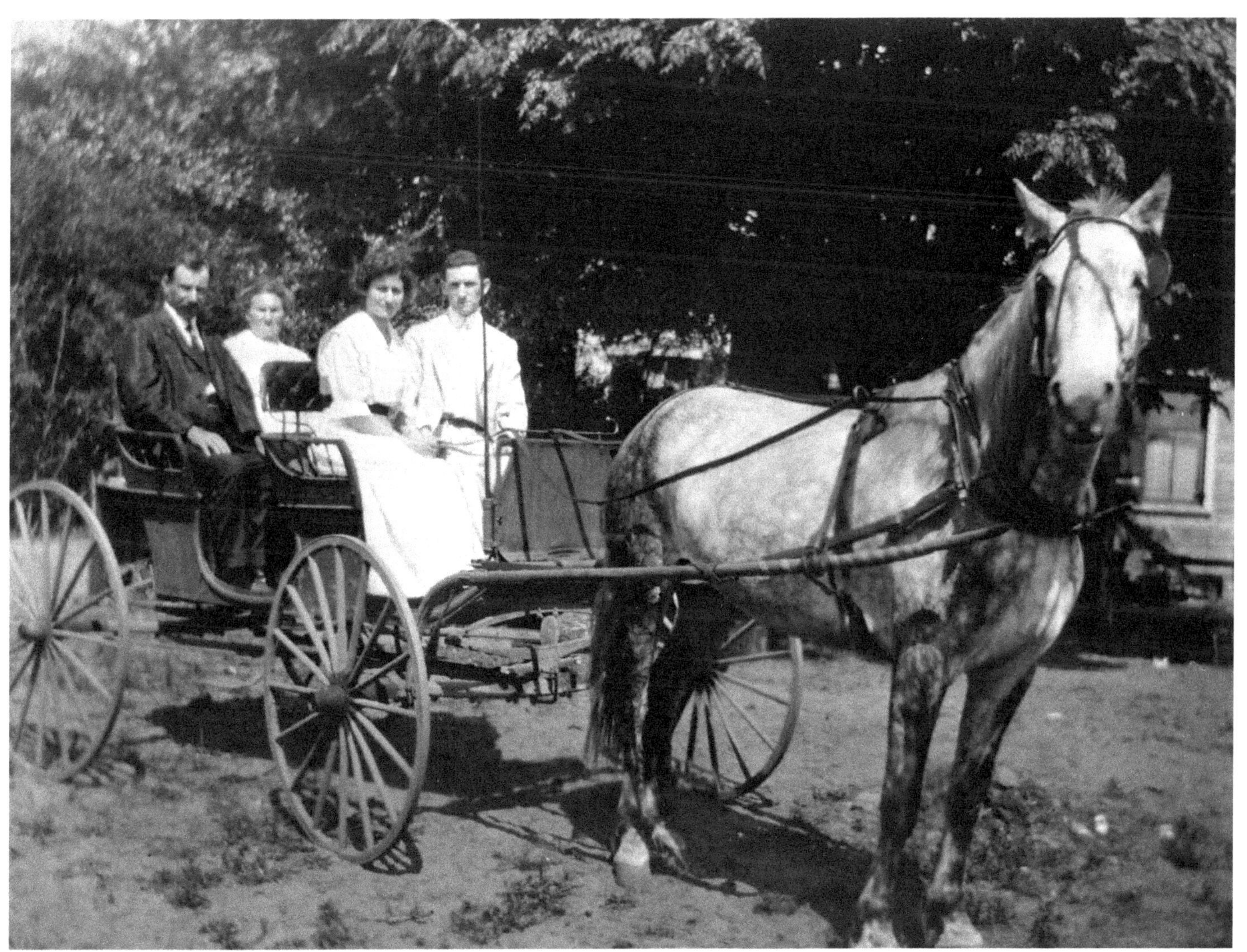

The Levine family, Gershon and Esther in back with Morris and Miriam Levine in front, taking a ride in a horse-drawn carriage around 1916. Counting only ten families by 1920, the twenties brought the first large influx of Jewish settlers and tourists and by 1926 the growing Jewish community finally had its own rabbi.

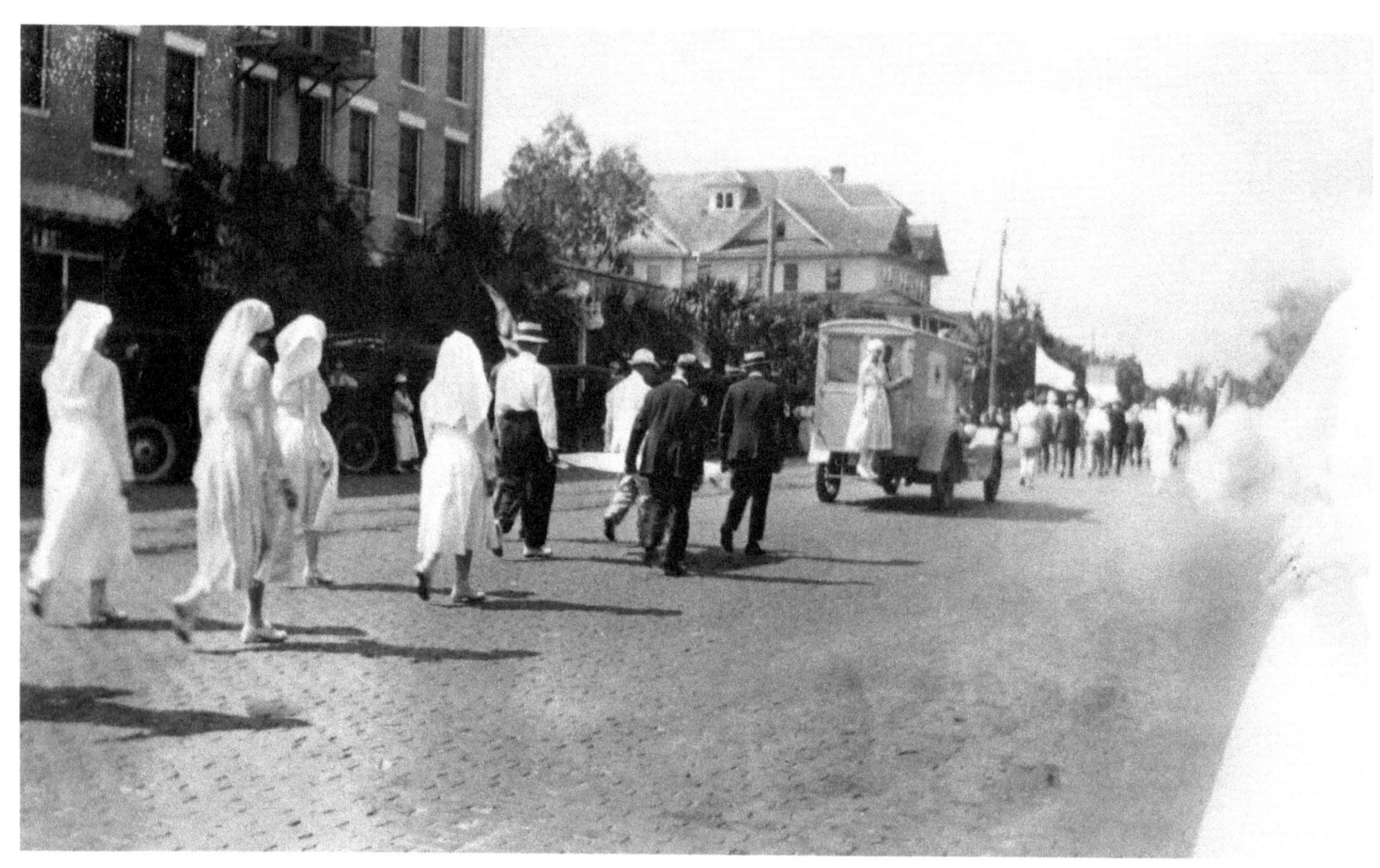

One nurse rides behind an ambulance while men carry an empty stretcher in a wartime parade during 1918. Civic improvements and development were temporarily put aside when the United States entered World War I. Hundreds from St. Petersburg joined the military and 16 gave their lives in service.

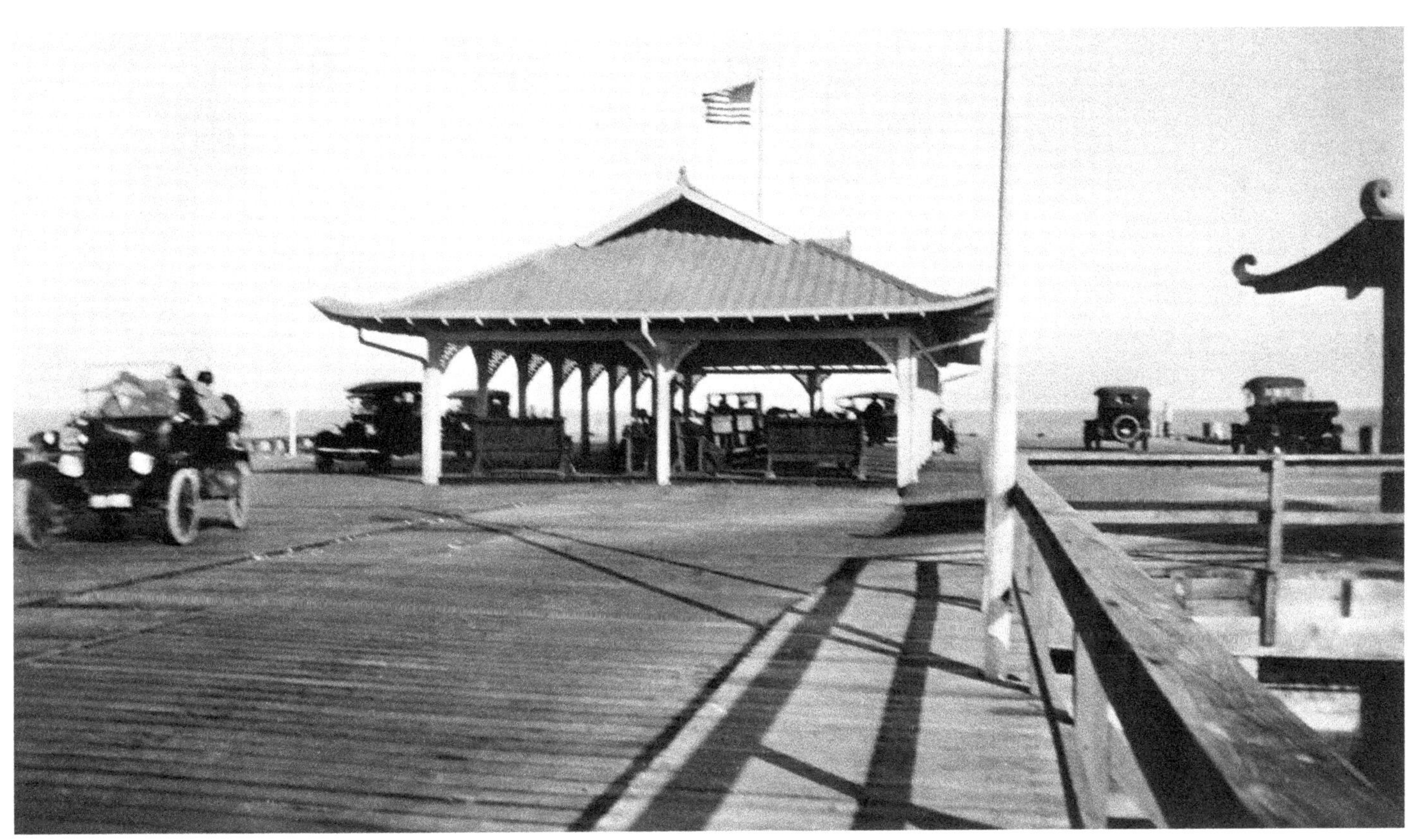

Visitors park under the covered shelter during a windy day at the end of the Municipal Recreation pier. At the foot of Second Avenue north, this pier was constructed in 1913, the same year the nearby electrical pier was torn down. Driving to the end of the pier was a popular pastime in the years following the First World War.

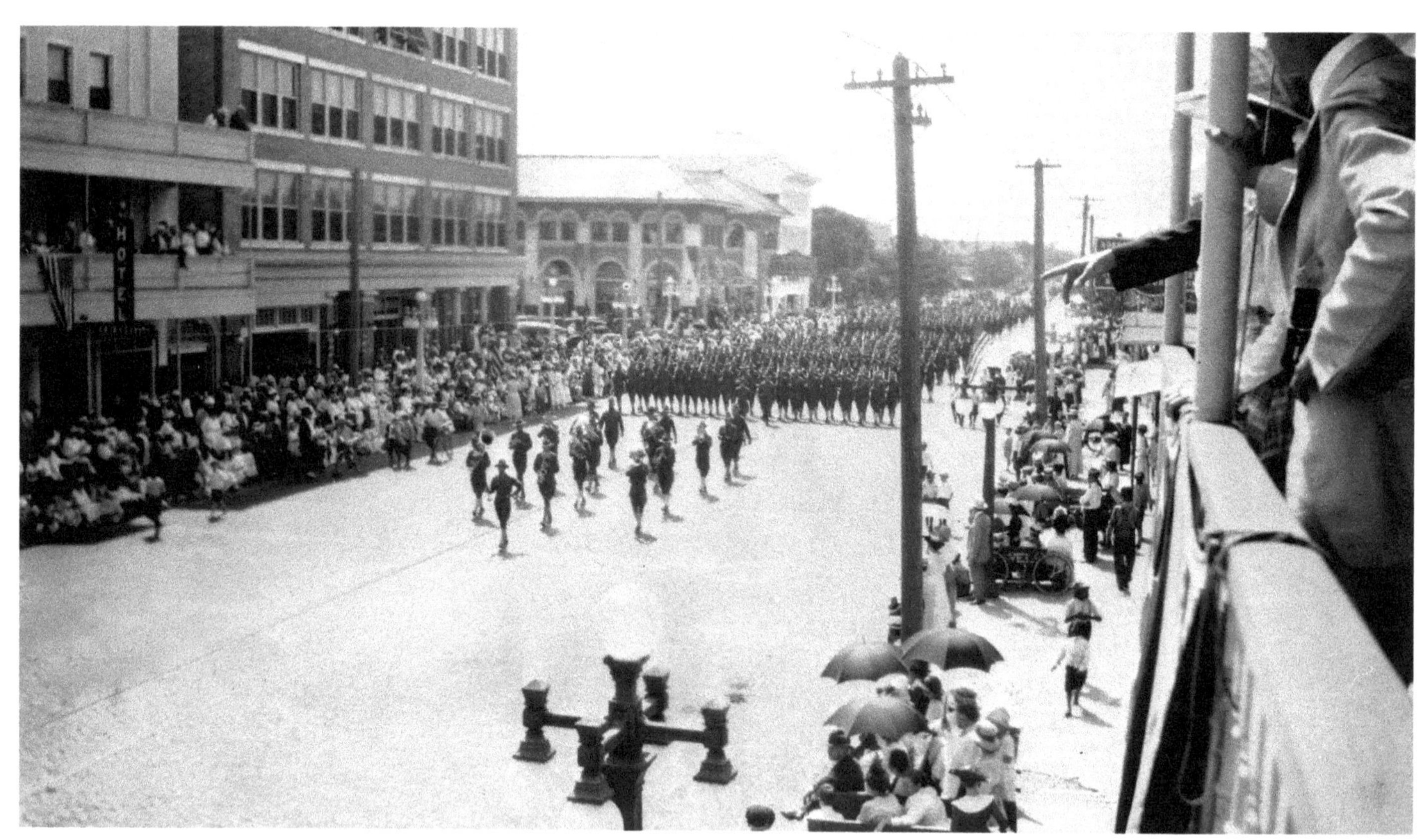

Soldiers parade down Central Avenue on February 22, 1918, while residents wave from porches and use umbrellas to shade themselves. The war was not the only problem facing St. Petersburg. Its economy struggled when the business empire of H. Walter Fuller faltered and went into receivership in April 1918.

Sunny Skies: The Boom Years

(1919–1926)

St. Petersburg benefited from the Florida land boom of the twenties as much as or even more than other towns in the state. Certainly the town's development by late 1918 positioned it to take advantage of the national circumstances. The nation's economic upswing toward the end of World War I provided most families with adequate income. Coupled with available transportation by automobile or train, people now had the ways and means to visit the state. The war and the turbulent period immediately afterward, beset with steel strikes, labor unrest, and race riots, provided the motivation to find somewhere peaceful and quiet. Where better to escape than sunny exotic Florida and the Sunshine City.

The town has always attracted ambitious and talented individuals ready to take the risks necessary for development. Young John Lodwick was one of these remarkable individuals. In 1919, he took over public relations for the town, declaring that the town could determine his salary after he finished a season's work. He proved to be a master of the art of publicity, as this 1921 town brochure demonstrates:

"When man seeks rest from the cares and wearing-out processes of life, he goes out of doors to find it. America's Sunshine City—St. Petersburg Florida invites you to come and see for yourself the satisfaction of spending your winter months where you may live in the great outdoors under unsurpassed climatic conditions. Health, pleasure and life find their greatest measure of expression here."

The publicity campaign worked better than expected and for the next six years tourism increased dramatically. They came to St. Petersburg from all across the country—some came to play, and others came to stay. The rich who came to play needed suitable accommodations, inspiring some of the most luxurious hotels in the state: the Vinoy, Don CeSar, Soreno, Pheil, and Rolyat. Those who stayed dabbled in the land speculation that became the core product of the boom period. Building permits increased from 2.8 million in 1920 to 24 million in 1925. Developers such as C. Perry Snell, Jack Taylor, and Walter P. Fuller promoted multi-million-dollar subdivisions such as the Jungle, Snell Island, Roser Park, Pasadena, and Shore Acres.

The booming real estate market provided a strong tax base and the investment capital necessary to meet the recreational and business requirements of the growing city. The focal point of the rising downtown skyline was the magnificent Snell Arcade. Other byproducts of the boom were the Million Dollar Recreation Pier, Million Dollar High School, and the Gandy Bridge. The city, along with the famous State societies and other clubs, provided numerous activities and events. Tourists could enjoy the Festival of States parade; watch the World championships of horseshoes; meet baseball stars from spring training camps; participate in group outings for fishing, swimming, and sightseeing; or visit the Coliseum and the Pier Casino for nightlife activities.

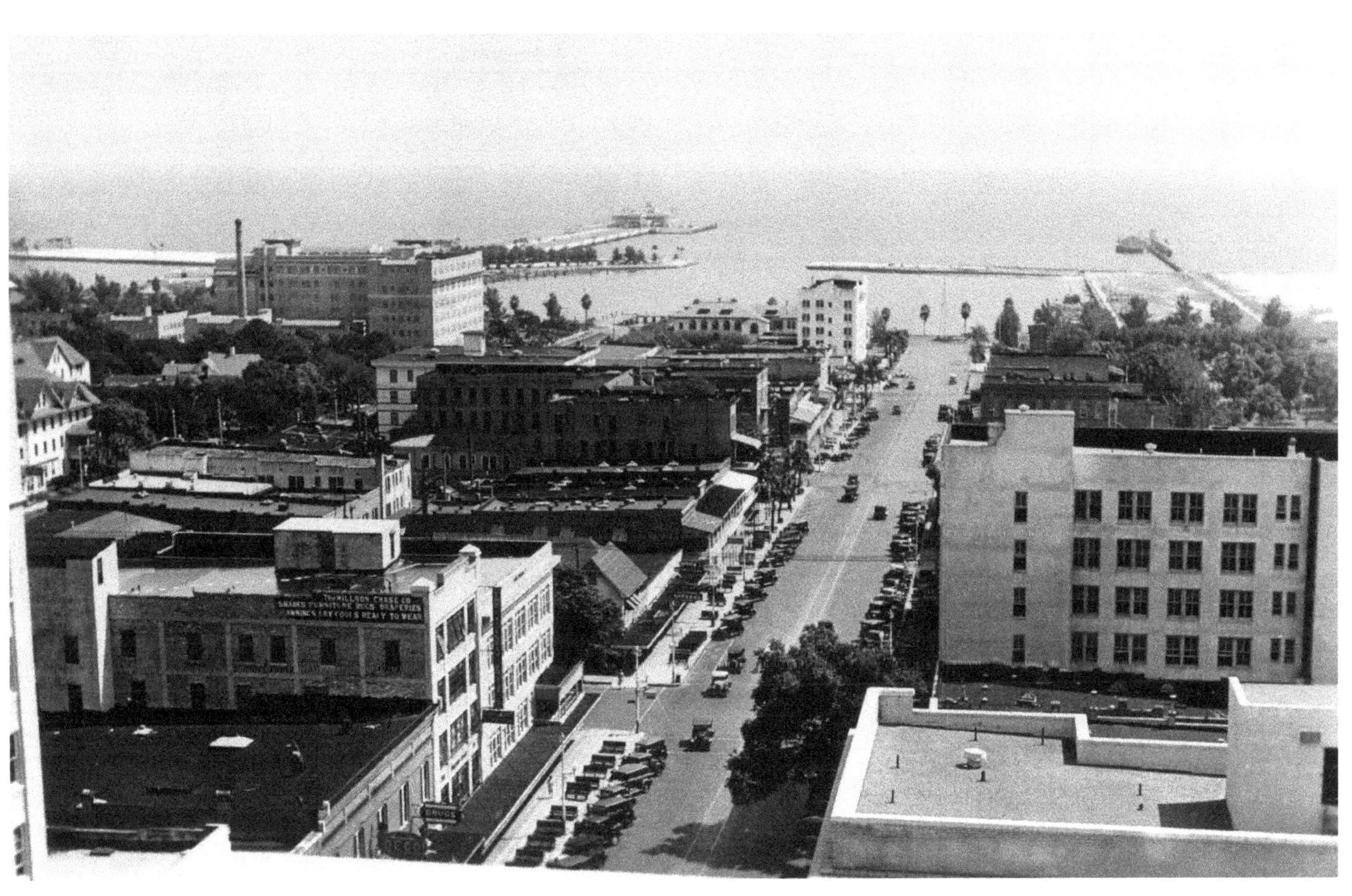

Behind a thriving tourist industry, St. Petersburg entered a boom period in the 1920s. East Central Avenue in 1922 already shows evidence of the prosperous and growing city—in stark contrast to the earlier dirt streets and wood storefronts. The new 85-room Ponce de Leon had just opened at the end of Central Avenue near the waterfront.

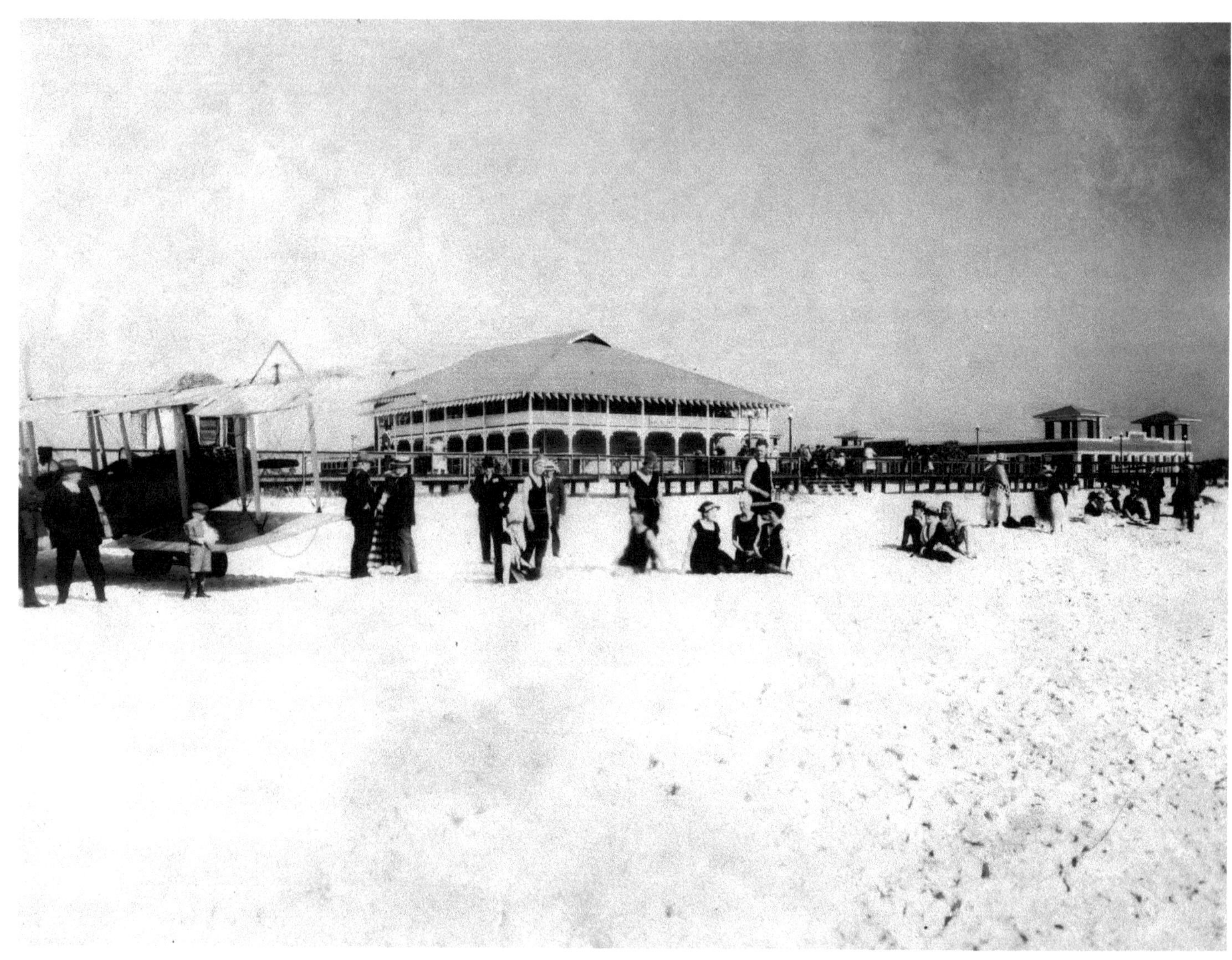

This biplane at St. Petersburg Beach around 1920, could be part of a stunt by Johnny Green, a local aviator who often took residents and tourists on their first flight. Before 1919, residents of St. Petersburg had preferred the readily available beaches of Tampa Bay to the Gulf beaches, which were accessible only by ferry.

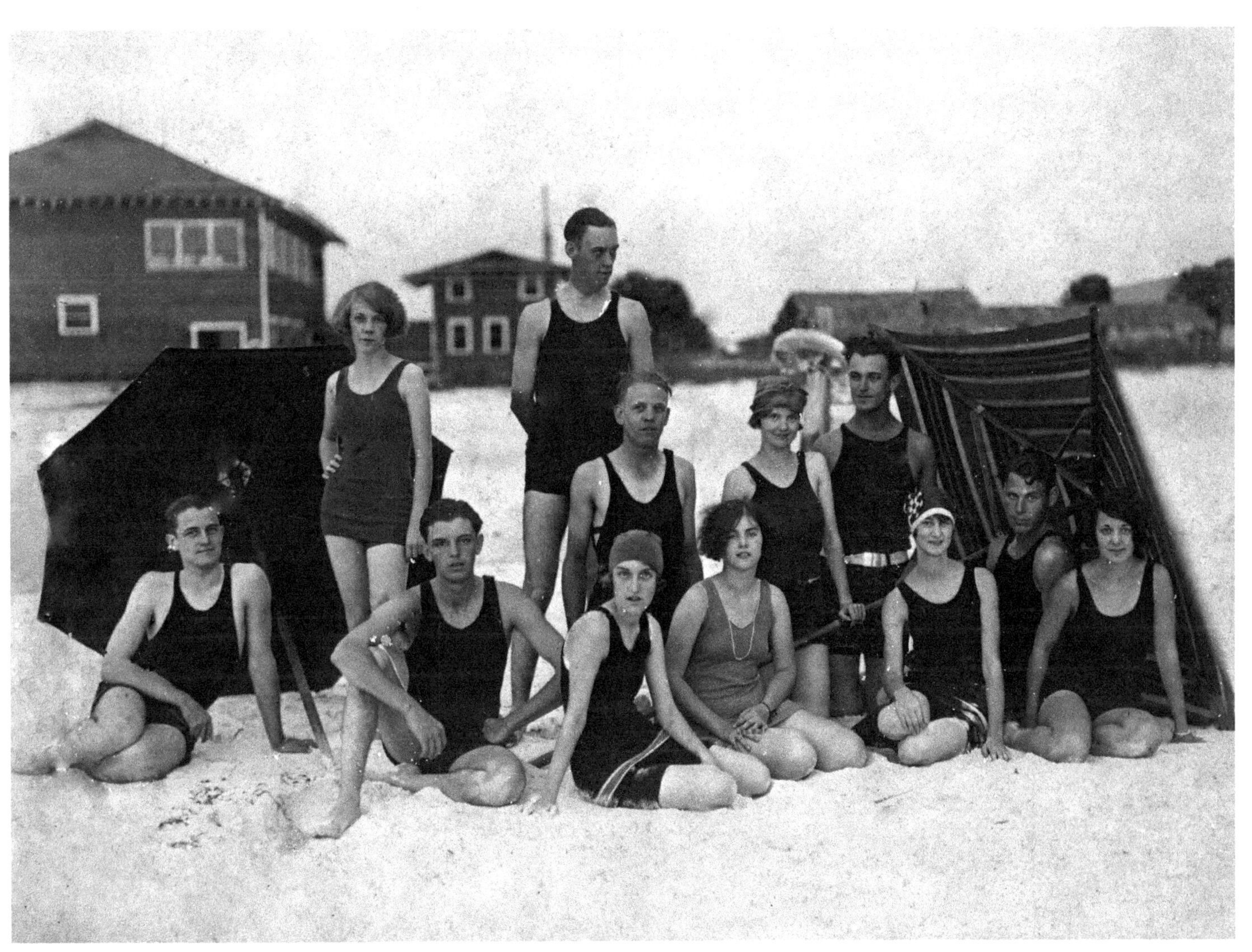

These bathers at St. Petersburg Beach in the 1920s may have used the new Pass-A-Grille bridge. Opened on February 4, 1919, and built by W. D. McAdoo, the wooden toll bridge instantly had a strong impact—with the new bridge in place, the gulf beaches at Pass-A-Grille and St. Petersburg Beach were only half an hour's drive from the city.

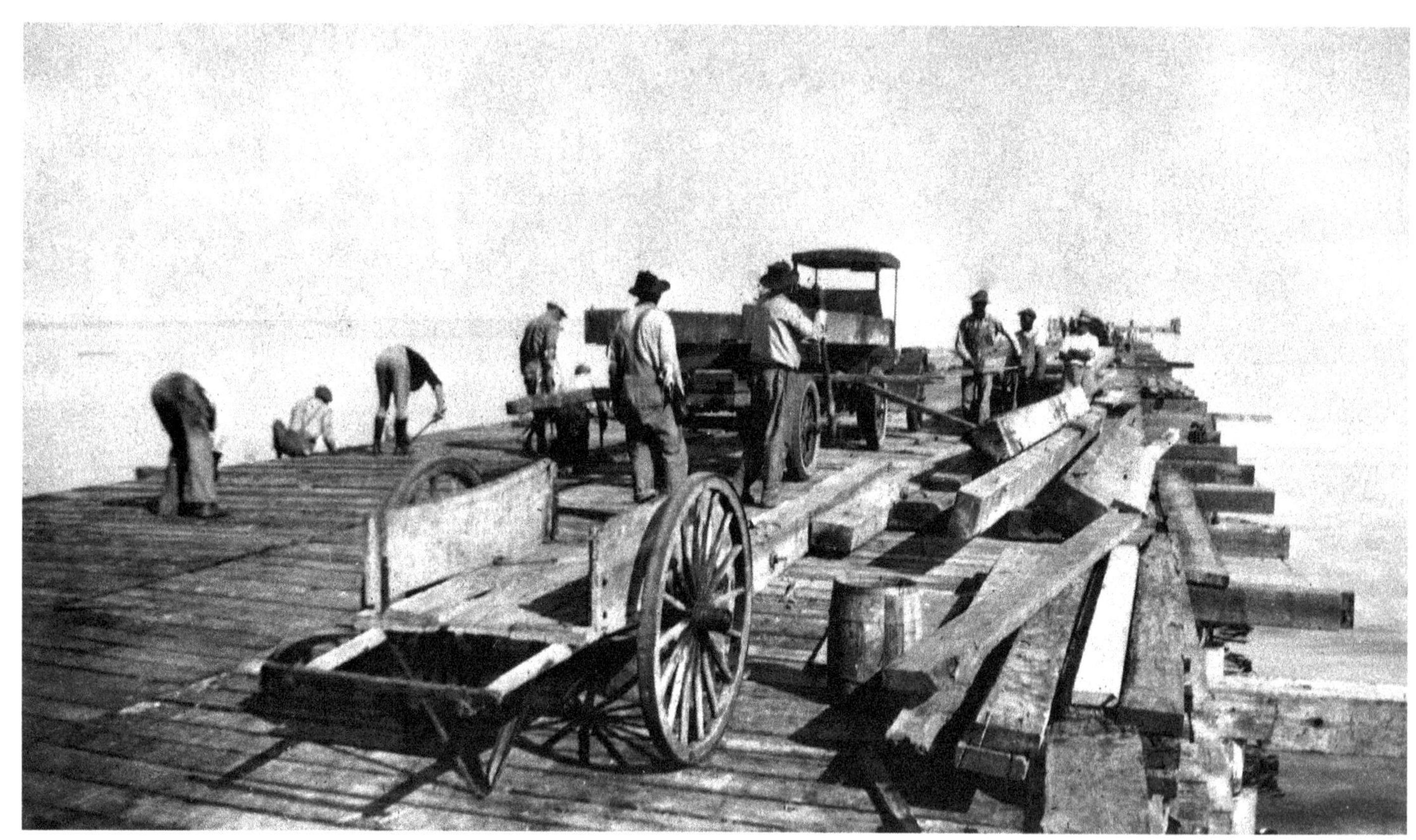

Workmen finish repairs to the recreation pier after the October 25, 1921, hurricane that hit the Tampa Bay area, heavily damaging the St. Petersburg waterfront and piers. Led by newspaper publisher Lew Brown, money was raised for repairs and the recreation pier reopened in January 1922. City engineers learned however that the pilings had been weakened; a new pier was needed.

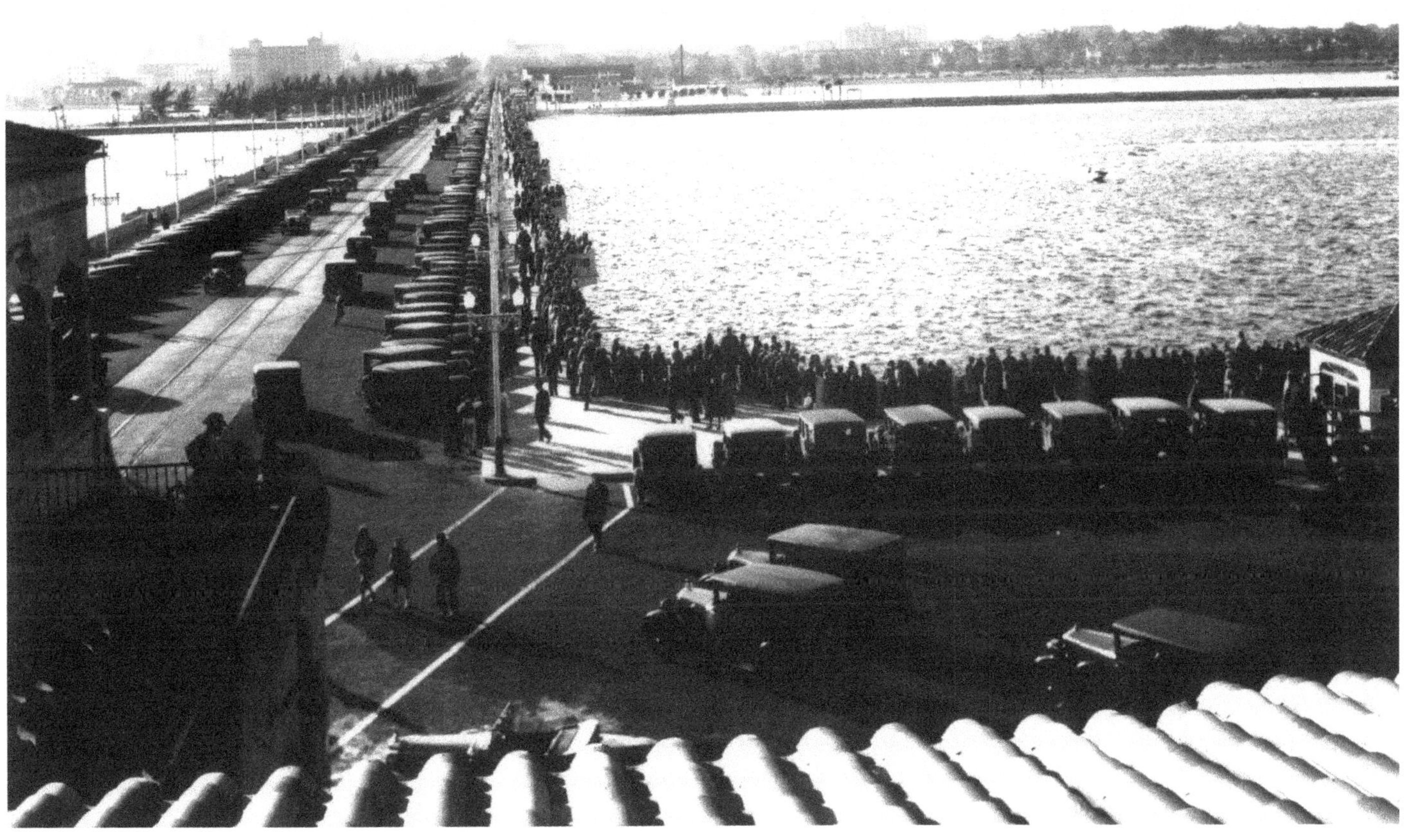

Facilities at the "Million Dollar Pier" included Spa Beach, a solarium, and a bait house. At 2,000 feet long by 100 feet wide, the two-lane road also had room for diagonal parking and fishing balconies. The street railway extended to the end of the pier, where the casino hosted dancing, concerts, and entertainment.

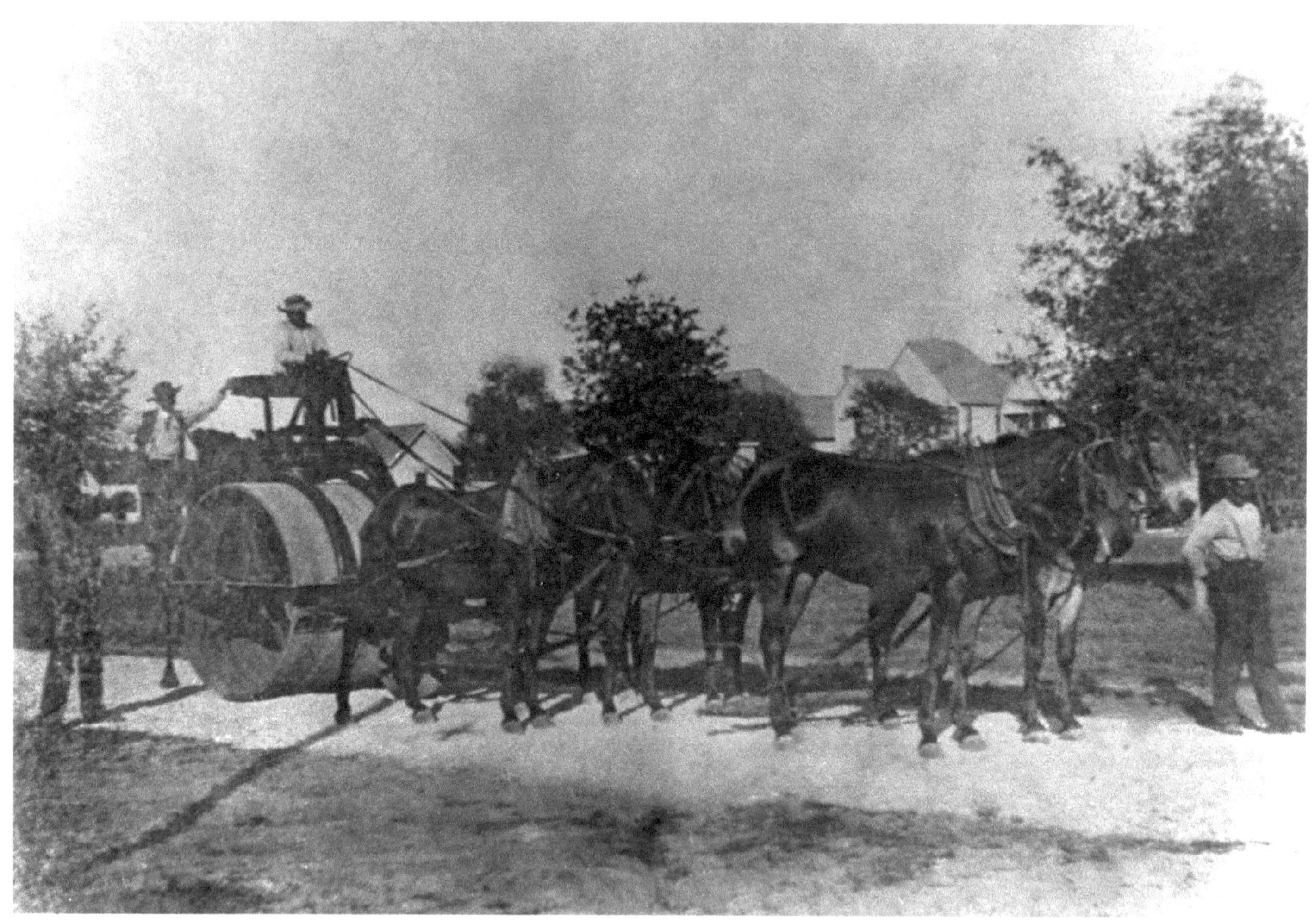

Owing to heavy recruiting of labor workers from Alabama and Georgia, the black community tripled from 2,400 to 7,400 during the 1920s to reach about 18 percent of the total population. Despite gains in wages and jobs, stringent "Jim Crow" laws were enforced.

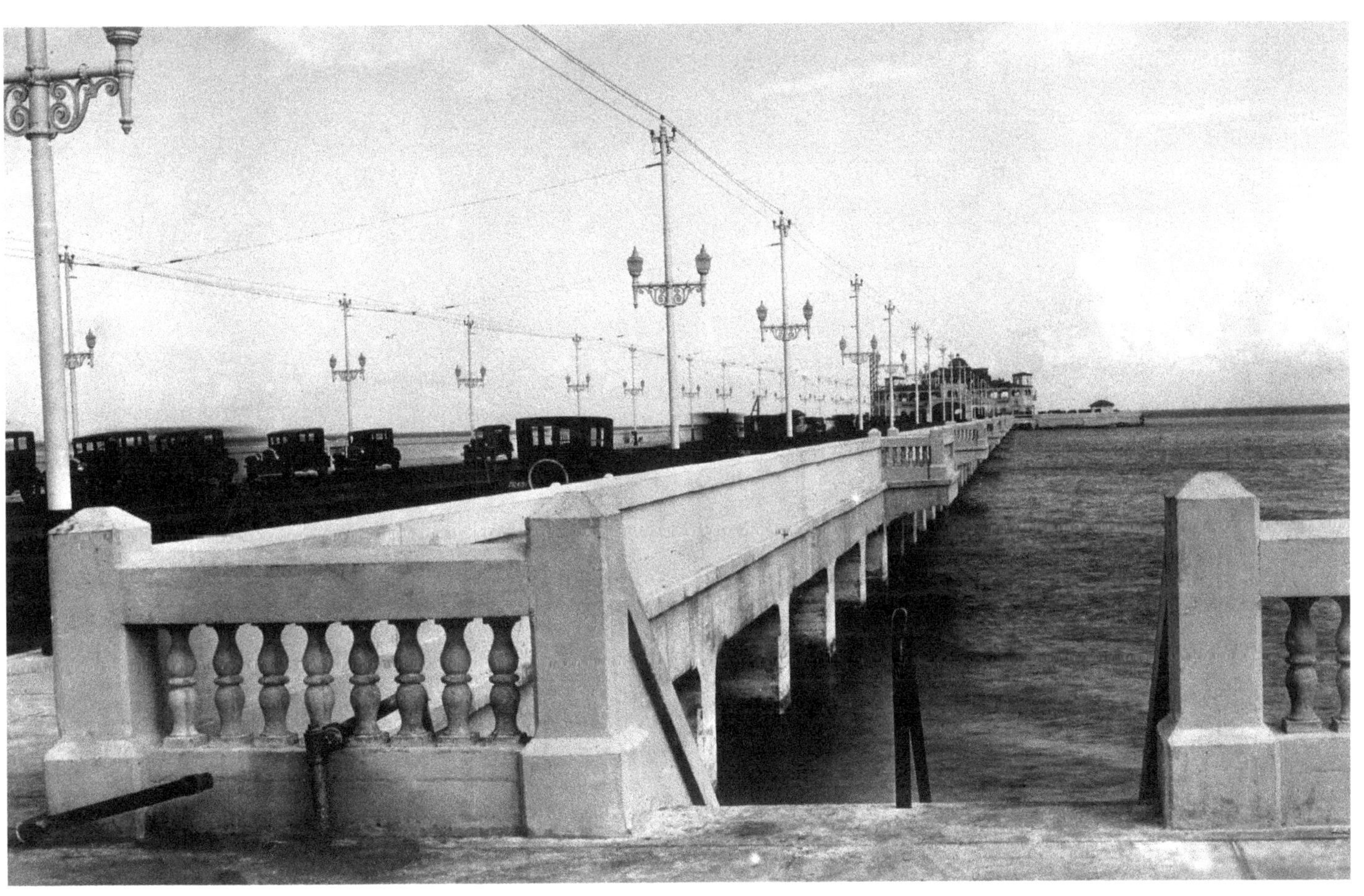

When Lew Brown of the *Evening Independent* newspaper touted the idea for a modern recreation pier, the city responded by issuing a million-dollar bond in May 1925. Construction began in September 1926 and was completed in just a few months. The "Million Dollar Pier" quickly became a city landmark and popular recreation spot.

The palatial Don CeSar, built by John Rowe, formally opened on January 16, 1928, on Pass-A-Grille Island. Designed by Henry Dupont, the pink, 312-room hotel cost $1.5 million and entertained celebrities like F. Scott Fitzgerald, Clarence Darrow, and Babe Ruth. "Just imagine," reported an early guest, "there's a toilet and bath with every room."

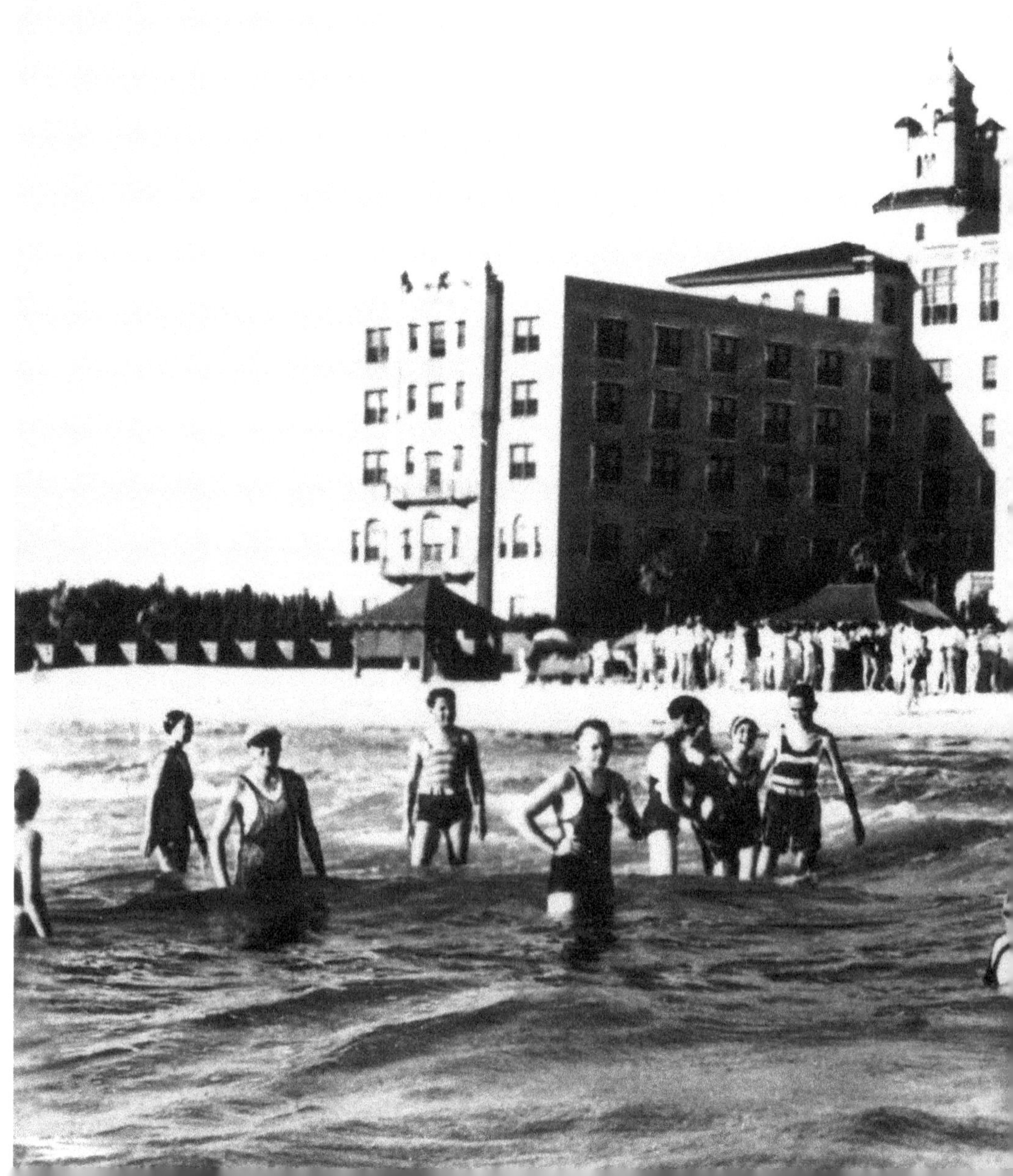

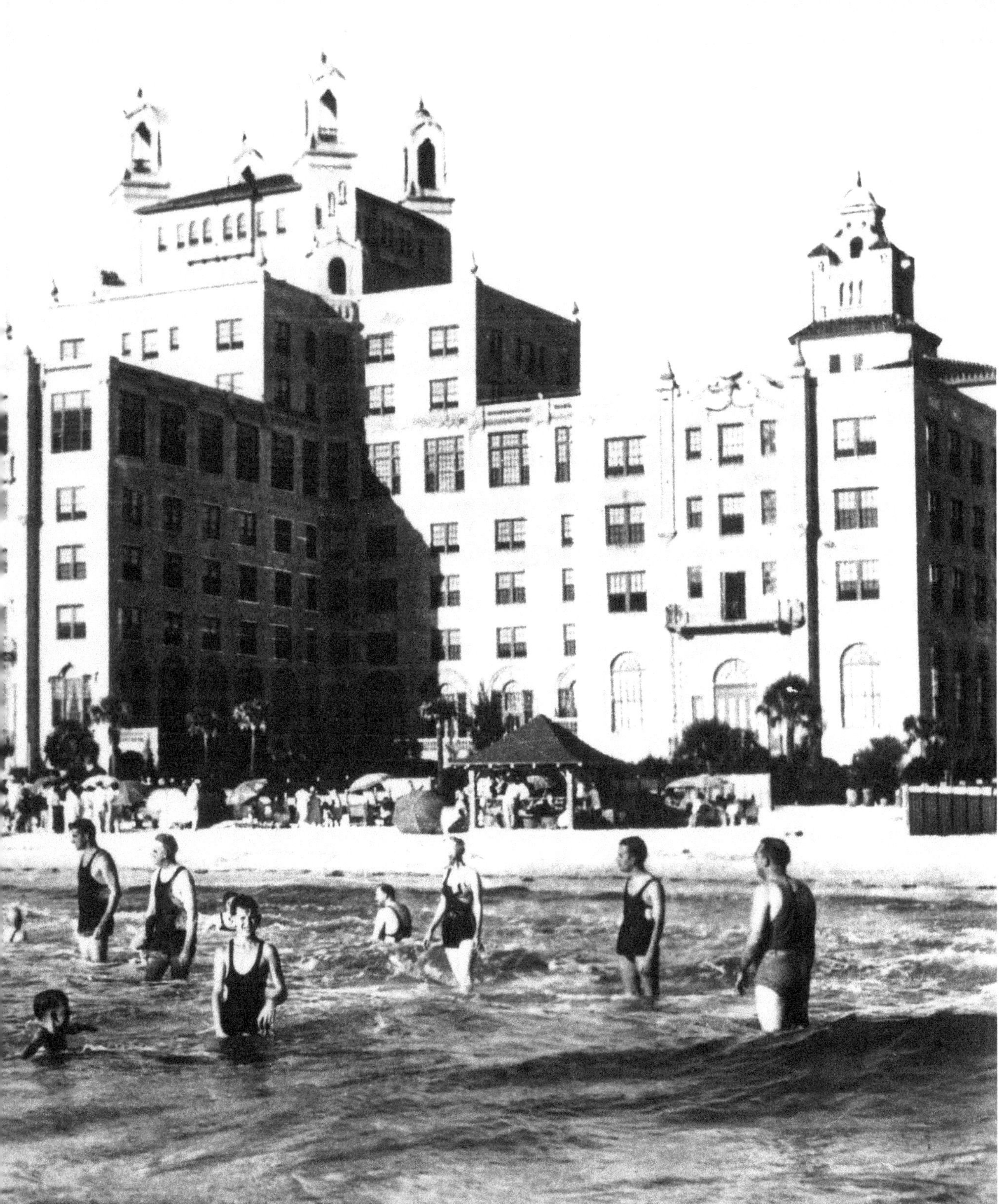

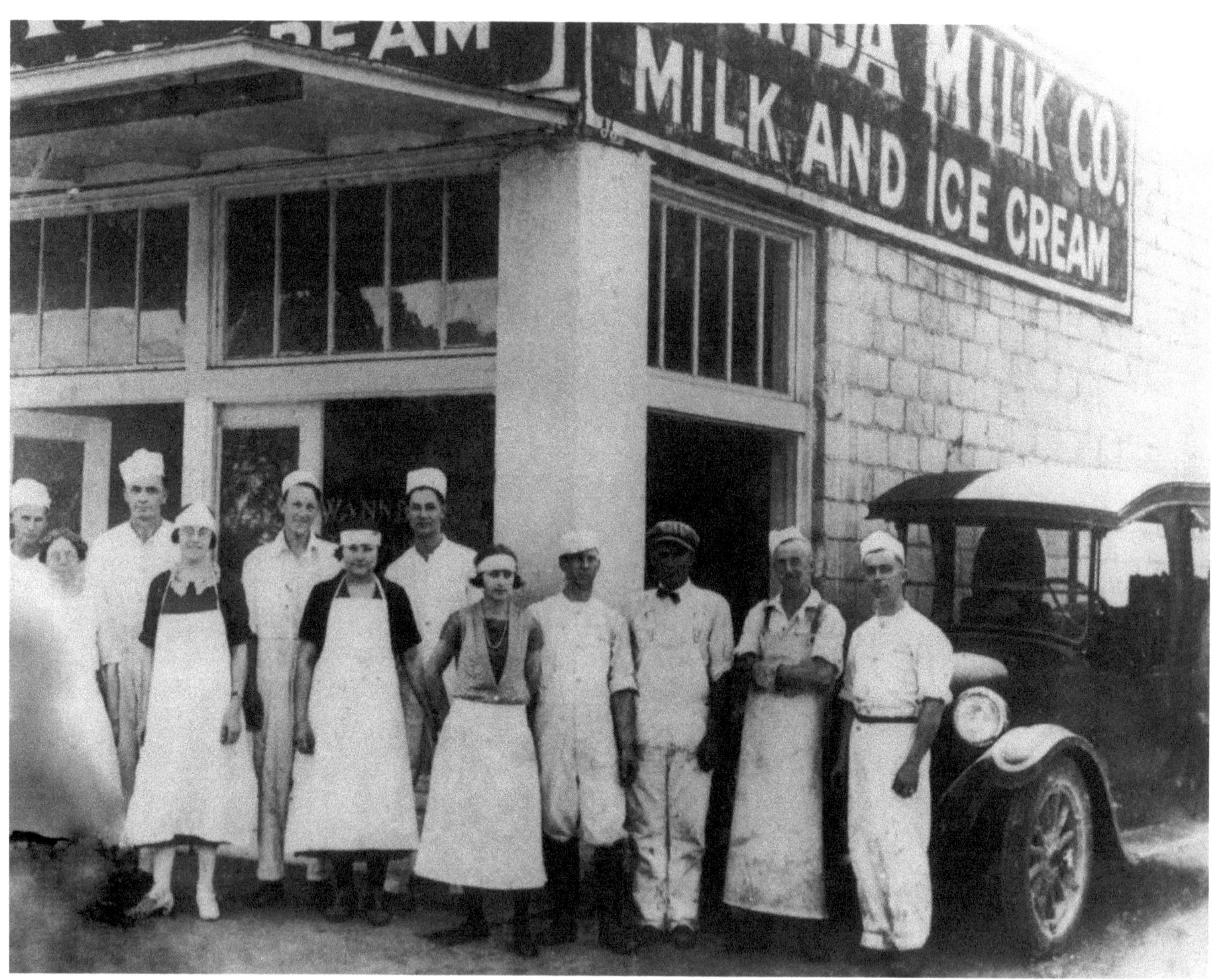

The Florida Milk Company, one of two local dairies, ran cattle on an open range they shared with Hood's Dairy. Reportedly, "feisty Elizabeth Hood" and "Cowboy Moody" fought over the strays. Moody tried to herd them to a city compound to collect a fee, while Mrs. Hood countered by roping the lead cow and leading the cows back to safety.

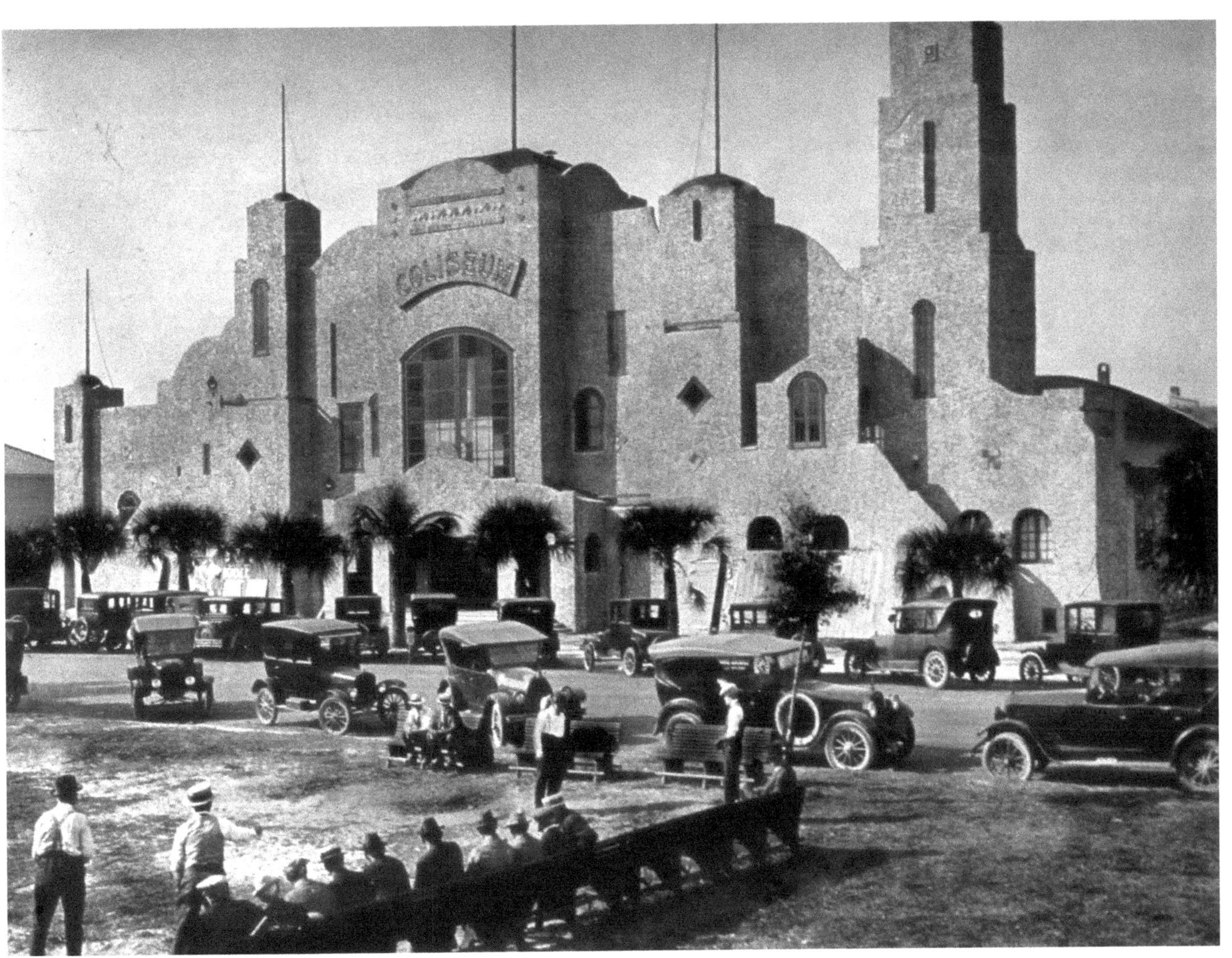

The Coliseum dance hall opened in 1924 and quickly became a symbol of the Roaring Twenties in St. Petersburg. C. F. Cullen spent $250,000 constructing this Fourth Avenue landmark with 28 carloads of lumber and 18,000 square feet of maple flooring. Mayor R. S. Pearce and three thousand guests danced at the opening.

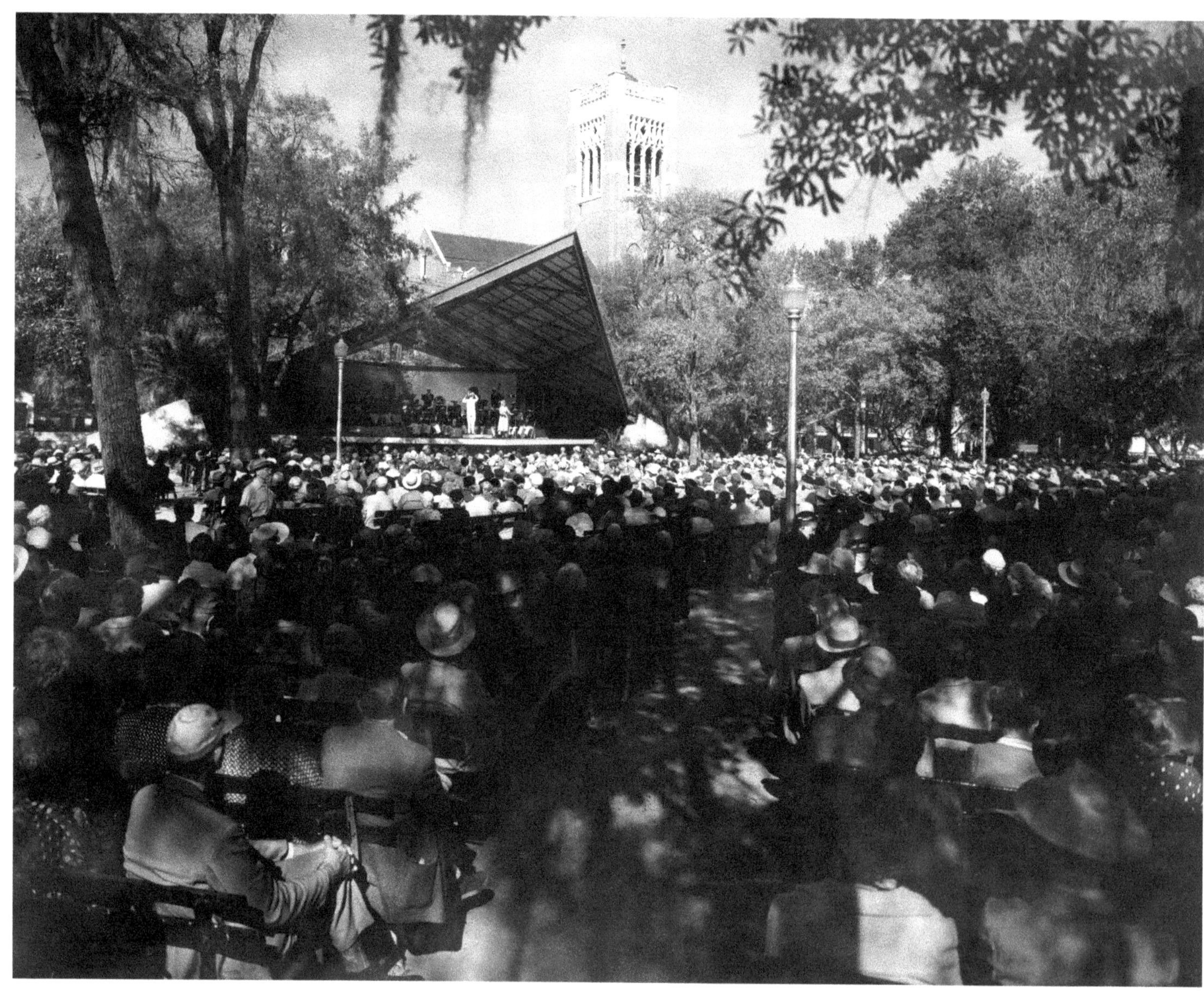

Erected in 1920 for $10,000, the new bandstand at Williams Park entertains a packed crowd, gathered for a band concert. The park became a sports center for horseshoes, chess, checkers, dominos, and roque (a variety of croquet). After courts and lanes were built, the Williams heirs sued the city to keep the park open to the public. As a result, the sports clubs were relocated in 1923.

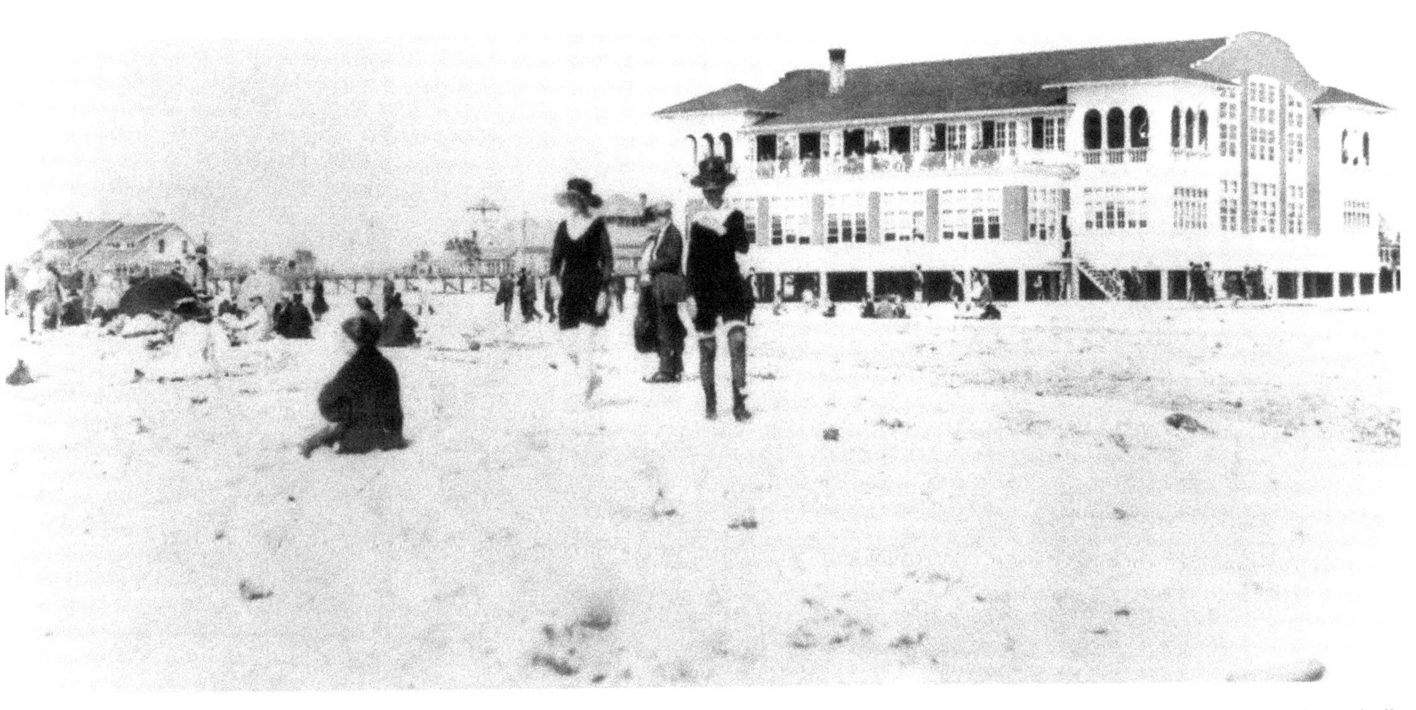

Originally a bathhouse and snack bar, the Pass-A-Grille Casino kept expanding, adding a second floor, a dance hall, restaurant, and finally a few hotel rooms. When the Pass-A-Grille Hotel burned in 1922, the Casino became the Pass-A-Grille Beach Hotel. It survived until 1967, when it also suffered a fire and was demolished.

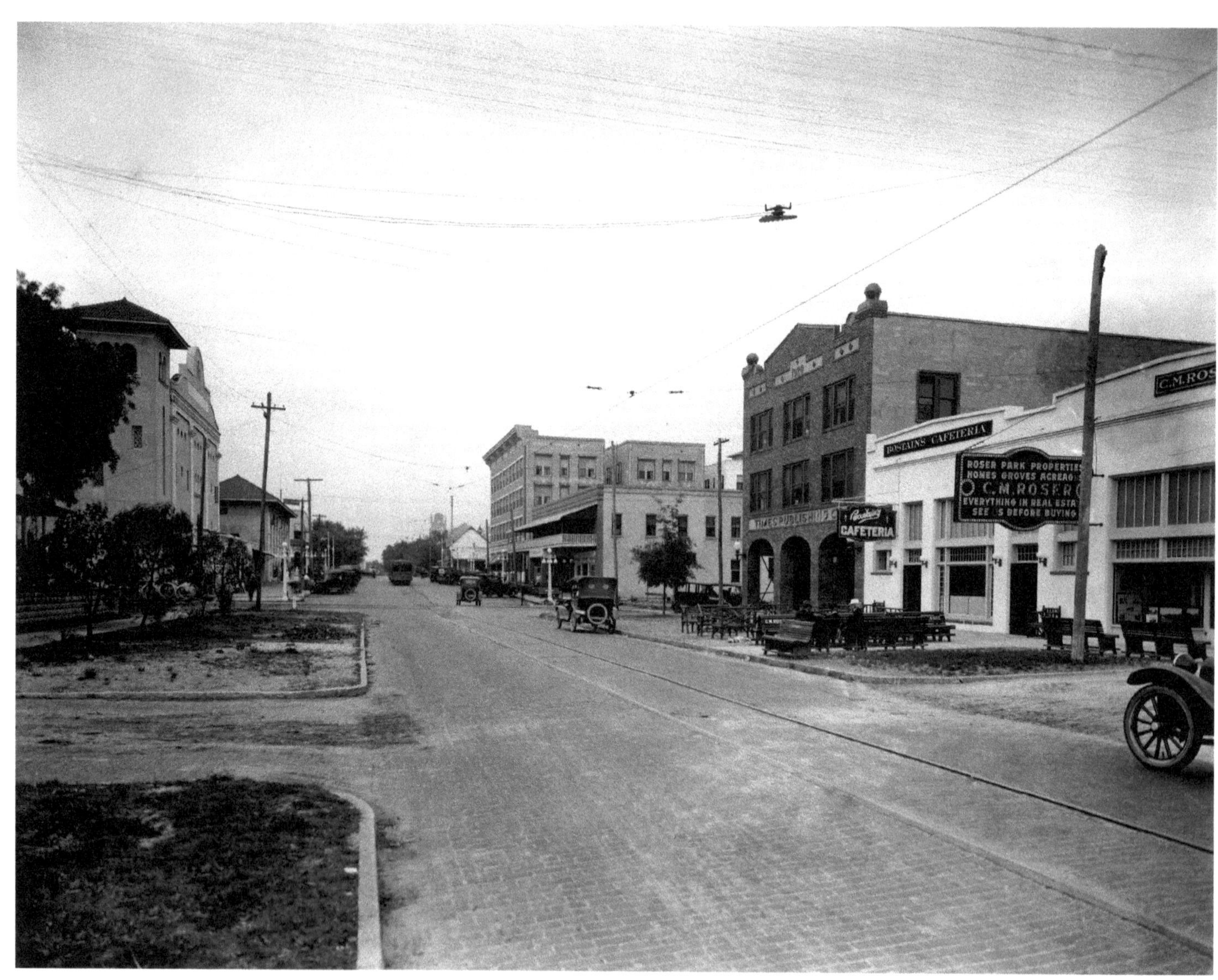

On the right, in this 1921 view of Fifth Street, is the St. Petersburg Times building and Charles Roser's Real Estate office. Opposite is the famous La Plaza Theater, built by George Gandy in 1913 at a total cost of more than $150,000. Towering over the city, it was initially dubbed "Gandy's White Elephant" but quickly became profitable.

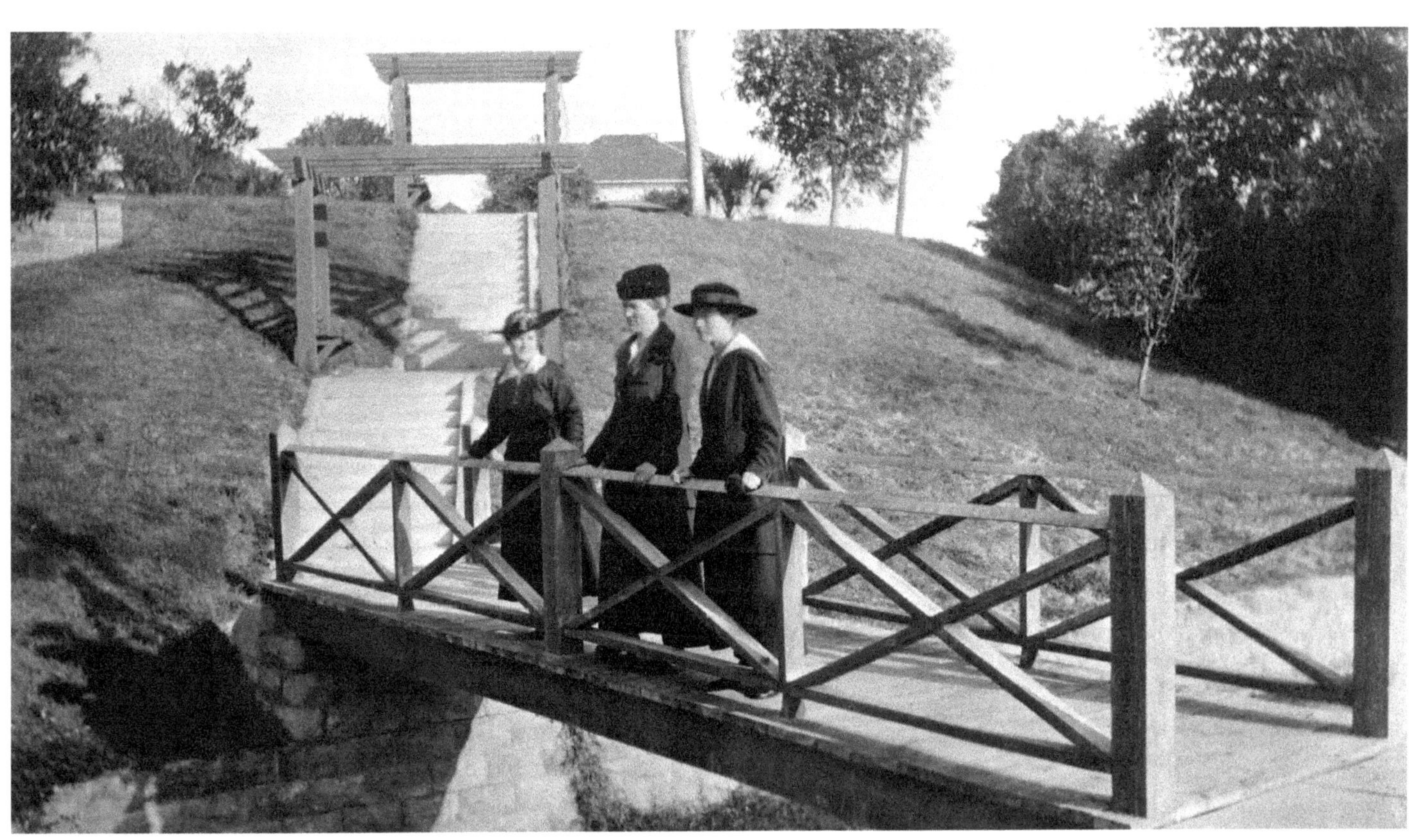

Winter tourists pause on a bridge across Booker Creek overlooking the beautifully landscaped terraces in scenic Roser Park. Charles Roser, a successful cookie manufacturer from Ohio and famous for the Fig Newton, moved to St. Petersburg and established this renowned neighborhood along Booker Creek.

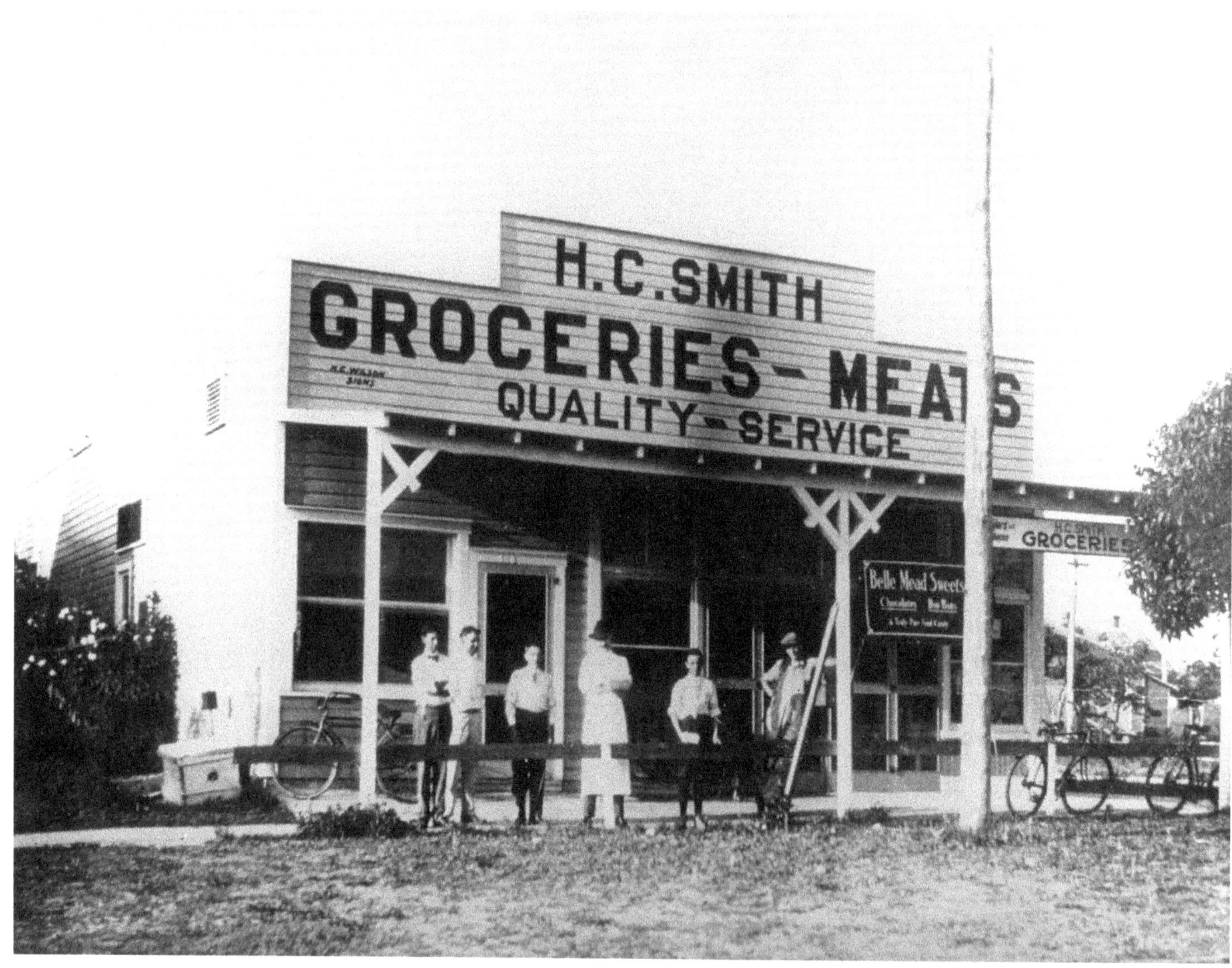

During the 1920s boom, a dozen new settlers a day moved into town. Neighborhood grocery stores, like this one, provided meats, fruits, and vegetables for the growing city. During the 1930s and 1940s, the "mom and pop" stores began to give way to larger supermarkets such as Nolen's Grocery, which boasted "6 car loads full of canned goods."

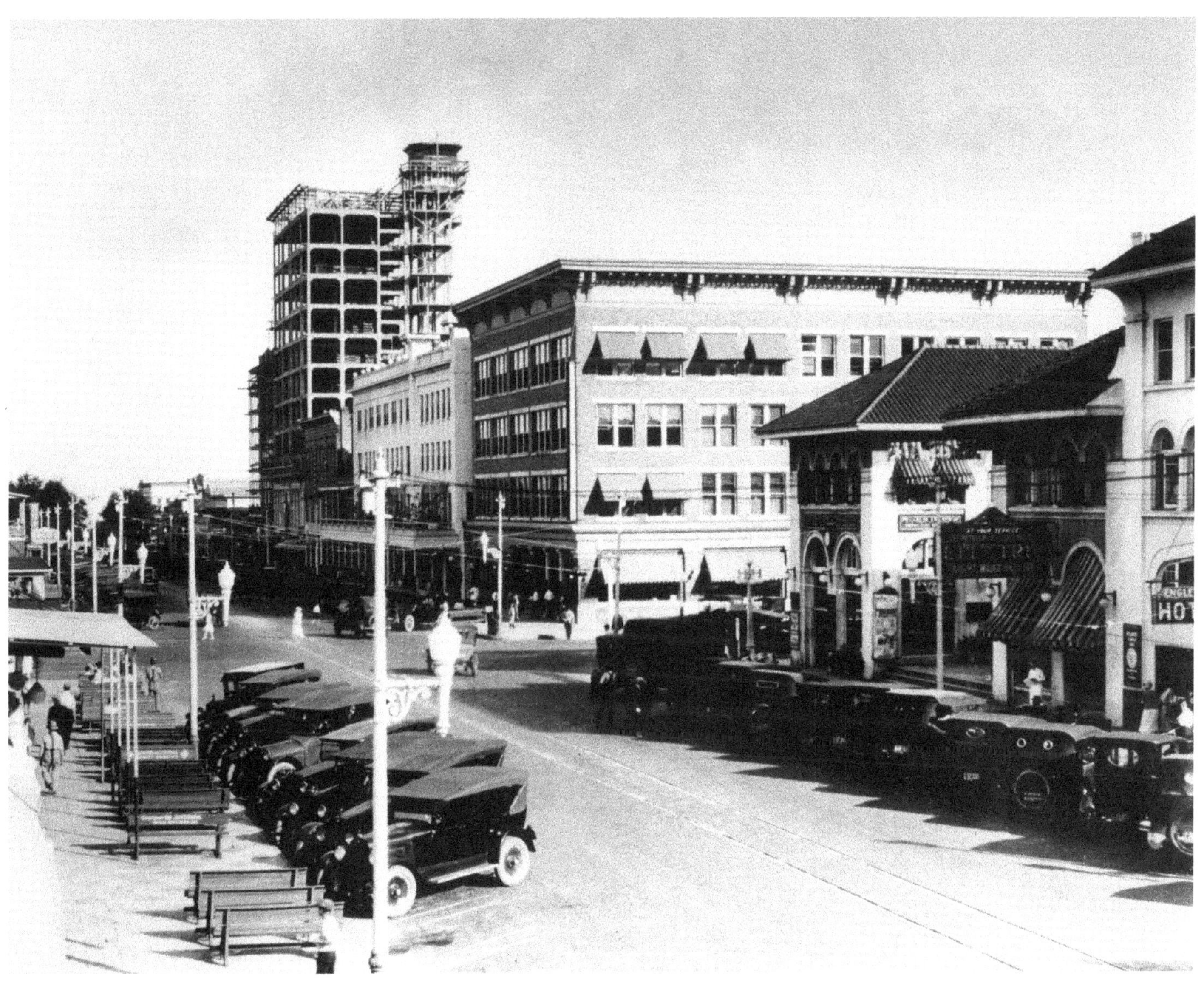

Between 1923 and 1926 ten new hotels were added to St. Petersburg to accommodate the sudden boom. Started in 1916, the eleven-story Pheil Hotel is still under construction in this view from 1922. Built by ex-mayor Abram Phiel, he died before it opened in 1924. It had gift shops, a domed ceiling, and a ground-floor theater.

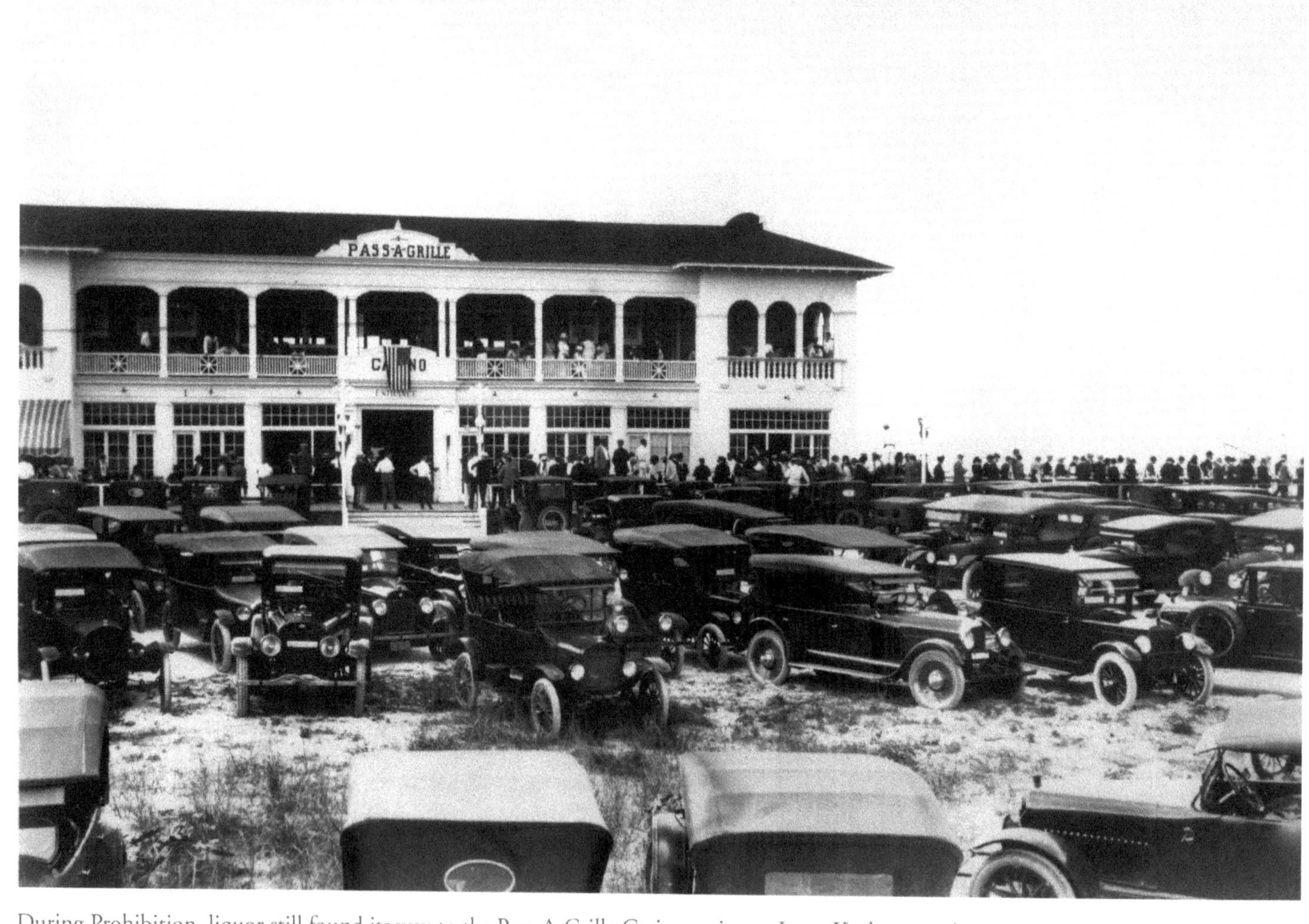

During Prohibition, liquor still found its way to the Pass-A-Grille Casino owing to Long Key's convenient Gulf location. In the area, rum sold for $20 a gallon, Canadian whiskey for $6 a quart, while moonshine fetched $5 a gallon. With set-ups supplied by the hotel, the drinks added to the casino's many conventions, parties, and dances.

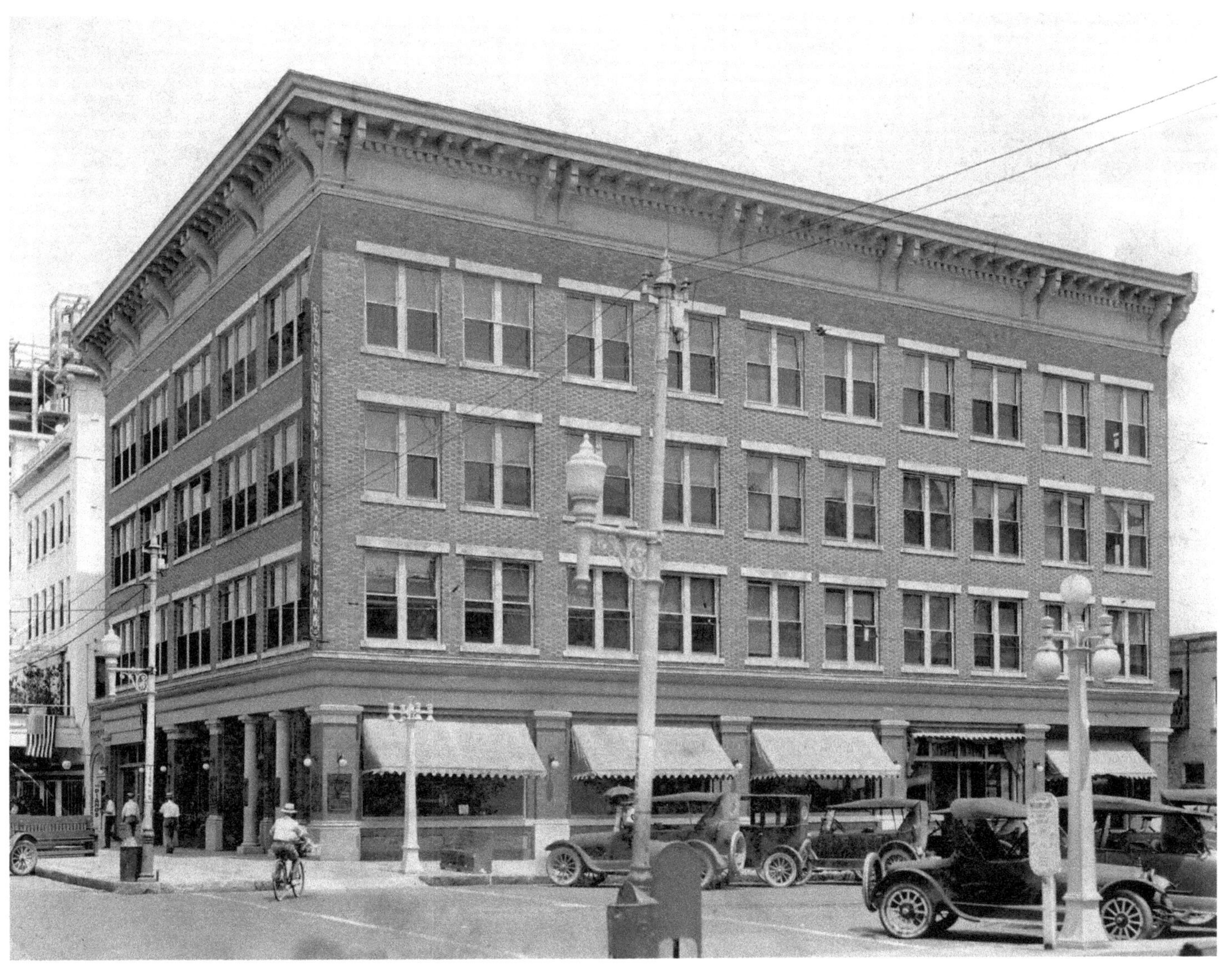

In 1920 the respectable First National Bank bought this building from the Florida Bank and Trust company at Fifth Street and Central Avenue. At the height of the boom era, bank deposits in St. Petersburg reached $46 million. This enabled First National Bank to enlarge the building to eight stories in 1925.

Young swimmers at the Spa Beach diving platform in 1923 display fashionable swimwear in outfits considered risque just a few years before. One of the first topless male swimmers in the area endured stares, giggling, scorn, and was almost arrested, but "there was no law against publicly displaying the bare male torso."

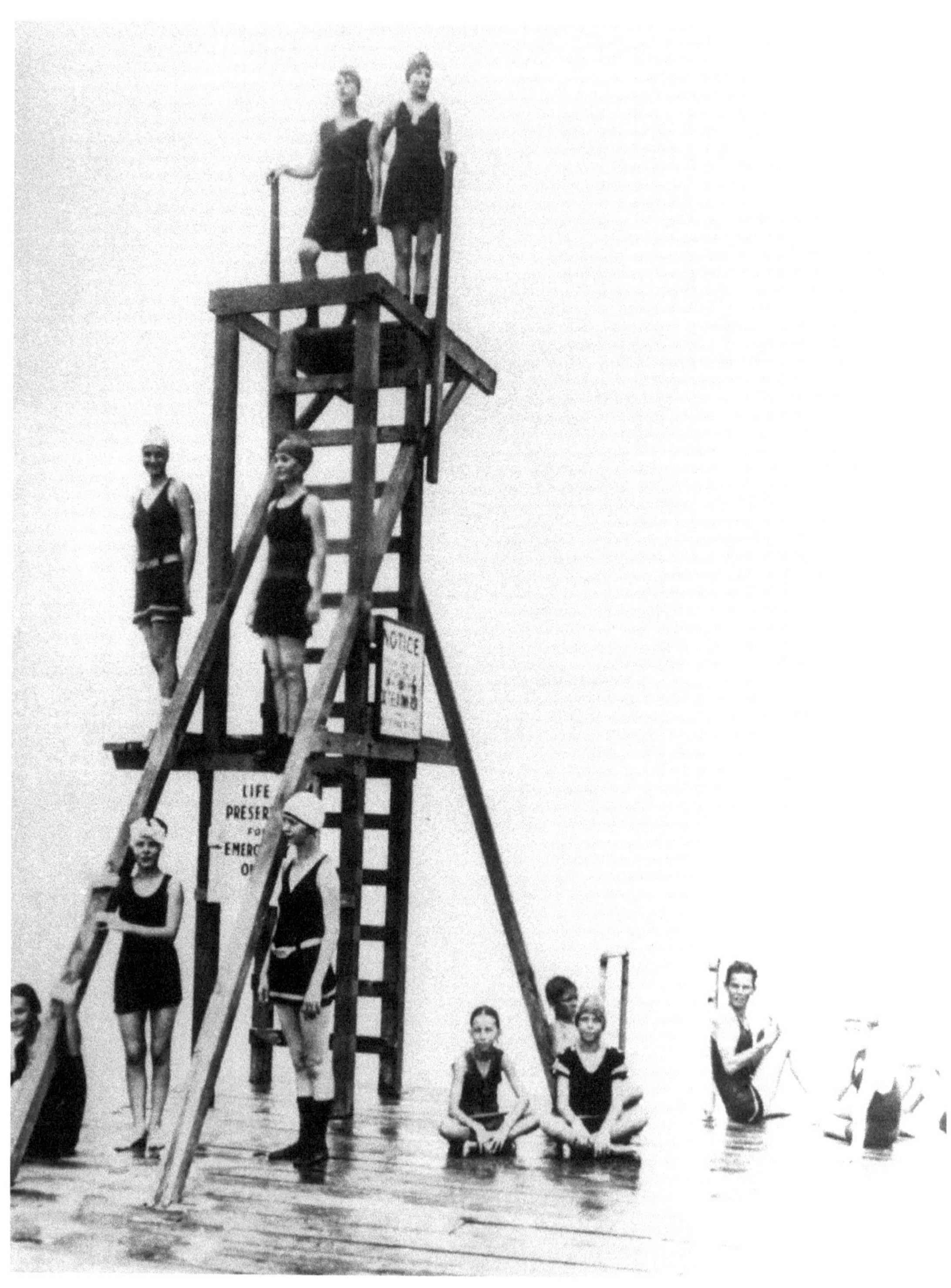

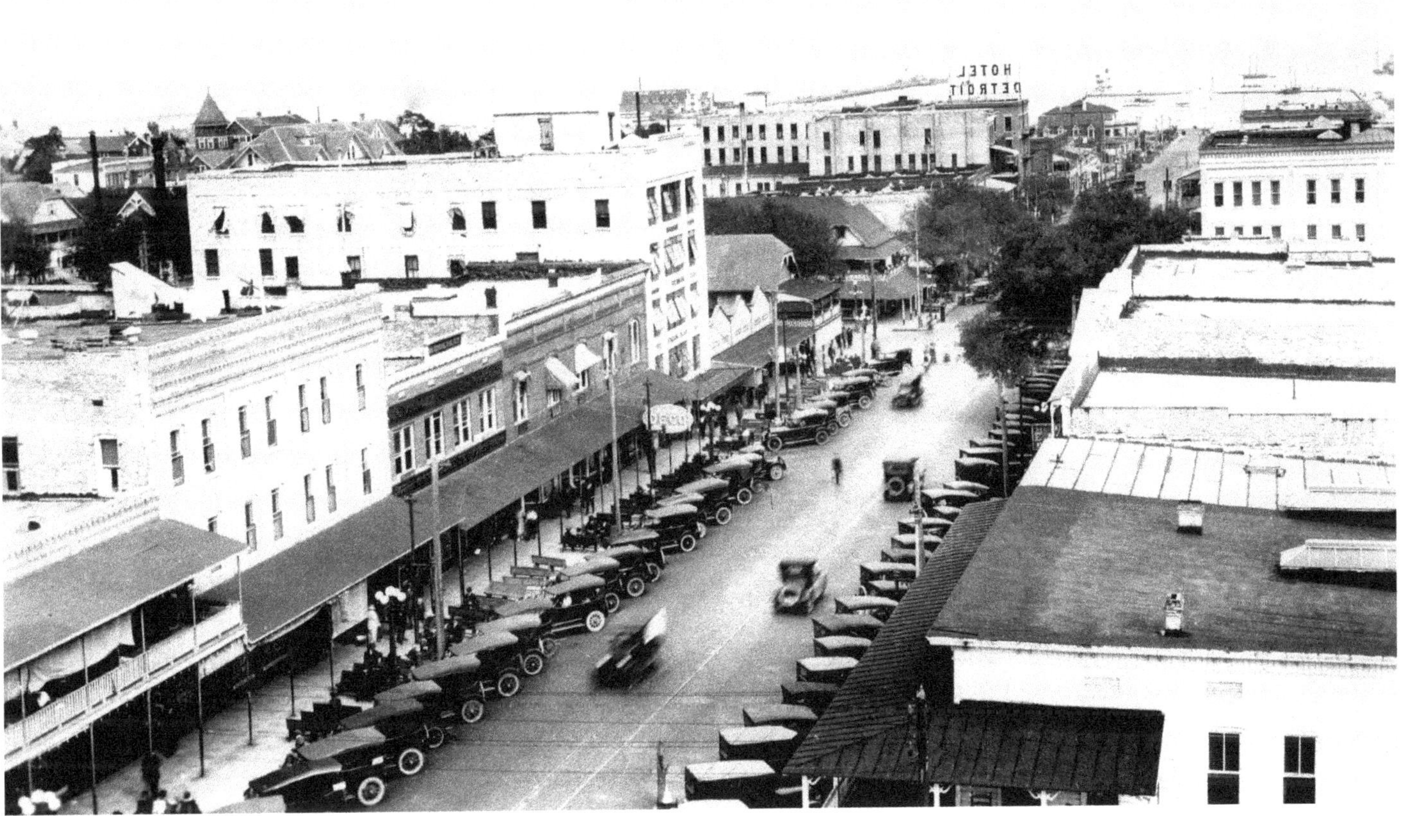

Visible on the left side of Central Avenue near the gulf, the Detroit Hotel is far from being the isolated building it was during its day as the only hotel in town. At the beginning of the boom, the town had fewer than 500 hotel rooms to handle the tourists and growing population. Between 1923 and 1926, seven large hotels were built in the downtown area.

The "Million Dollar Pier" opened Thanksgiving Day, November 25, 1926, with a gala celebration attended by Mayor Pearce, Senator Park Trammel, and ten thousand visitors. At the pier head, the Mediterranean revival–style Casino included a central atrium, an open-air ballroom, a radio studio for WSUN, and an observation deck.

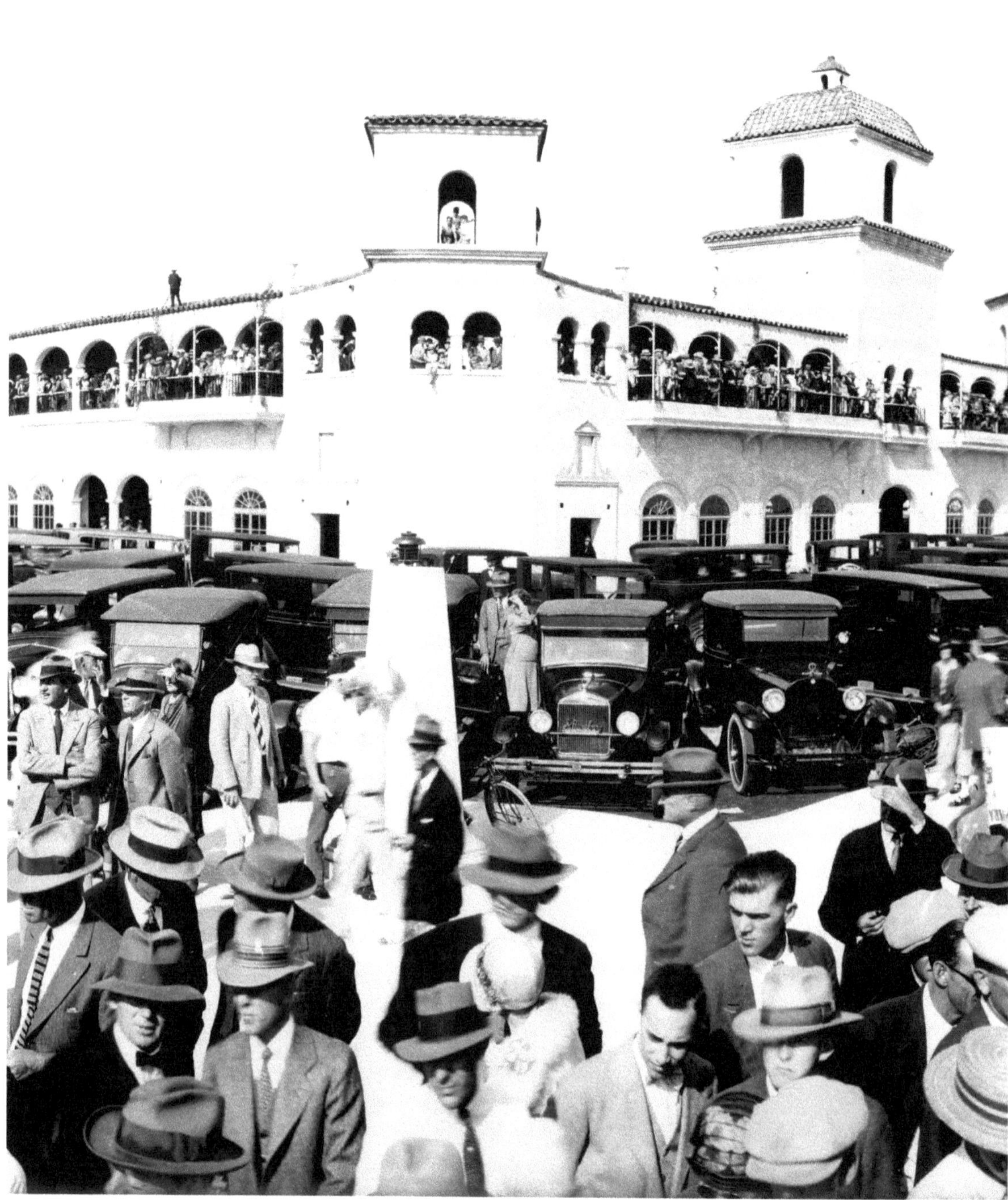

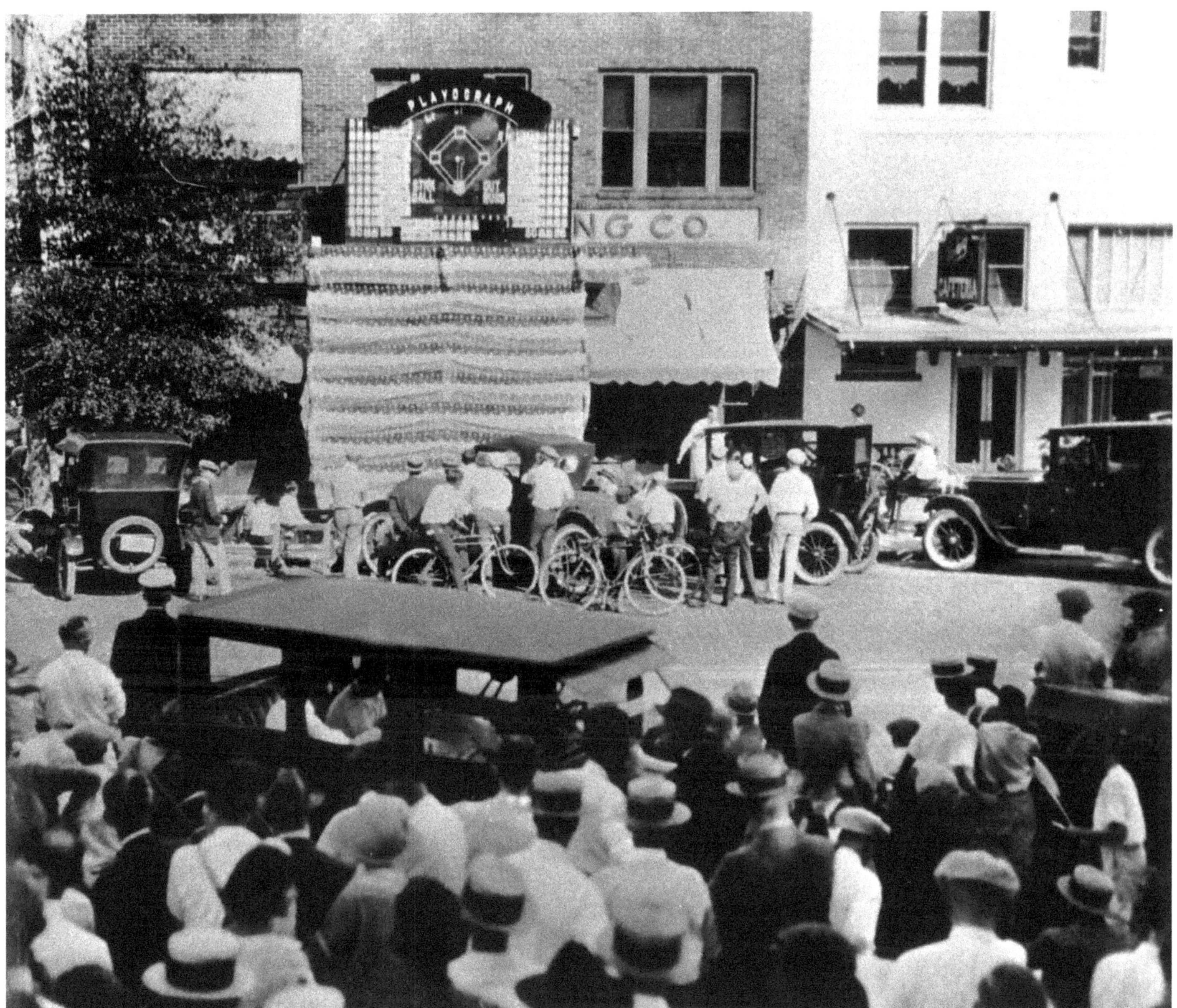

Before play-by-play radio broadcasts of baseball games, various devices like this "playograph" kept fans informed about a game. In front of the St. Petersburg Times building, fans catch up on the latest news, updated by telegraph, about the 1924 World Series. The Washington Senators beat the New York Giants in seven games.

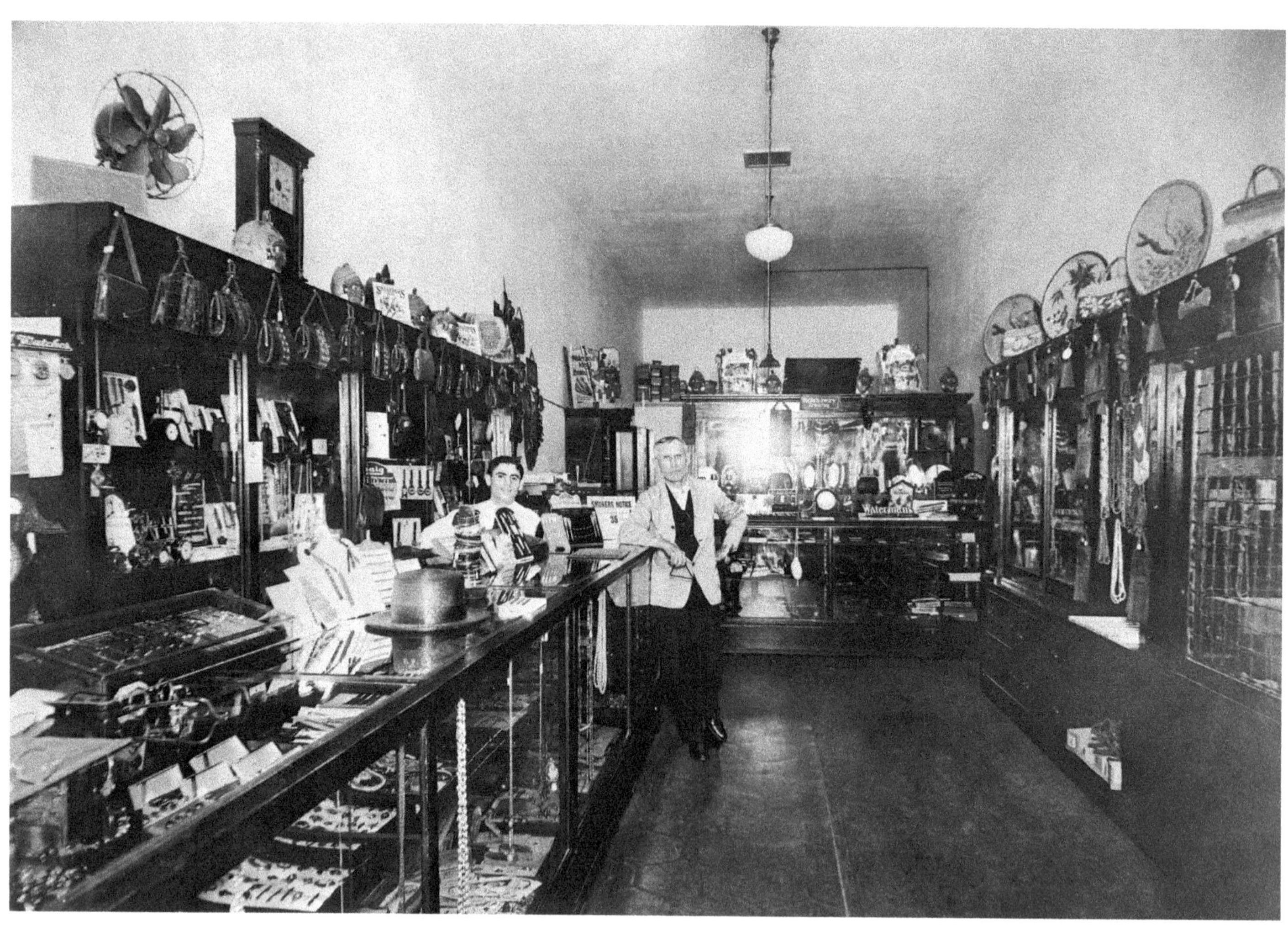

Leon Haliczer at his jewelry store, located at Central Avenue and 9th Street, in 1924. Haliczer was one of the founding members of Congregation B'nai Israel in 1923. As the Jewish community grew, anti-Semitism also grew, manifested in social restrictions that included many of the area's new upscale hotels.

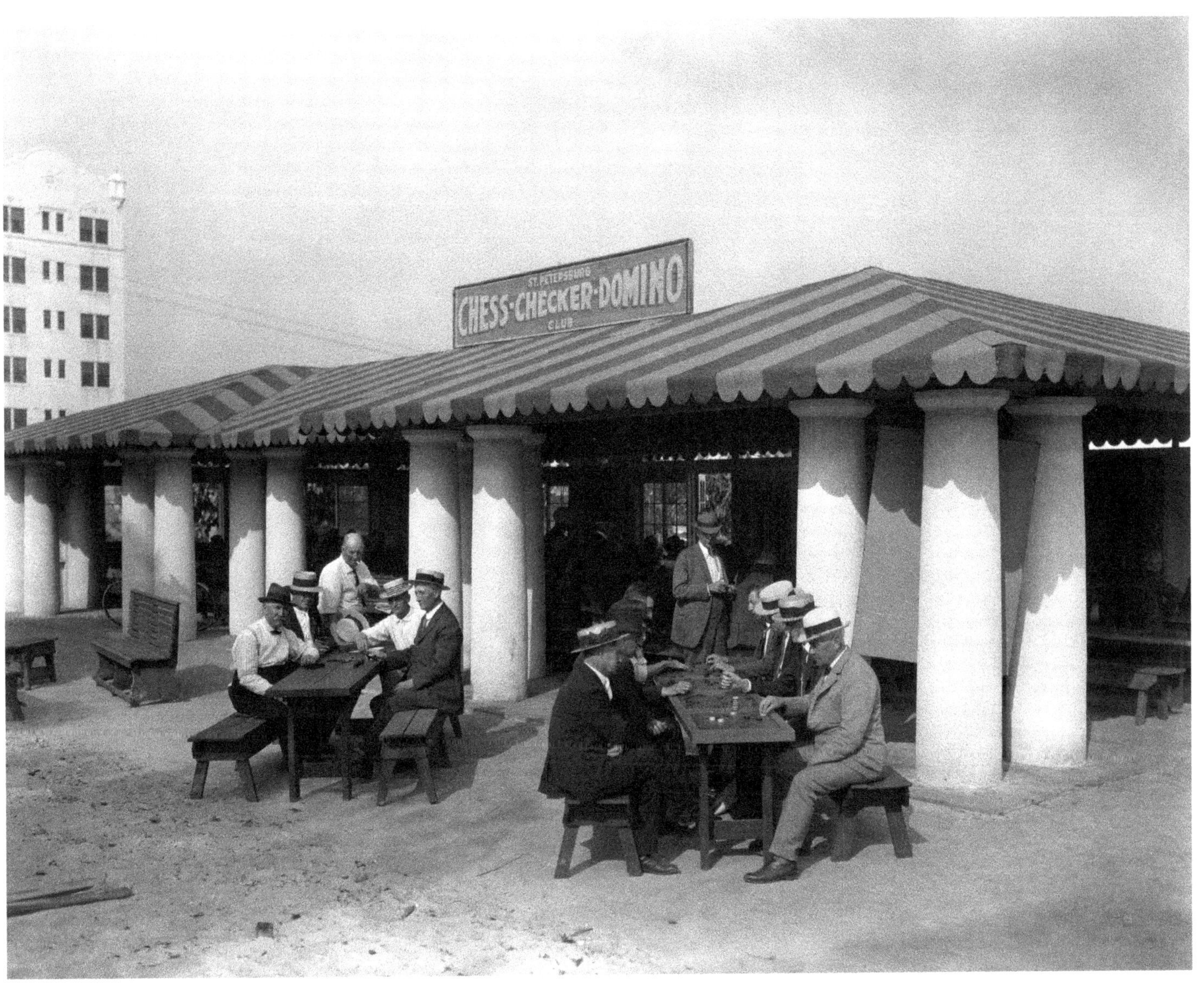

Many sports clubs moved to Waterfront Park, where they had room to expand. The Chess-Checker-Domino Club in Waterfront Park was photographed March 13, 1925. St. Petersburg promoters often held competitions billed as the "National" or "World Championships" of various "tourist sports," including shuffleboard, horseshoes, quoits, and roque.

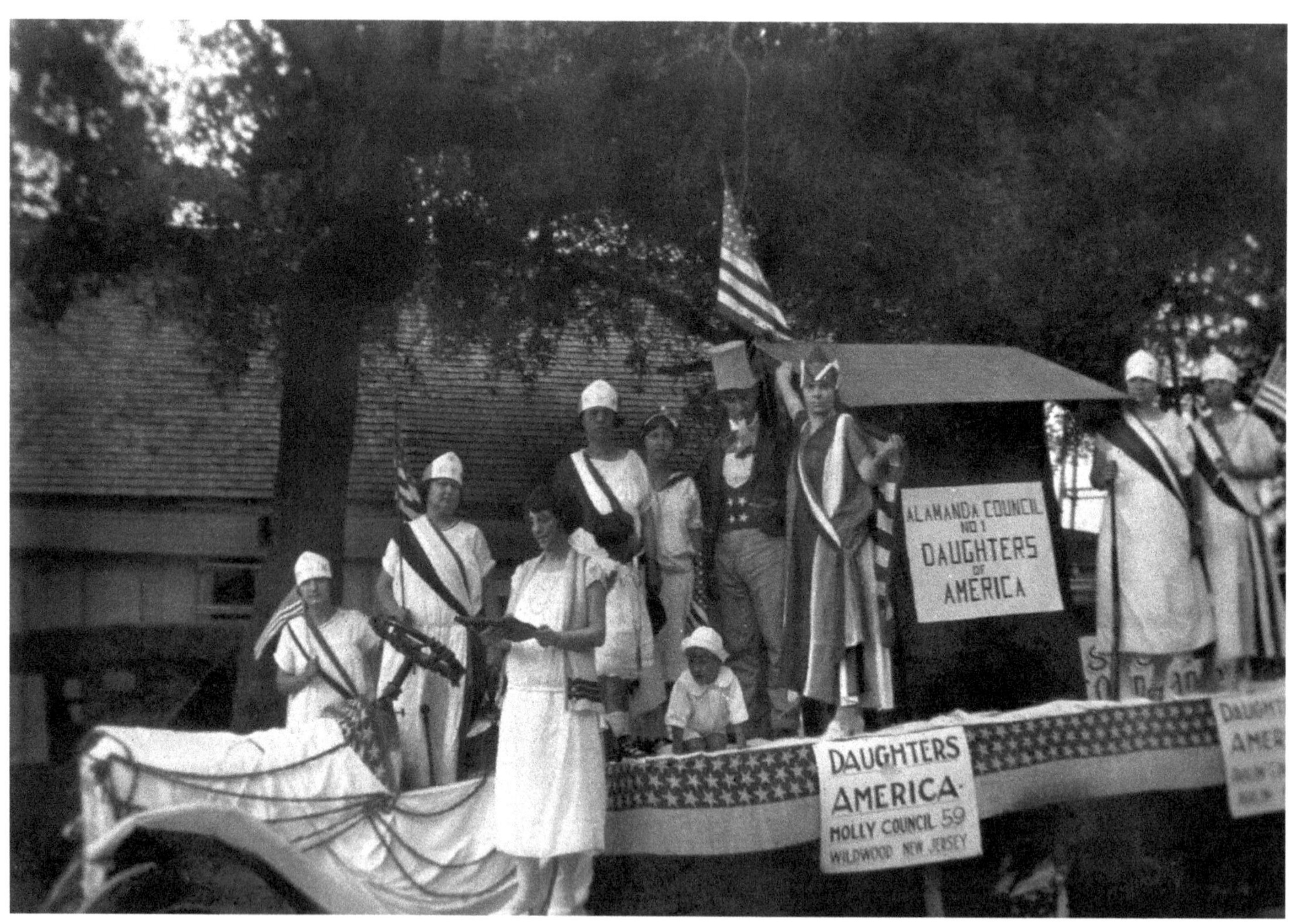

The "Daughters of America" show off their float for the 1925 Festival of States parade. Mayor Al Lang and Phillies baseball scout William Neal designed the parade in 1917 as a tourist attraction based on the many State societies organized in early St. Petersburg. Reinstated in 1922, the parade is a St. Petersburg institution.

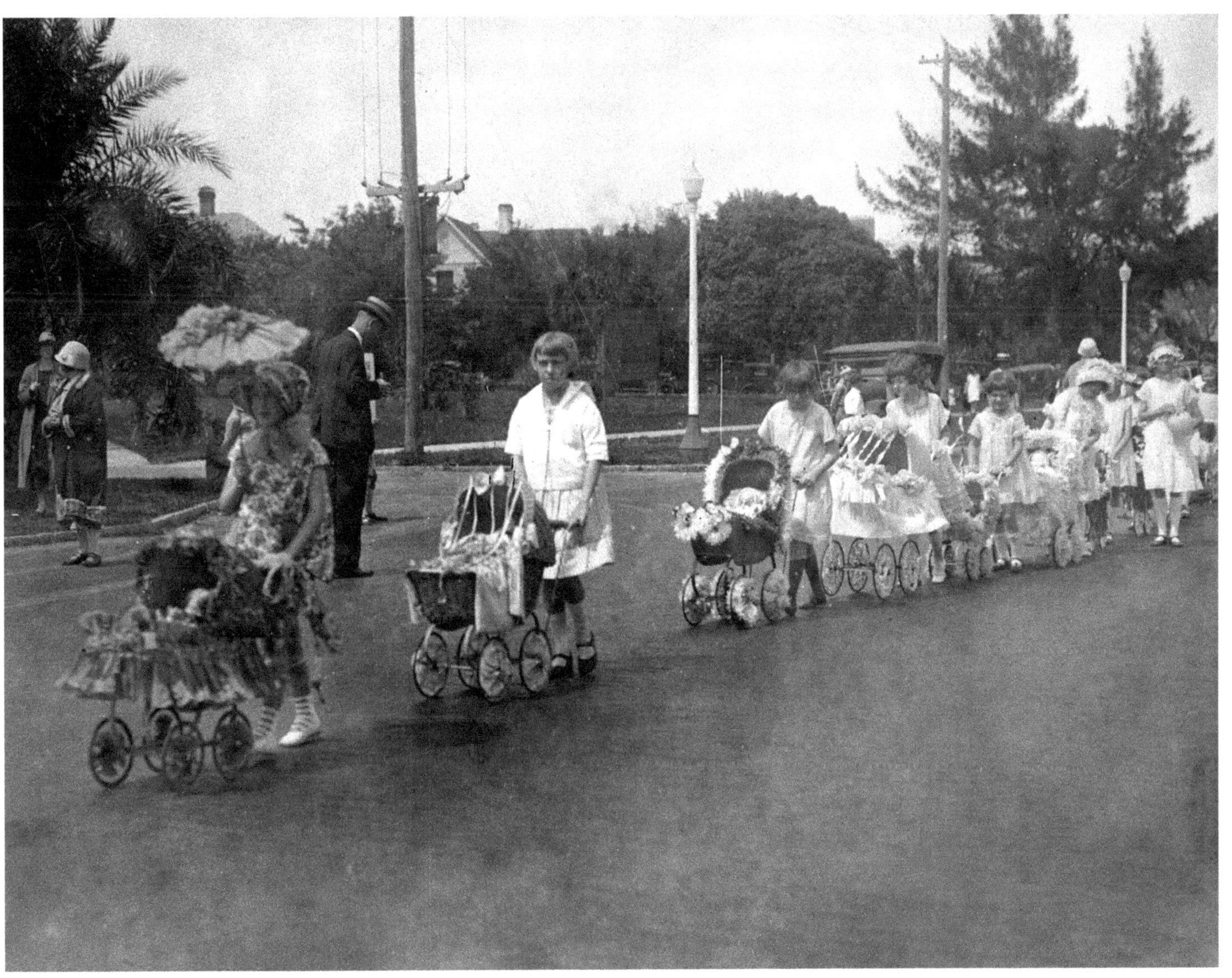

Young girls push their decorated baby carriages in a kiddies' parade, added in 1929 to the growing list of activities in the Festival of States. Other events were the crowning of the Festival Queen, the Coronation Ball, boat races in Tampa Bay, sailing regattas, various sports events, and finally the grand parade.

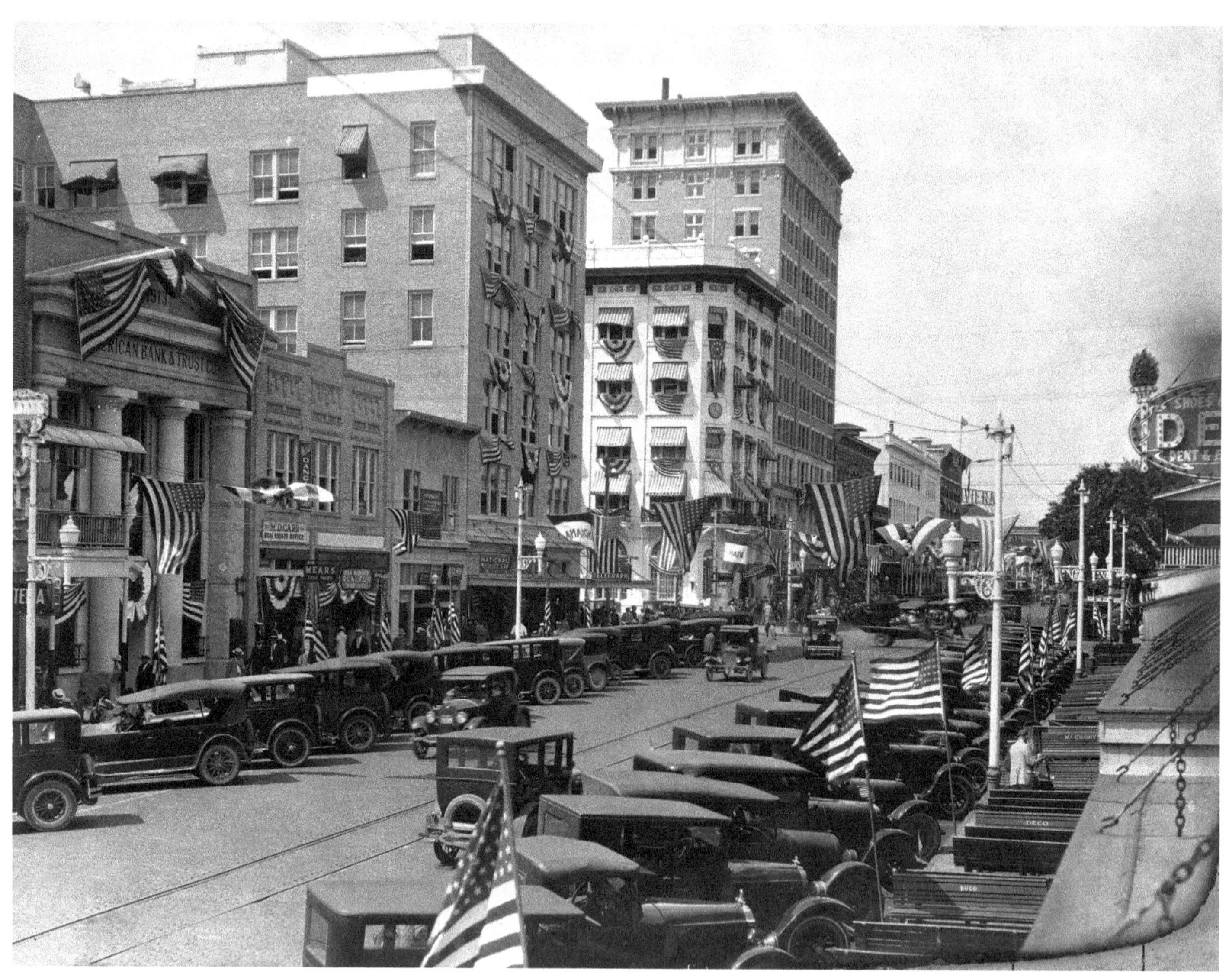

A decorated Central Avenue is ready for a Festival of States parade in the 1920s. This annual event is an offshoot of the State tourist societies. Joining a state society "for one little dollar bill" entitled members to enjoy beach trips, picnics, dances, concerts, musicals, and socials—all with people from their home state.

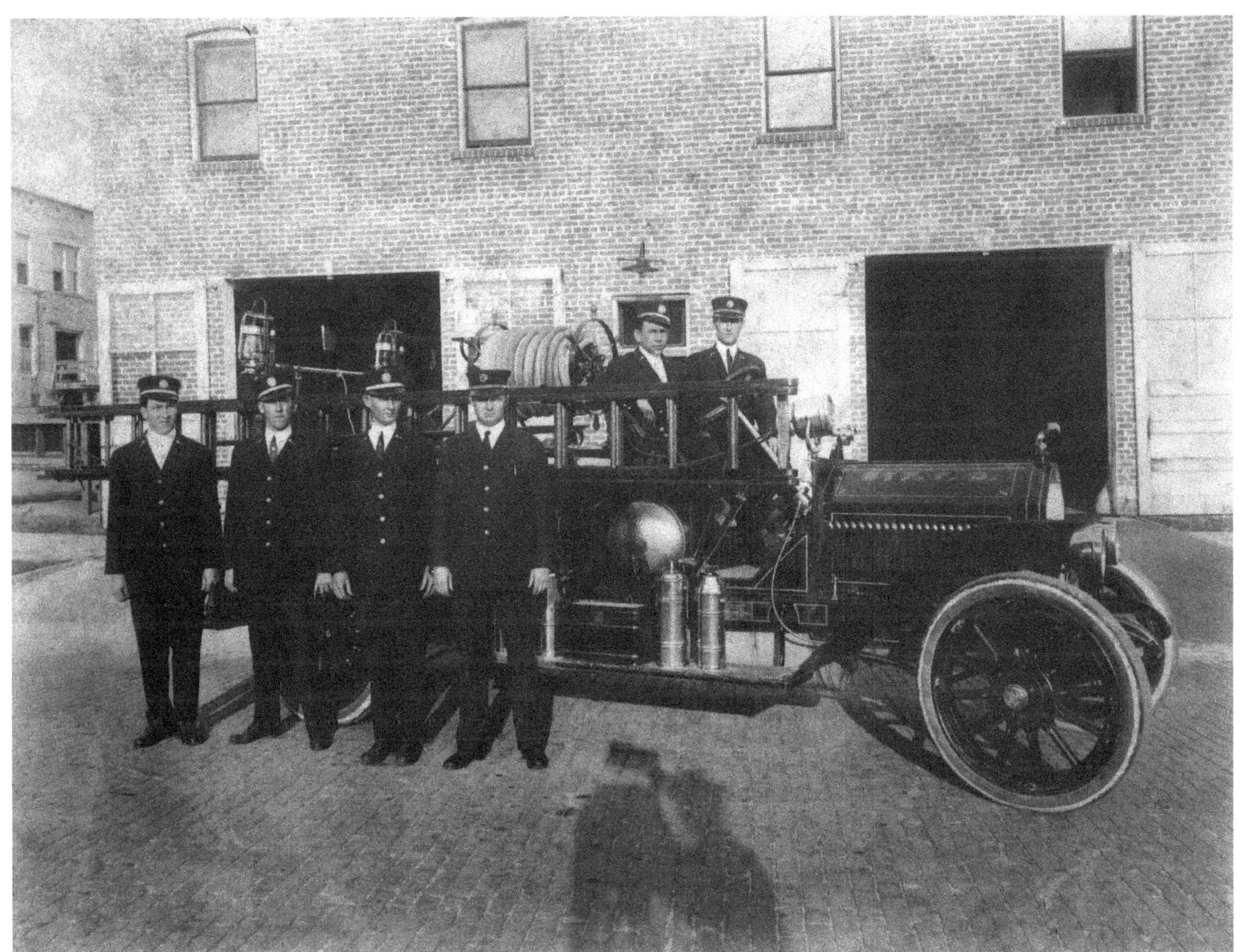

St. Petersburg fire chief J. T. McNulty, fourth from left, headed the Fire Department from 1913 to 1936. He was called "Chemical Crank," because he used chemicals instead of water where possible, to prevent water damage. In 1918, he obtained the city's first modern fire truck, featuring a hose, ladders, and a chemical tank. This photograph is from 1925.

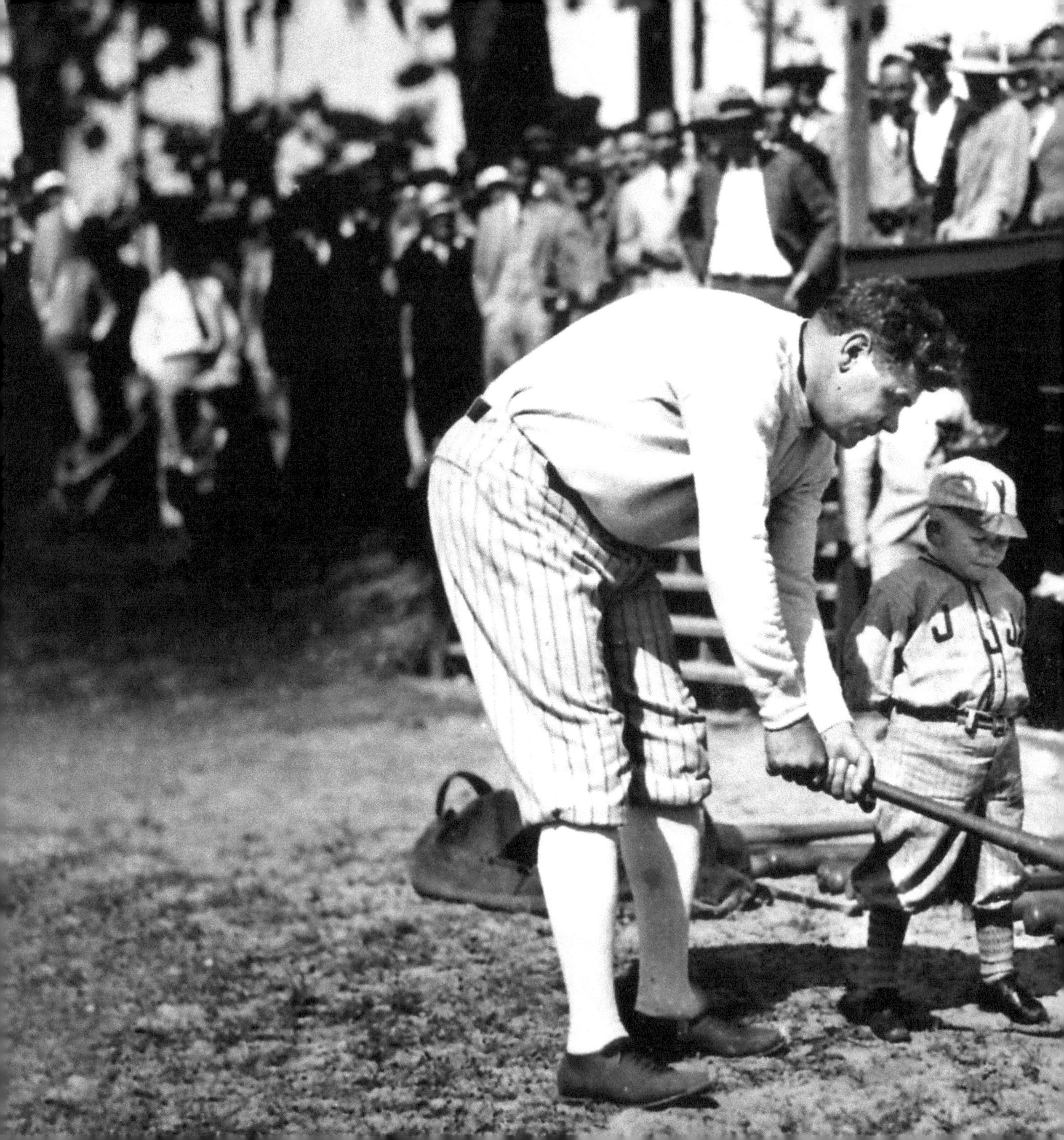

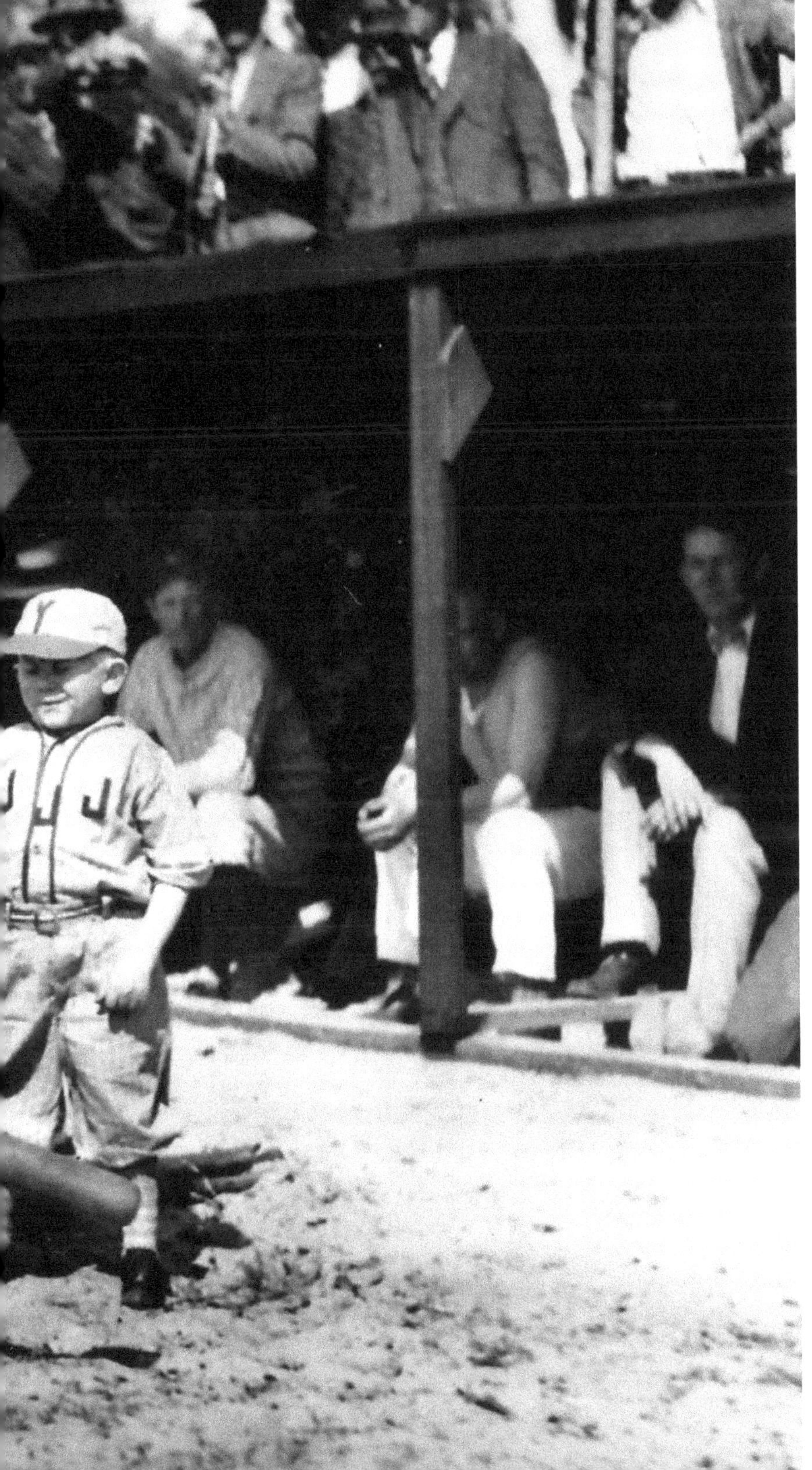

The legendary Babe Ruth demonstrates his grip to batboys Mike and Ike. The New York Yankees moved their spring training camp to St. Petersburg in 1925. To accommodate the Yankees, the city built a new ball park and clubhouse at Crescent Lake Park. Many Yankee players stayed at the Don CeSar Hotel; Ruth preferred the Vinoy.

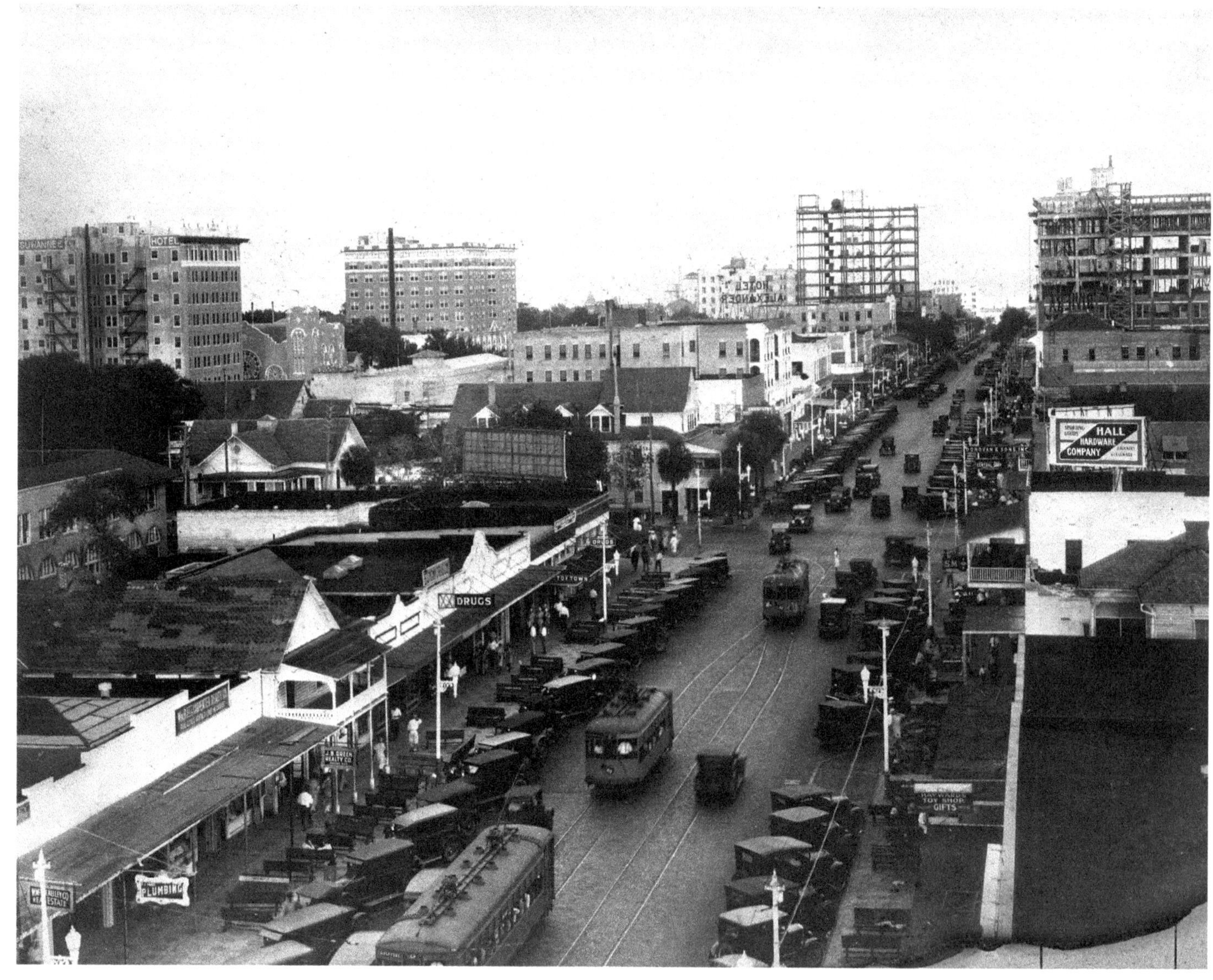

Owing to the tremendous increase in tourism, hotels seem to spring up overnight in downtown St. Petersburg during the boom era. In this view east on Central Avenue is the Suwannee, far left, opened in December 1923; the Mason, under construction in the center, renamed the Princess Martha in 1926; and the Pheil Hotel, far right, finished in 1924.

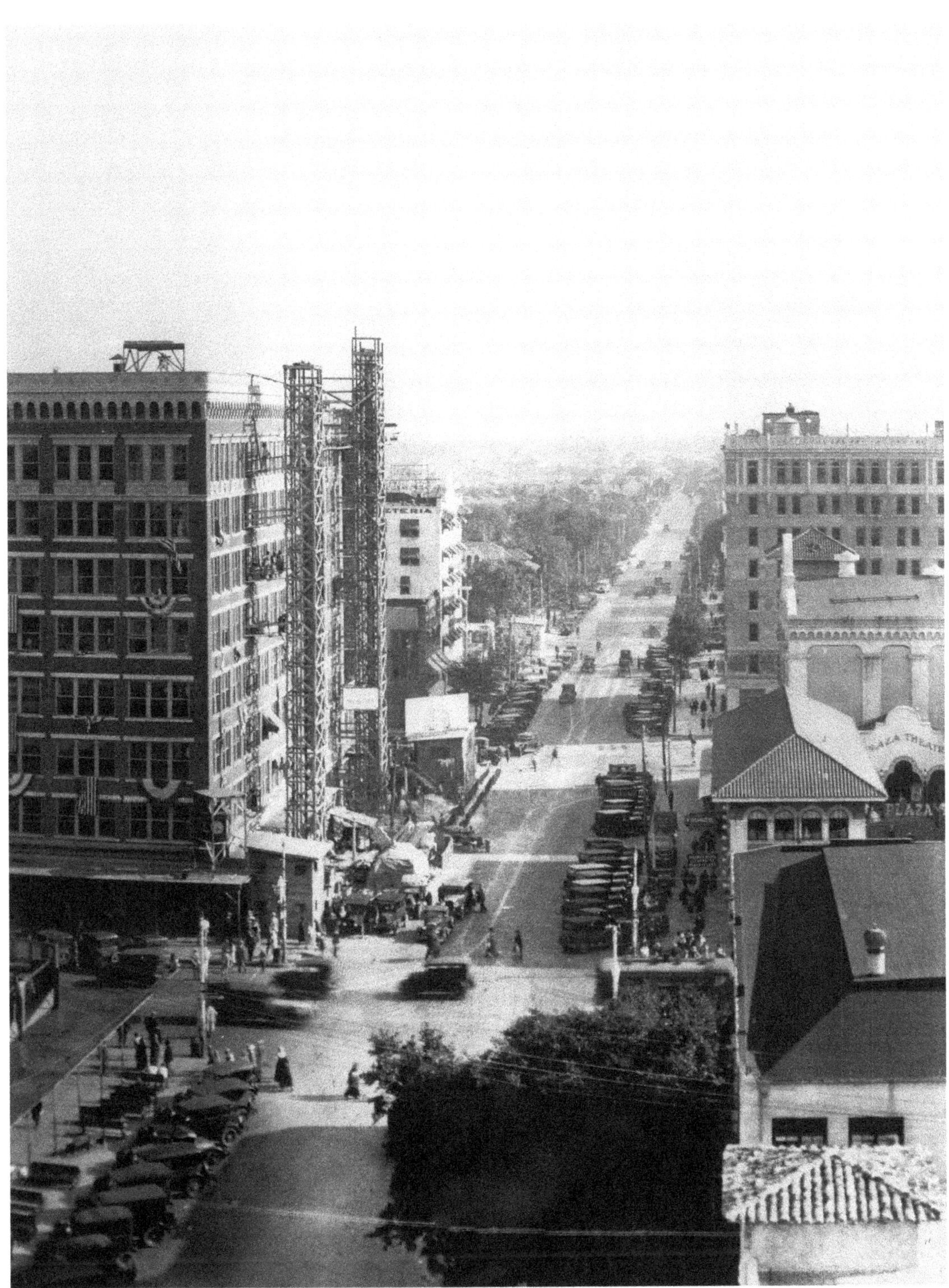

In 1926, this was the view south on 5th Street from the Suwanee Hotel. The first intersection is Central Avenue and to the right is the famous La Plaza Theatre. As the boom progressed, real estate values soared. One woman wanted to sell her land for $10,000 in 1921, but she was advised to wait. She did and sold the property for $200,000 in 1925.

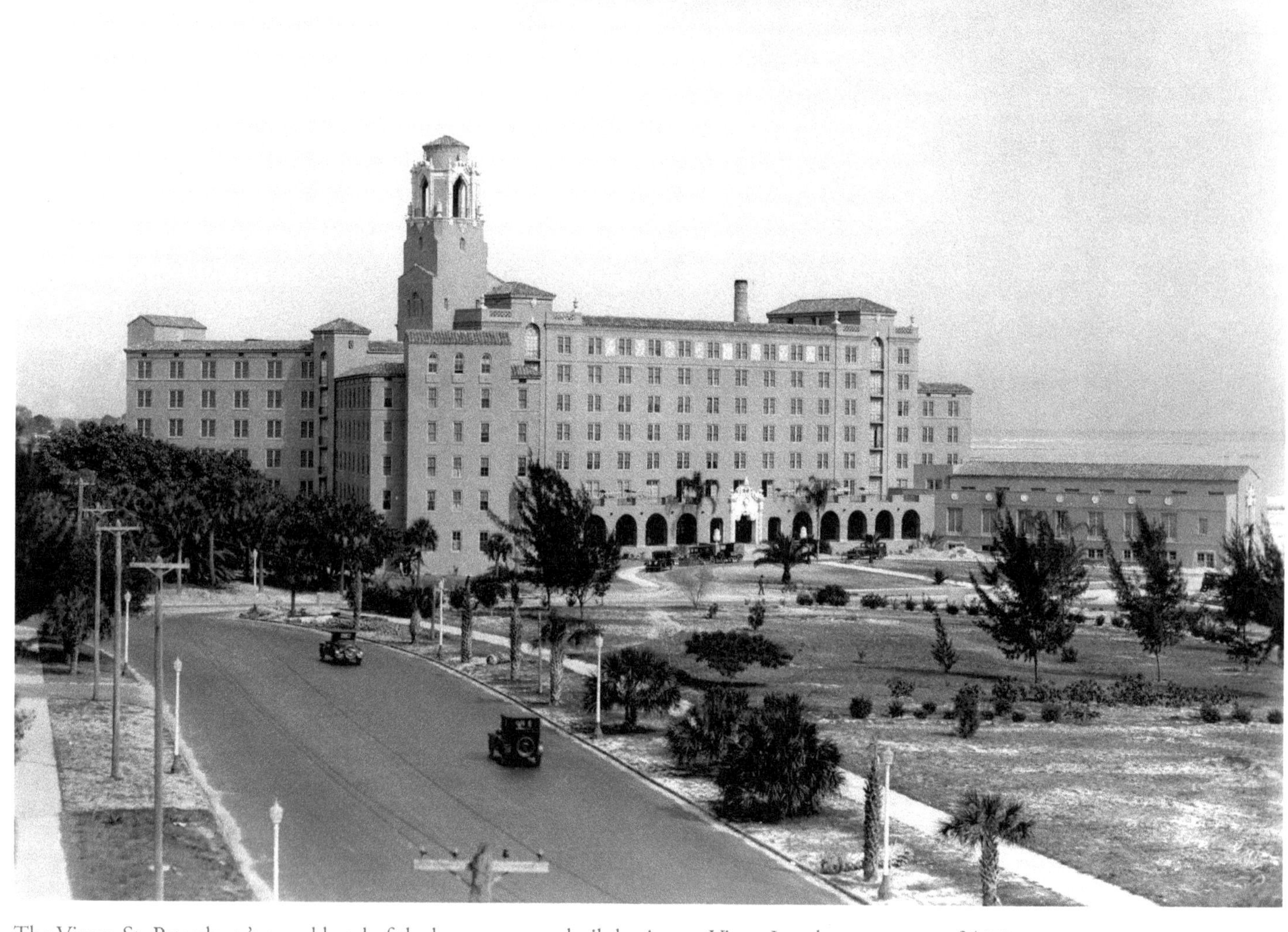

The Vinoy, St. Petersburg's grand hotel of the boom era, was built by Aymer Vinoy Laughner at a cost of $3.5 million. Constructed on the waterfront in 1925, the hotel sat on twelve acres, created with fill from dredging the North Yacht Basin. Designed by Henry L. Taylor, the Mediterranean revival–style hotel even boasted an observation tower.

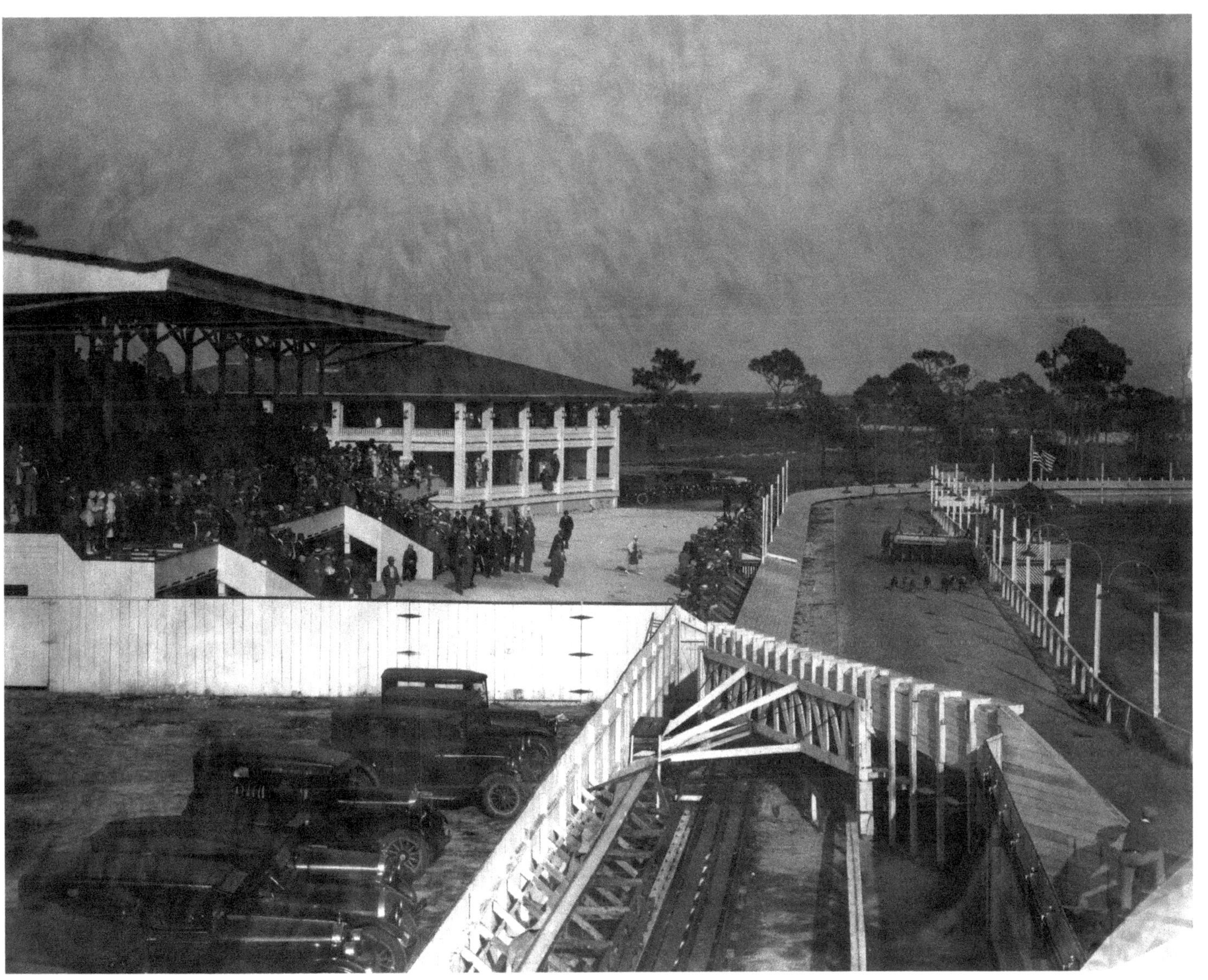

Organized in 1924, the St. Petersburg kennel club purchased land and built a track and grandstand on Gandy Lane. Since the day the races began, January 3, 1925, Derby Lane has become the oldest continuously operating dog track in the world. New York Yankees legends Babe Ruth and Lou Gehrig were frequent visitors.

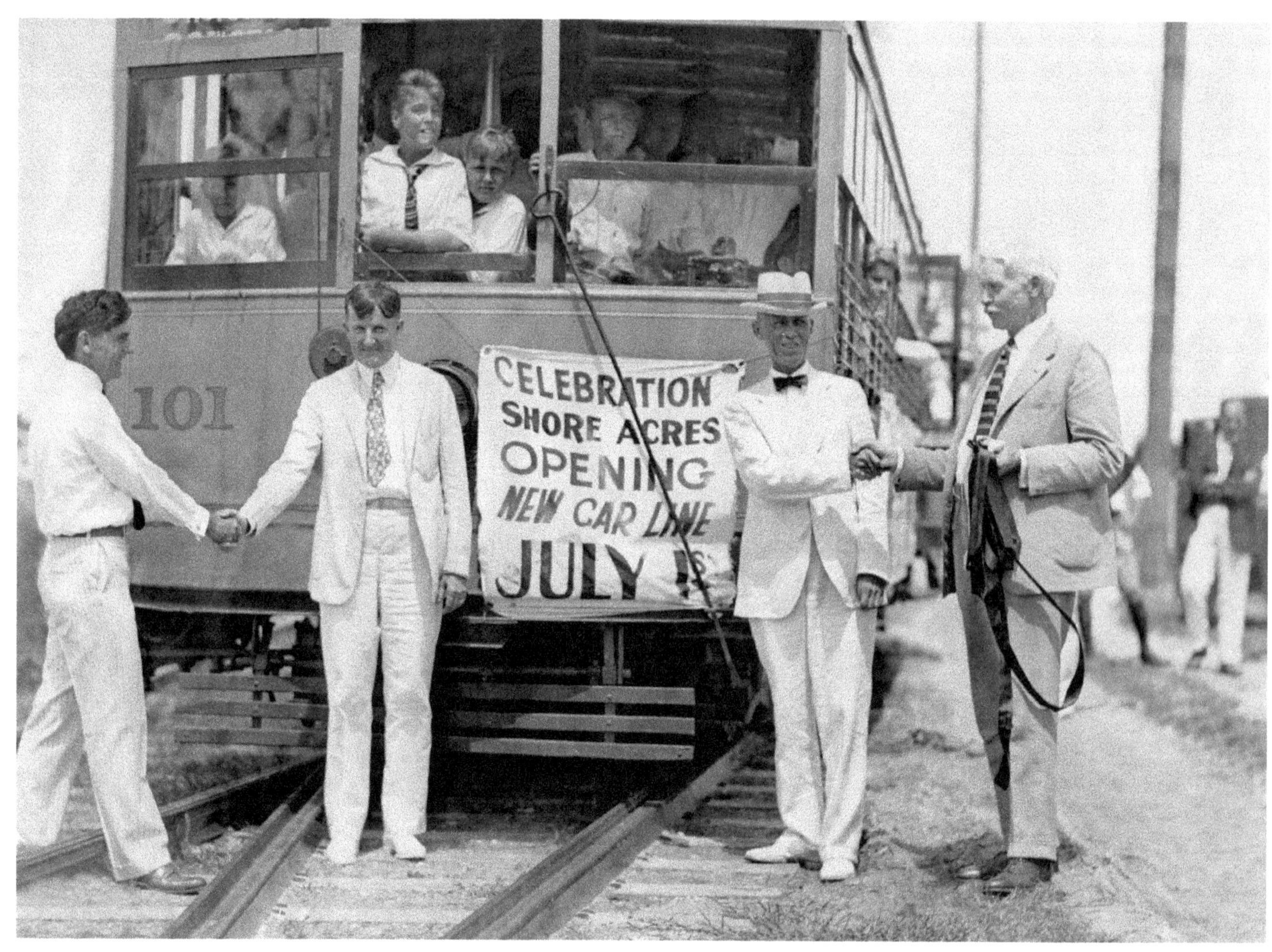

A trolley line opens to Shore Acres in 1926. Developed by Nathaniel J. Upham, twice president of the National Association of Realtors, it was originally pine woods, marsh, and palmetto. A long and expensive drainage project added new land. According to local legend, Al Capone purchased a home there that same year.

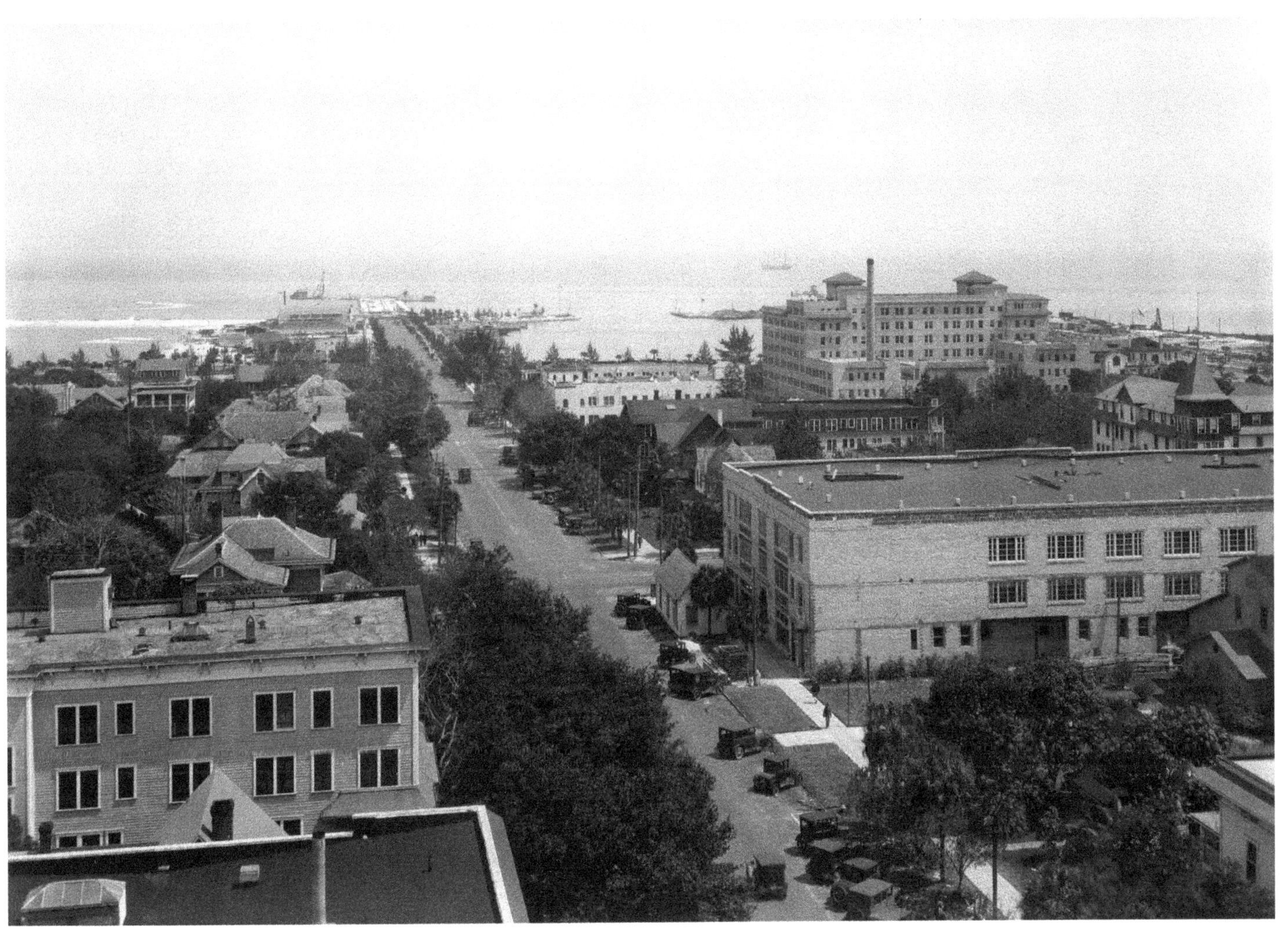

The Soreno Hotel (right, rear) was billed as the first million-dollar hotel in St. Petersburg and opened on New Year's Day 1924. The 300-room waterfront hotel was owned by Soren Lund, a Danish immigrant. During World War II, it became a training base for cooks and bakers. Its demolition was filmed in 1992 and added to the movie *Lethal Weapon III.*

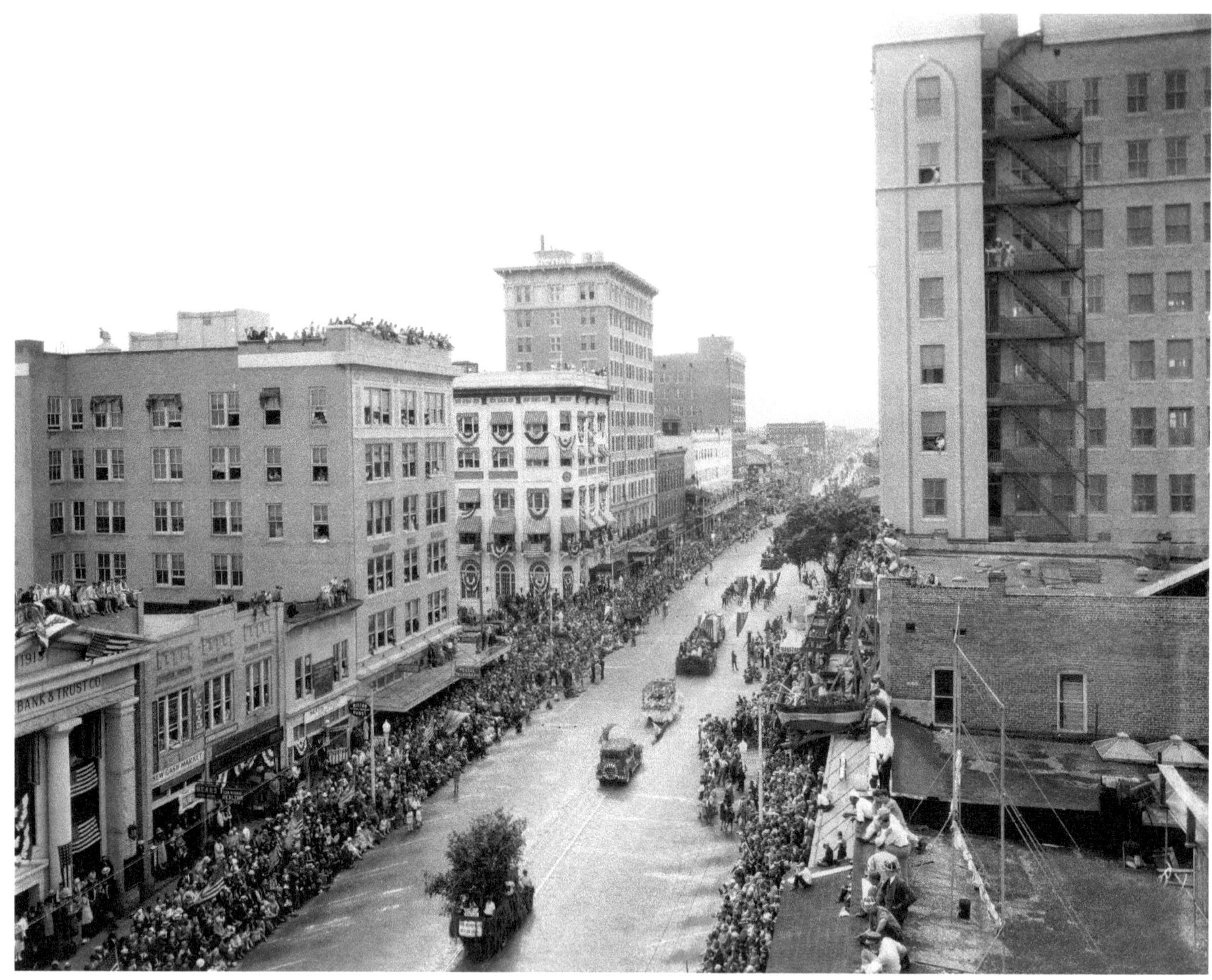

Central Avenue's one-hundred-foot-wide streets easily accommodate this large crowd at the 1926 Festival of States Parade. Spectators also line the buildings, porches, rooftops, parapets, overhangs, and windows. This bird's-eye view faces west toward the 13-story Phiel Hotel and theater.

A unique community landmark, the first "open air post office" was designed by Edwin Tomlinson and opened in 1907. Similar plans for a new structure were scoffed at by the postal service, but Postmaster Roy Hanna insisted that the open-air design was well suited for St. Petersburg and in 1917 the second Open Air Post Office, shown here at right, was dedicated.

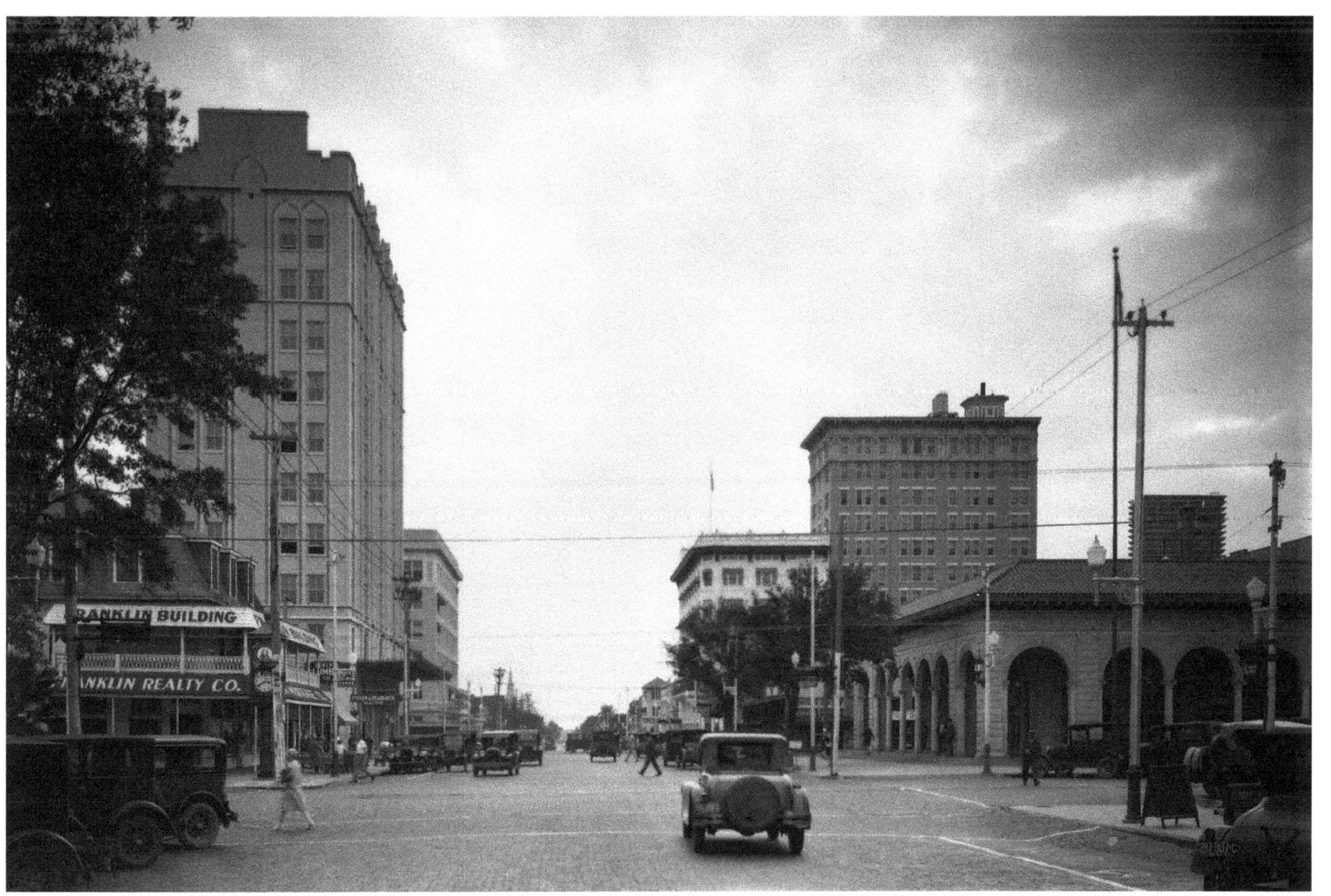

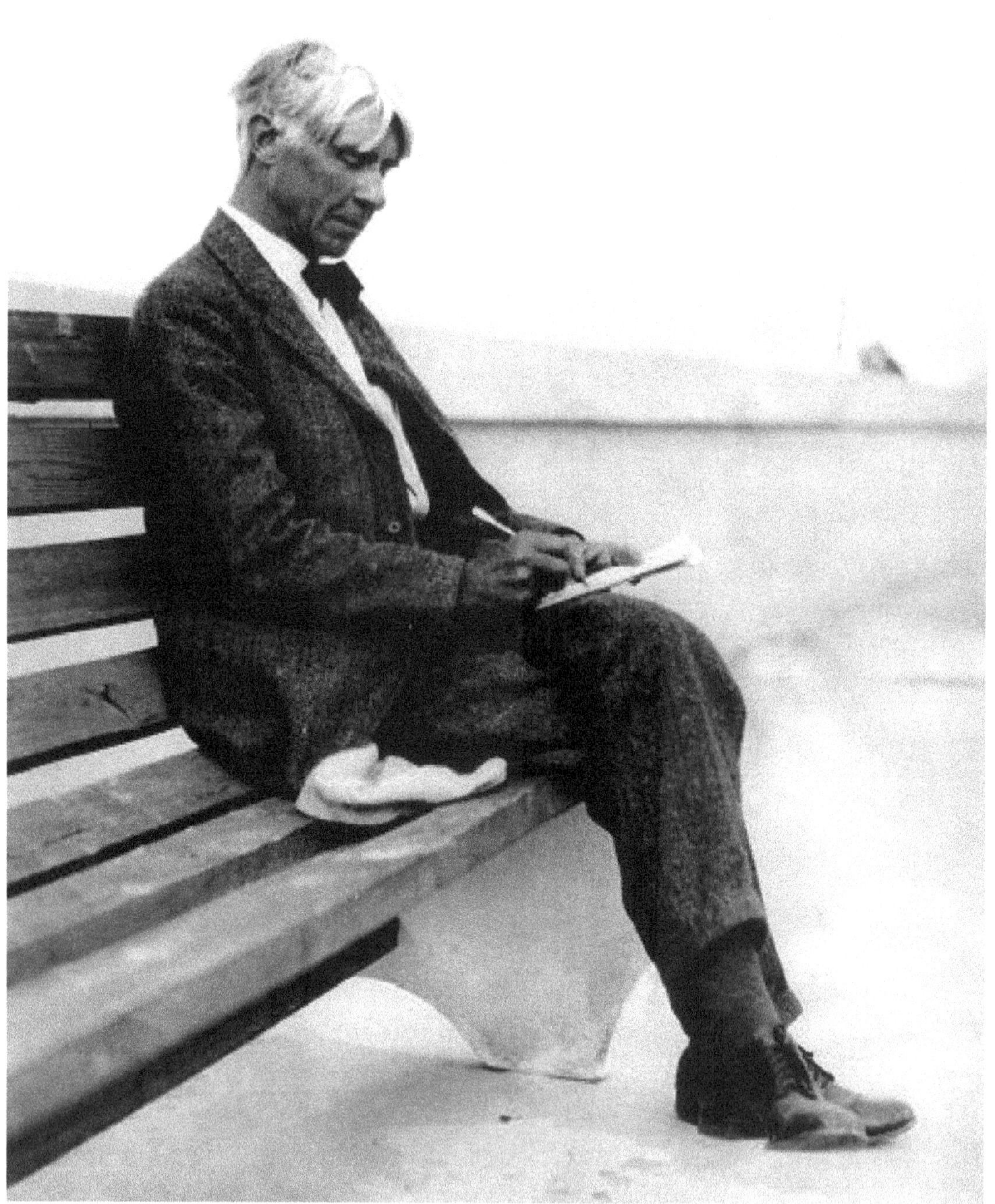

The poet Carl Sandburg once interviewed Babe Ruth in St. Petersburg: "At least a million hot ball fans in this country, admirers of yours, believe in the Bible and Shakespeare as the two greatest books ever written, and some of them would like to know if there are any special parts of those books that are favorites of yours." Babe Ruth replied, "A ballplayer don't have time to read."

Overcast: Bust and Depression Years (1927–1940)

The Florida land boom of the twenties ended abruptly late in 1926 with a dramatic collapse of real estate prices that crippled the town and the state for years. Fortunes were lost and development came to a virtual standstill. As the city attempted to recover, in 1929 the stormclouds of the Great Depression rolled in.

Speculators, hoping to turn a fast profit, had been the driving force behind the real estate boom, greatly inflating the market. When the bubble burst, sales started to slow and many of them were unable to meet their notes. Many residents intending to cash in on the boom lost everything, and for years partly completed subdivisions deteriorated quietly on the roadside. Daily auctions for taxes saw lots that once had sold for $10,000 to $60,000 go for delinquent taxes of $4 to $450. Hotels, business blocks, houses—everything went at bargain prices. All businesses were affected, many were caught with large inventories that they could not sell, and customers defaulted on bills. Many merchants went bankrupt. Severe Florida hurricanes in 1926 and 1928 only added to the statewide misery.

The great stock market collapse of October 1929 led the United States into the Great Depression and hit St. Petersburg as it was trying to recover from the real estate collapse. Within a year all the banks in the city had closed, many city merchants closed their doors permanently, and others were forced to lay off workers. The visitors who did show up had little money, barely enough for necessities.

The city persevered. It had fewer unemployed residents than large industrial cities, since most of the construction workers of the boom years had simply moved elsewhere. With its wonderful climate and peaceful surroundings, the city could still promote its Sunshine City image as a great place to wait out the depression. City publicity agent John Lodwick advertised this image throughout the nation, emphasizing the Florida fantasy bathing beauty photograph. One observer concluded, if all the publicity were true, that one must believe "the city was populated solely by beautiful women and their grandparents."

By the mid 1930s, the number of winter visitors started to increase, driving construction permits forward, which rose from 1.5 million in 1934 to 3 million by 1937. City officials also advocated for federal Works Progress Administration projects. The WPA spent $4 million, employing more than 1,000 a year in local city projects, which included Whitted Airport, St. Petersburg Junior College, Bartlett Park, Jordan Park, and the National Guard Armory.

As the nation struggled with the effects of the depression, remarkably St. Petersburg and the area continued to grow. These were not the heady, prosperous years of the boom, but years of slow, steady growth. During the decade of the depression, the county population increased 47 percent, from around 62,000 in 1930 to more than 90,000 in 1940. Despite this growth, tourism remained the city's primary economic engine—by 1940 more than 60 percent of employees worked in the retail or service sectors.

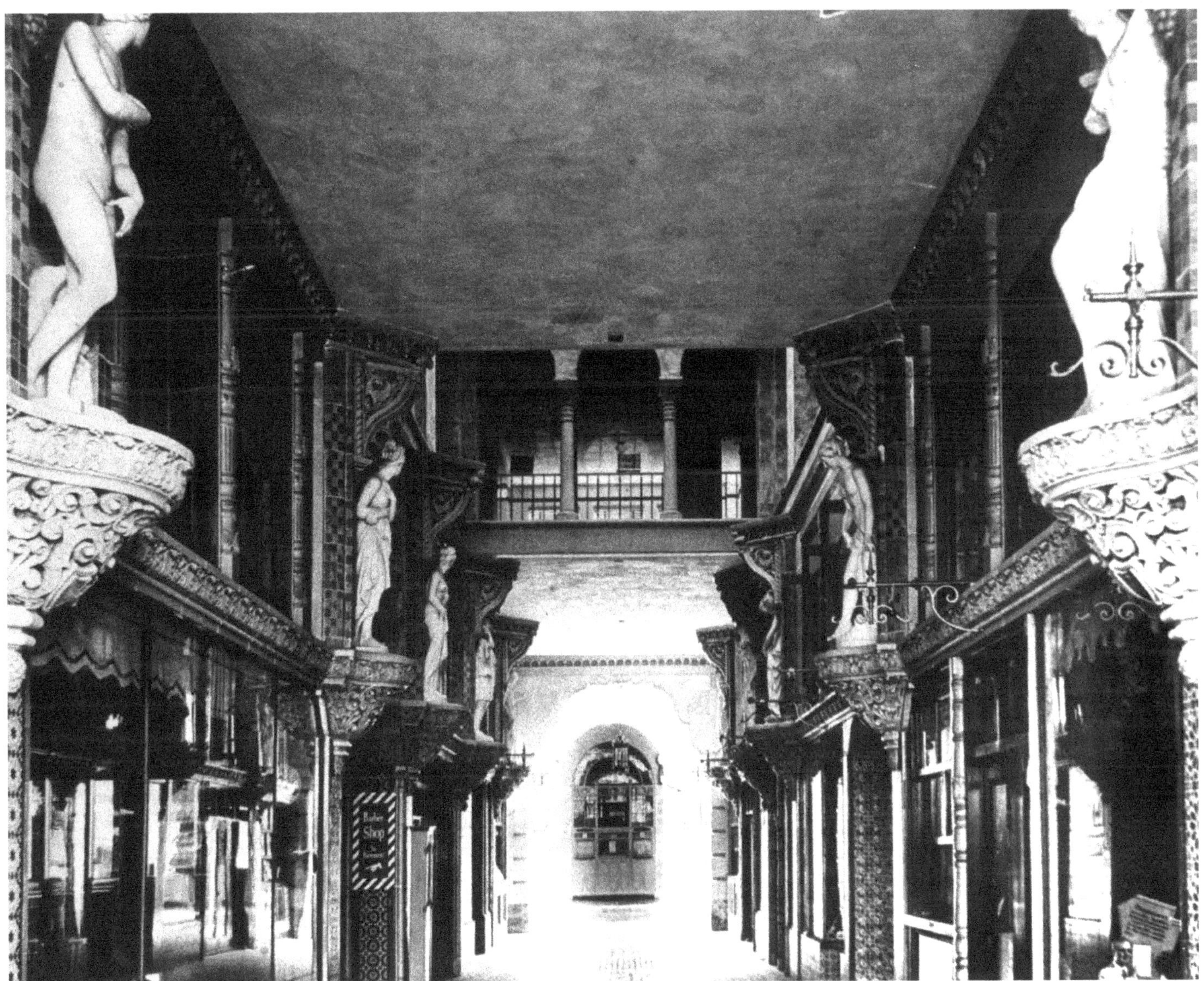

The elaborate ornamentation of the Snell Arcade is clearly exhibited in this first-floor hallway leading to the open-air post office. Included in the arcade were mosaics, tiles, and statuary that Perry Snell had collected from all over the world, resulting in a fusion of Mediterranean revival–style with Gothic and fantasy elements.

This image shows the Snell Arcade soon after its 1926 completion. Offered $1 million for this northwest corner of Fourth and Central, real estate developer C. Perry Snell instead spent $750,000 building the landmark structure. He soon lost it in a foreclosure to an insurance company. Designed by Richard Kiehnel, this architectural landmark featured a terra cotta exterior, bas-relief details, and an ornate parapet. During a revitalization project in the 1980s, columns, arches, and other unique architectural details were discovered, including a seventeenth-century mosaic hidden from view since the 1950s, when the arcade was modernized.

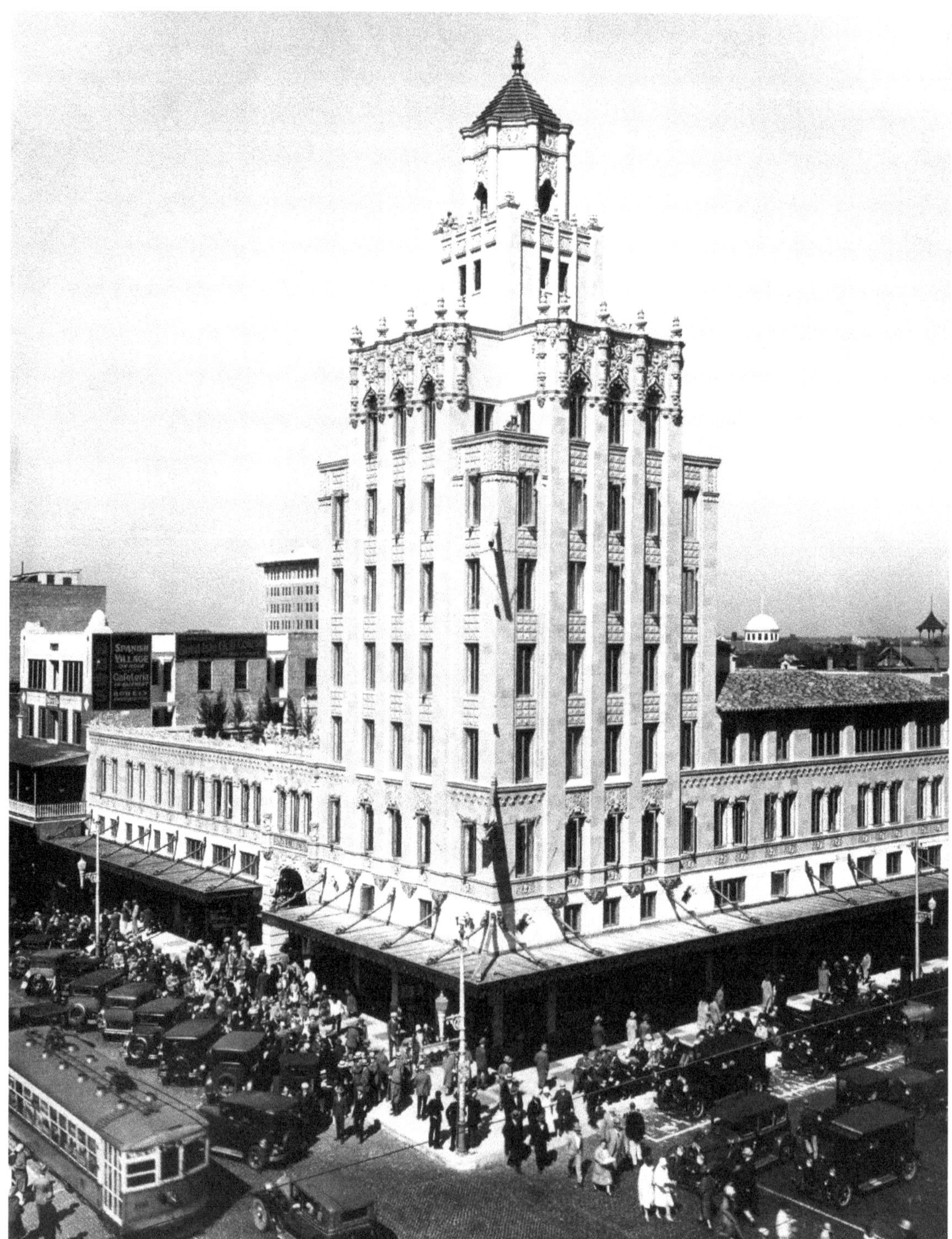

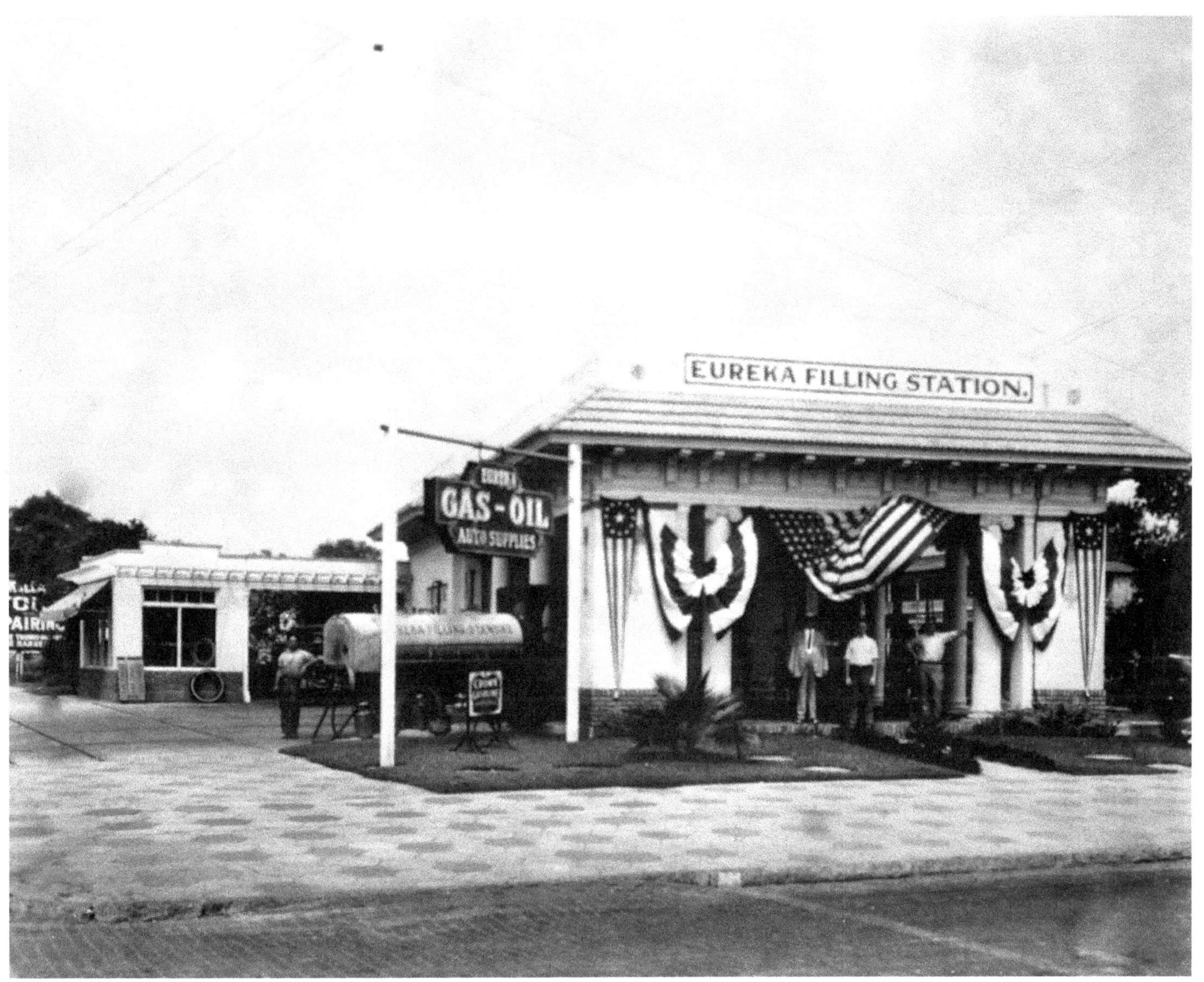

The Eureka Filling Station, located on 4th Street near 9th Avenue, appears to be decorated and ready for its first customer. This image is from the National Cash Register Company archives, which kept photographs, taken after a register was installed, to use as promotional material.

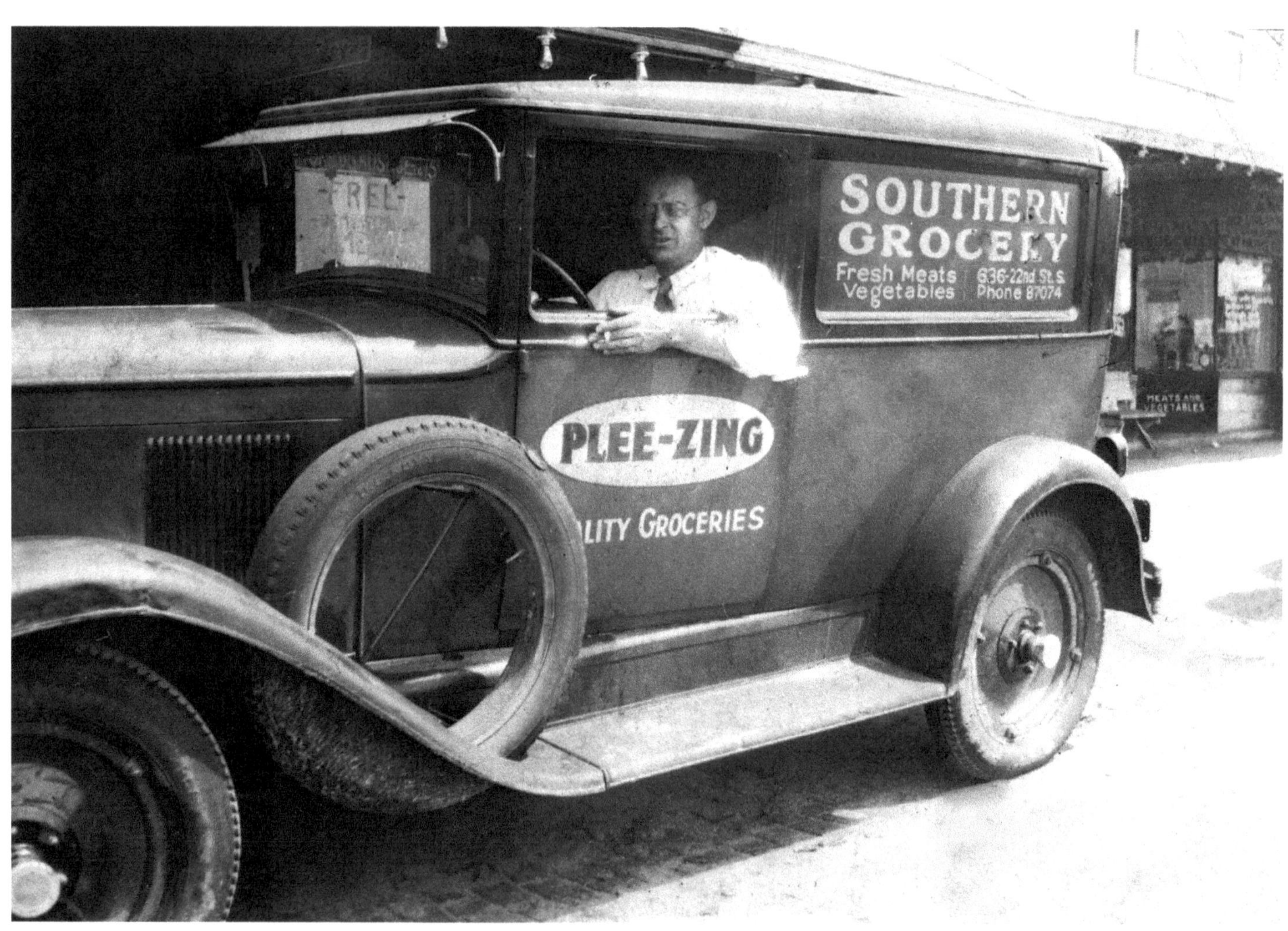

David Rothblatt, owner of Southern Grocery located at 636 22nd Street South, poses for a photograph in his delivery truck. Isaac Jacobs, who had moved from Chicago and opened the store, invited his daughter, Ethel, and her husband, David Rothblatt, to join him in the family business. The couple came to St. Petersburg from Milwaukee.

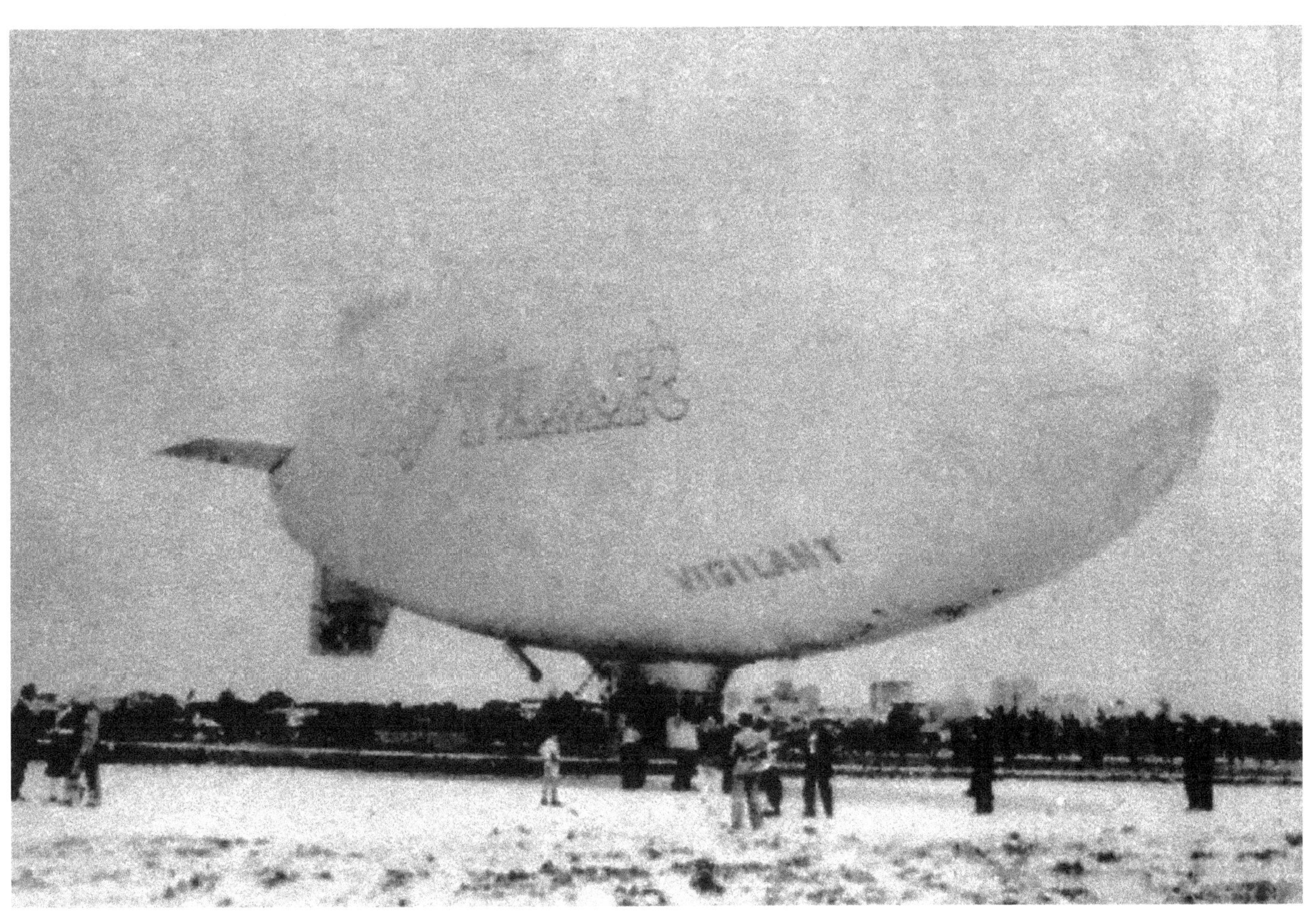

City publicity agent John Lodwick persuaded the Goodyear Tire and Rubber Company to station one of their blimps at the new Albert Whitted Airport in St. Petersburg. The city spent $33,062 for a municipal blimp hangar and Goodyear stayed in St. Petersburg for 15 years. The Goodyear *Vigilant,* shown here in 1930, was christened at Whitted in 1929.

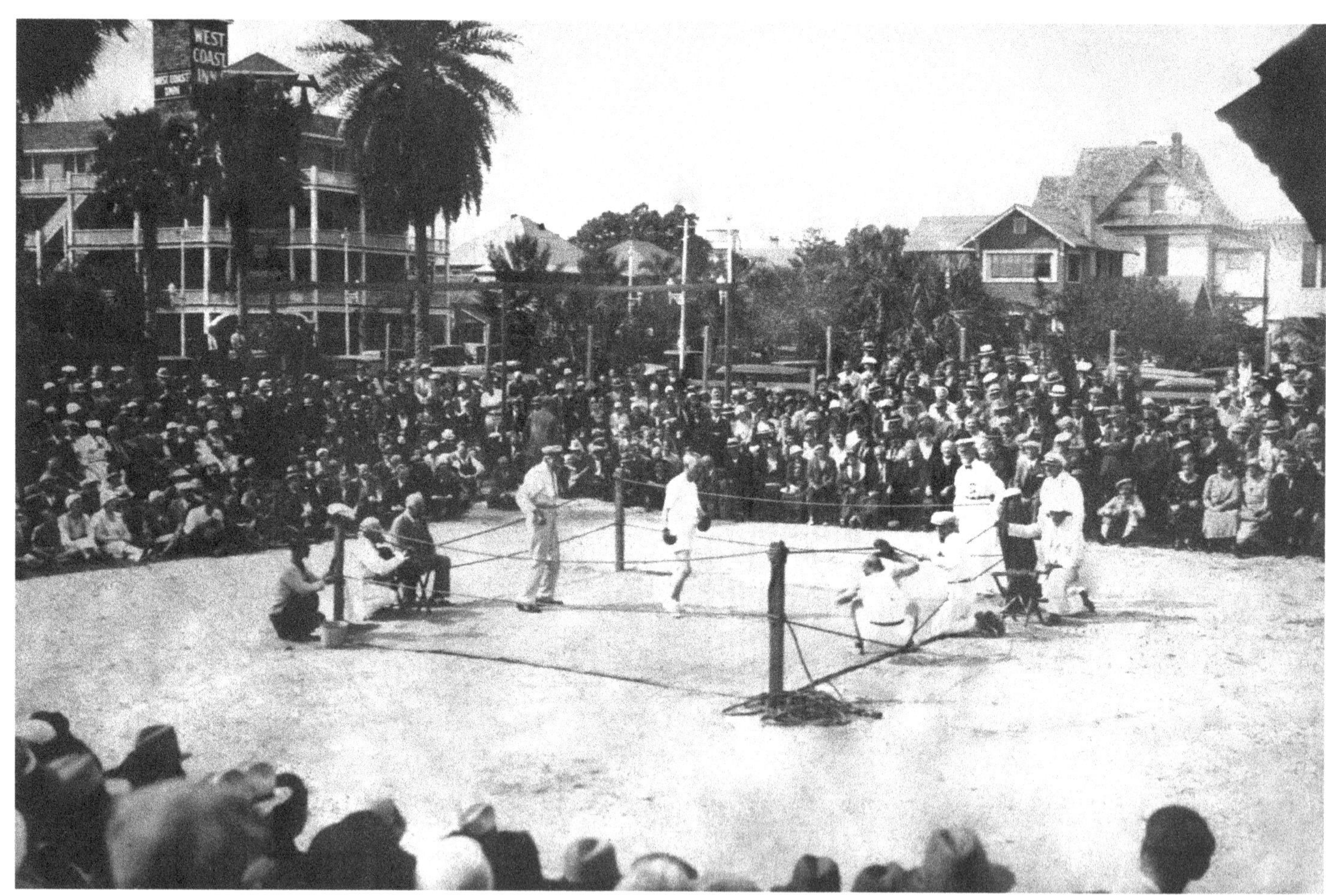

With the advent of the 1930s and the national economic downturn, St. Petersburg was promoted as "the perfect place to sit out the depression." There were always activities for retirees, even boxing matches. This one is taking place in front of the West Coast Inn, with its distinctive shingled tower and wraparound verandas.

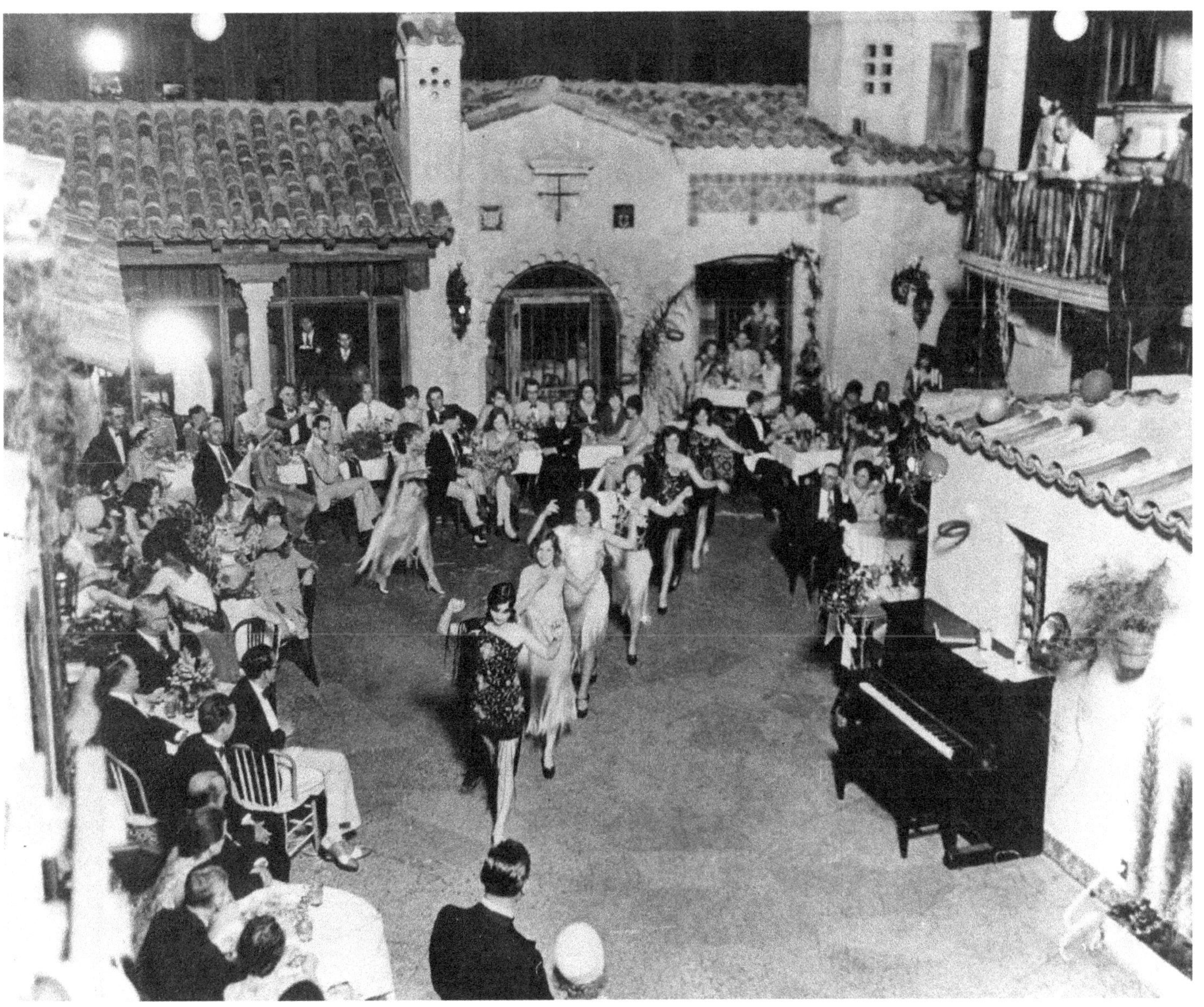

An audience watches the dancers at Spanish Bob's nightclub on the third-floor terrace of the Snell Arcade. Bob's was a popular hot spot and a favorite of Babe Ruth's. In 1937, Walgreen and Company purchased the arcade for $500,000, adding $100,000 in remodeling.

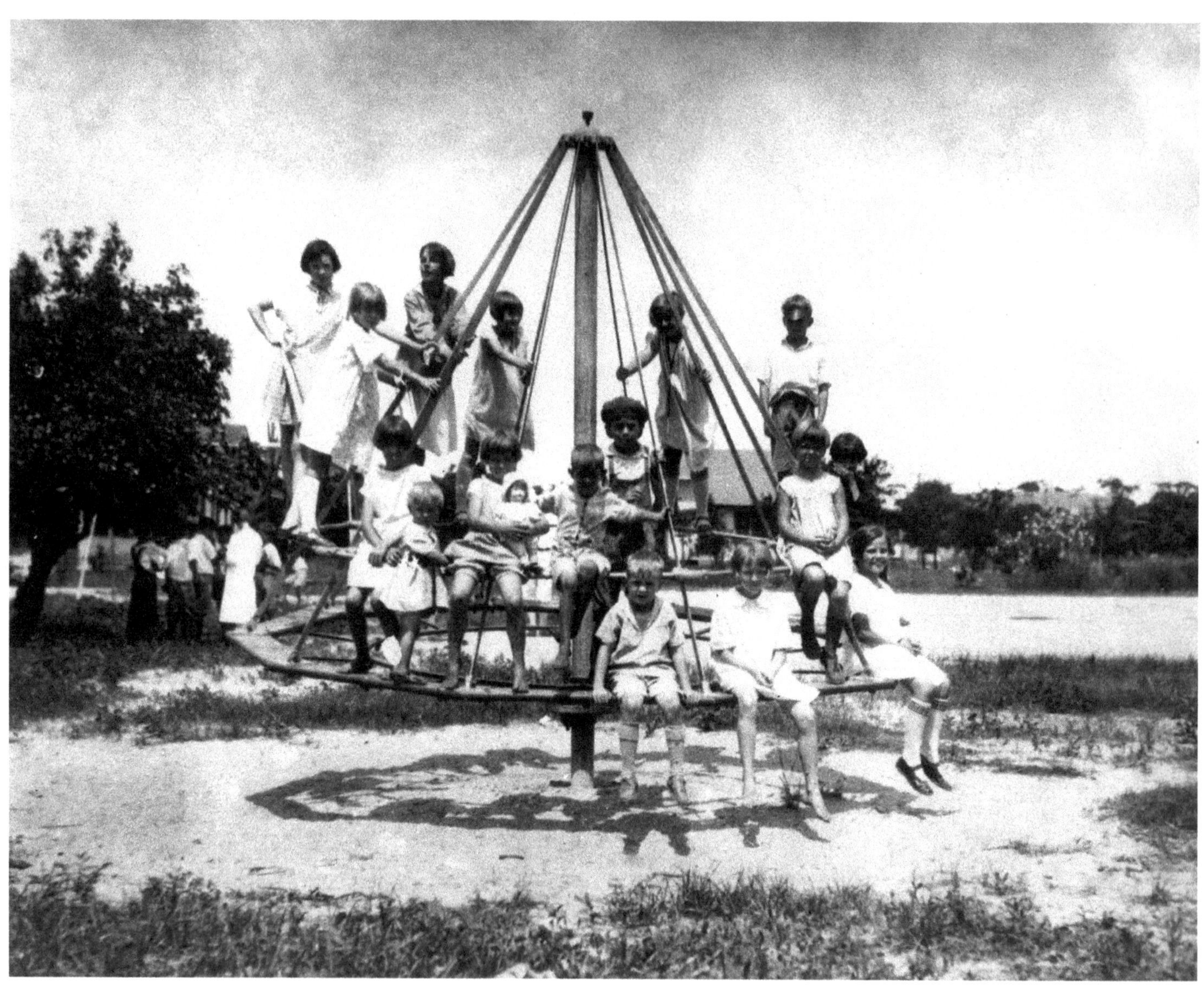

Children continued to have fun at this playground, but elsewhere in 1930, St. Petersburg like the rest of the nation was feeling the effects of the Great Depression. There were local attempts at relief—a Citizen's Emergency Committee even issued scrip used to pay wages and honored by most area merchants.

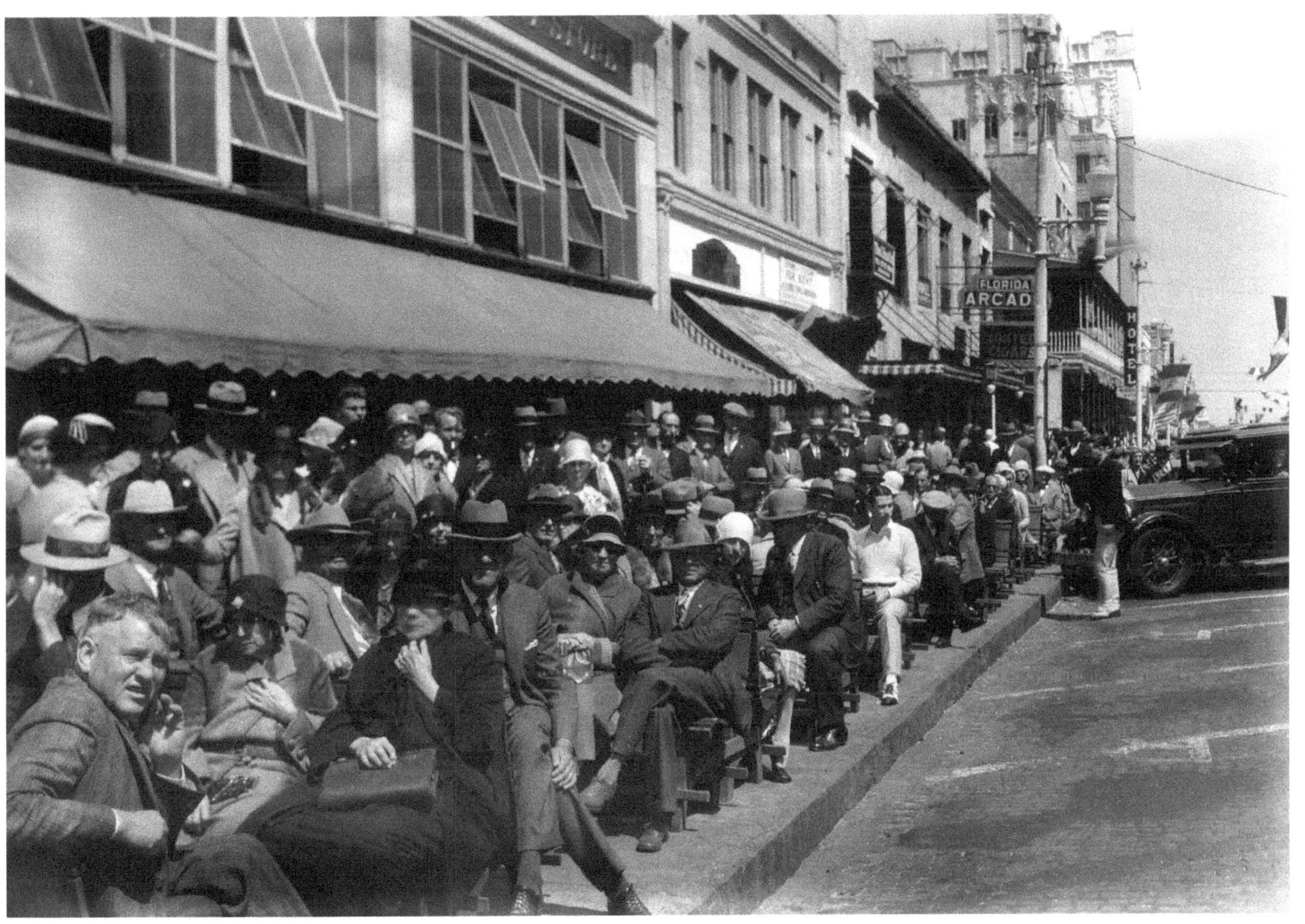

This view of a crowded street on March 26, 1930, inspired someone to note that one "may easily get acquainted and enjoy passing a few hours on these benches." The depression forced many unemployed to join the retirees and tourists on the famous green benches. The few tourists who did come had limited funds and added little to the economy.

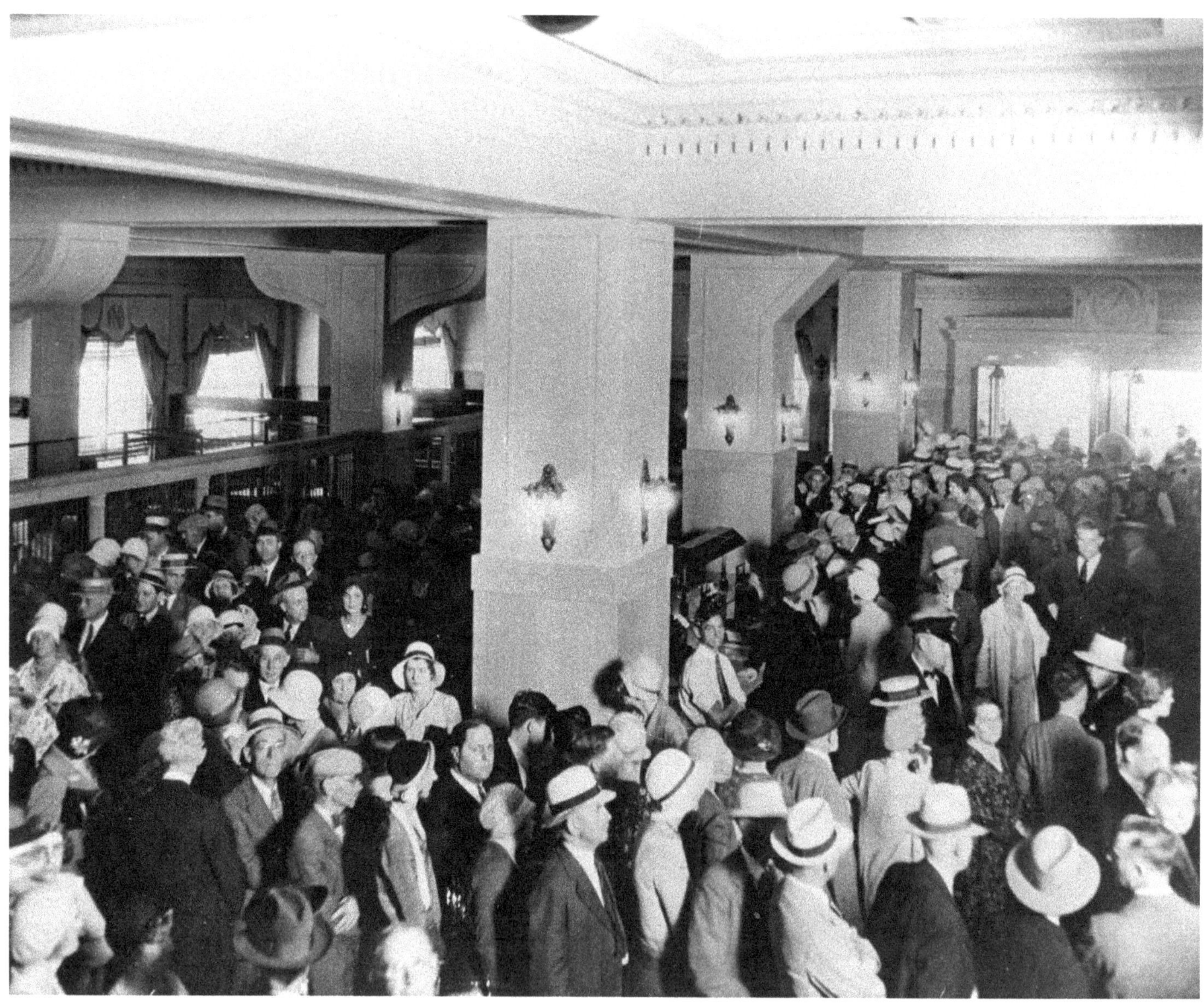

Anxious depositors wait in line during a run on the Florida National Bank on April 17, 1931. Since the preceding April, most of the nine St. Petersburg banks had closed and ultimately only one bank survived. More than $10 million in depositors' assets were frozen and less than half of that was ever recovered. Many people had to settle for just cents on the dollar.

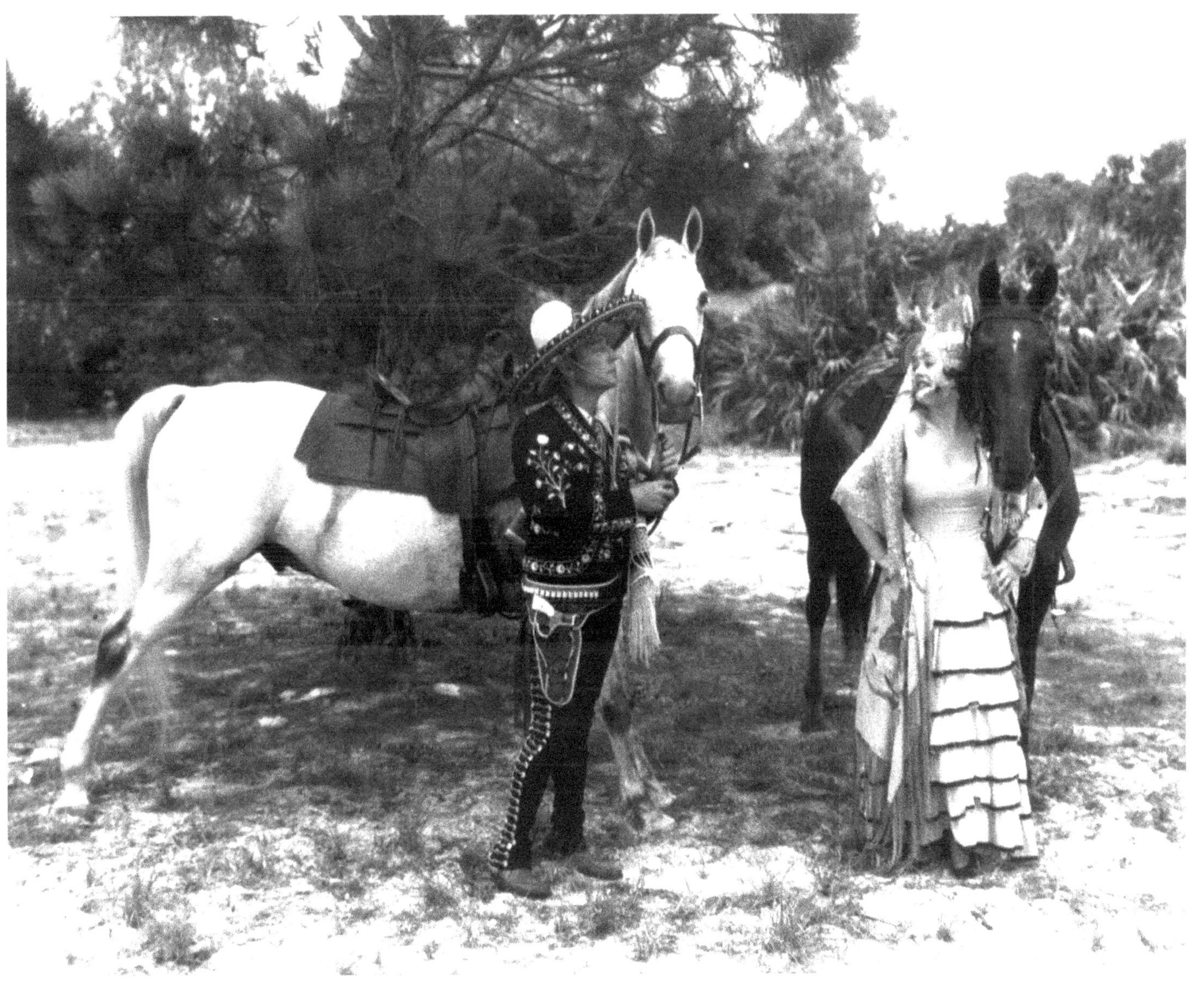

Buster Keaton and Molly O'Day appeared together in many "shorts" in the 1920s. Unsettled by a divorce, Keaton signed a contract with Kennedy Productions, which planned to build a production center in St. Petersburg. In May 1932, he arrived in the city, but soon the production company failed and Keaton returned to Hollywood.

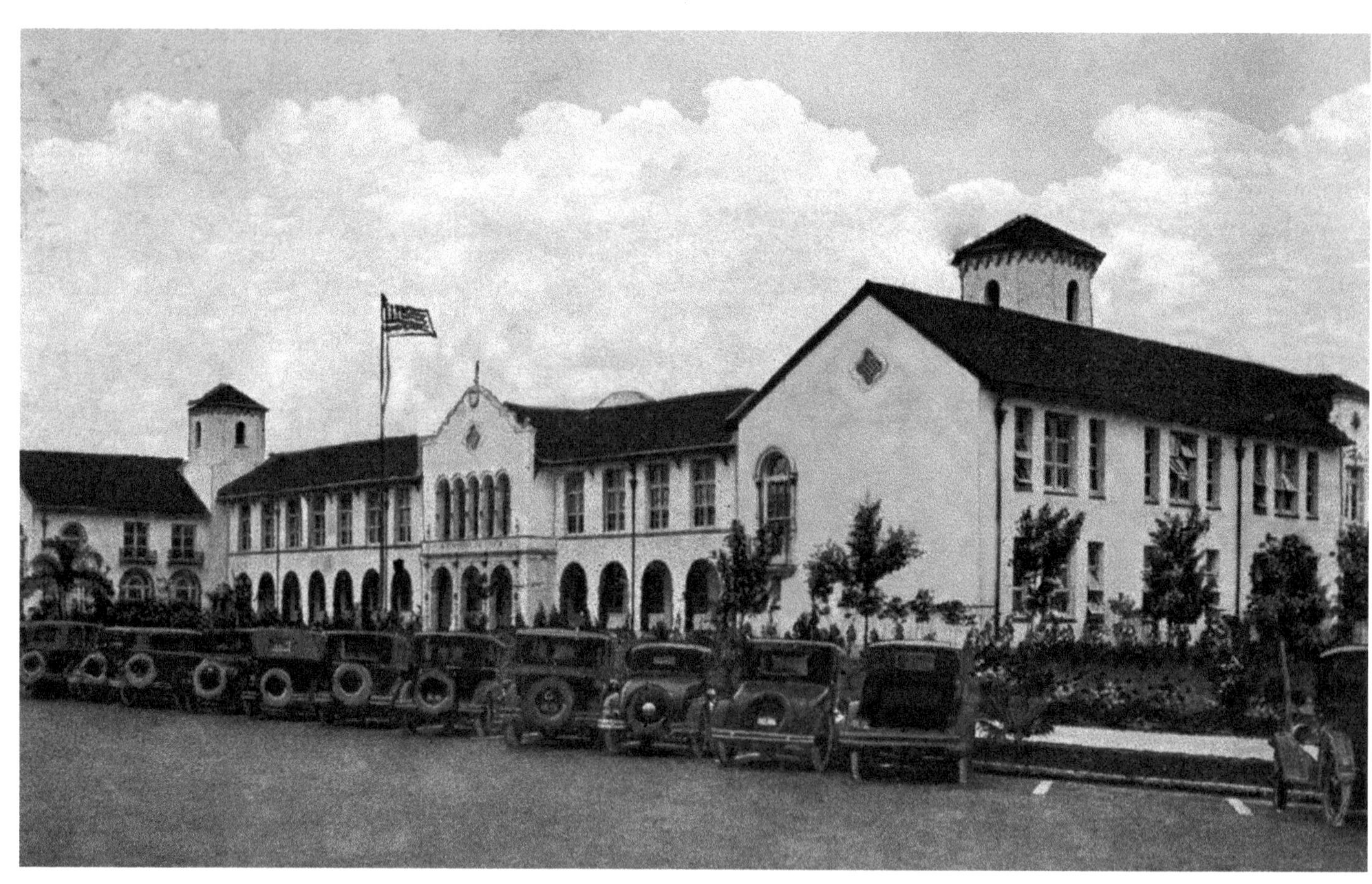

The school paper described the new 1926 "Million Dollar High School" as "the finest school building in the South . . . rambling Spanish architecture makes the three-story building look long, low, impressive . . . an inspiration to walk toward it . . . to see the sun on the red-tiled roof . . . inside, one is almost lost at first." Shown here is the school in 1931.

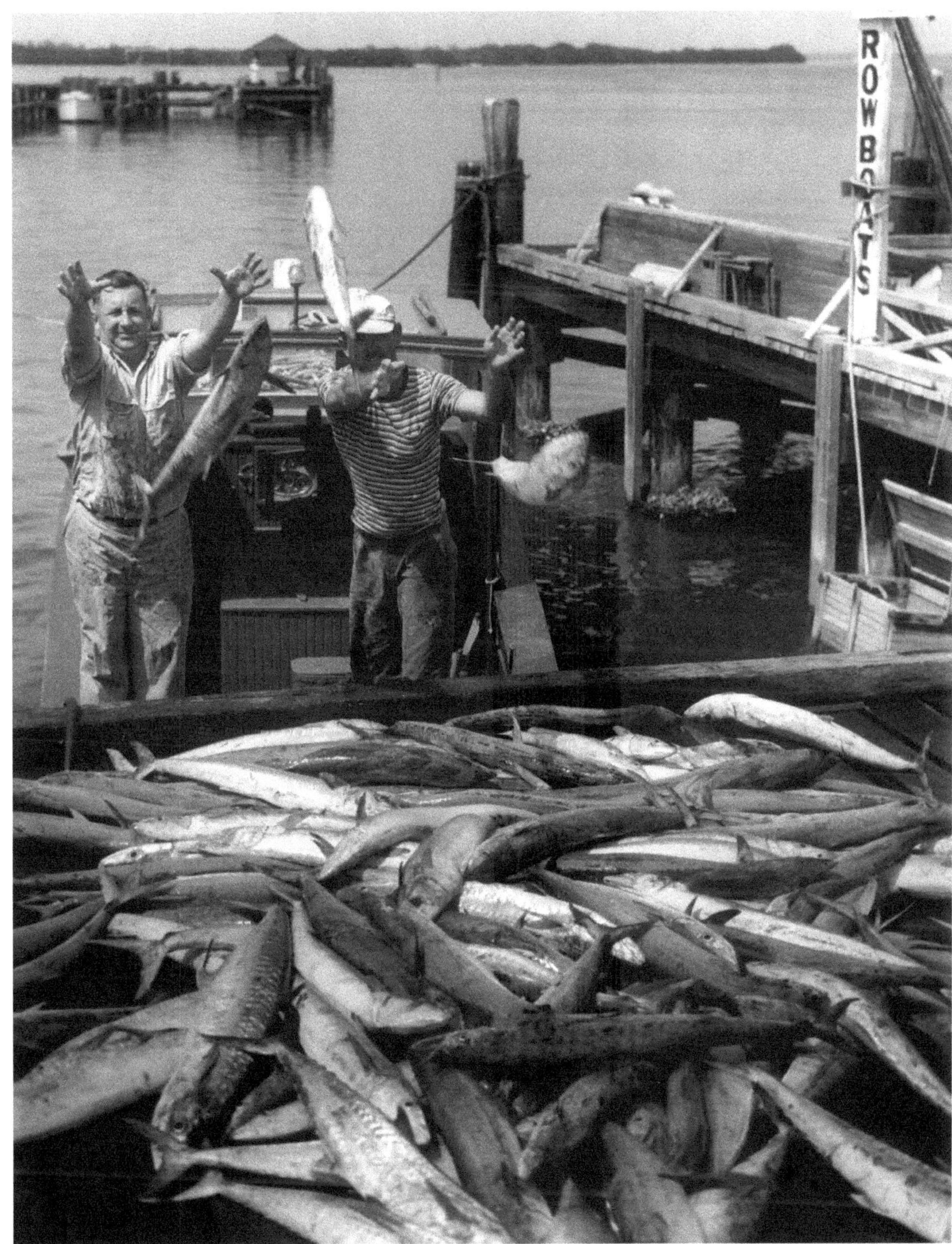

A day's catch at Pass-A-Grille in 1935. Eccentric but wealthy Sir Charles Ross thrilled the Chamber of Commerce with his testimonial: "I have fished everywhere, but I have never caught a greater variety of fish than I have at Pass-A-Grille. This season I have caught over 10,000 pounds of fish, and I'm coming back for more."

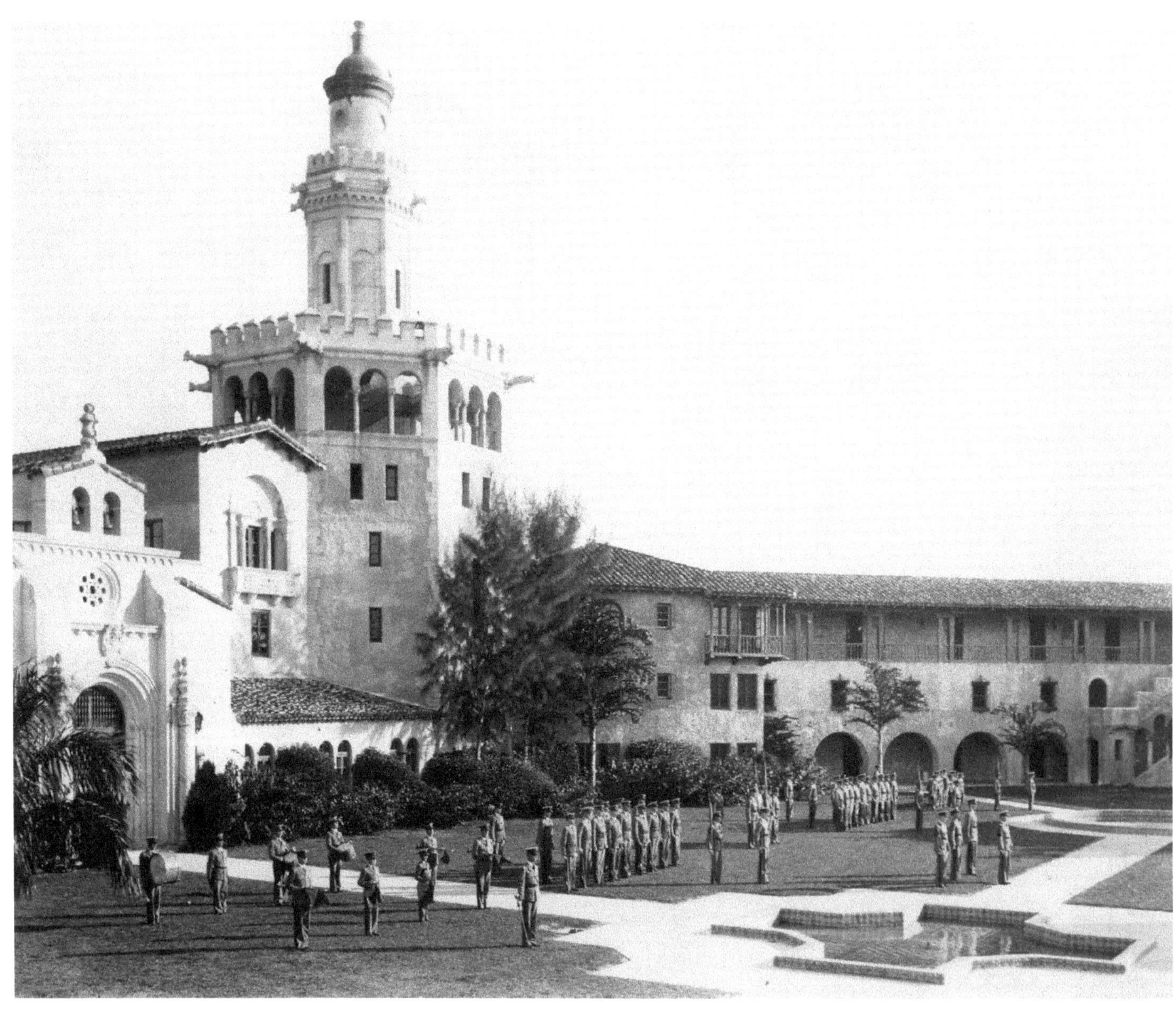

The Florida Military Academy purchased the Rolyat Hotel in 1932. The hotel, built by colorful "Handsome Jack," opened in January 1926. Inspired by Spain's feudal period, it featured a courtyard with a well and two large fountains, two towers, and an elaborate main entrance. ("Rolyat" is Taylor spelled backward.) This view is from 1939.

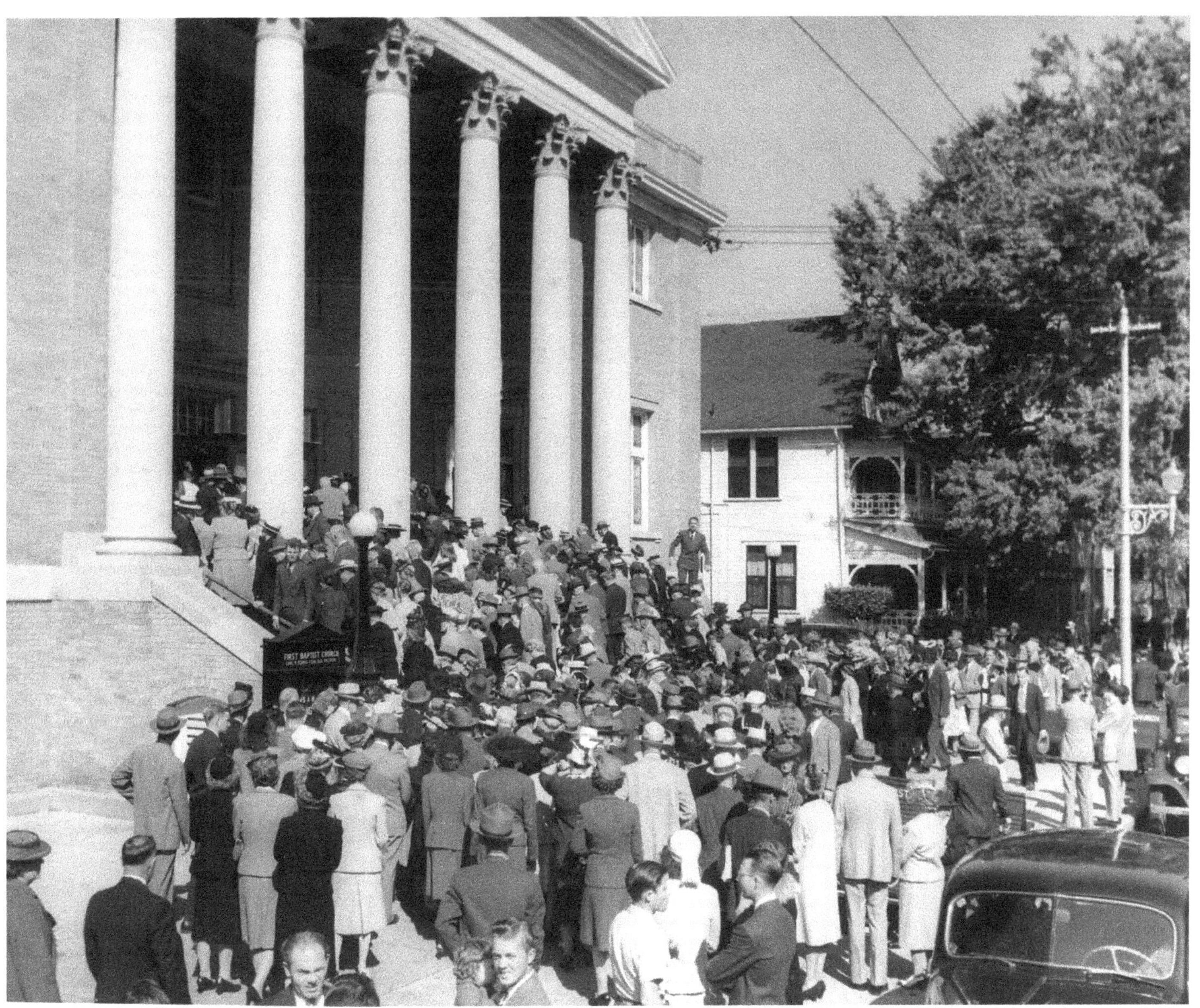

A crowd enters First Baptist Church in 1935 for services. The congregation was organized in 1892, and moved to several locations before buying a lot on Fourth Street North opposite Williams Park. This neoclassical-style building, erected in 1923, is one of only 28 buildings of this style remaining in St. Petersburg.

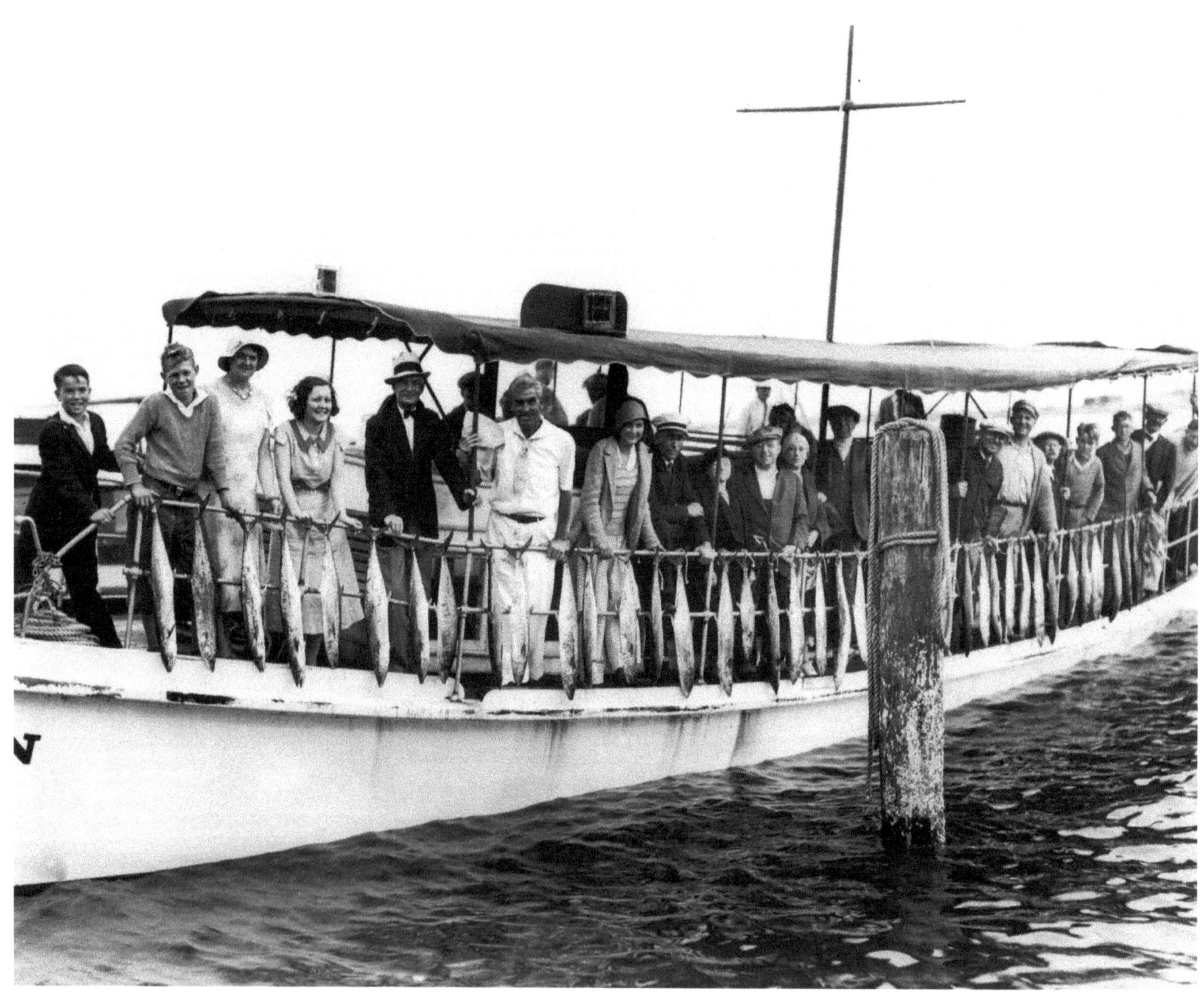

It's all smiles as this party boat displays their catch in 1938. Around that time, as the story goes, a mullet fisherman got more than he bargained for when mullet started jumping out of his nets into his little dory and it started sinking. A witness to the event, J. W. Prichard recalled, "I'll never forget the look on his face when he found himself neck-deep and going deeper."

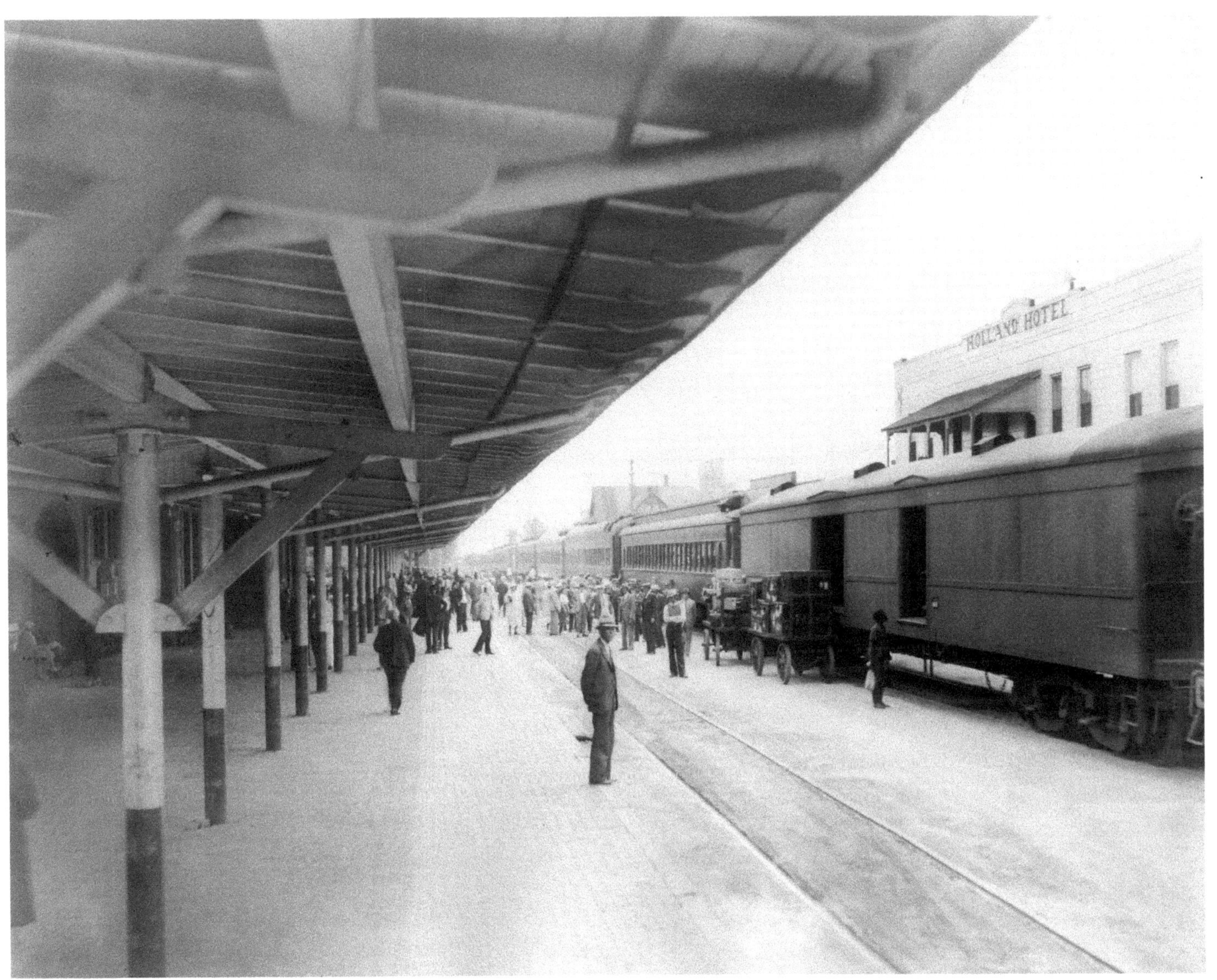

Passengers meet and debark at the Atlantic Coast Line railroad station in 1936. After absorbing the Plant railroads in 1902, the ACL spent $5 million to upgrade service. The first through-train from New York to St. Petersburg arrived in 1909, and in 1915 a $100,000 passenger depot was completed on First Avenue South.

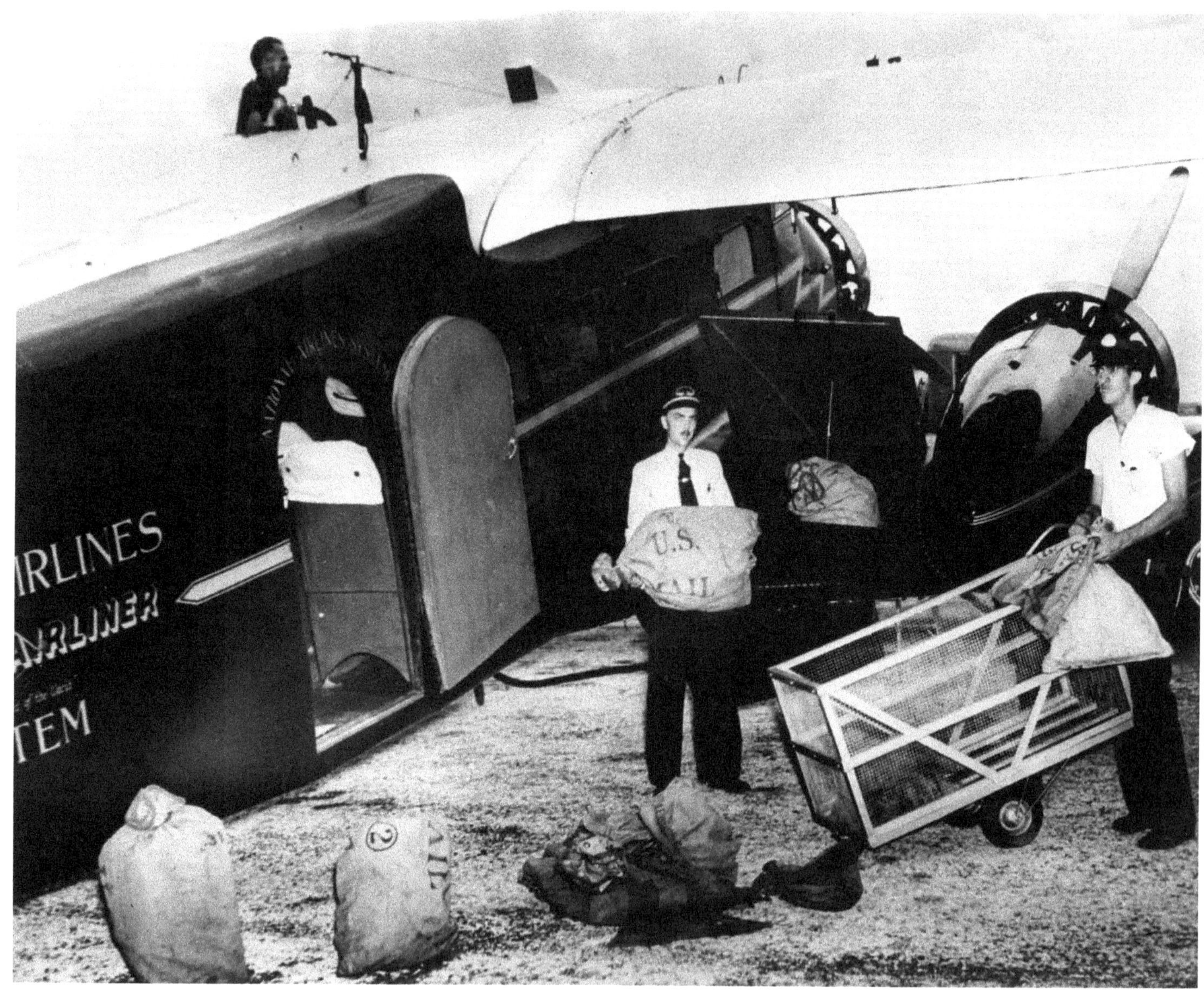

In 1936, National Airlines station manager David Amos loads mail while Lee Hederman gasses the left fuel tank at Whitted Field. This Stinson Trimotor, labeled a "Giant of an Airplane" by the *St. Petersburg Times,* held eight passengers and a crew of three. G. E. "Ted" Baker started National in 1934 with two aircraft and five employees.

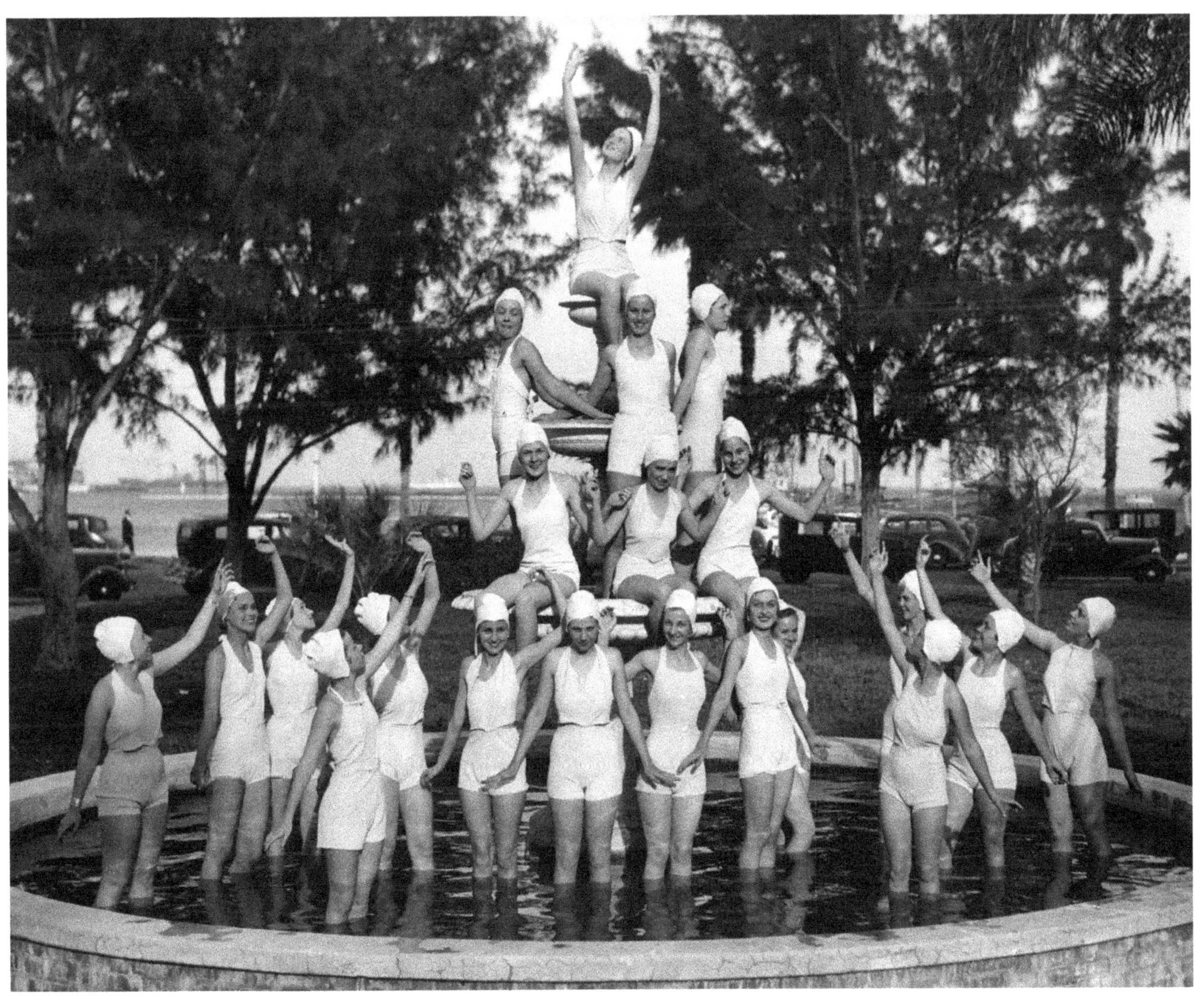

A 1936 publicity shot of young girls in bathing suits. Publicity agent John Lodwick masterfully promoted St. Petersburg for 23 years. In one stunt, Lodwick had Mayor Frank Pulver battle a fictitious Purity league that demanded a bathing suit inspector to ensure that women's bathing suits covered at least half their body.

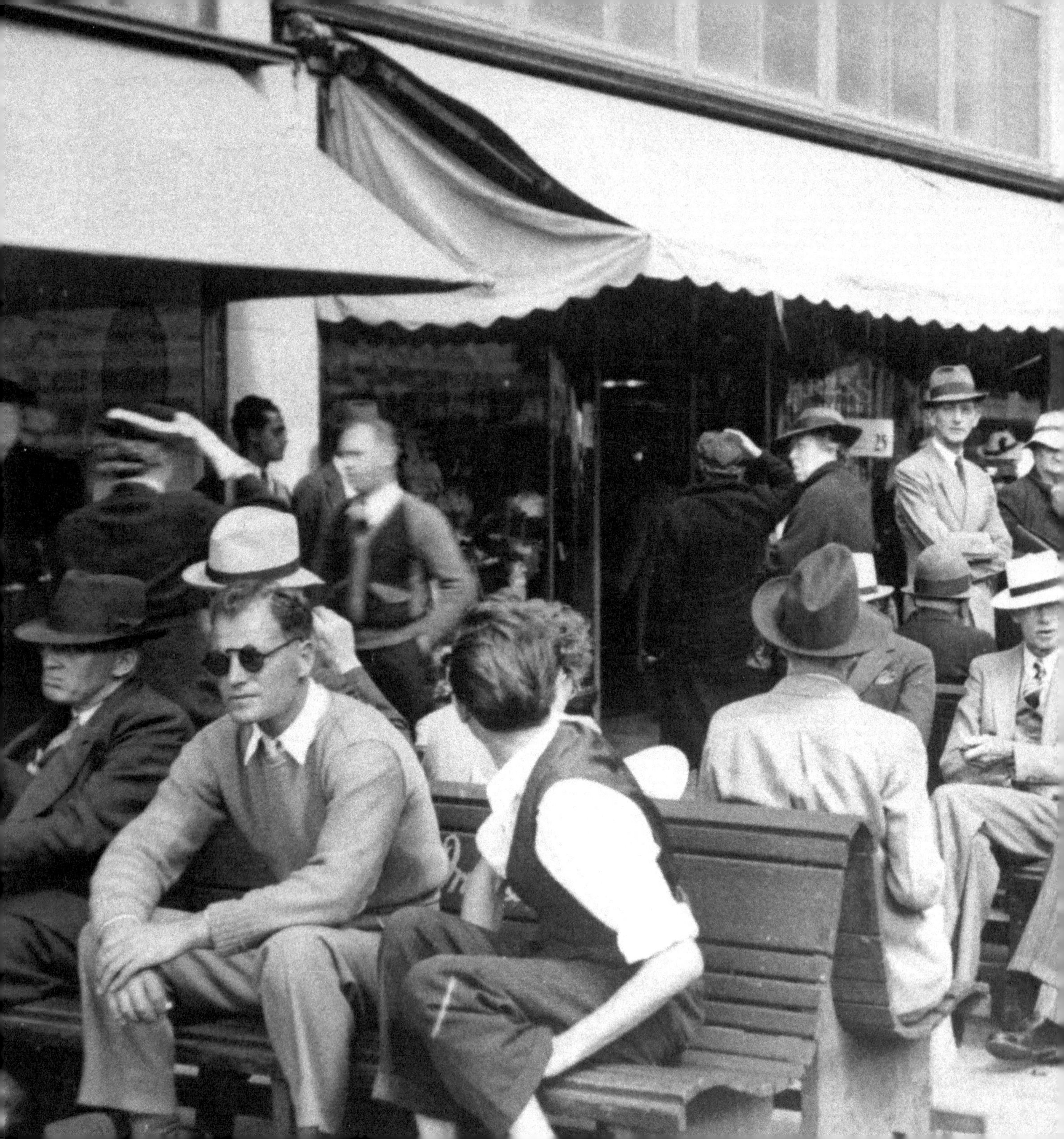

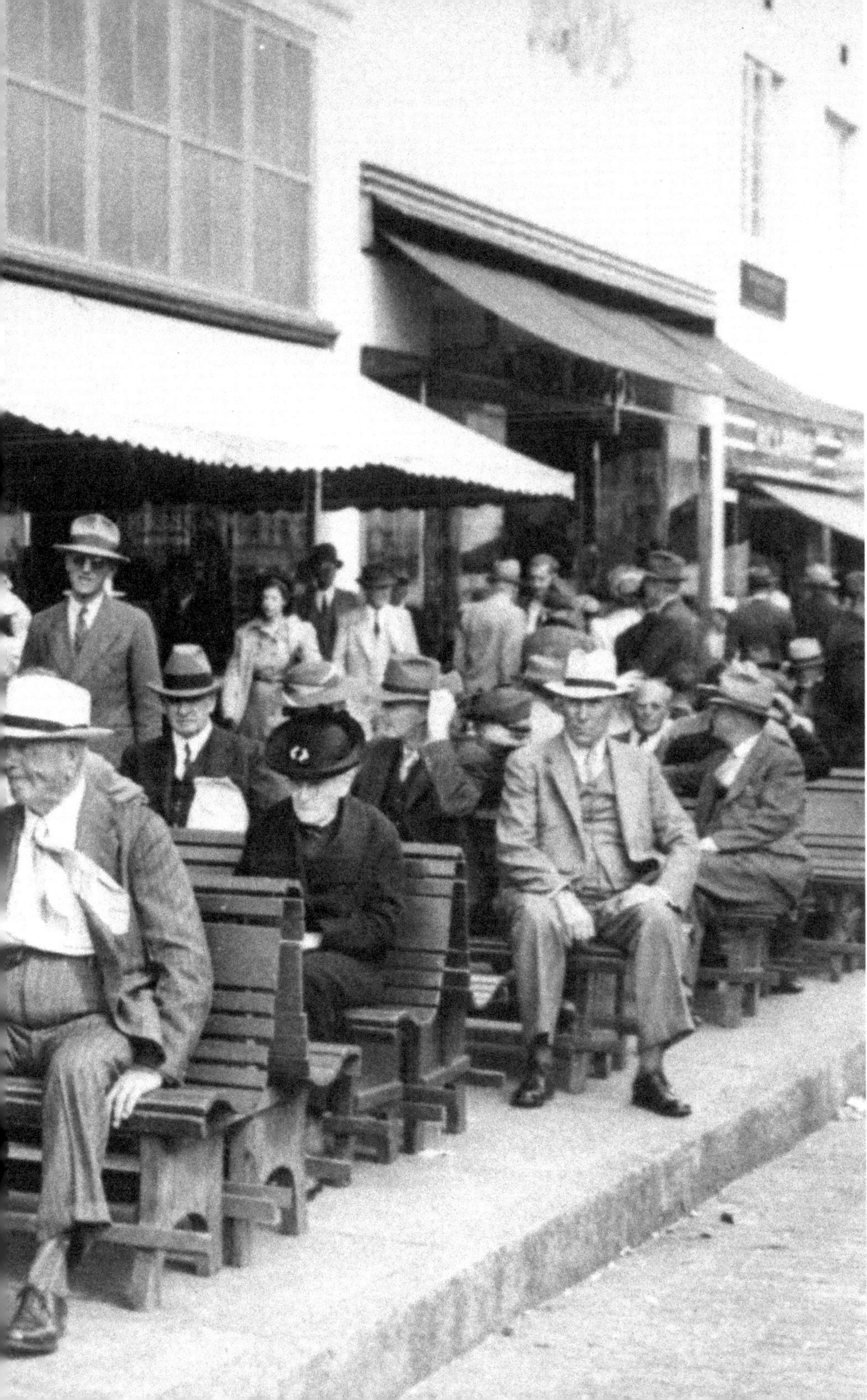

In 1907, Noel Mitchell built orange benches outside his real estate office to attract customers. Others soon copied him but in various colors and sizes. A 1916 ordinance regulated bench size and stipulated the color green, hence the famous green benches of St. Petersburg. Pedestrians socialize while resting on the benches here in 1938.

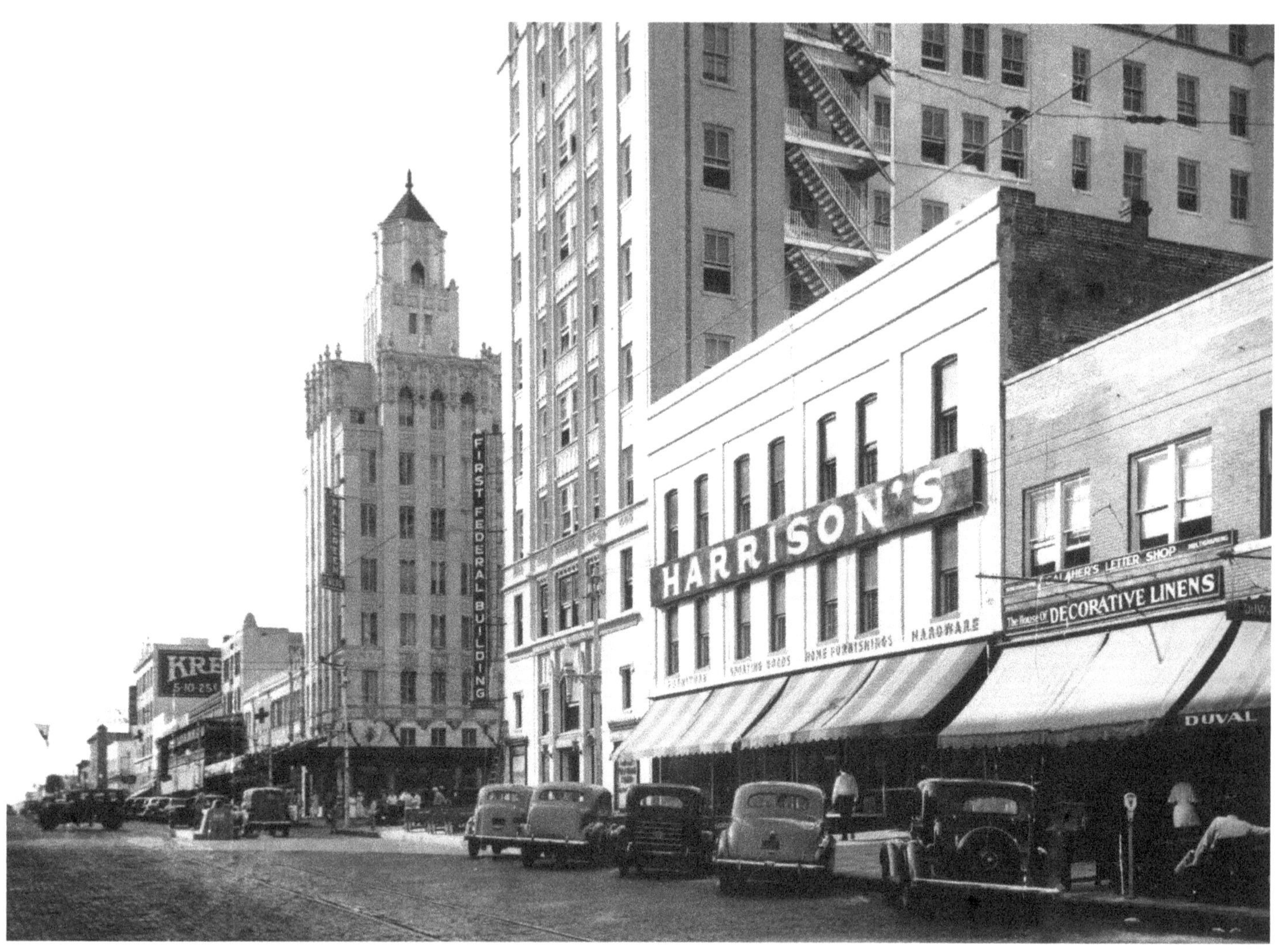

Central Avenue seems relatively quiet in 1938, flanked by Harrison's Hardware, the Snell Arcade, and the First Federal Building. Early residents Edgar Harrison and his two sons started a general store in a small, 25-foot by 50-foot area. In 1907, they built Harrison's hardware and furniture store in the town's first large, brick building.

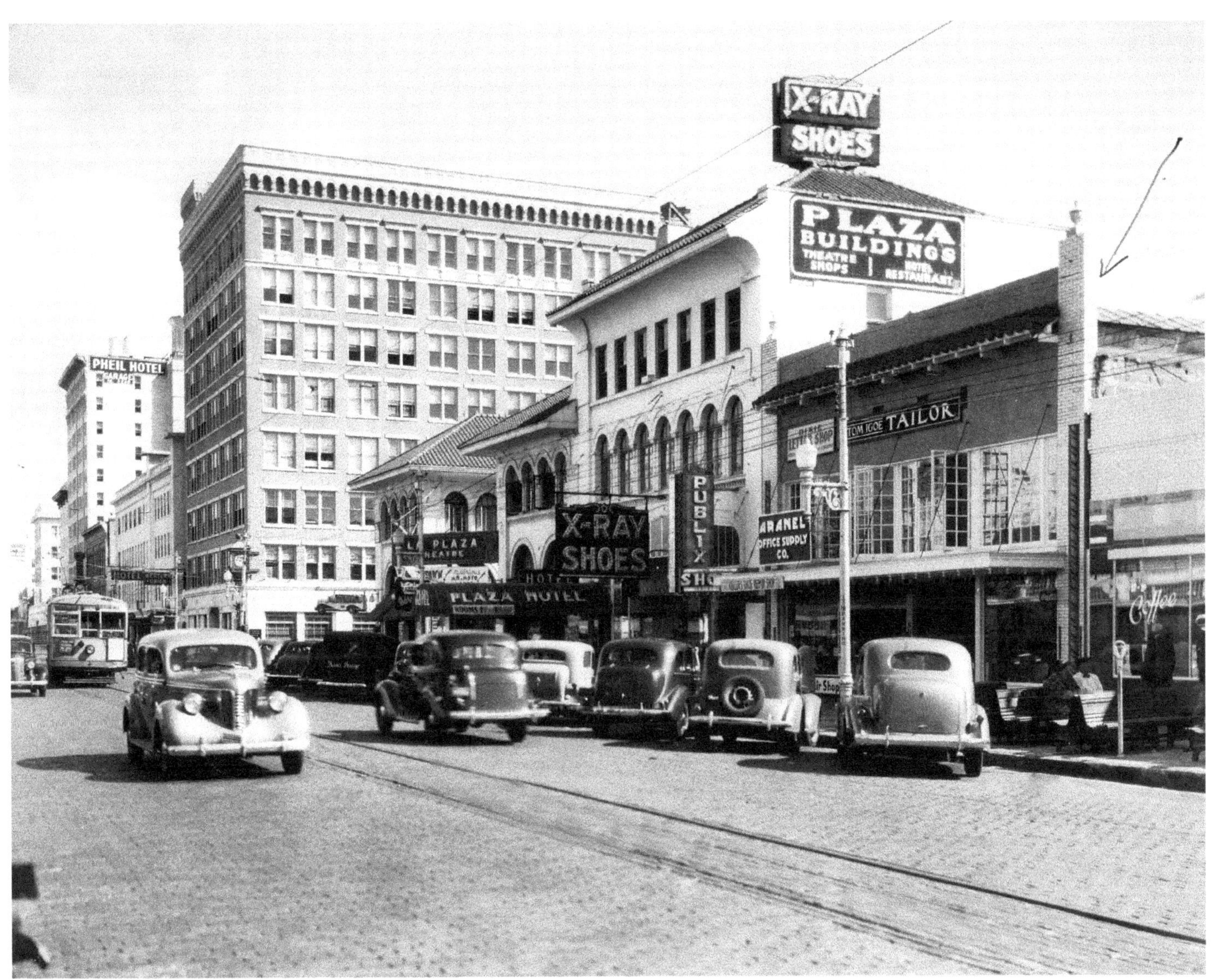

The Plaza buildings in 1938 are adorned with advertising for the theater, shops, hotel, restaurant, and shoe stores. In the 1930s, many of the leading shoe stores had X-ray shoe-fitting machines that used an X-ray tube to produce an image of the feet within the shoes. Many states eventually banned them owing to radiation hazards.

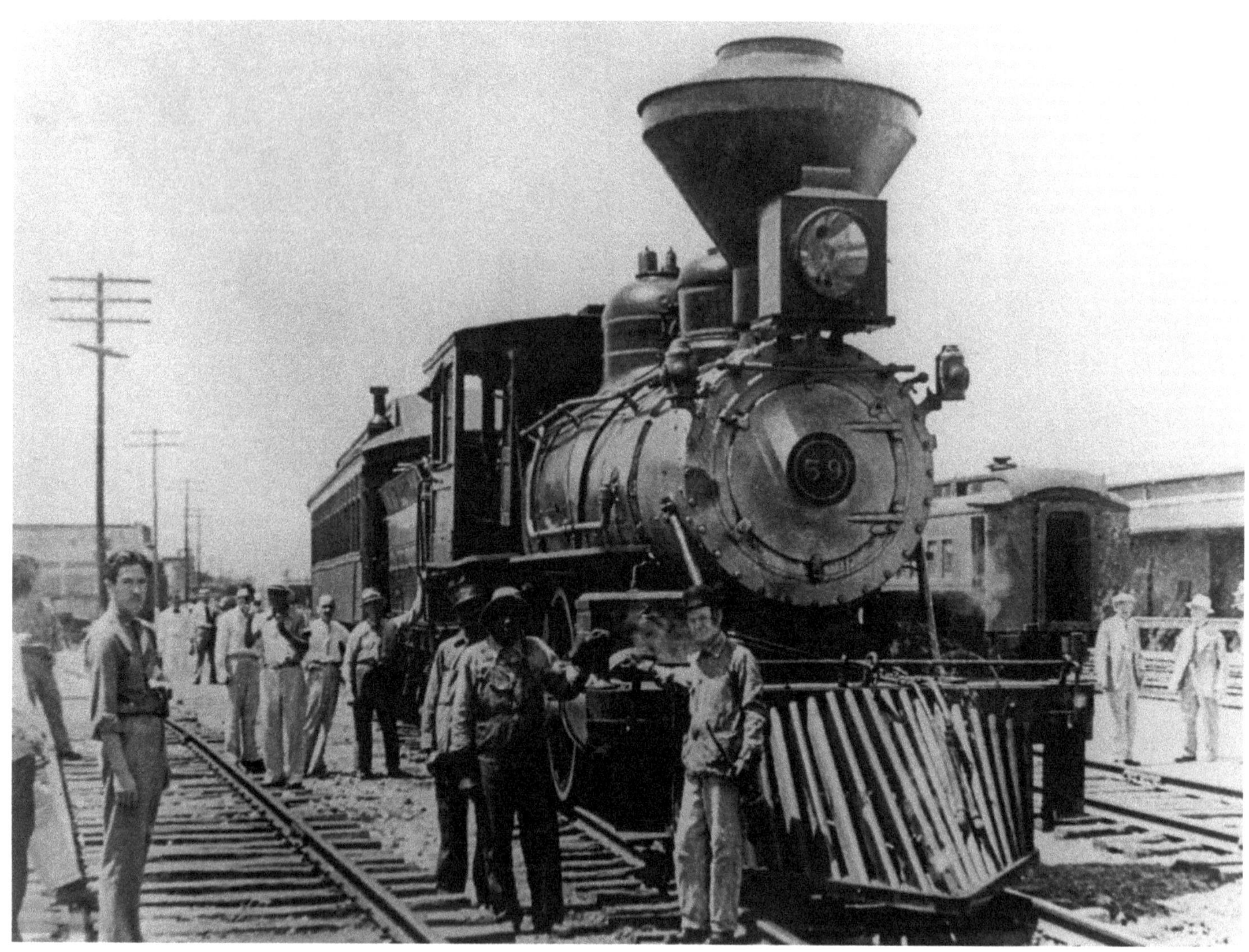

In 1938, on its 50th anniversary, restored steam locomotive no. 59 reenacted the arrival in June 1888 of the first Orange Belt Railway train. Originally the locomotives of the Orange Belt were second-hand narrow-gauge engines and represented many different builders—Baldwin, National, and Pittsburgh.

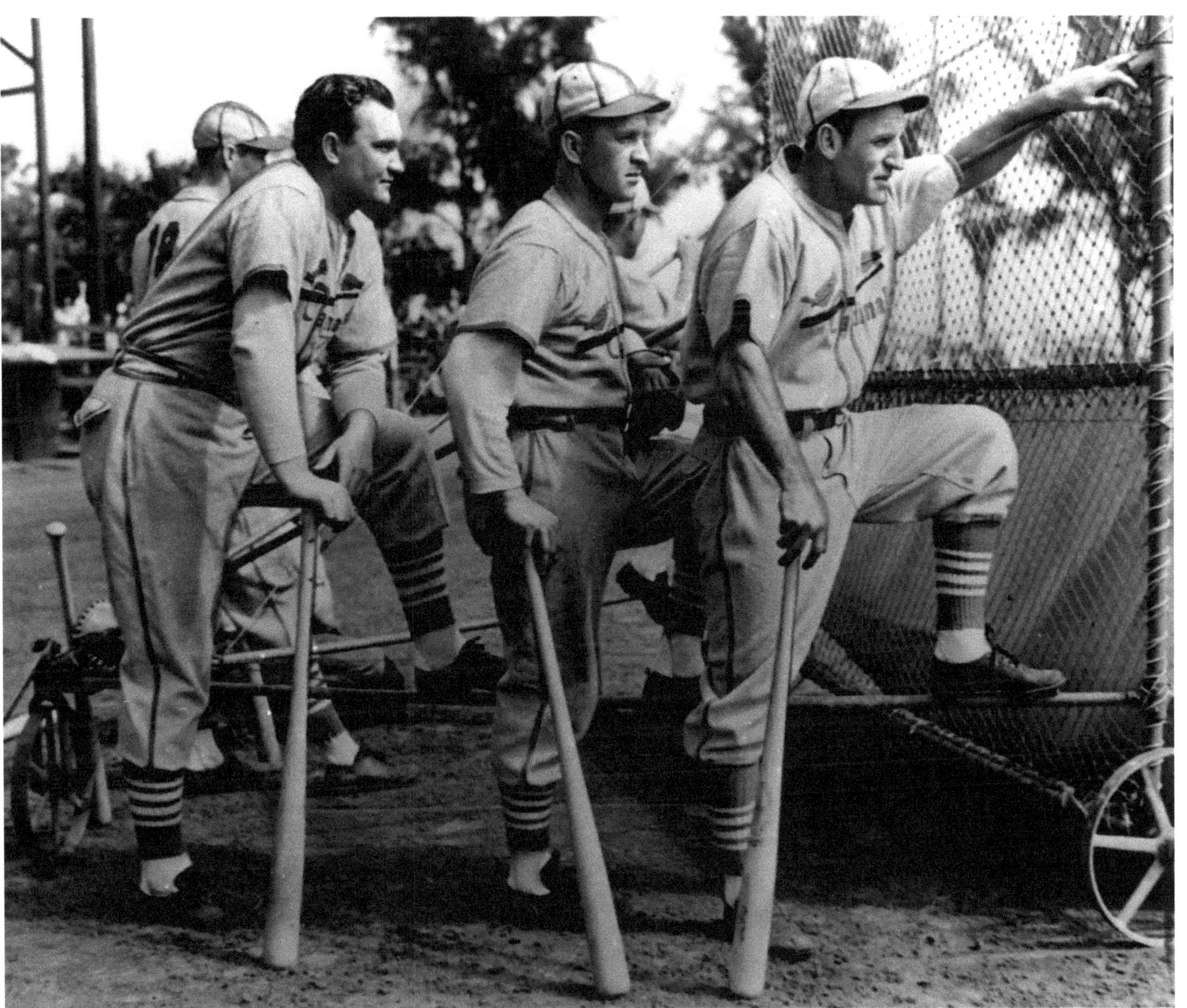

In 1937, the Boston Braves moved to another location after 16 years. The following year the St. Louis Cardinals held their spring training in town. Player-manager Frankie Frisch and the gas-house gang were one of the best teams of the 1930s, winning two World Series titles and enjoying four second-place National League finishes.

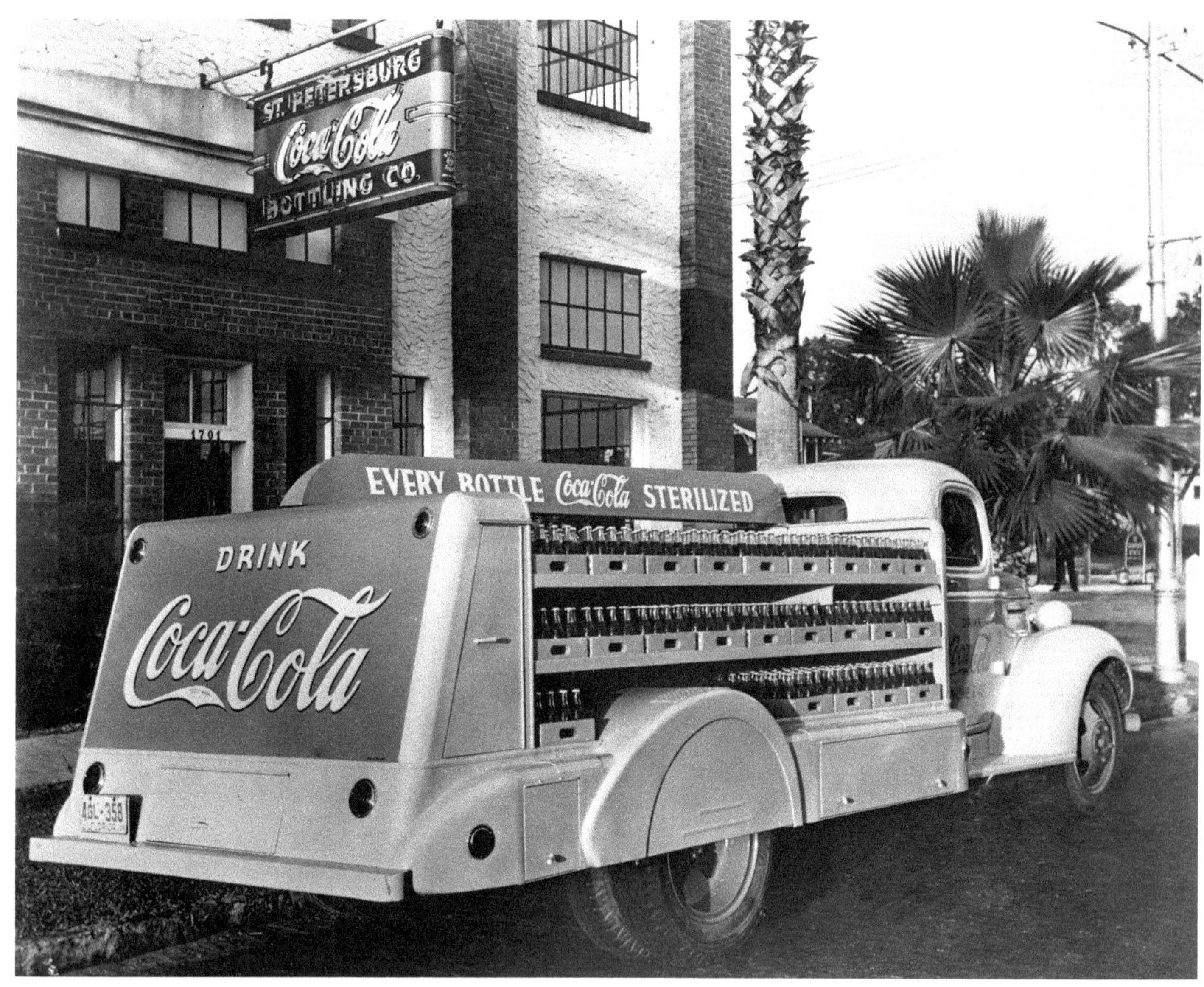

A Coca-Cola truck appears ready to start its delivery runs outside the old bottling company building. In 1940, the St. Petersburg Bottling Company relocated to the American Legion Armory and had it completely remodeled. In 1967, the Turner family acquired that building and added it to Sunken Gardens as a gift shop.

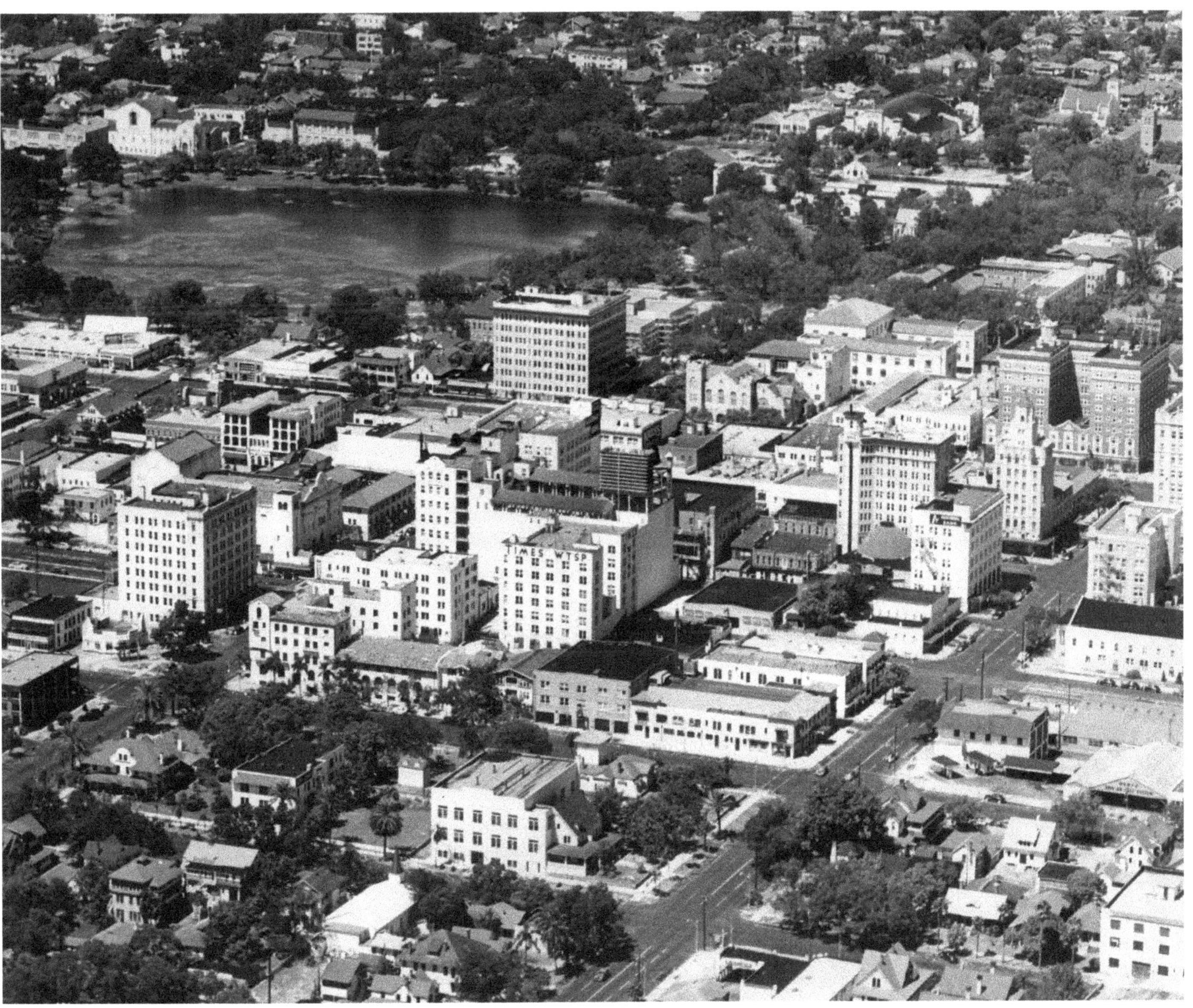

This 1939 aerial view of downtown features Mirror Lake toward the north. Despite the Great Depression, the city continued to grow—during the decade the population increased by approximately 50 percent, to 60,812. The Snell Arcade, center-right, is at the city's main intersection of Central Avenue and Fourth Street.

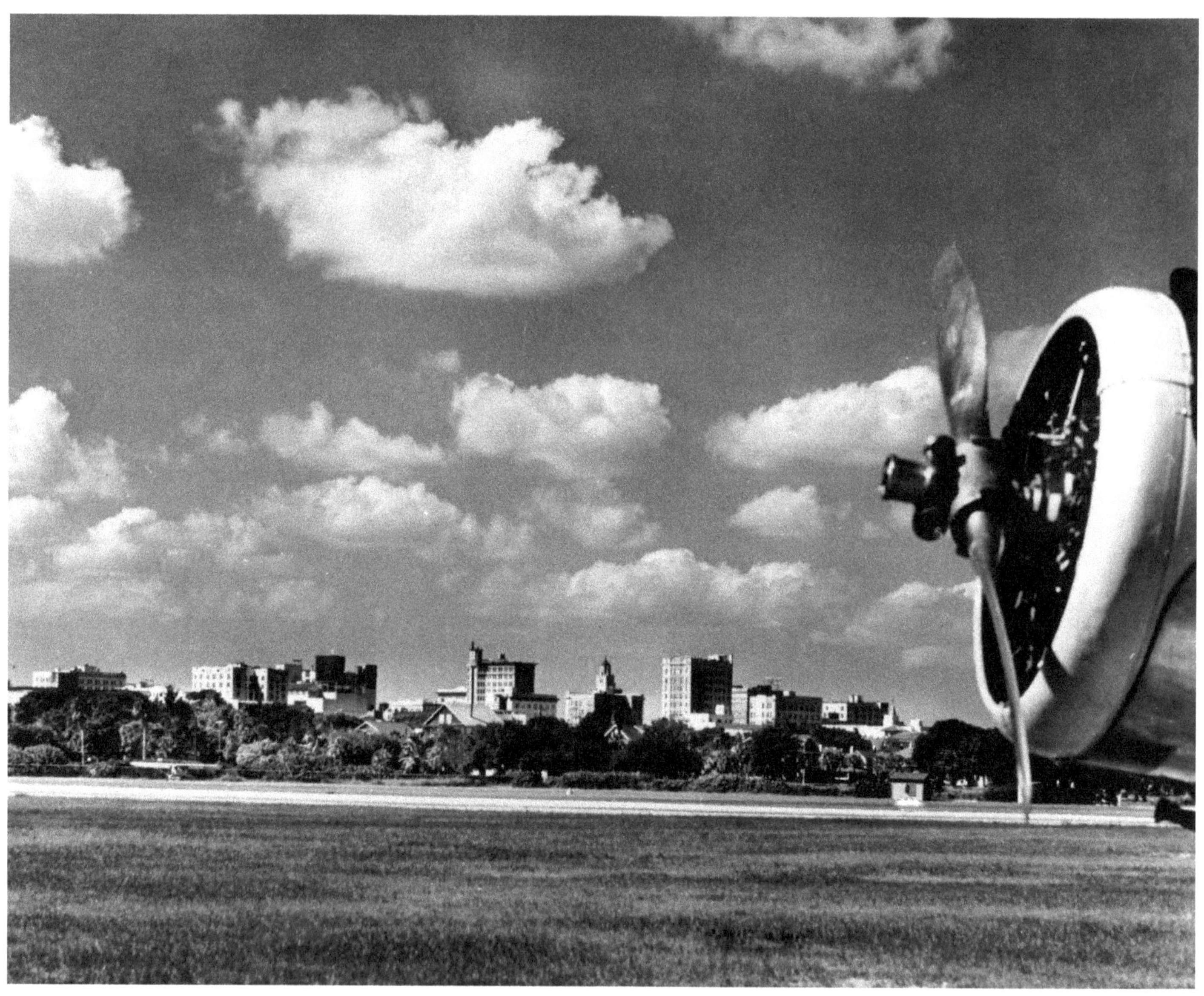

In view here is the city skyline, as it appeared in 1940 from Whitted Airport. The airport was named in honor of hometown Navy aviator James Albert Whitted, who died in a crash near Pensacola in 1923. The airfield opened in 1929 on the south side of the waterfront with only one short runway. Whitted was home to the Goodyear blimp and the first home to National Airlines.

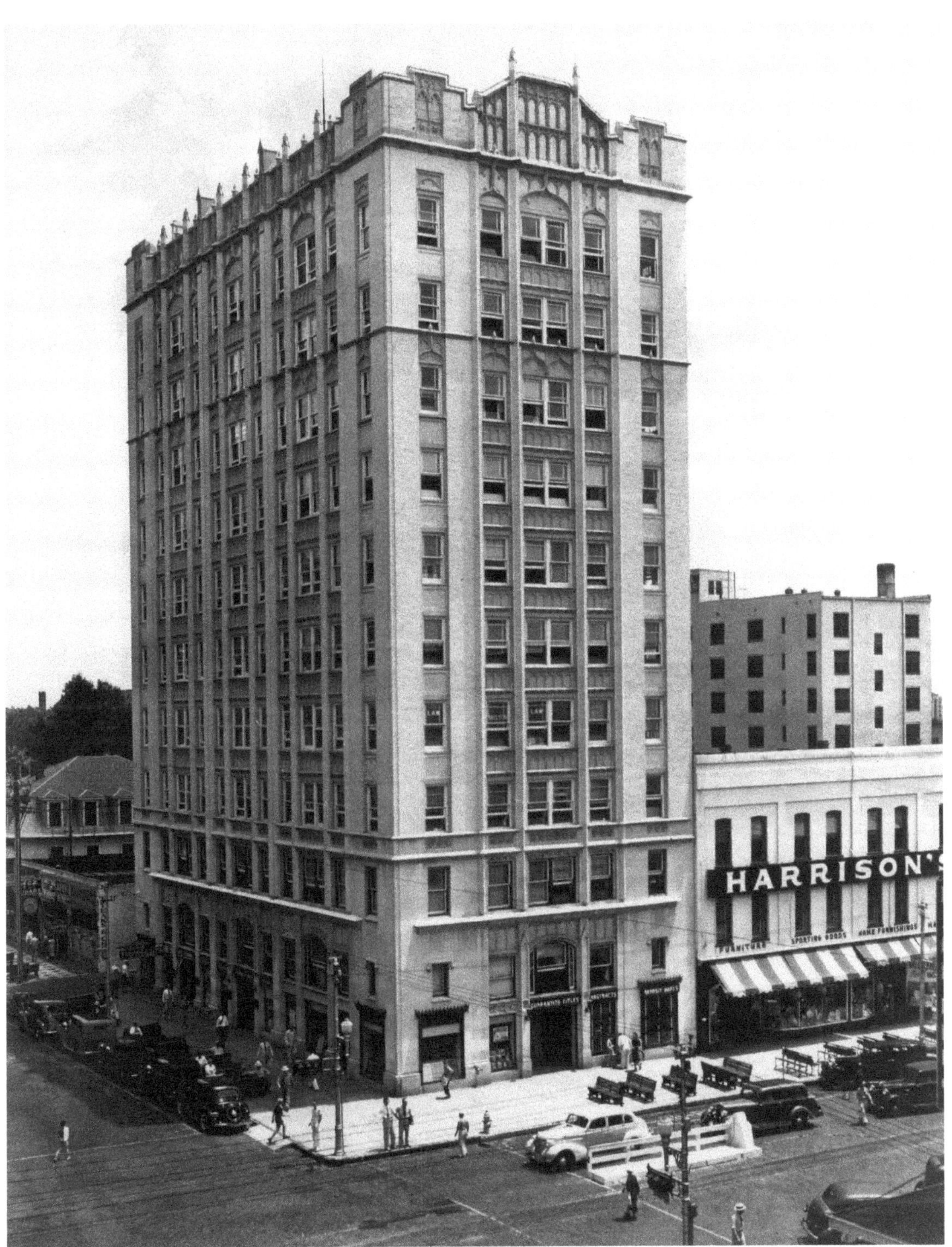

Originally the Equitable Building, this structure became known as the First Federal Building in 1940. During the depression, the federal government chartered savings and loan associations. St. Petersburg's First Federal Savings and Loan Association received the third federal charter on August 26, 1933, and was the first to open for business.

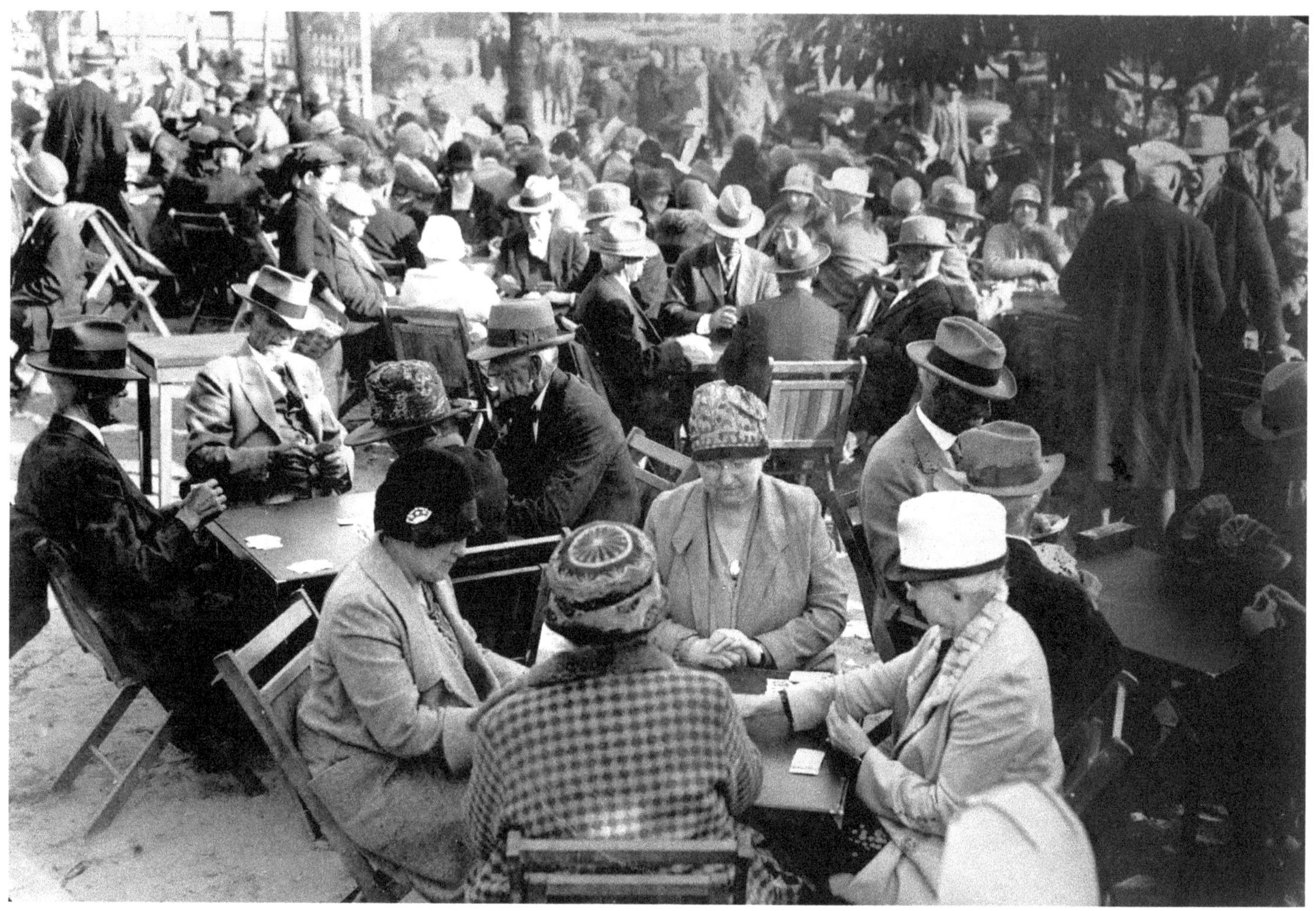

This card tournament at Mirror Lake Park was a welcome economic signal. Tourism was picking up by the 1940s and it was becoming common again to see hundreds of cardplayers around tables in the parks enjoying bridge and other card games. According to one promotional tract, "Bridge players come from every state in the Union."

Traffic hurries along Central Avenue on another sunny day in the downtown area in 1940. The St. Petersburg Motor Club published the following traffic regulations: "Traffic moves on green lights only," "No person riding a bicycle shall hold onto a streetcar," and "No person under fourteen years of age shall operate a vehicle."

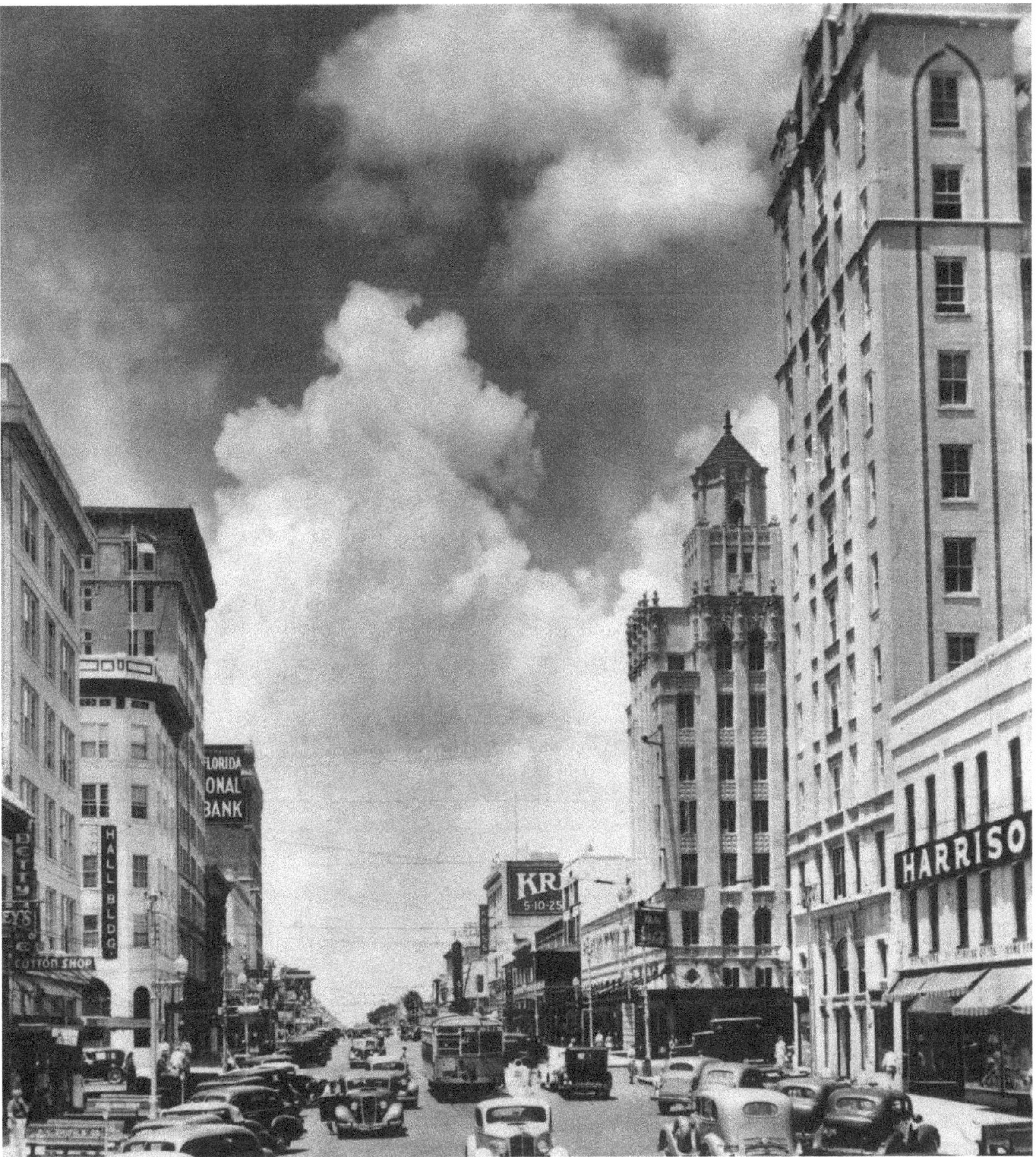

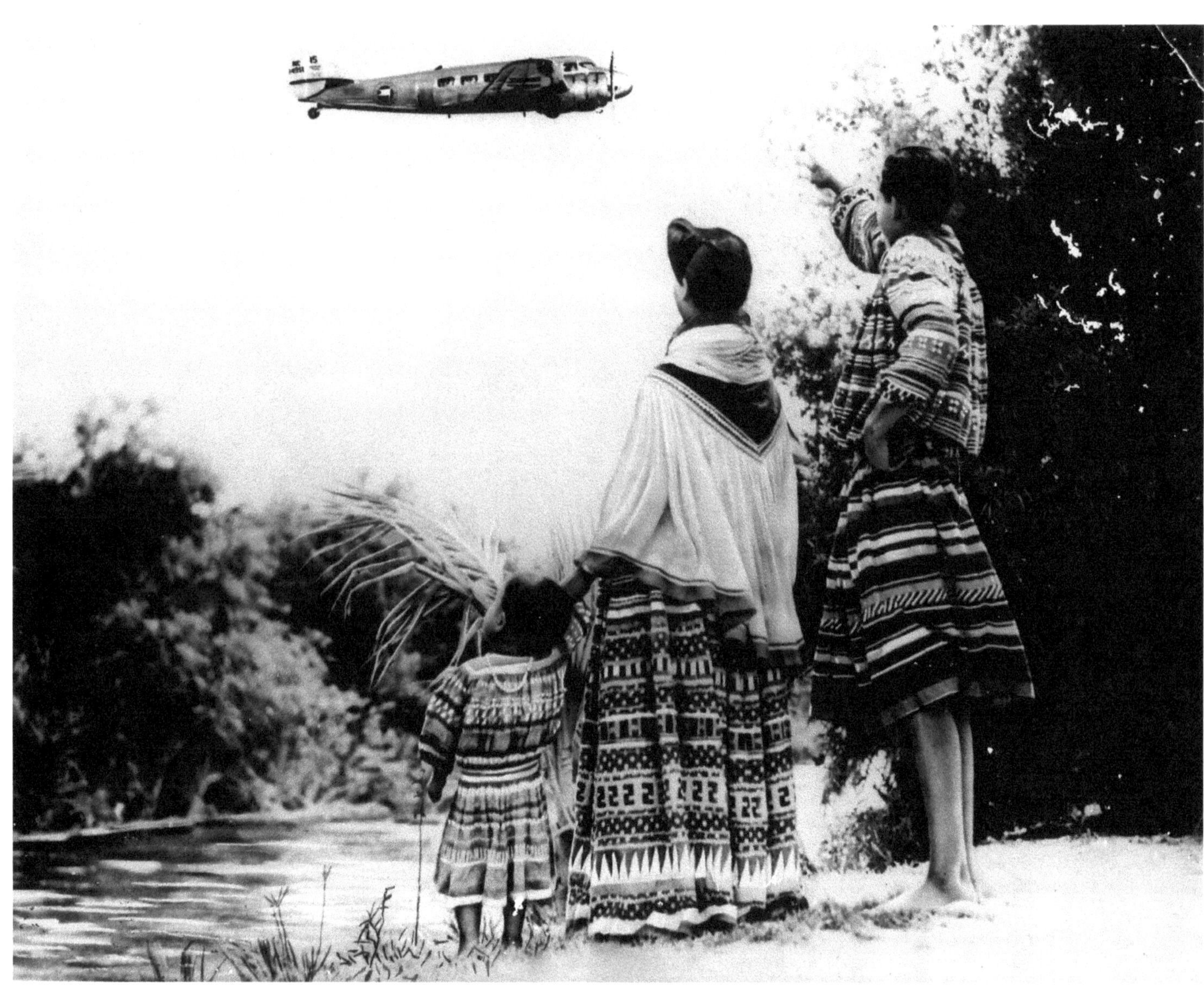

Shown here is a promotional photograph originally captioned "National Airlines over the Everglades." On July 8, 1937, the company was chartered under the laws of the State of Florida and new routes were added. Seminole Indians were used in some advertisements about the airline's new routes.

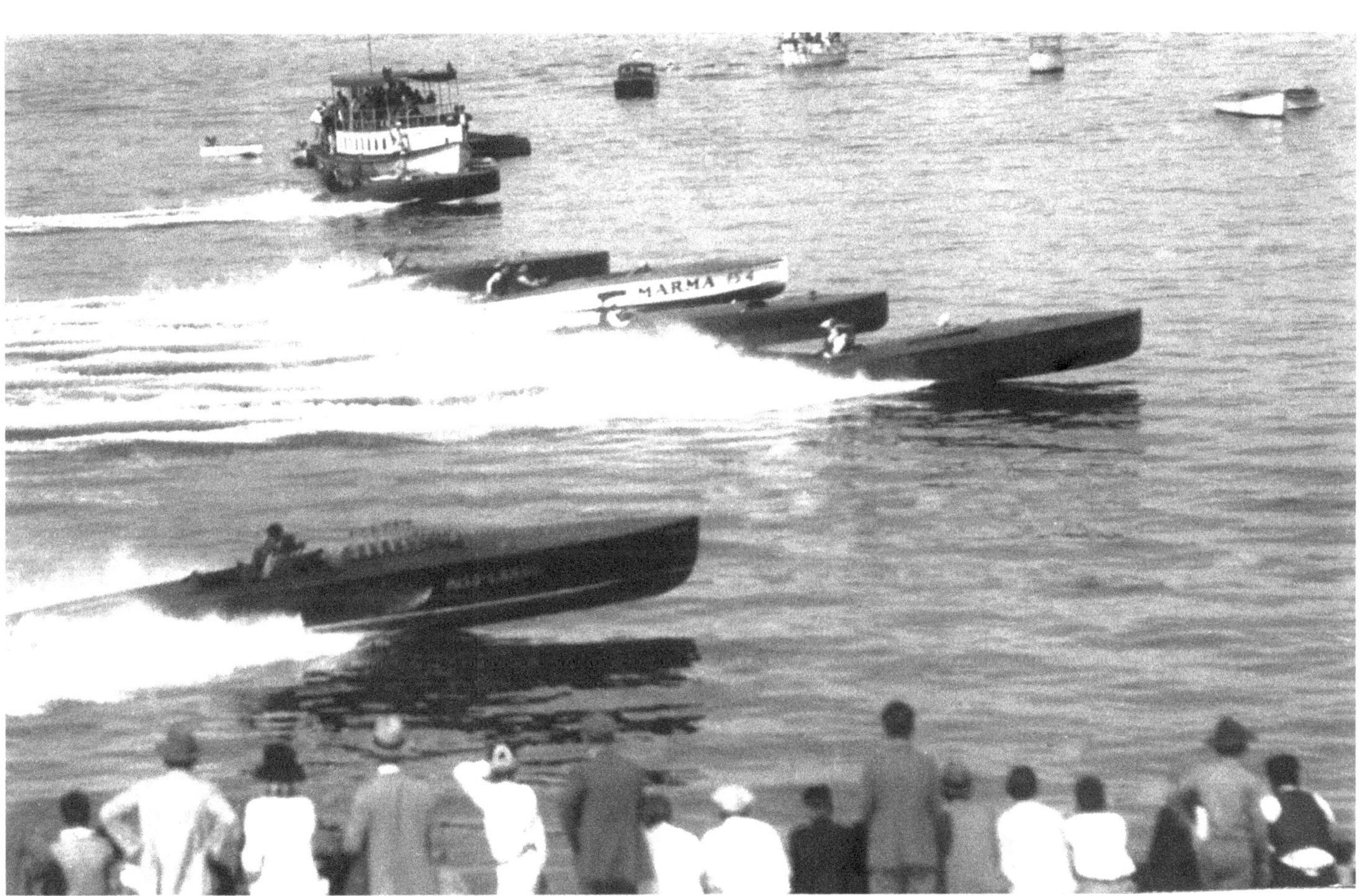

The Southland Sweepstakes Regatta gained national prominence when Commodore Harry M. Shaw of the St. Petersburg Yacht Club selected the race as a principal activity of the Yacht Club's Winter program. Starting in the winter of 1939-40 and originally held in the bay off the pier, the races were moved to the smoother waters of Lake Maggiore.

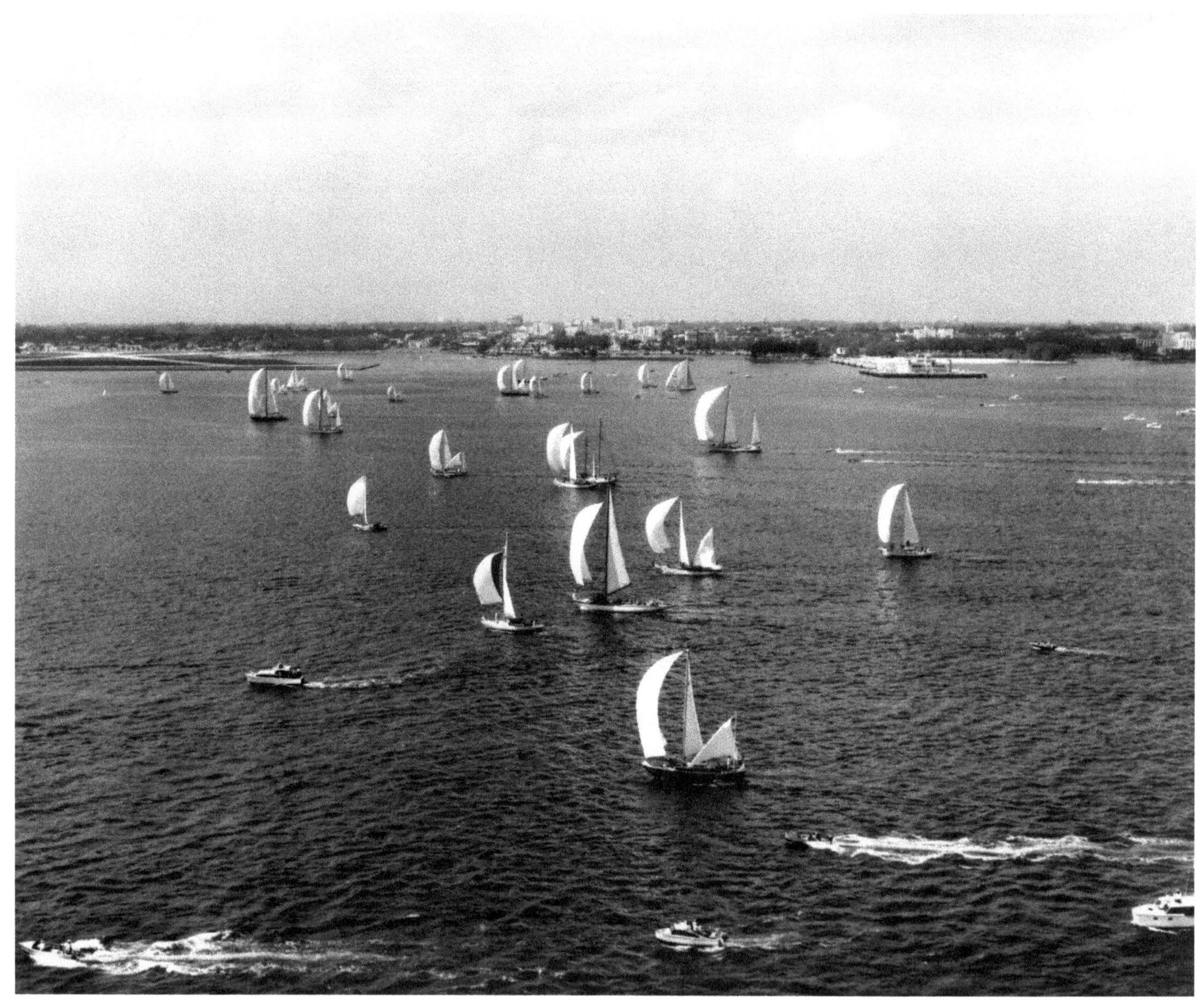

The 1940 start of the St. Petersburg to Havana, Cuba, sailboat race, sponsored by the St. Petersburg Yacht Club. There were sailboat classes for the 284-mile course: boats under 50 feet in length and those between 50 and 85 feet. Eleven boats participated in the first event. Held annually in March, the races ended in 1959.

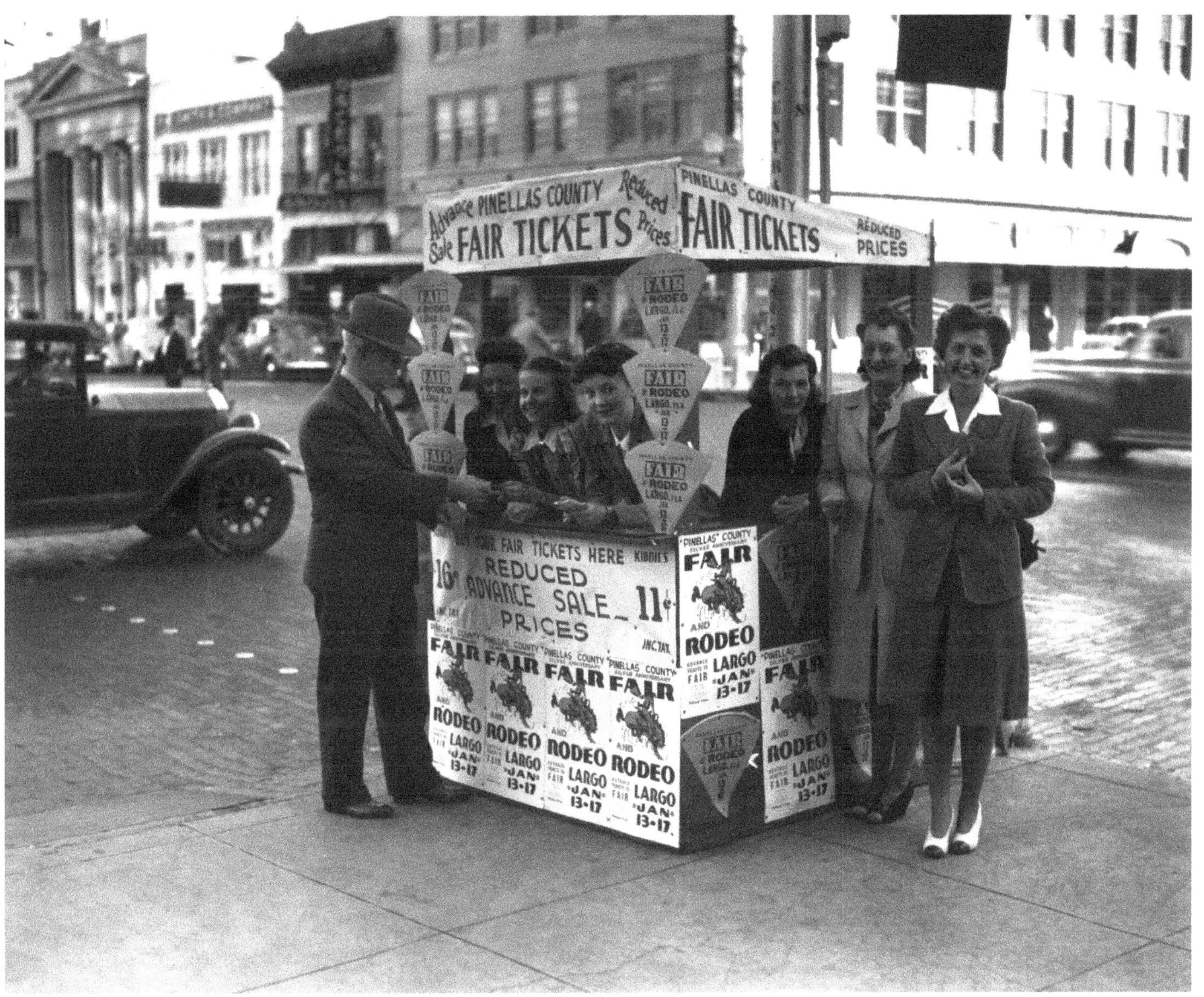

The Women's Club of Largo held the first county fair January 25-27, 1917, aimed at showing the county's resources to the winter tourist and visitor. Low on finances, the first agricultural building was made from lumber scraps and palmetto leaves. Owing to its success, the Pinellas county fair was transferred to the county in 1925. Shown here is a ticket booth for the 1940 fair.

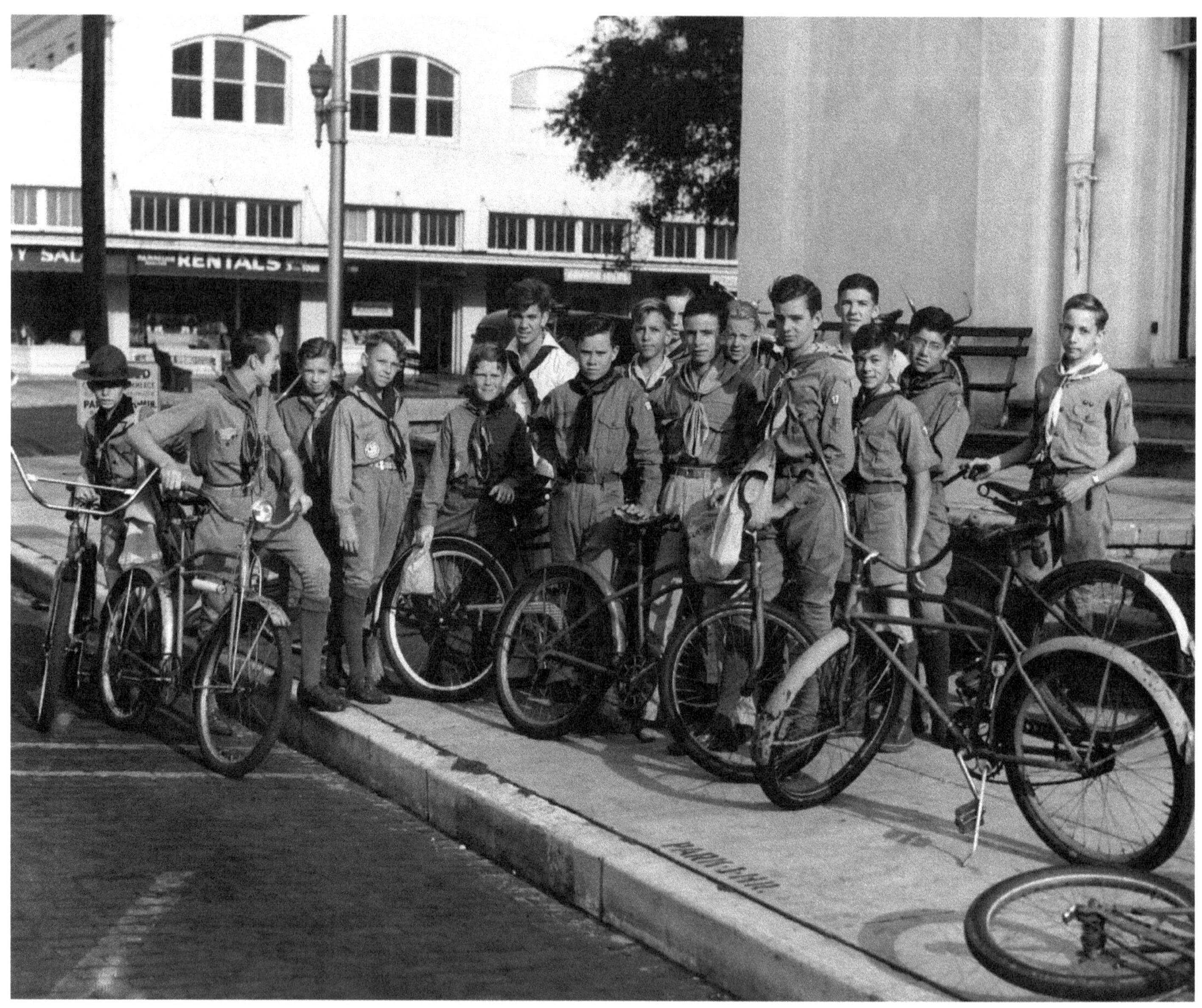

The first Boy Scout troop in St. Petersburg was organized by a woman, the remarkable Katherine Tippets. The first Scout Master of the Pinellas Boy Scouts was developer Walter P. Fuller. The first St. Petersburg recipient of the Distinguished Eagle Scout Award was William R. Hough, who may be part of this 1940 troop.

Clearing Skies
World War II and Postwar Boom

(1941–1979)

At the beginning of World War II, St. Petersburg lacked an industrial base to manufacture products for the war effort; however, its warm climate and available housing made it an ideal site for training bases. The Army Air Corps, U.S. Navy, Coast Guard, and U.S. Merchant Marine all established military bases or training centers in Pinellas County. Besides personnel assigned to bases in the vicinity, service members on leave from other bases in Florida came to visit for recreation and relaxation. Wives and families of service members rented homes in St. Petersburg, which caused a housing shortage and led to temporary price controls. The inflow of newcomers during the war years led from seasonal to year-round prosperity for businesses. Municipal utilities set up a special surplus fund for postwar civic improvements.

The national postwar economic boom provided a considerable influx of veterans; many were already familiar with the city when stationed here during the war. While some came to visit, many came to stay, initiating the postwar building boom. This boom differed from the earlier one by focusing on residential houses and apartments. Located outside the downtown business district, the construction extended the city in all directions, creating the suburbs. The twenties boom-era subdivisions, which had languished silently for years, suddenly became a valued commodity as building permits dramatically rose from 4.5 million to 11 million in one year. City attractions also tried to keep pace—the new Al Lang ball park opened in March 1947 as the spring training center of the New York Yankees and St. Louis Cardinals.

The building boom continued throughout the fifties, with 100,000 housing units constructed as the city doubled its population, reaching 180,000 by the end of the decade. This expansion brought distinct changes to St. Petersburg and Pinellas County. Transportation improved with the opening of the Skyway Bridge in 1954, providing speedier access to Manatee County and the south. The economic base broadened with the relocation of several space industries that produced light manufacturing goods. The demographics also changed—a quarter of the population was now 65 or older.

By the sixties, the beach communities had grown so fast that dredging the bay was required to provide land to keep pace with development. Newcomers gave impetus for adding recreational activities and more business services, causing a switch in construction from housing to businesses and infrastructure. The debut of the Bayfront Center in 1965 provided a setting for recreational and entertainment events and spurred a revitalization of downtown. New buildings were constructed while many older ones received face lifts. Even the city's symbol—the Million Dollar Pier—made way for a newer edition, complete with the city's latest landmark, the Pier with its inverted pyramid design.

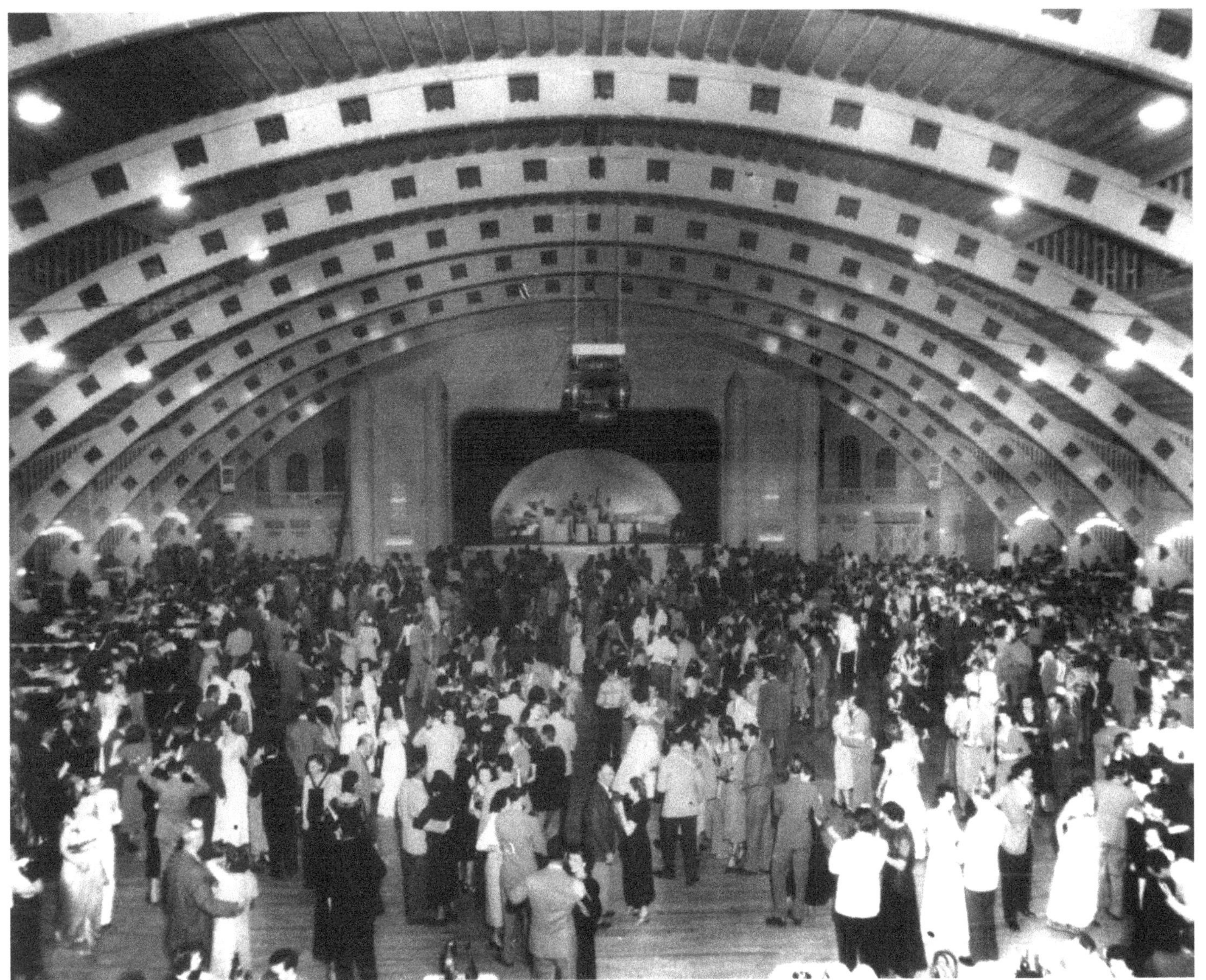

Couples at the Coliseum dance to the sound of a swing-era band. The unique Rotary Jewel lighting system comprised four cone-shaped cylinders fastened together to form a square, each cone covered with mirrors. Electrically operated, the "Jewel" revolved slowly for moonlight dances.

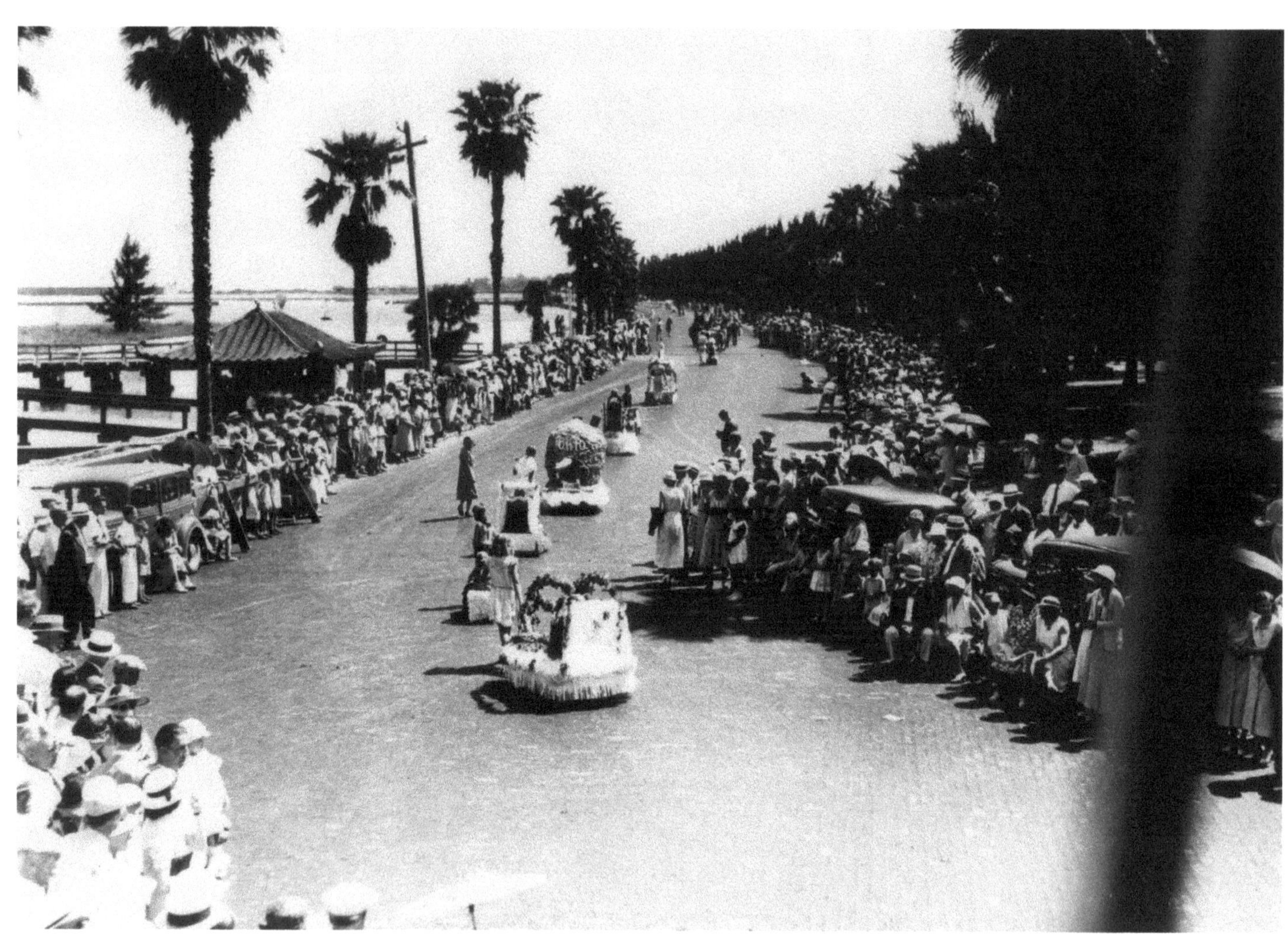

The Festival of States parade was curtailed during the first years of the Great Depression. By 1935, as tourists began returning, the annual parade gradually became more elaborate. The event reached a pinnacle in 1938, the 50th anniversary Golden Jubilee of the founding of St. Petersburg. In view here is the festival for 1941.

Young women wait in line for volunteer registration. All of St. Petersburg joined the war effort, but maintaining the home front fell to young and middle-aged women. They worked as nurses with the Red Cross, teachers, clerical staff, trolley operators, and at many other roles ordinarily filled by men, who were overseas engaging the enemy.

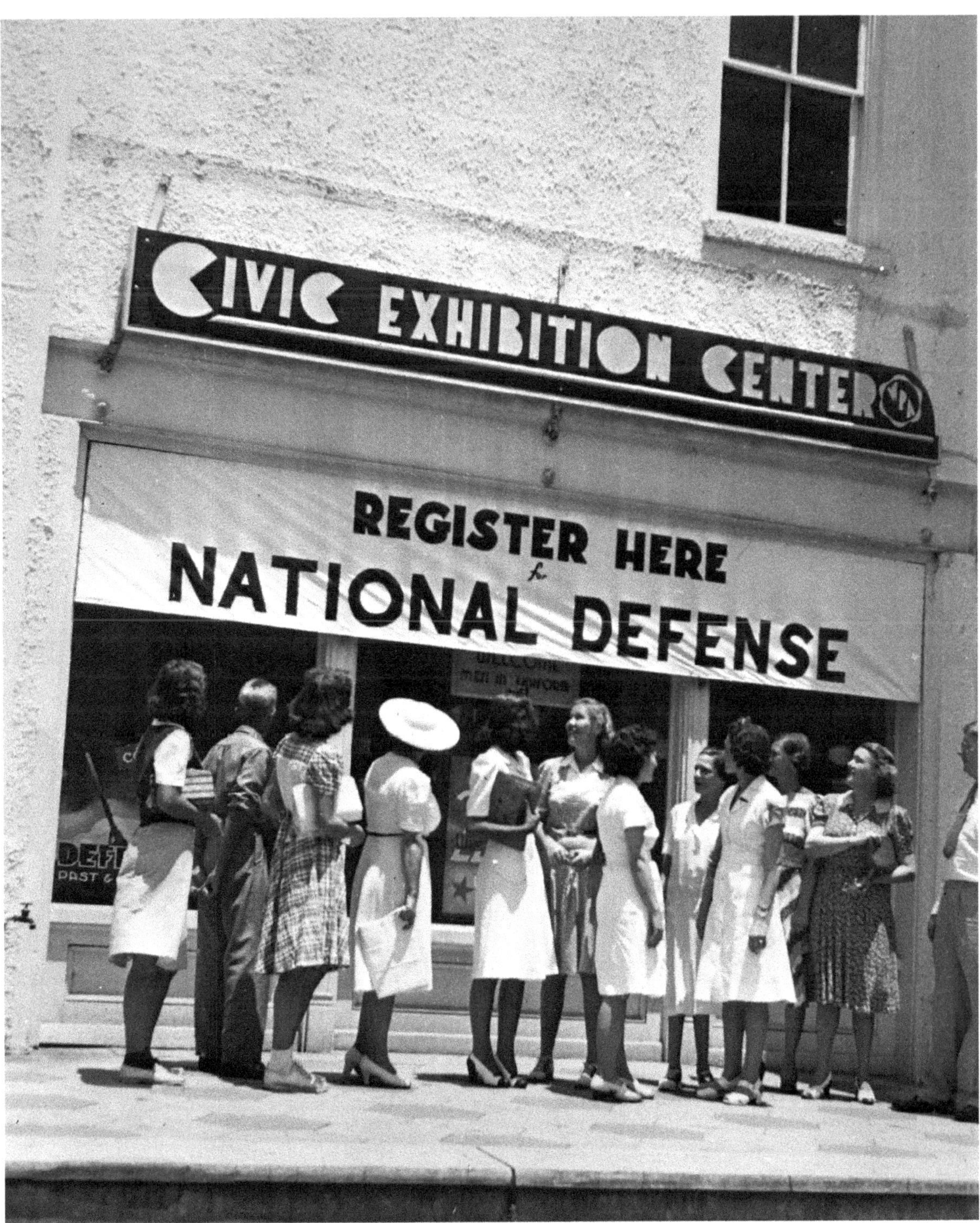

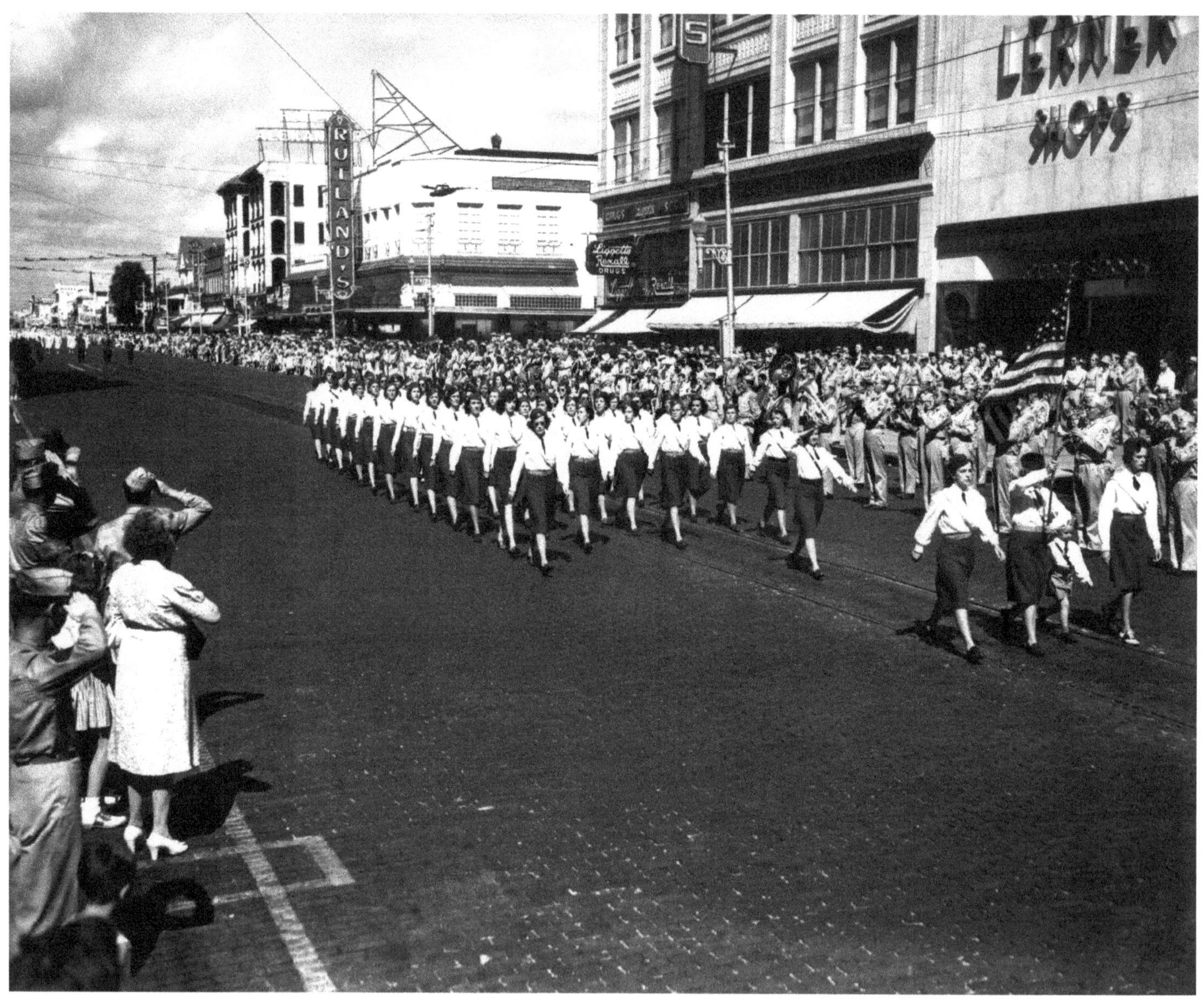

The honor guard of this Women's Army Auxiliary Corps proudly carries the flag in a military parade in 1942 downtown St. Petersburg. Converted later into the Women's Army Corps, the corps involved many women from St. Petersburg. The WACs were the first women other than nurses to serve in the United States Army.

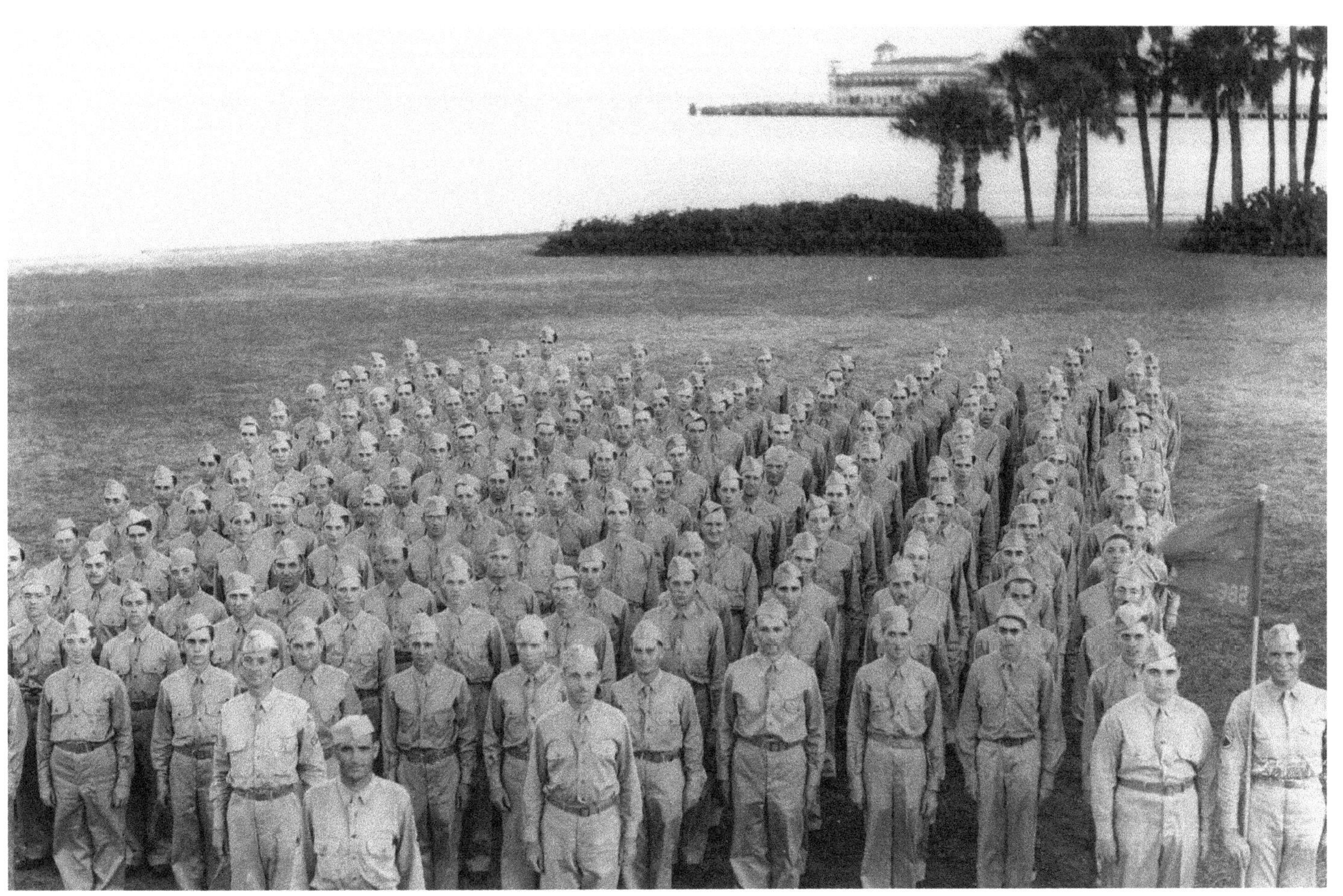

Formerly catering to tourists, the town's hotels now provided living quarters for Army Air Corps trainees, like this unit near Vinoy Park. In 1942, the town was selected as a basic training camp for the Army Air Corps Technical Services. More than 100,000 servicemen had trained at the center by the time it closed in July 1943.

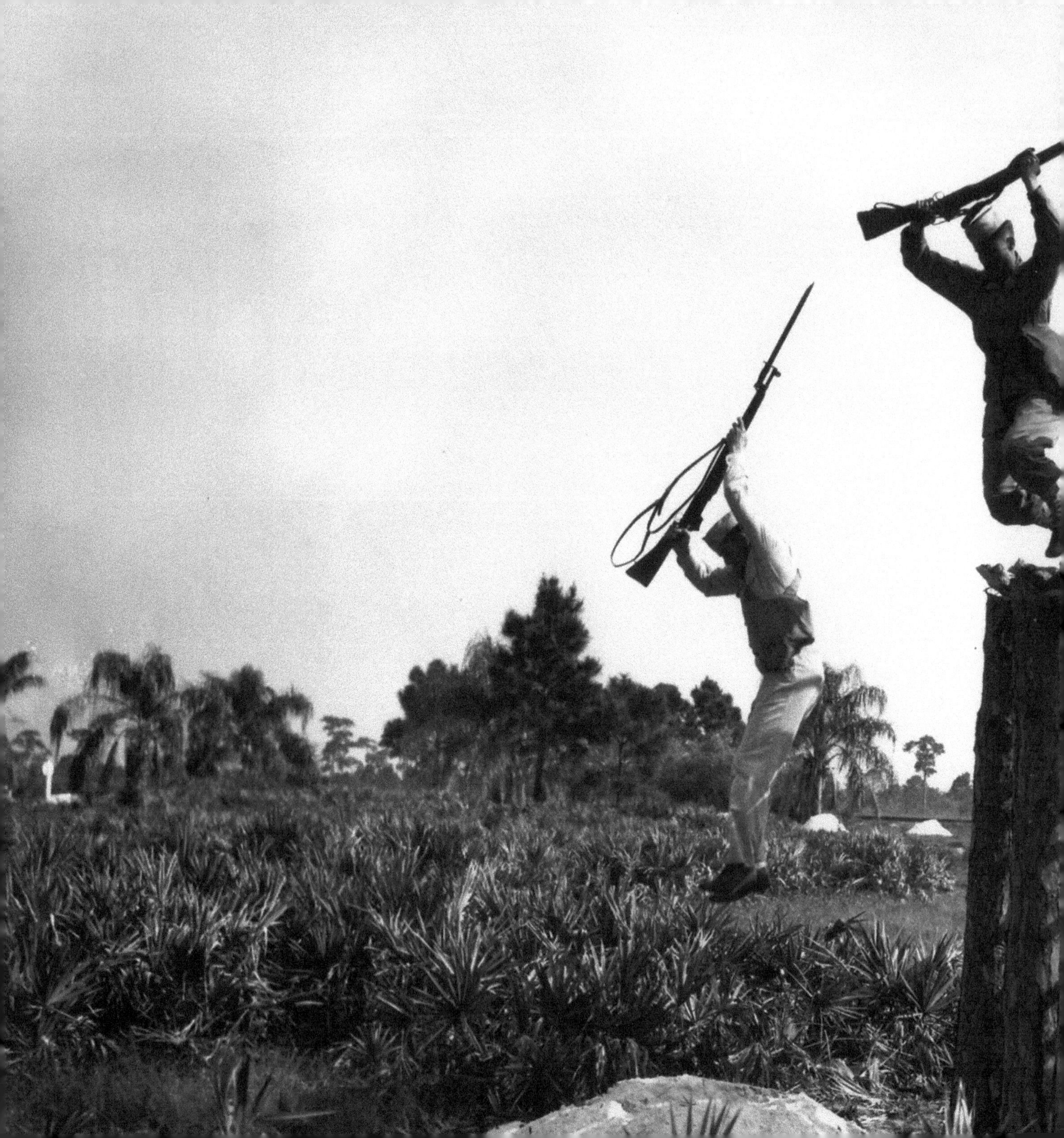

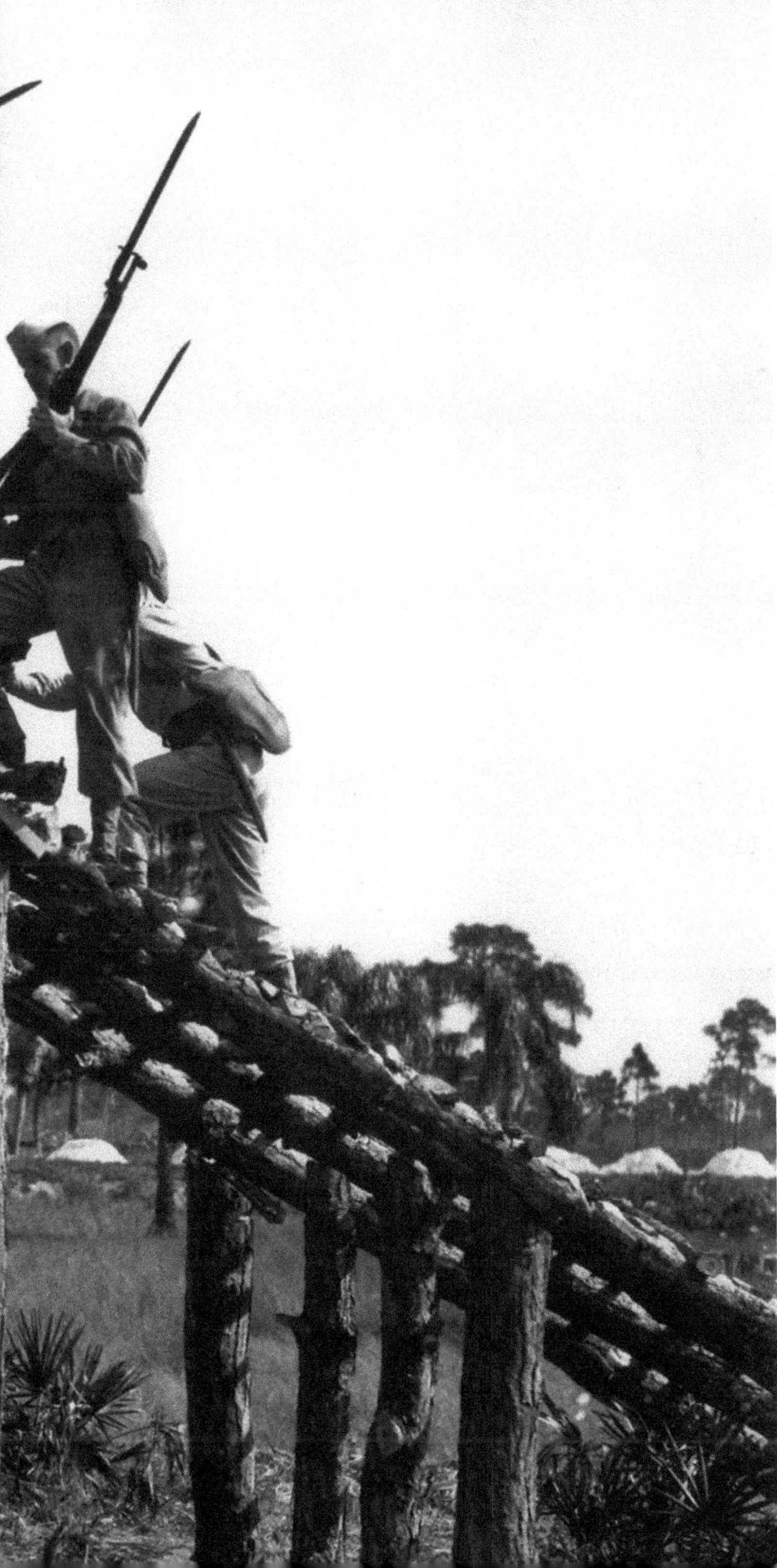

Soldiers work their way through an obstacle course near St. Petersburg. Throughout the war the town was crowded with servicemen from all over Florida on furlough, creating a boom in the local economy. Visiting wives and families relocated to St. Petersburg to be near their servicemen, many families staying after the war.

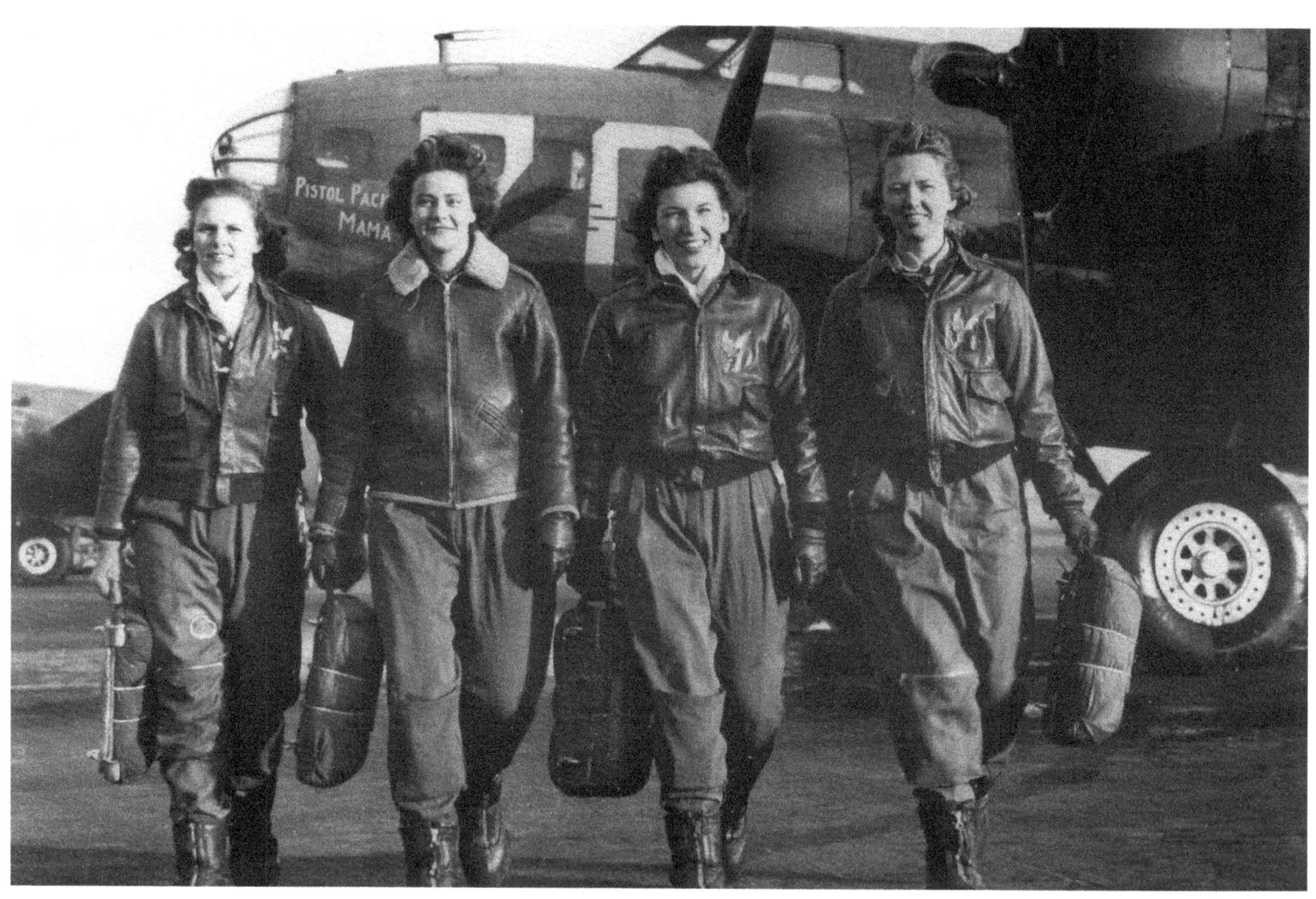

These Women's Air Force Service pilots served the war effort by ferrying bombers between military bases. The Tampa and St. Petersburg areas were vital sites for the training of Army pilots. Many service personnel visited or relocated to St. Petersburg, increasing the population from 60,000 to 85,000 by 1945.

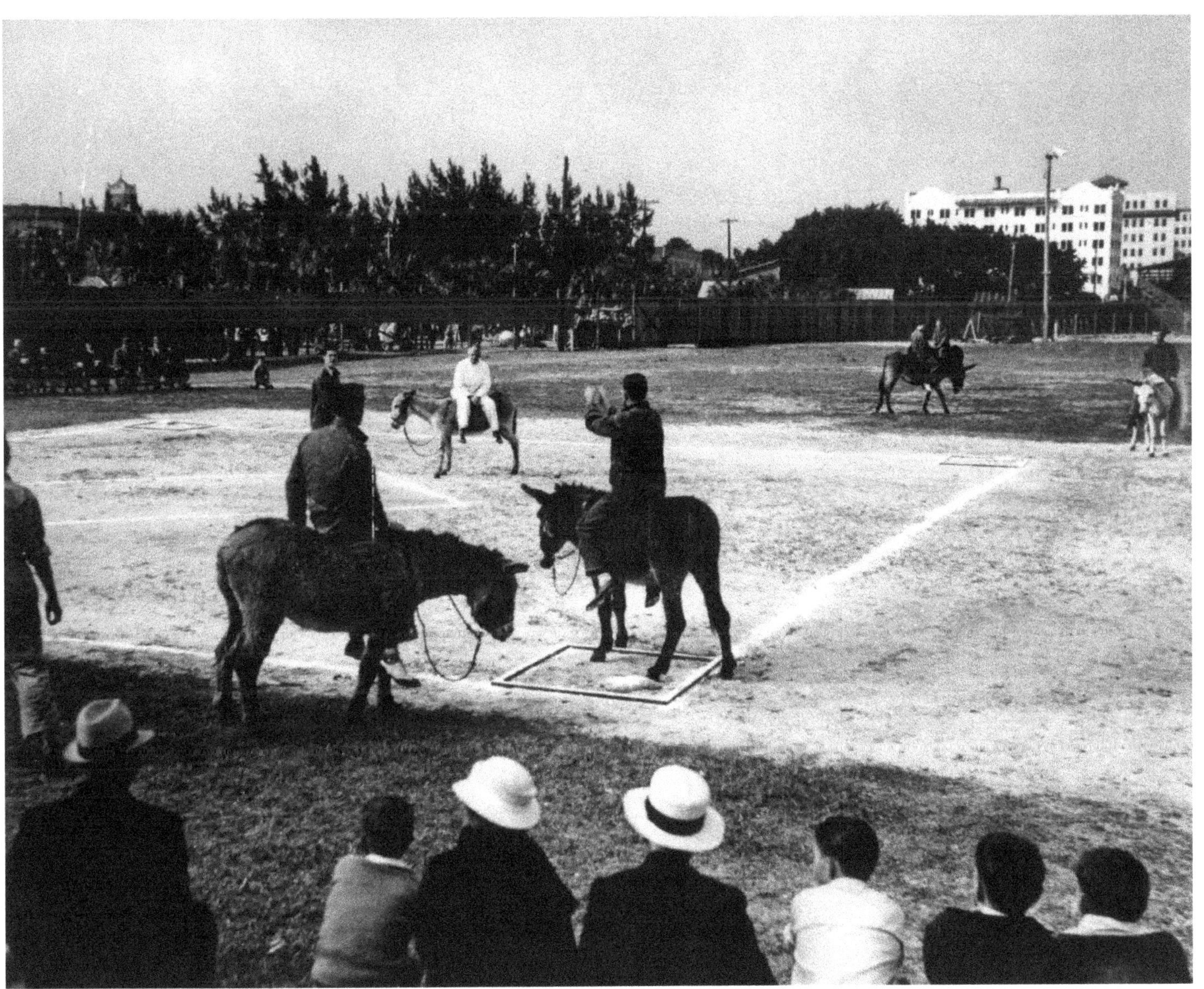

On a field near the West Coast Inn, this baseball game was played with men on donkeys. With suspension of the usual tourist-oriented activities, the city provided numerous activities for servicemen. From 1943 to 1945, there were no Festival of States parades, no yacht races, and no spring-training camps.

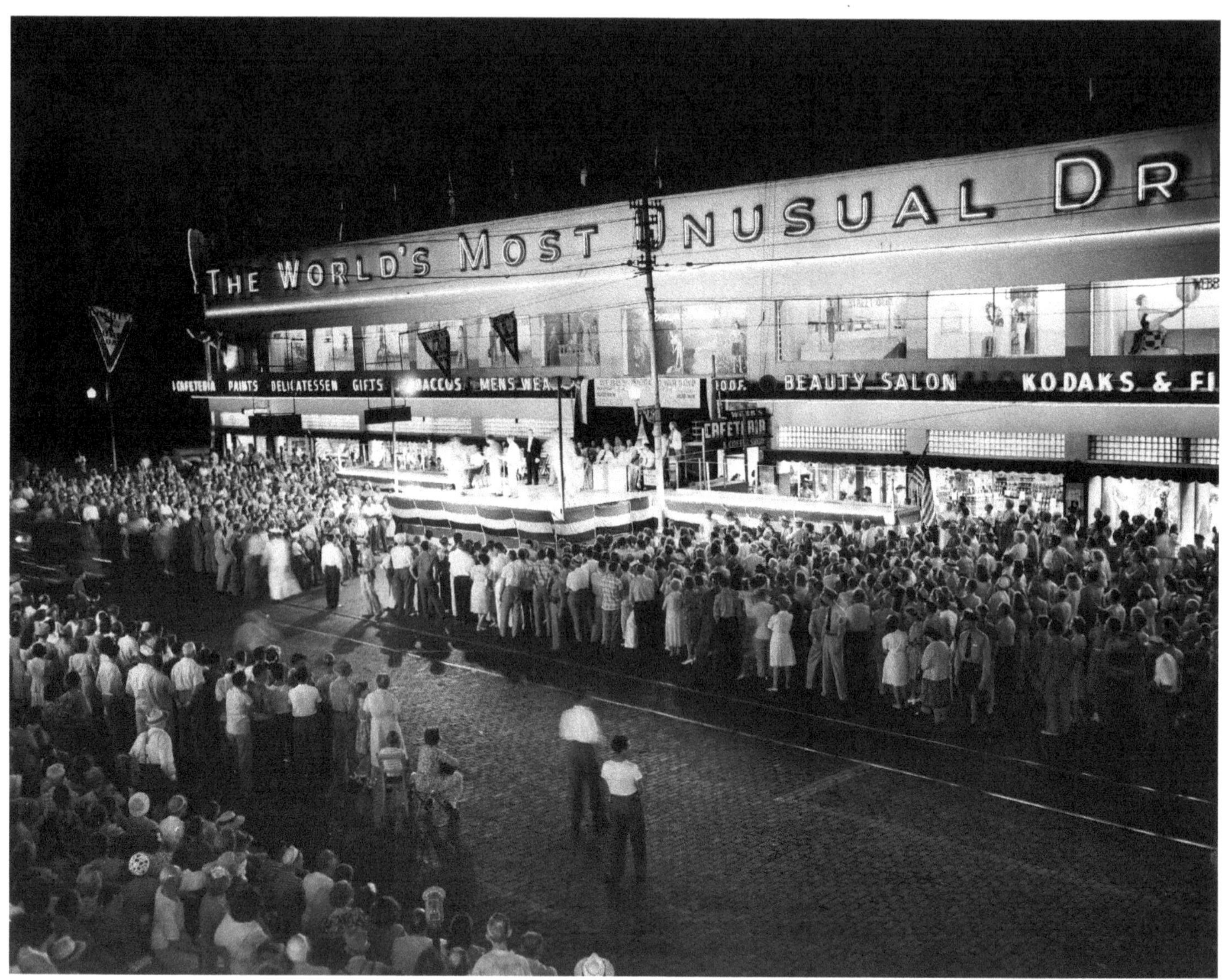

A war bond drive is held on a night in 1942 at Doc Webb's "Most Unusual Drug Store." James Earl "Doc" Webb, known as the master showman of volume sales, bought a small drugstore and through the 1930s, by concentrating on volume sales, turned it into a complex of stores known as Webb's City. Its annual sales in 1941 surpassed $4 million.

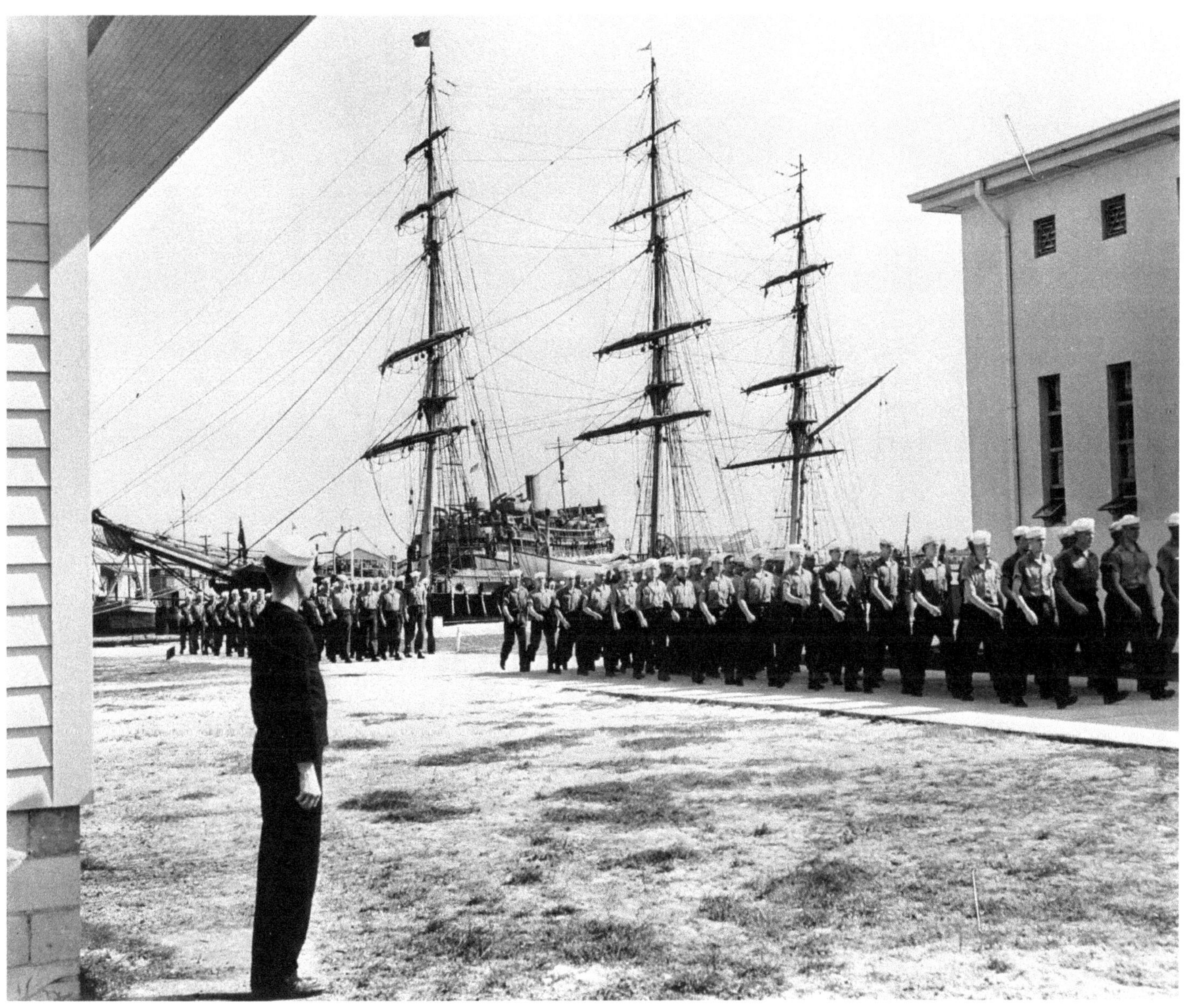

At the beginning of the war, the Coast Guard operated a training facility at Bayboro for merchant seamen, with approximately 250 recruits and two training ships, the *Joseph Conrad* and the *American Seaman.* In 1942, the facility was transferred to the United States Maritime Service, and a large barracks housing 800 men and a classroom building were added.

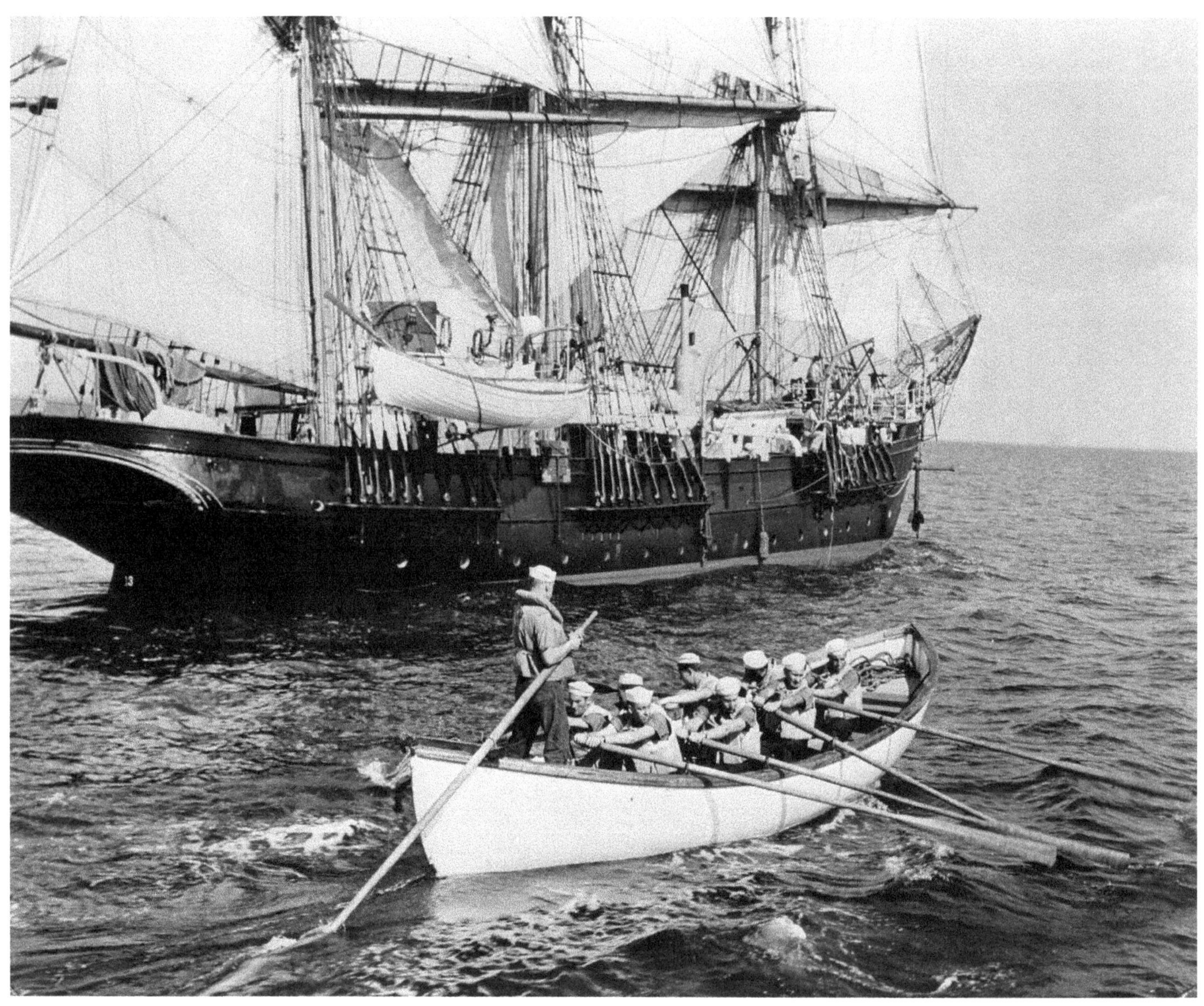

In 1943, trainees handle a lifeboat in an "abandon ship" drill at the United States Maritime Service training station. Hotels and businesses stayed busy as the Maritime Service facility at Bayboro was expanded, training 25 thousand seamen by the end of the war.

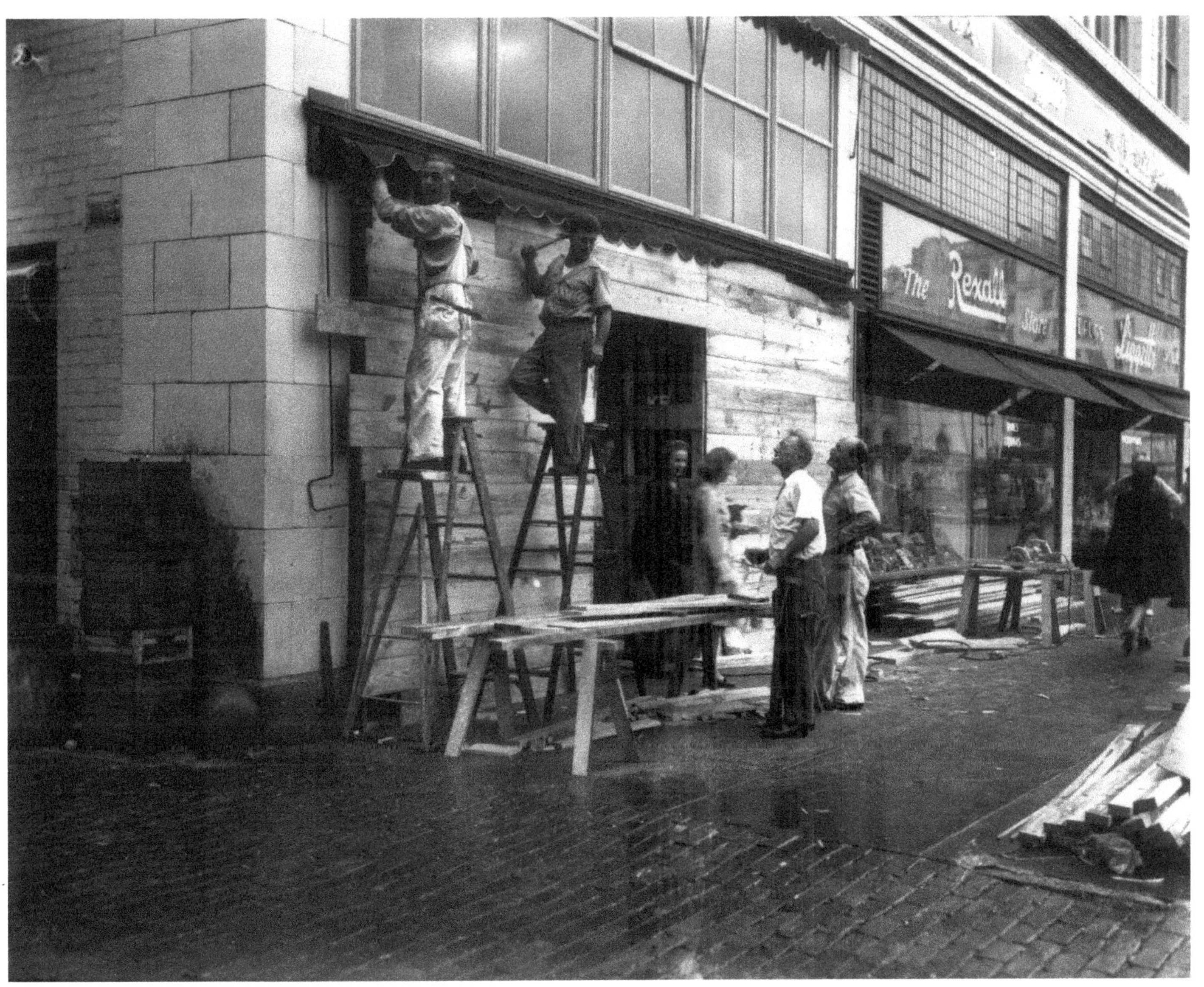

Businesses are boarded up in 1945 as a hurricane threatens the area. An early storm that season had dissipated greatly when it hit Cedar Key on June 24. On September 4, a second tropical storm skirted the west coast of Florida, causing minor damage. A category 4 hurricane hit Miami on September 15 and turned north over the peninsula, resulting in four deaths and millions of dollars in damages.

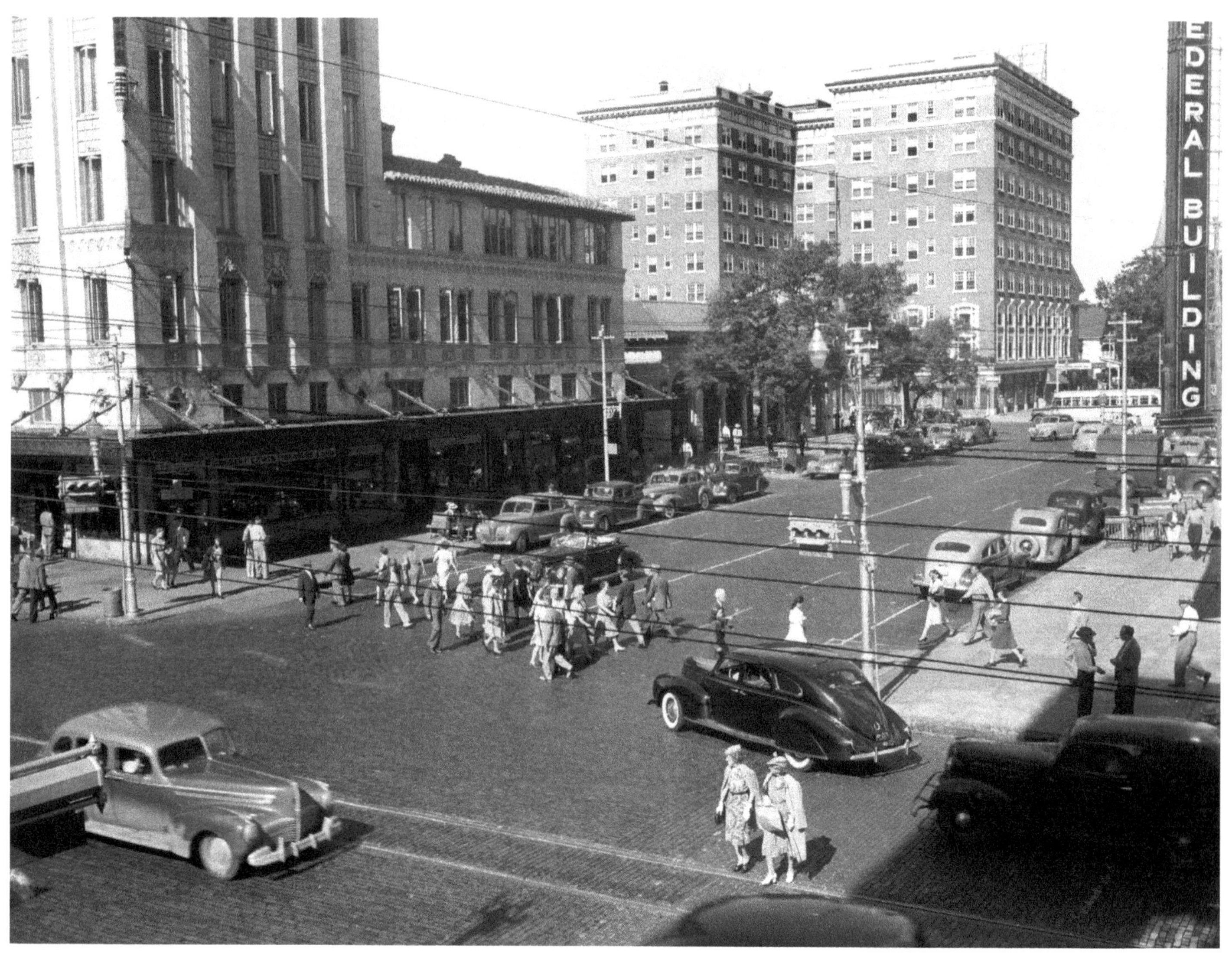

St. Petersburg quickly returned to a civilian footing after the war as newcomers from across the nation relocated. Supplementing this postwar boom was a fund the city had built up from wartime municipal utilities. The city spent the fund, in excess of $1 million, to improve parks, streets, baseball fields, and the waterfront.

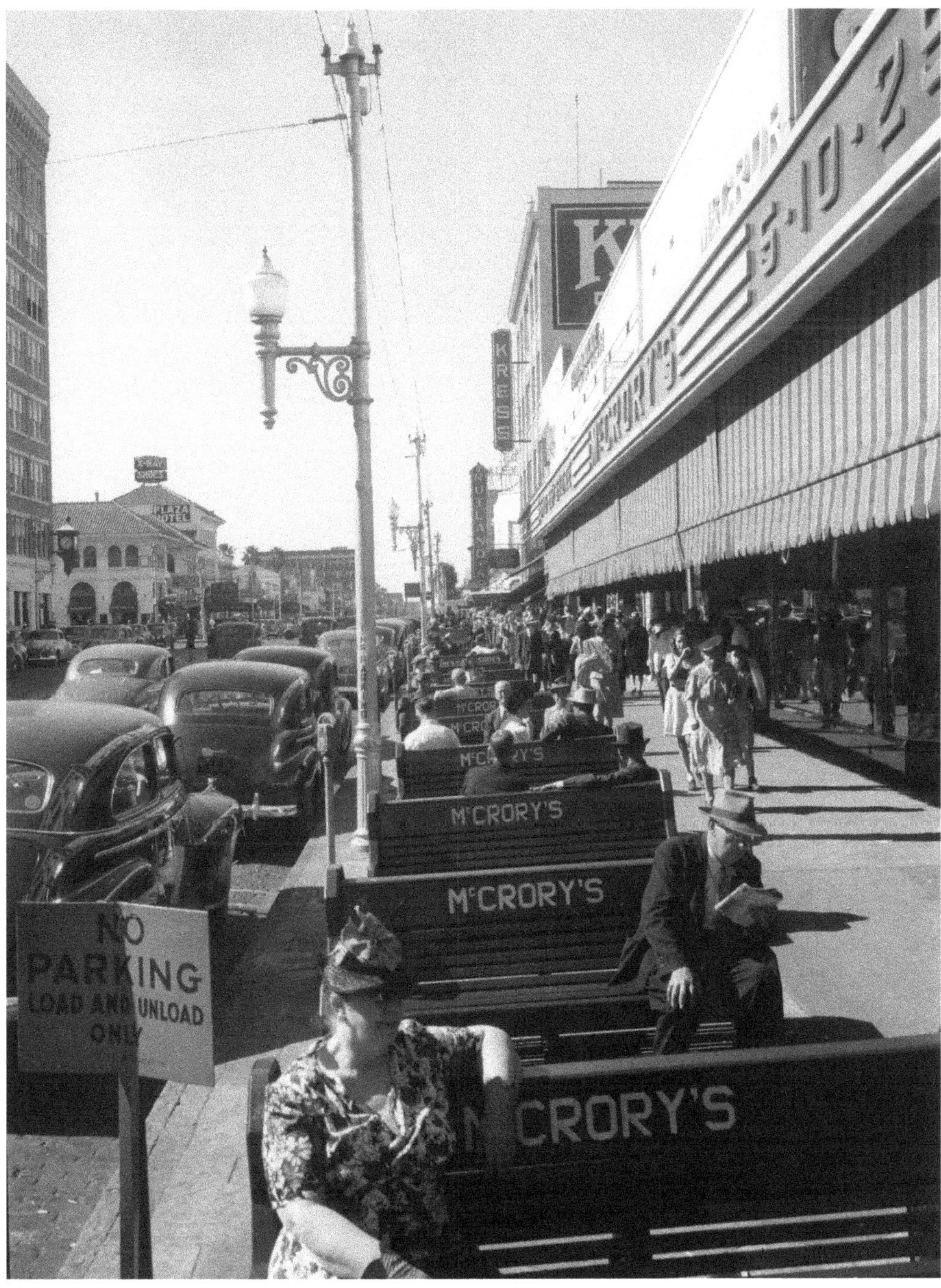

Alongside the familiar green benches, downtown Central Avenue stores are busy with postwar customers here in 1946. On the right, pedestrians stroll past McCrory's, Kress, and Rutland's department store. On the left is the Plaza Theatre, which was demolished in 1957.

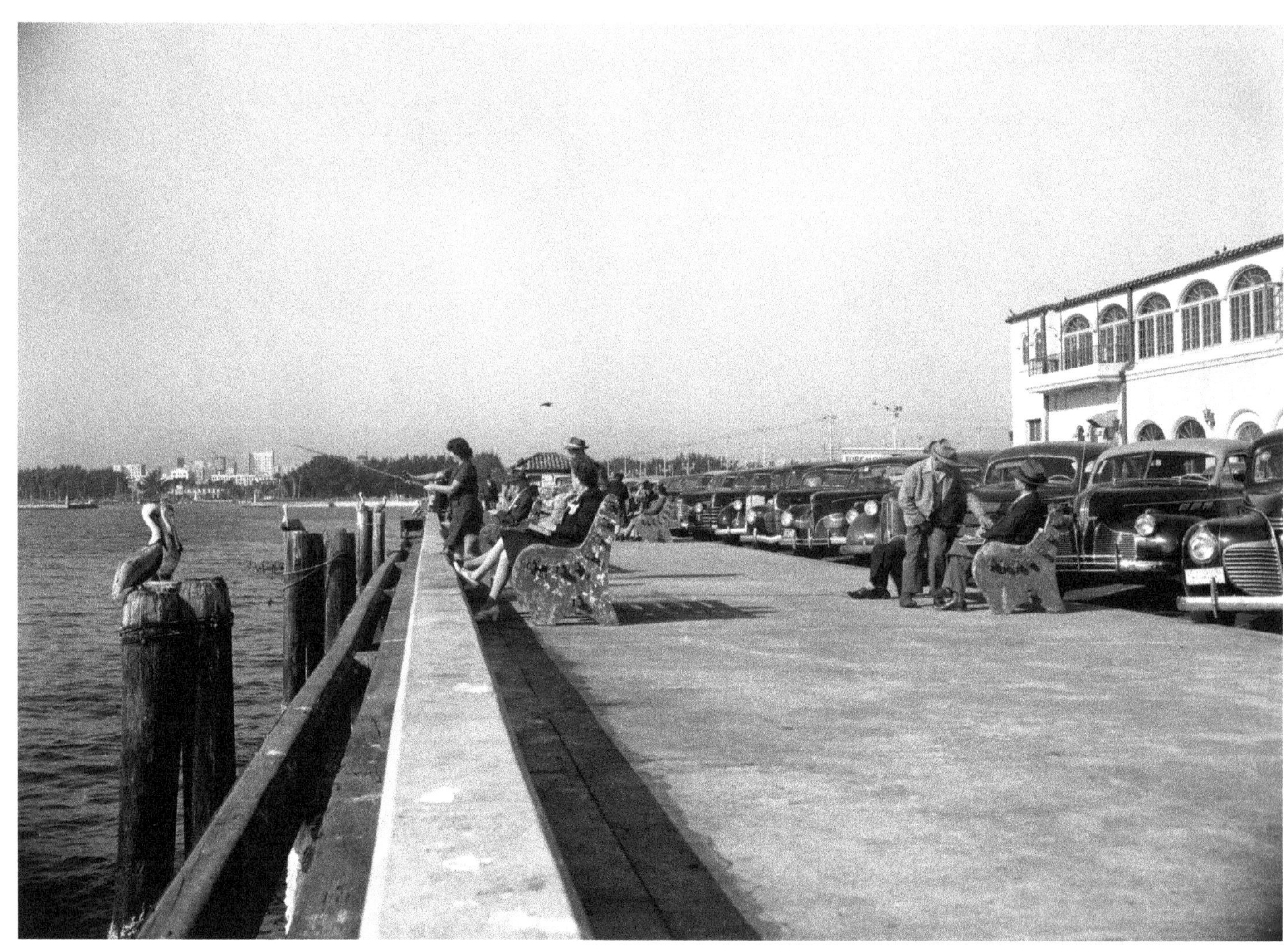

People are fishing and cars are parked along the Million Dollar Pier in 1946. The city had used postwar funds to repair the pier, which remained popular as a gathering place for cardplayers, tourist meetings, community sings, and fishing tournaments. Once again it became a popular fishing spot for mackerel, trout, and redfish.

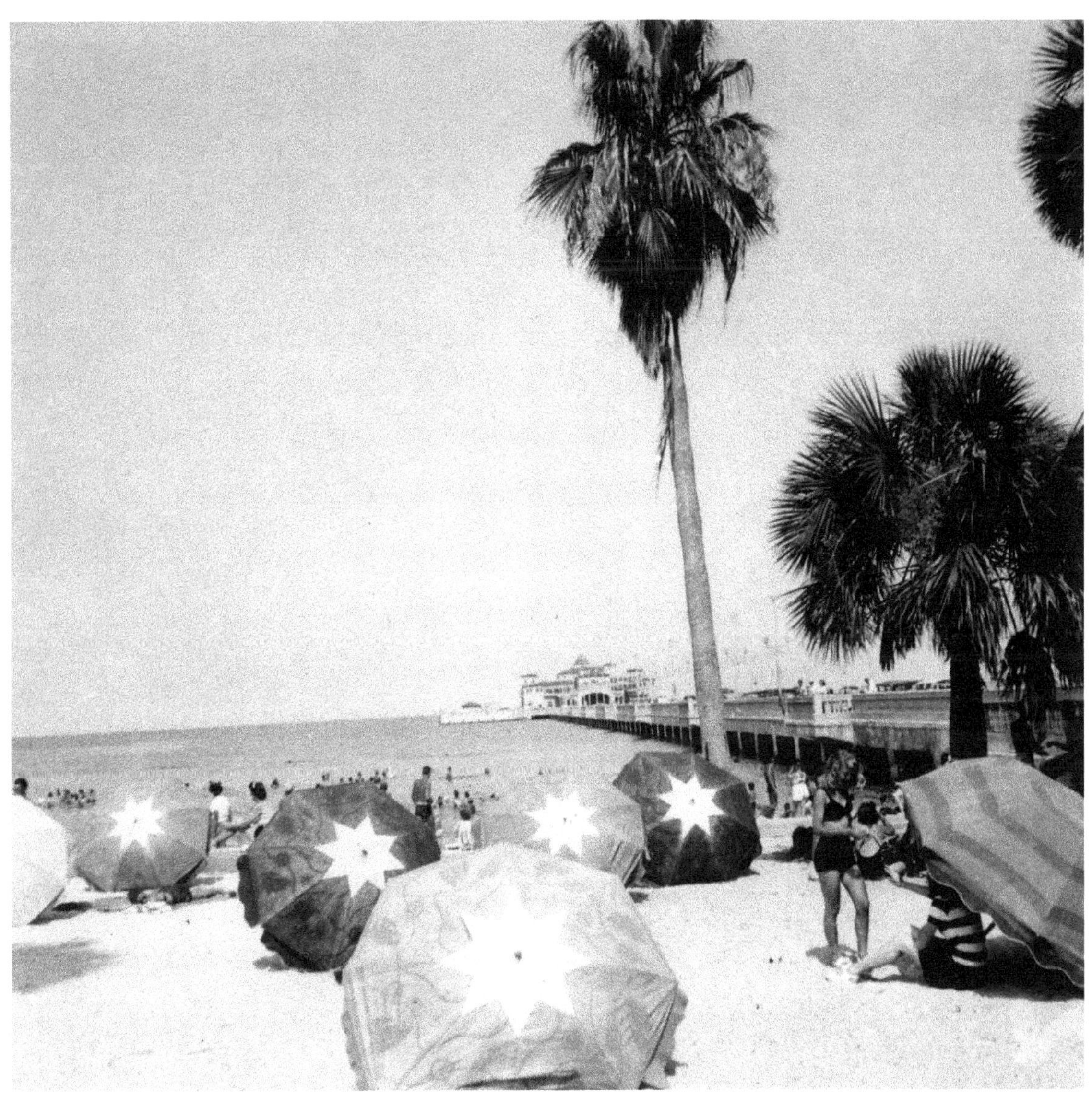

This 1946 publicity image was used as a lure to entice Americans to visit the area. Florida state agencies participated in producing and distributing promotional literature to encourage Florida tourism, an effort that succeeded. In St. Petersburg, the population increased from 85,000 in 1945 to more than 90,000 in two years.

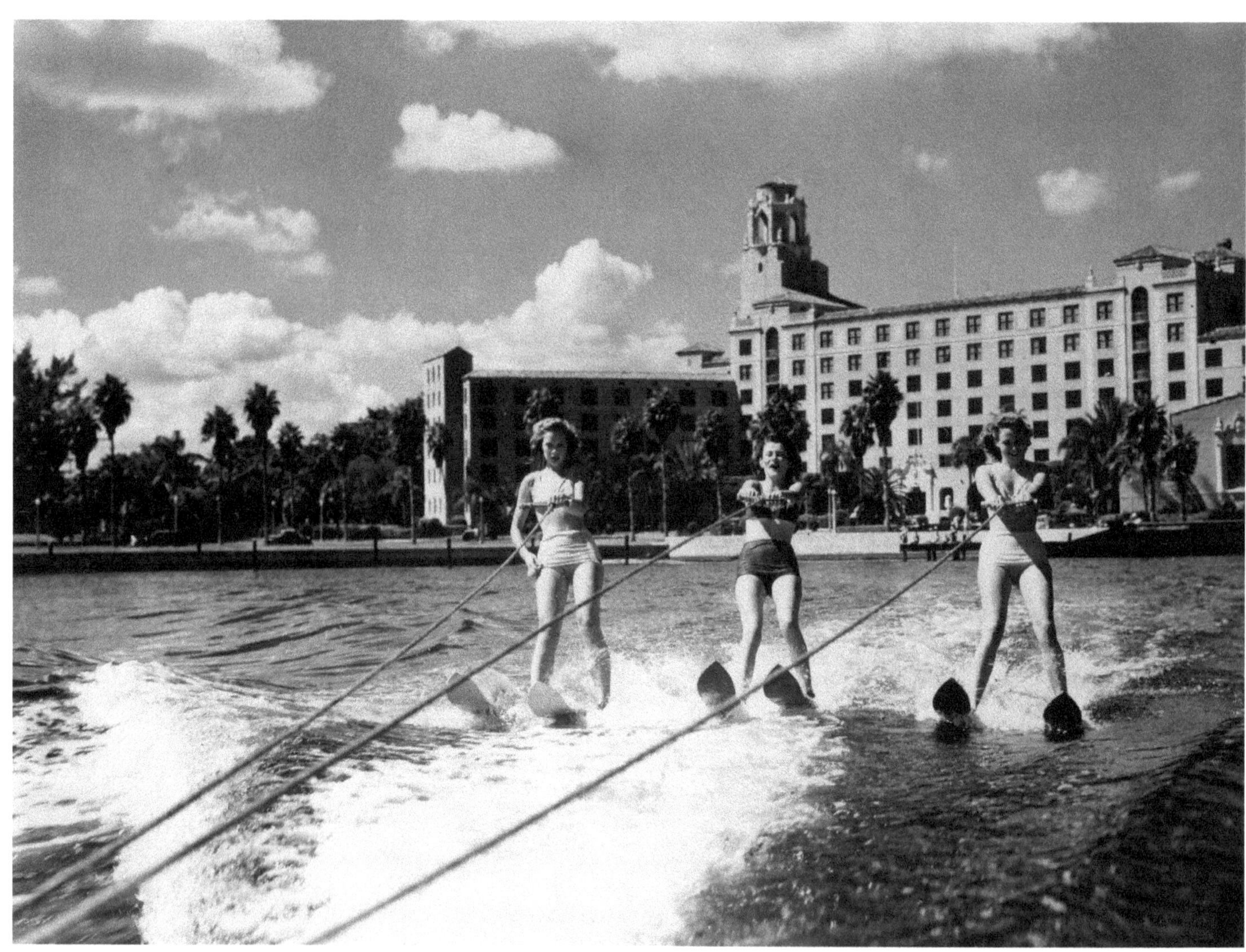

The Vinoy Hotel became a training center for army cooks and bakers during the war. Kitchens that had served lavish meals now served as classrooms, and troops bunked in rooms where millionaires had resided. Briefly closed for repairs, the Vinoy opened again for guests in 1946 and resumed its place as a favored winter destination.

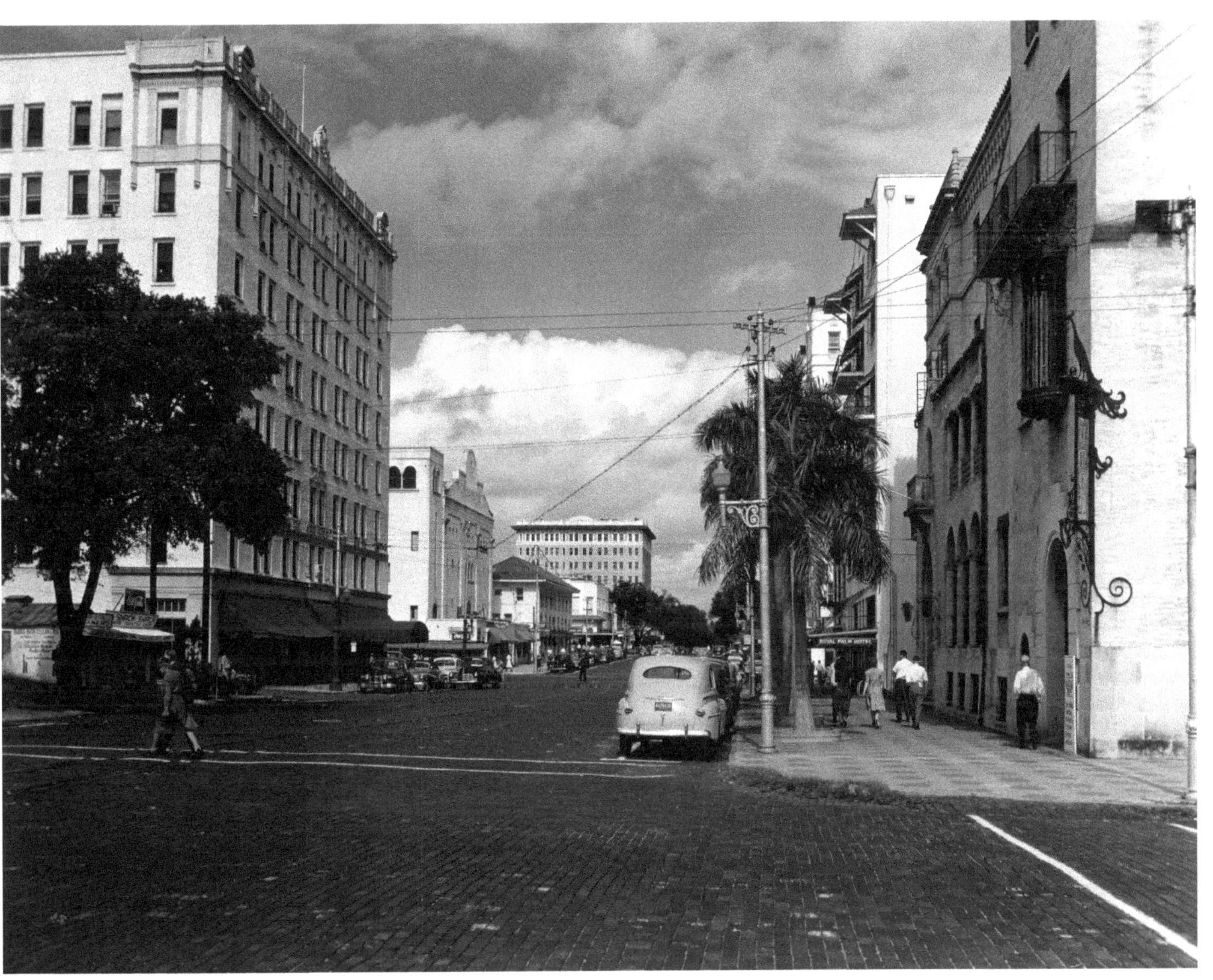

Fifth Street seems empty on this February day in 1947. As the postwar boom unfolded, St. Petersburg experienced the suburbs. As home construction permits rose from just 11 in 1943 to more than 1,500 in 1946, vacant twenties-boom-era subdivisions came to life again, and development throughout the area drew people away from downtown.

A view across Mirror Lake in November 1947. Motivated by the growth of the suburbs, the city government focused on improvements aimed at rejuvenating downtown. The ambitious program included street improvements, a new sewer system, a large city park, Lake Maggiore, and a new athletic park.

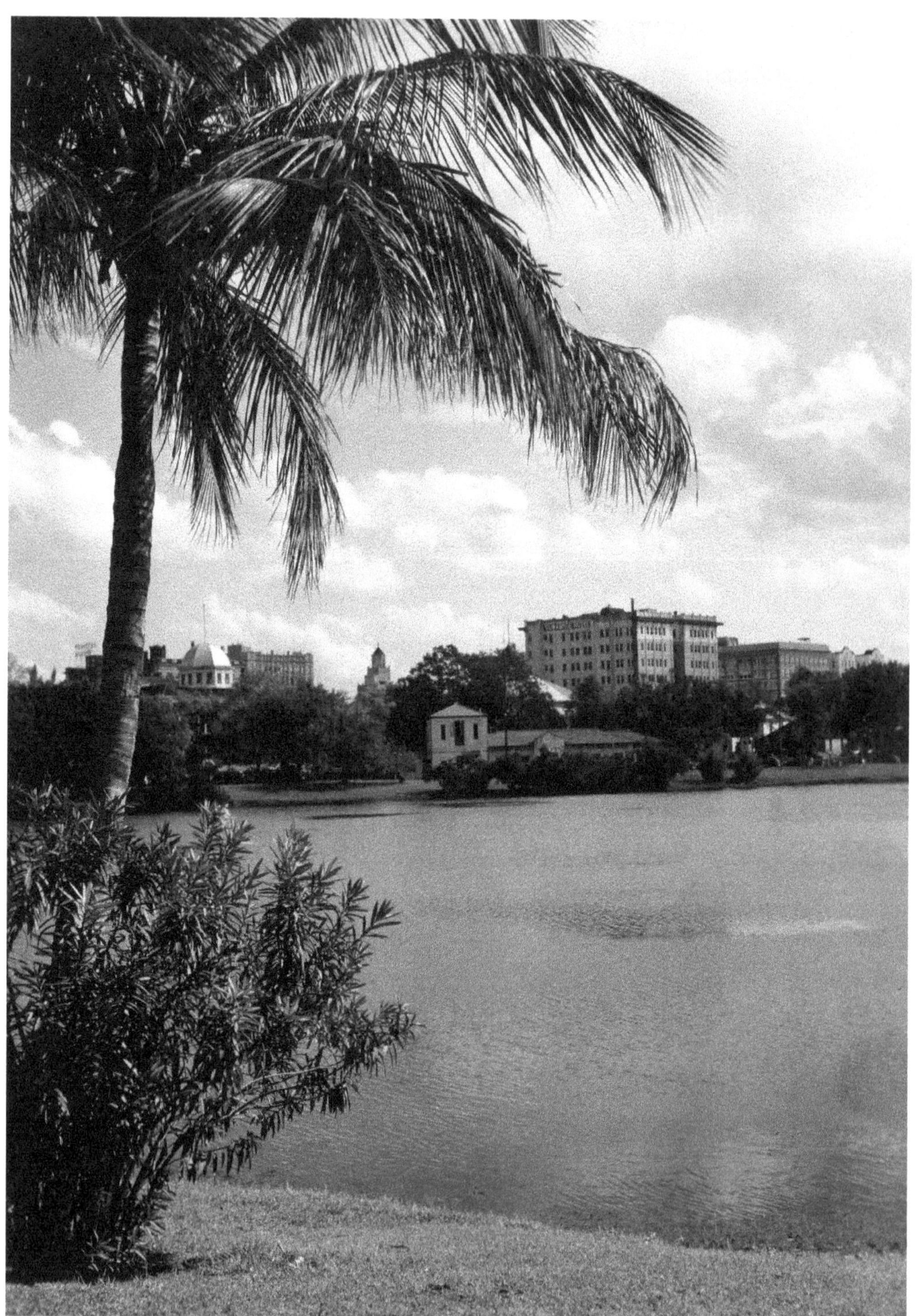

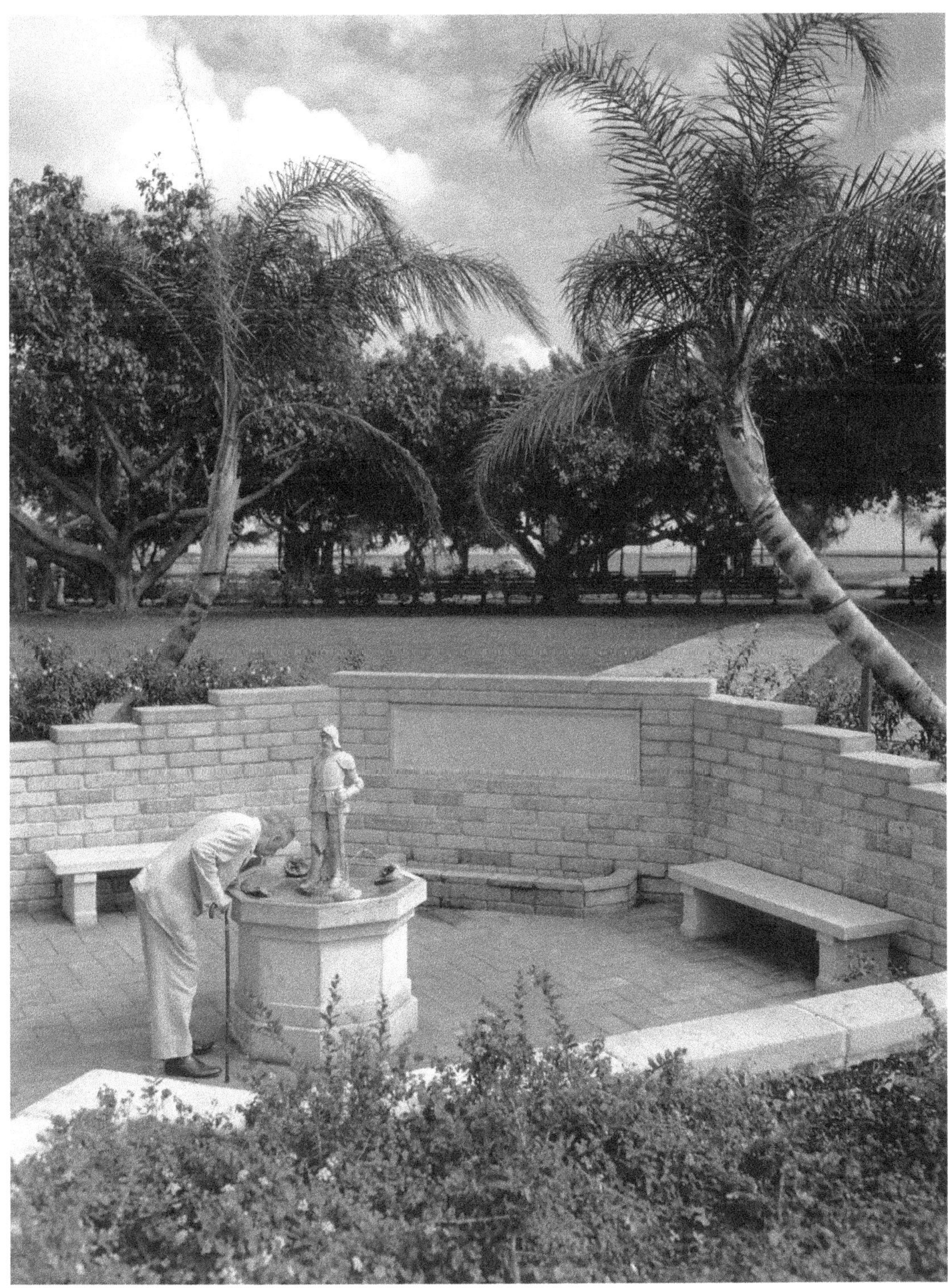

In 1947, a man takes a sip from the Fountain of Youth. This attraction, created by Edwin Tomlinson in the early 1900s, was a reminder of the city's past. The famous artesian well was welcoming more and more retirees as newcomers. St. Petersburg's percentage of locally born residents dipped below 20 percent for the first time in 1950.

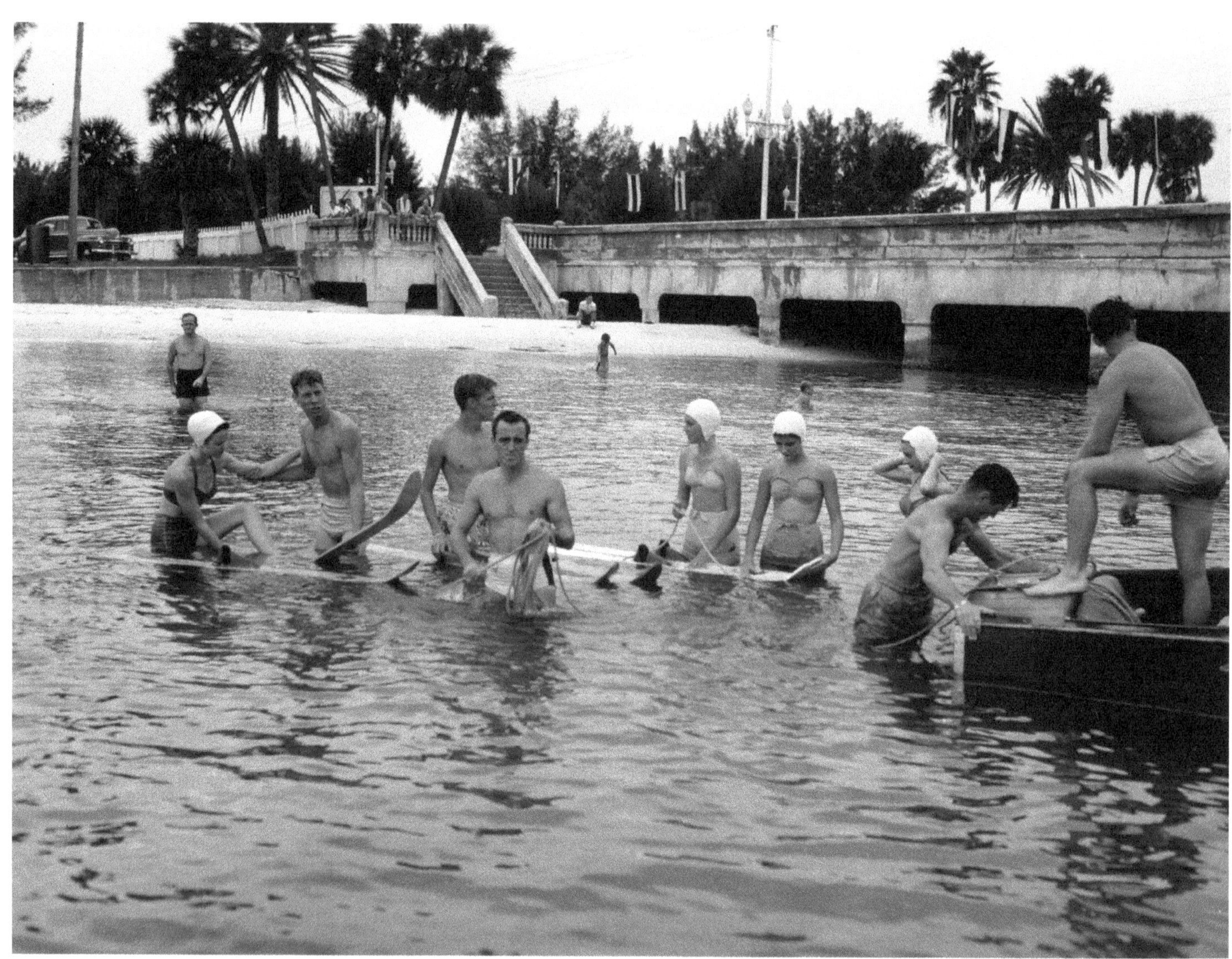

This group of water skiers is preparing to skim the waves. As the local population increased, interest in adding recreational activities also rose. This Jaycee activity was one of many recreational activities they have provided the area since 1933. Others include the Soap Box Derby, the Miss St. Petersburg pageant, the Tarpon roundup, and the Mutt Derby.

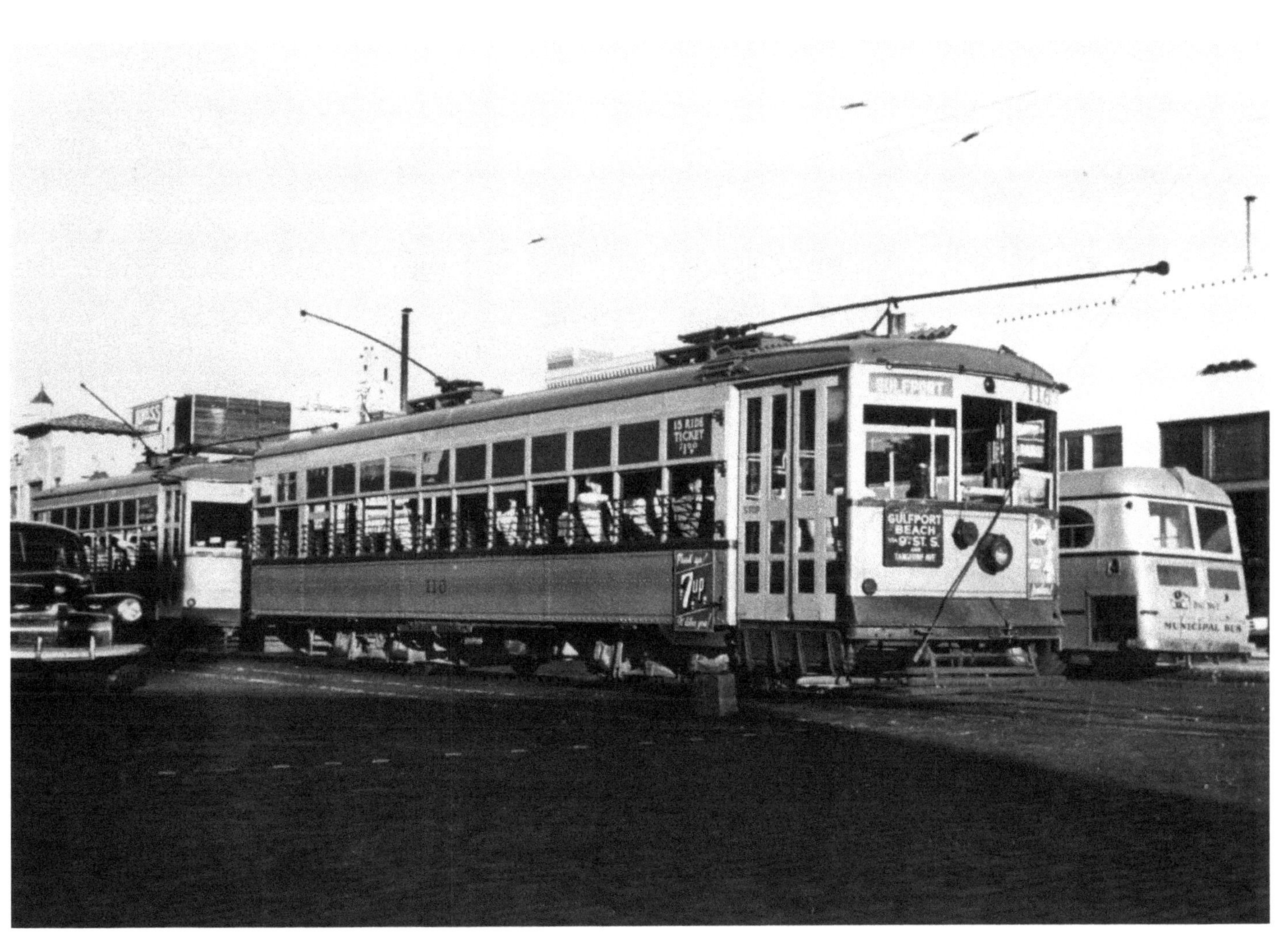

In 1904, the St. Petersburg and Gulf Electric Railway became operational. It was purchased by the city in 1919. The city extended and modernized the transit system in the twenties and replaced most of the streetcars. Many of those same electric trolley cars were still operating when the transit system switched to buses in 1947.

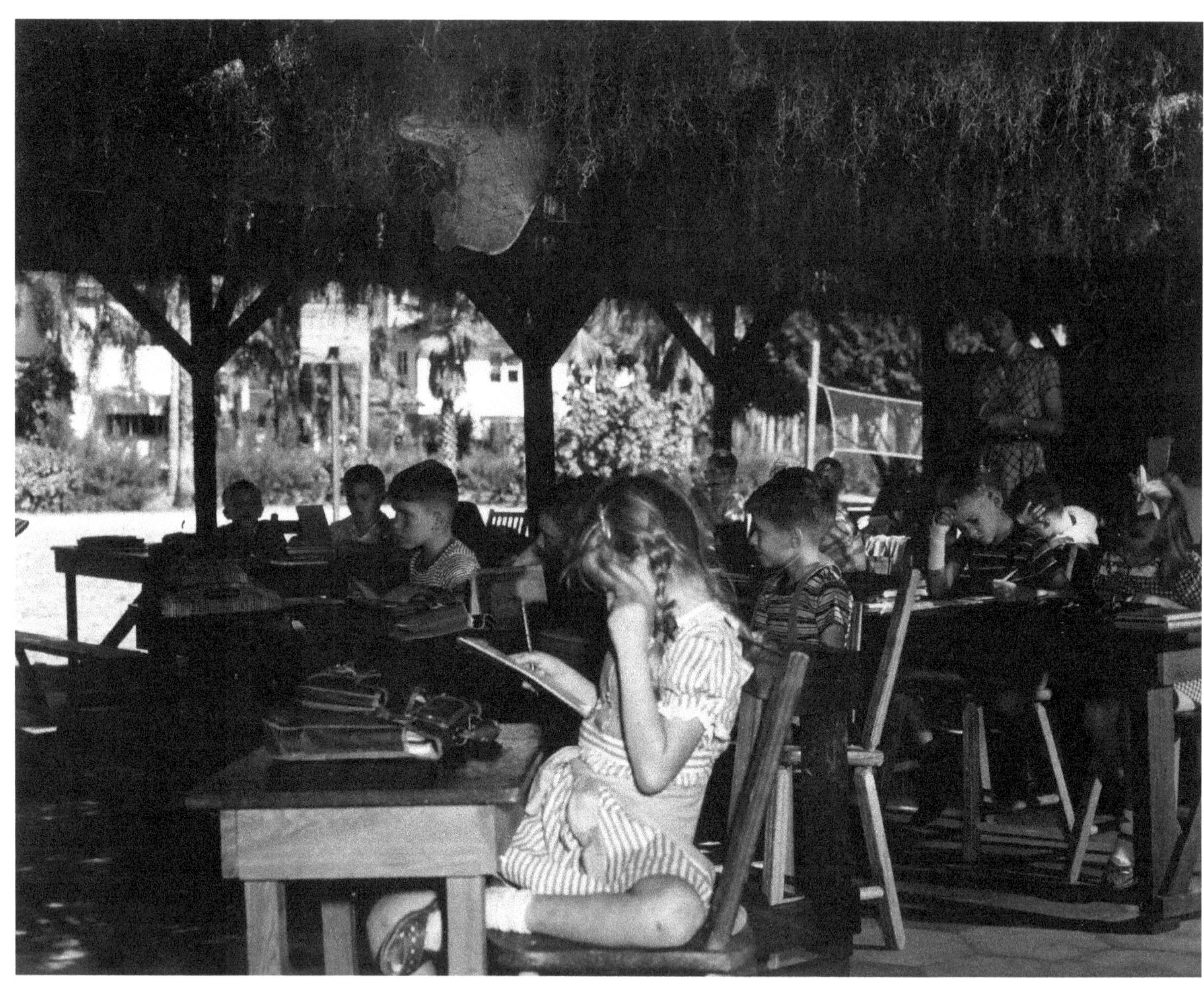

Established in 1923 to provide instruction for children of winter families, Shorecrest Outdoor School is Florida's oldest independent day school. Classes were held in open-air classrooms covered with thatched roofs and students literally learned outdoors. The original campus was 15 feet from water's edge.

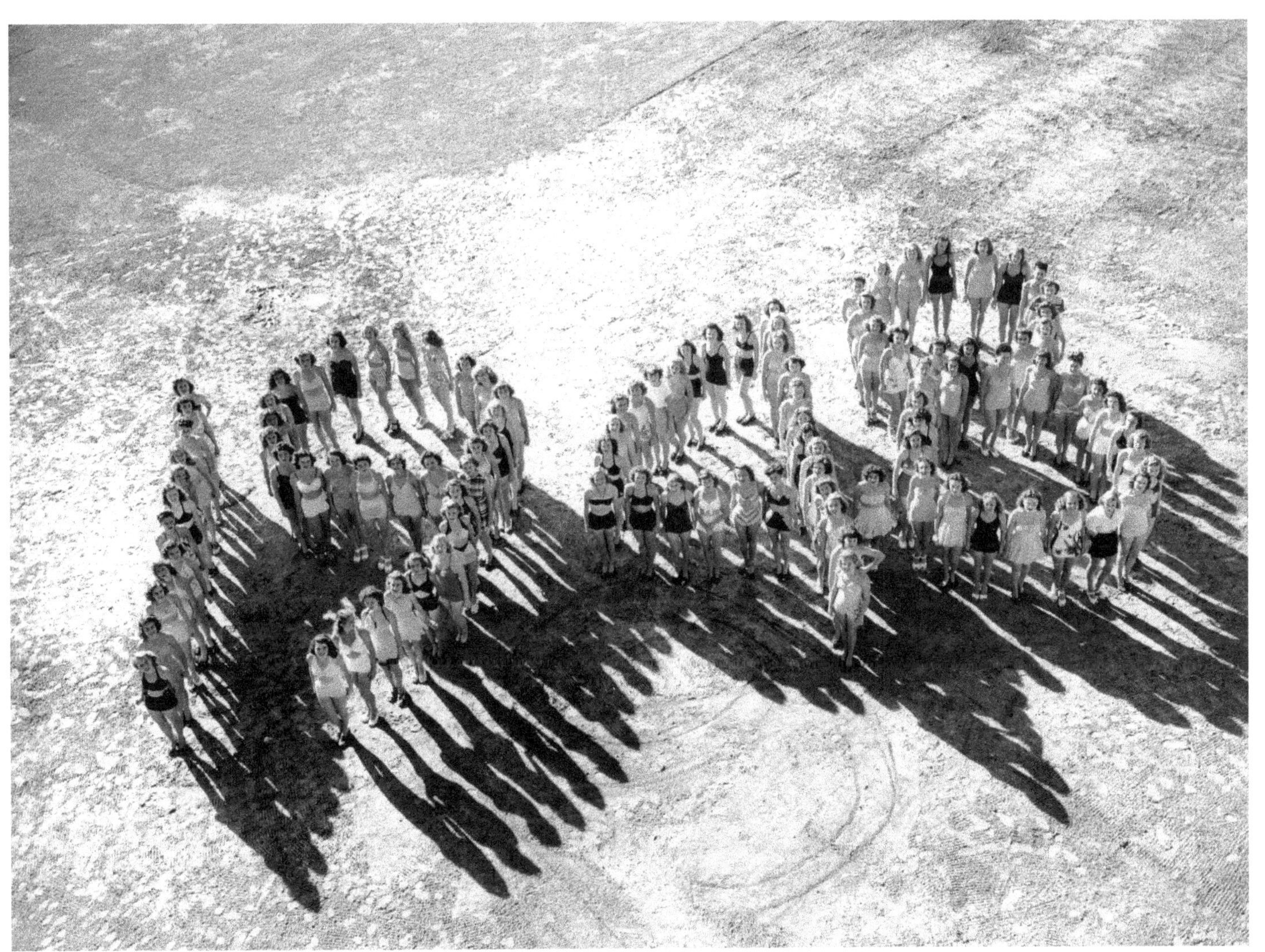

Beauty contestants stage a publicity shot, entitled "entries to charm school for the 1948 year." The year before, Miss St. Petersburg, Eula Ann McGehee, also won the Miss Florida title. St. Petersburg beach and the other beach communities benefited greatly from the postwar recovery of the tourist trade.

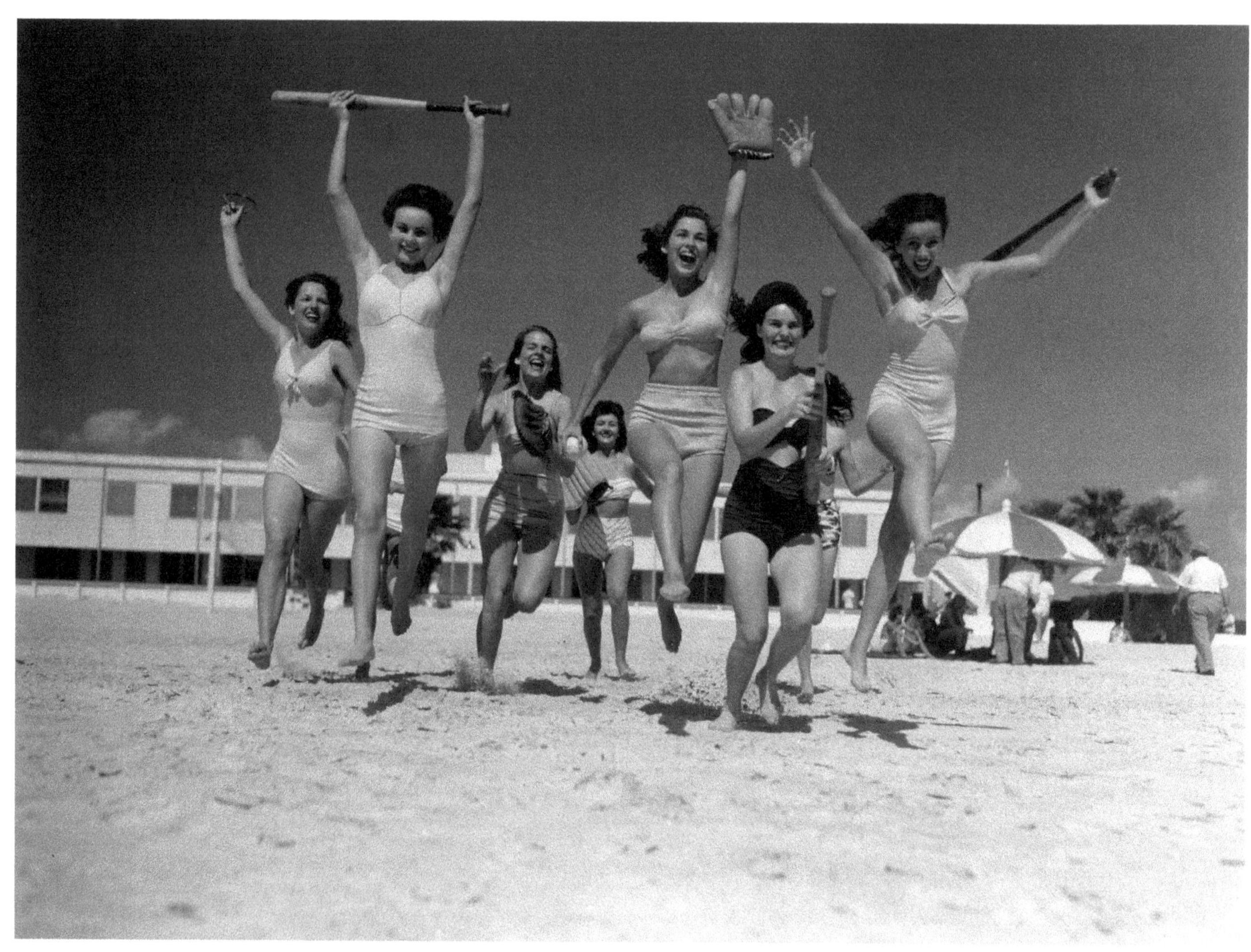

A "baseball team" runs into the surf, on a beautiful sunny day in 1948, for an advertisement promoting the area's world-famous beaches. John Lodwick, the city's chief publicity agent from 1919 to 1942, regarded this promotional approach as a key resource, referring to it as the "Florida fantasy" bathing beauty photograph.

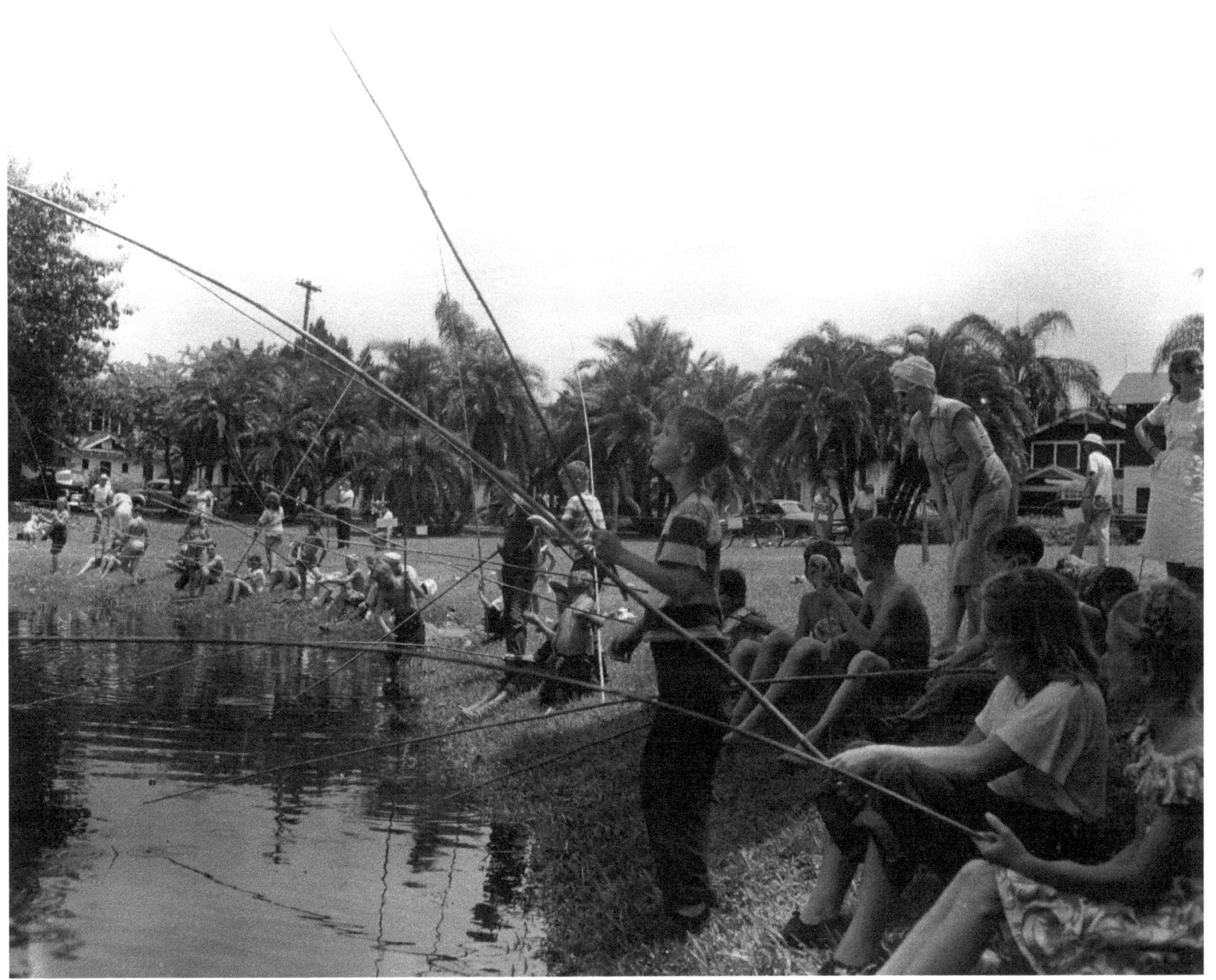

Shown here in 1948, the annual St. Petersburg Children's Fishathon provided fishing poles, bait, and prizes. One girl related that on the morning of the event she asked her father, could she keep the first prize, a bicycle, if she won? The parents had been reluctant to let her have a bike; however, when in fact she won first prize by catching a 2-pound bass, Dad consented.

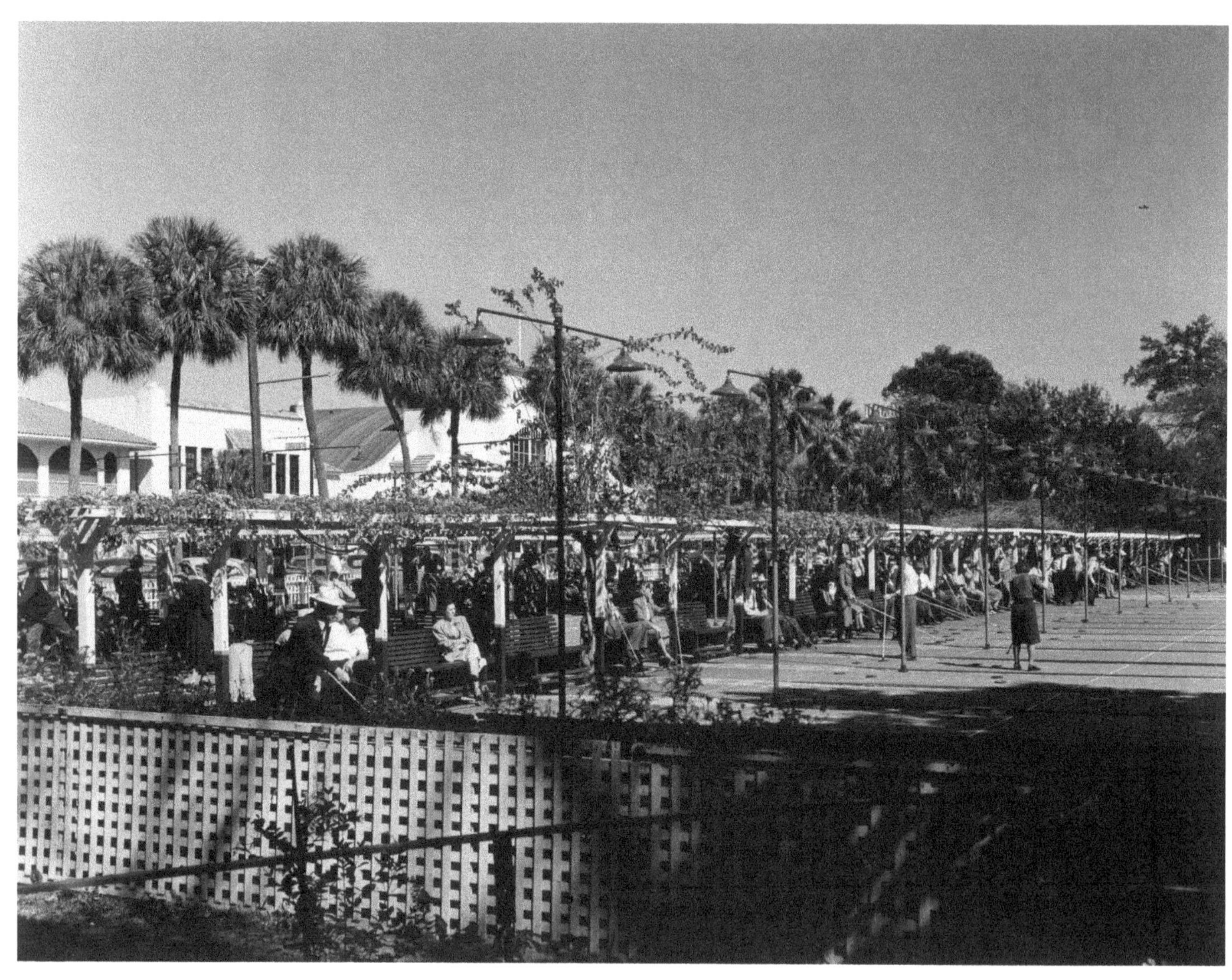

The shuffleboard club at Mirror Lake Park boasted 7,000 members in 1949. Originally built in 1923, the complex has grown to an assembly of 65 masonry courts, 4 buildings, and a grandstand. As city historian Karl Grismer noted, "St. Petersburg wouldn't be St. Petersburg without the shuffleboard courts."

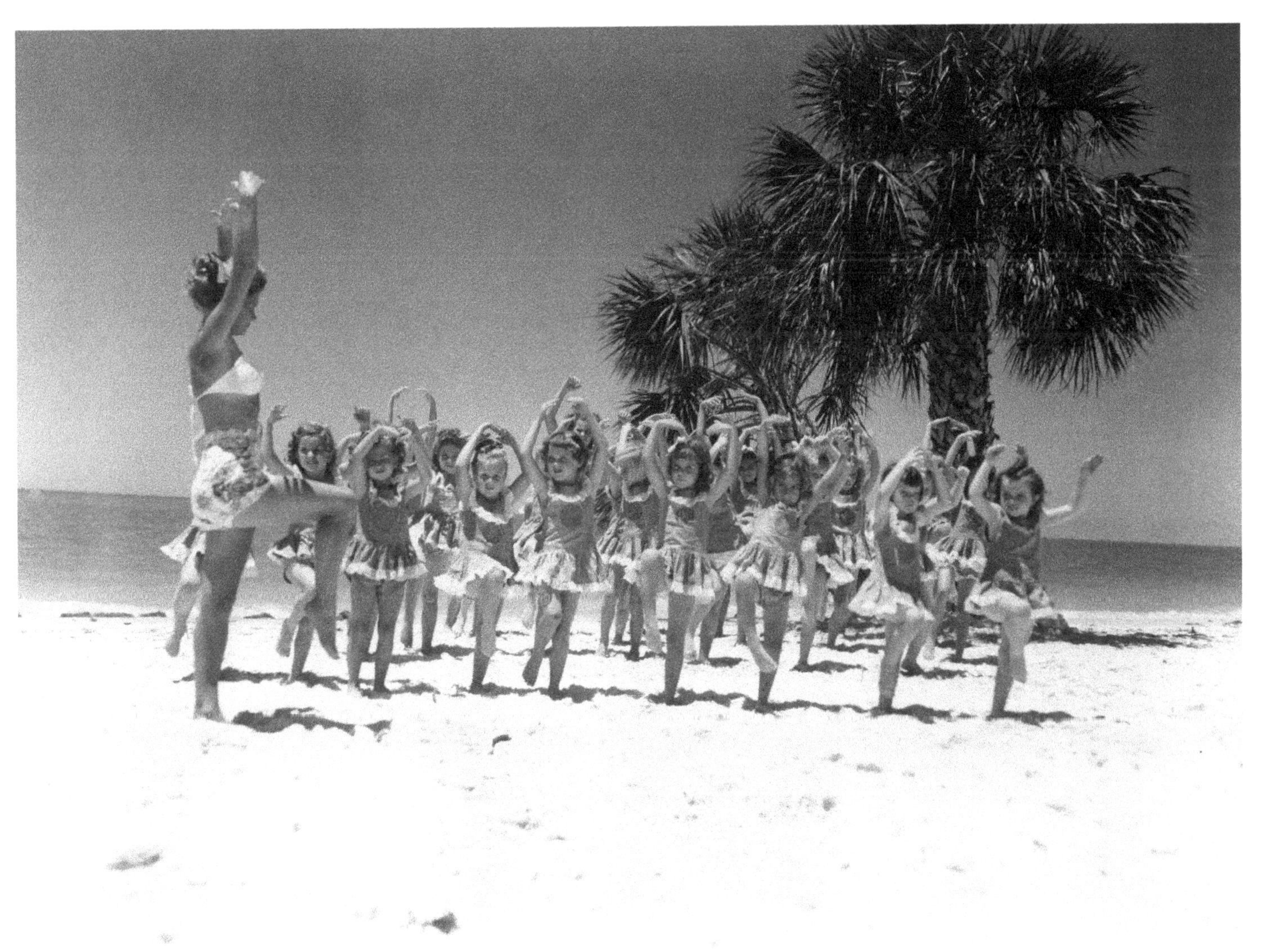

The Eborn School of Dance Art's modeling and ballet class practices on the beach in 1949. Organized children's programs were a valuable community asset. One of St. Petersburg's few dance teachers, Lois Eborn, taught child modeling and ballet. She also had a parasol group, make-up class, and a majorettes and drum-major group.

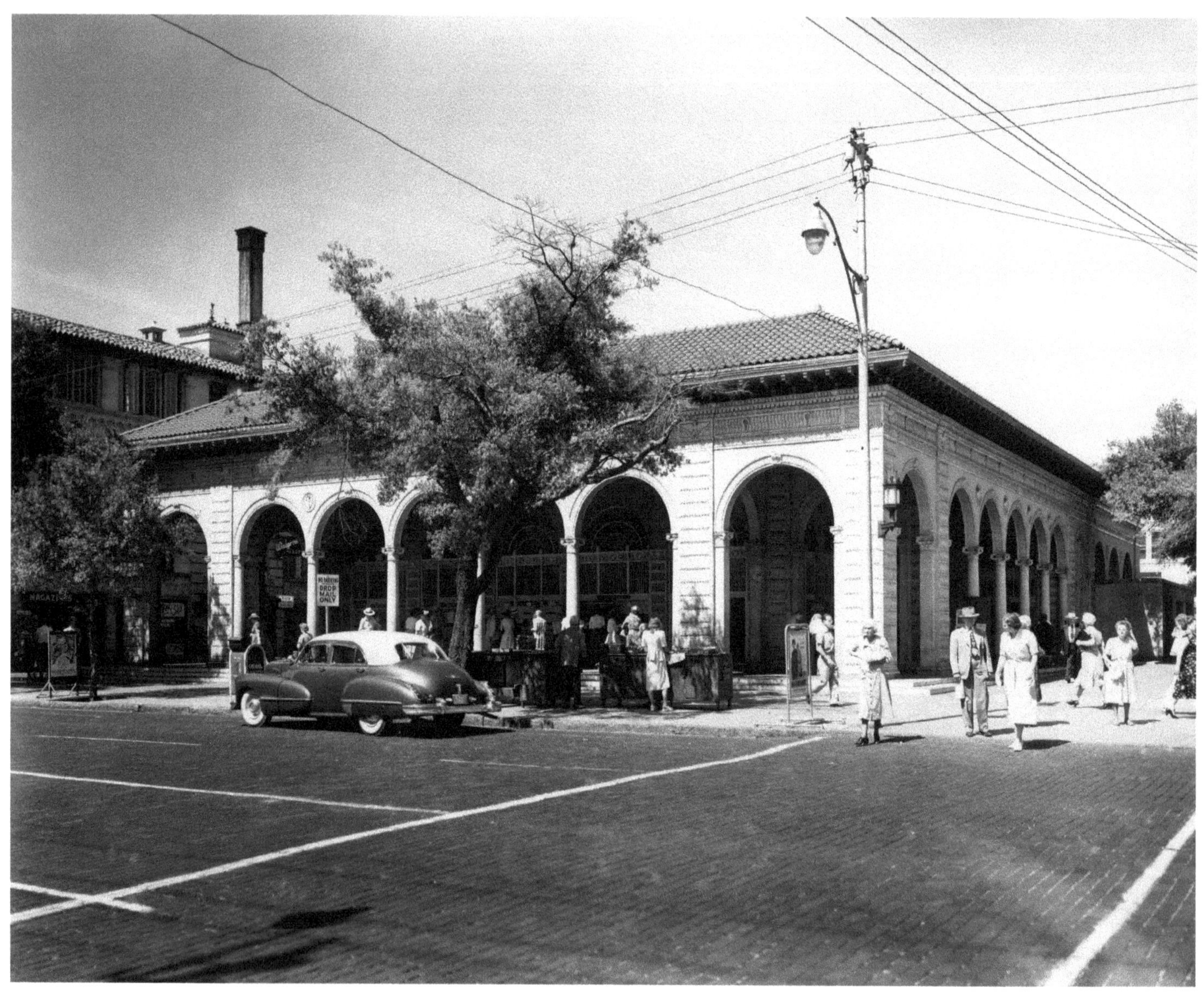

In 1916, Postmaster Roy Hanna had a design for a new "open-air" post office, in which three sides were left open to the street. The architect refused to discuss the design, so Hanna, in frustration, threw the plans on the architect's desk and walked away. When the new blueprints arrived, architect George Stewart had incorporated almost all of Hanna's design elements. The post office is shown here in 1949.

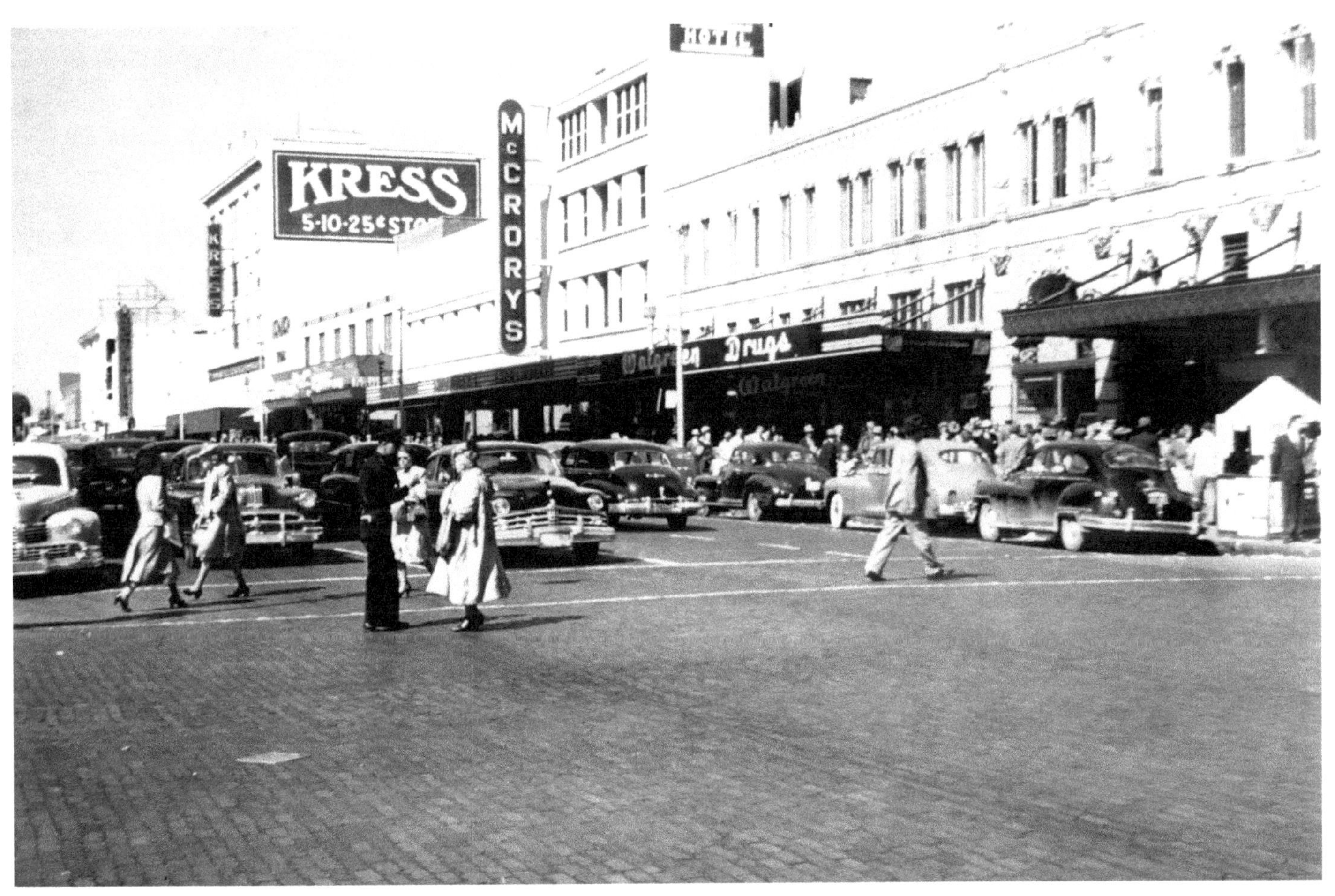

Some pedestrians seem slow to cross Central Street. The 1950 census had revealed significant changes taking place in the community. The population had increased from around 60,000 to 96,000, and the city's profile indicated that it was getting older—22 percent of residents were now older than 65.

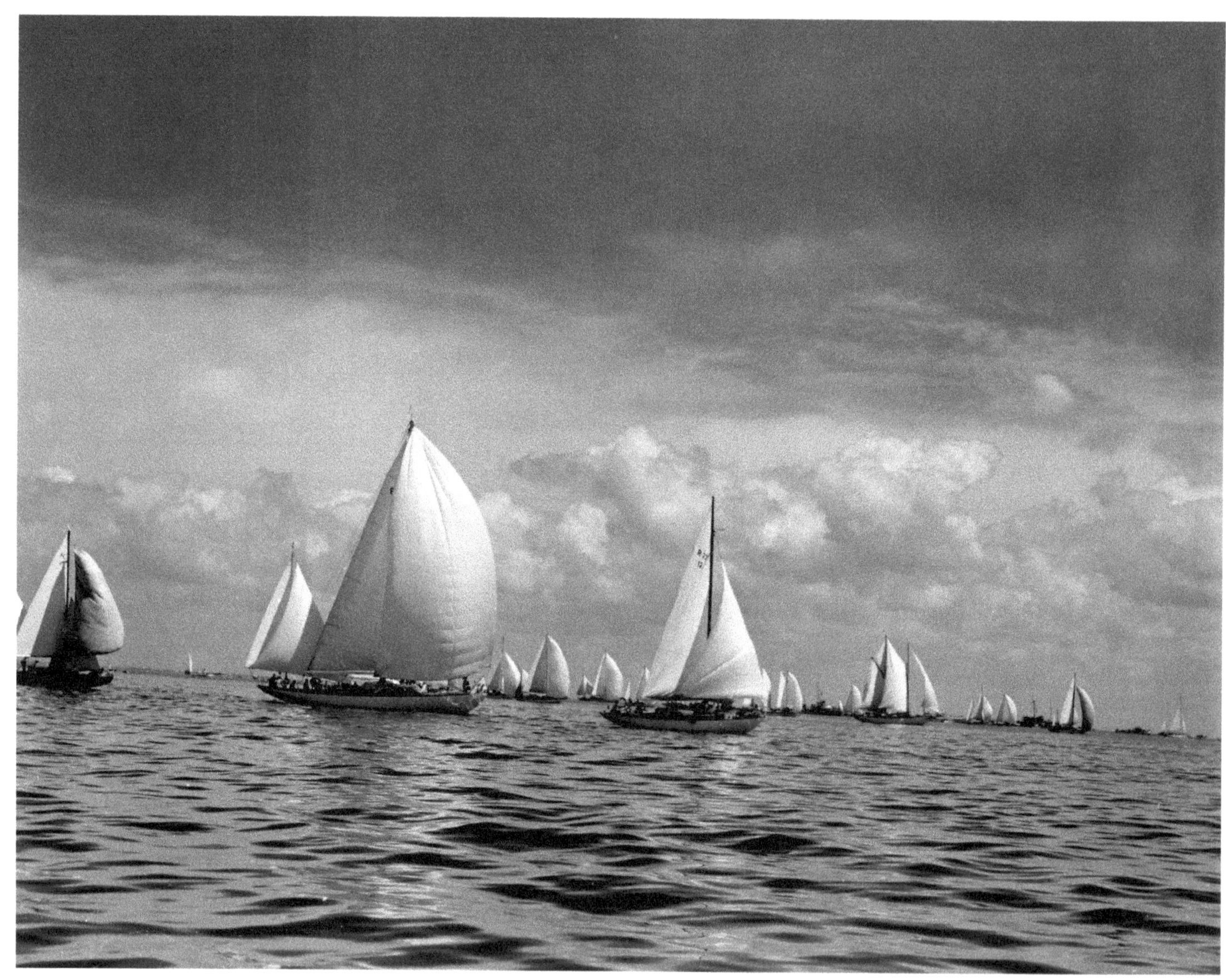

The St. Petersburg–to–Havana, Cuba, sailboat race had some interesting moments. One observer mistook firecrackers for gunfire as their boat neared Cuba. A disputed crew-list resulted in an all-women team being dropped. (They raced anyway.) One yacht lost the race after stopping to fish. Said one team member, "It was a question of priorities."

As the oldest law school in Florida, Stetson Law School relocated to Gulfport in 1954. Originally Jack Taylor's Rolyat Hotel, it next became the Florida Military Academy and then became Stetson. The first dean at the Gulfport Campus was Harold Serbing, former chief justice and judge at the Nuremberg war trials.

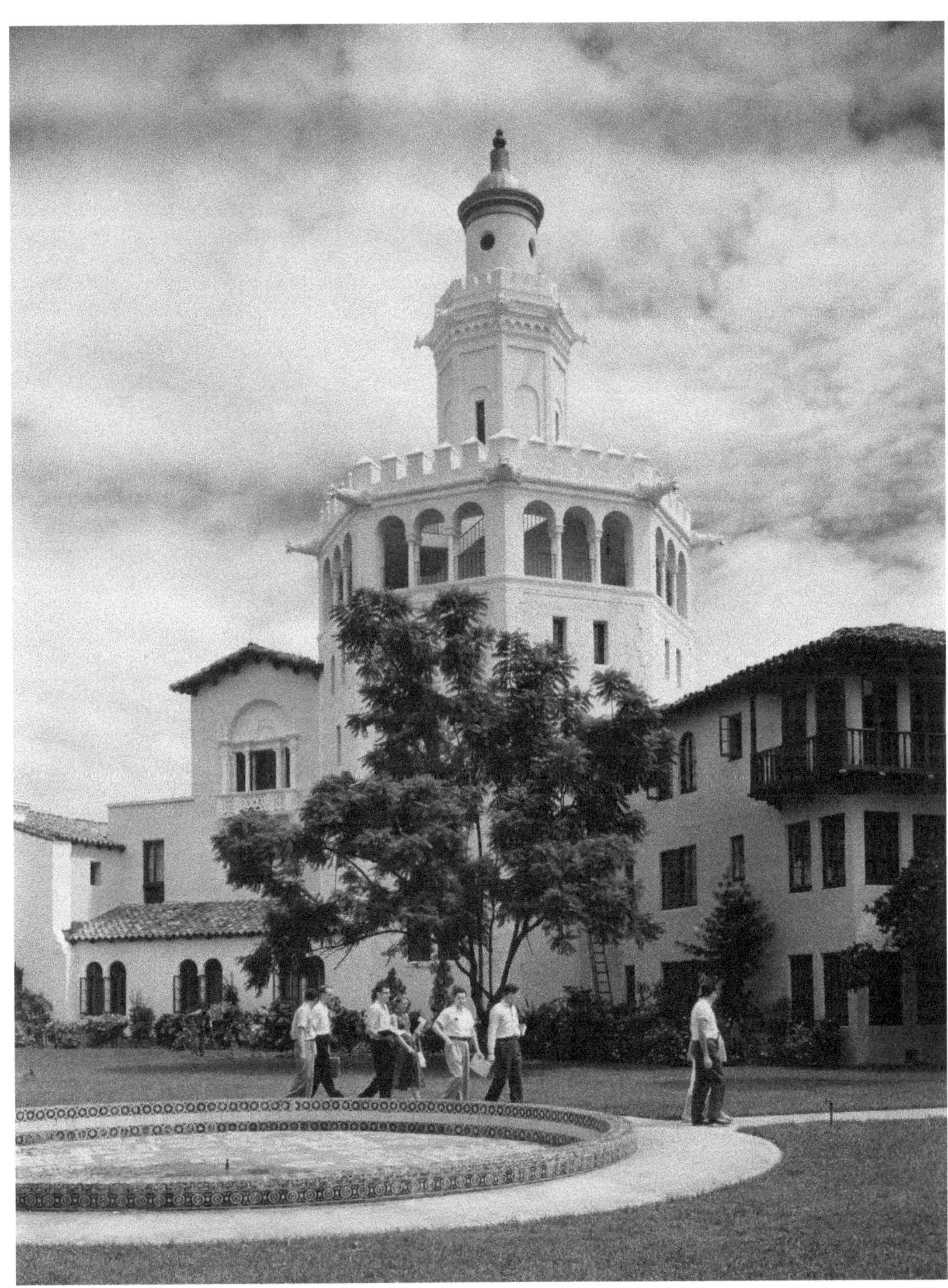

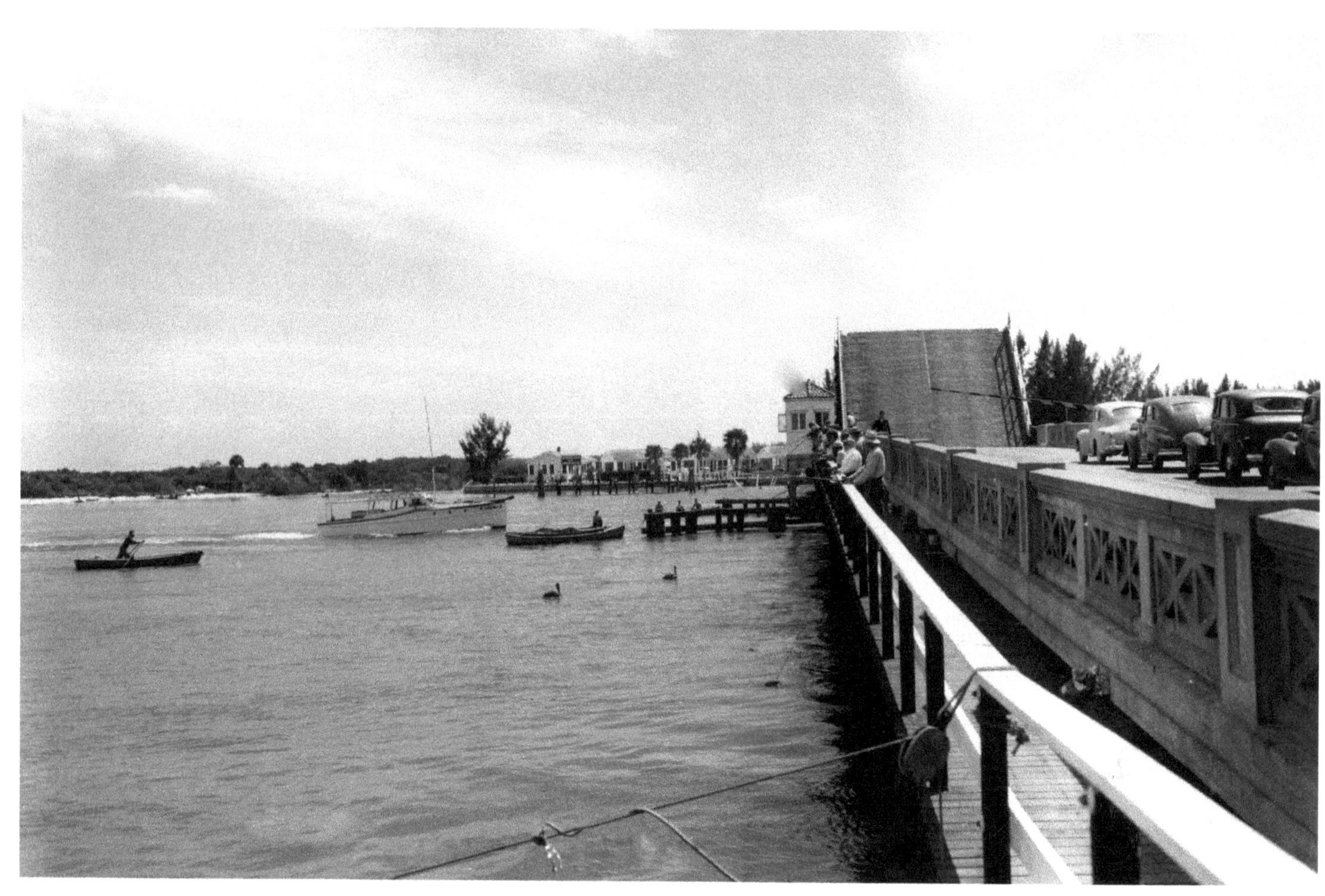

A busy scene at the Johns Pass Bridge in 1951. The postwar years saw tremendous development on the Pinellas Suncoast and the barrier islands. Before the bridge was built in the early 1920s, "Red" Clingman, "deaf as a post, but a great guide," ferried tourists to Johns Pass, where Mrs. Clingman served stone-crab dinners on picnic tables.

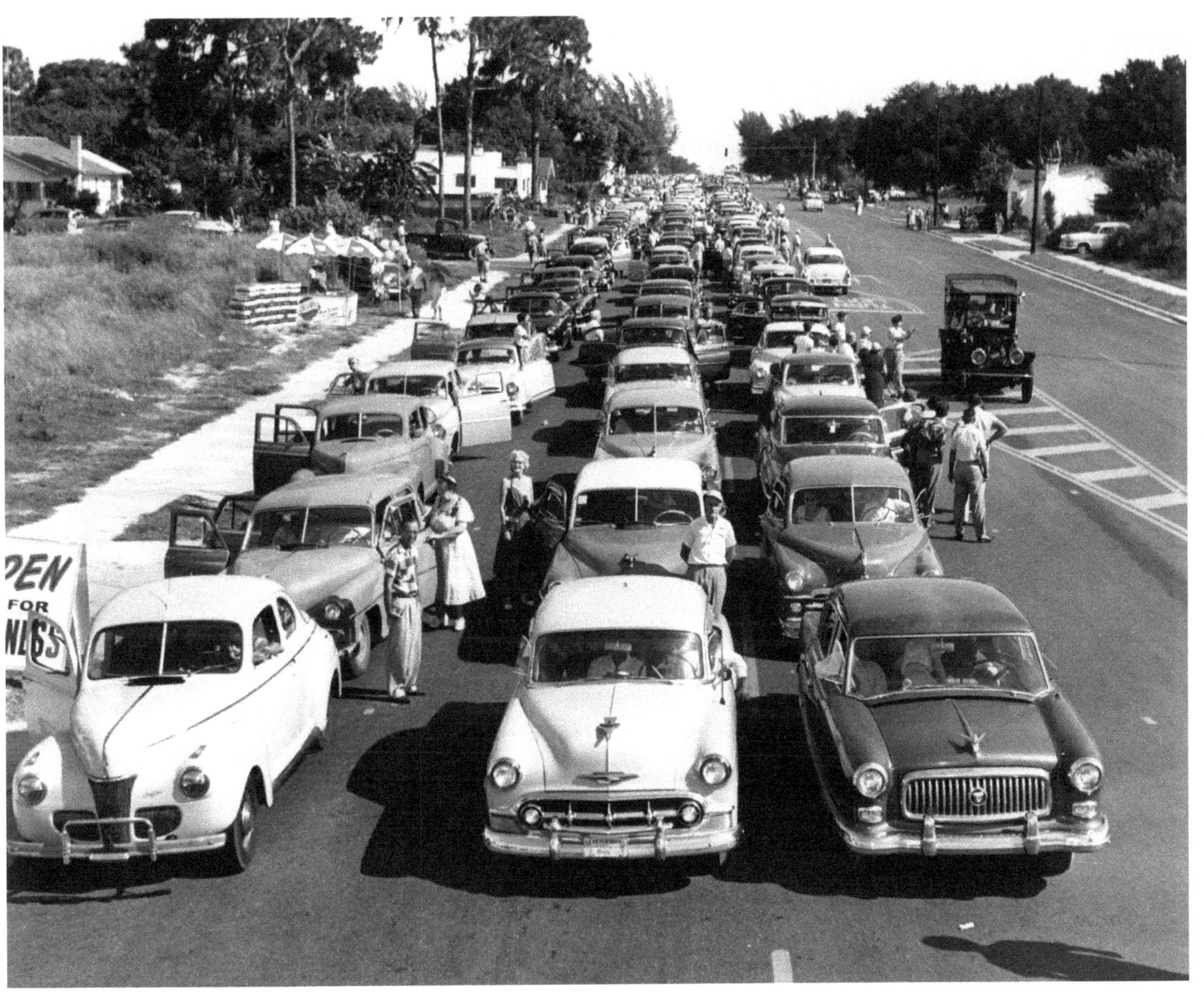

Residents of St. Petersburg eagerly await the opening of the Sunshine Skyway bridge linking Pinellas County roads to the south and Sarasota. Thousands of cars waited on new U.S. 19 to cross the fifteen-mile-long, $22 million bridge. It was a toll bridge, but was free until 11:00 P.M. More than fifteen thousand vehicles made the trip in the first 11 hours.

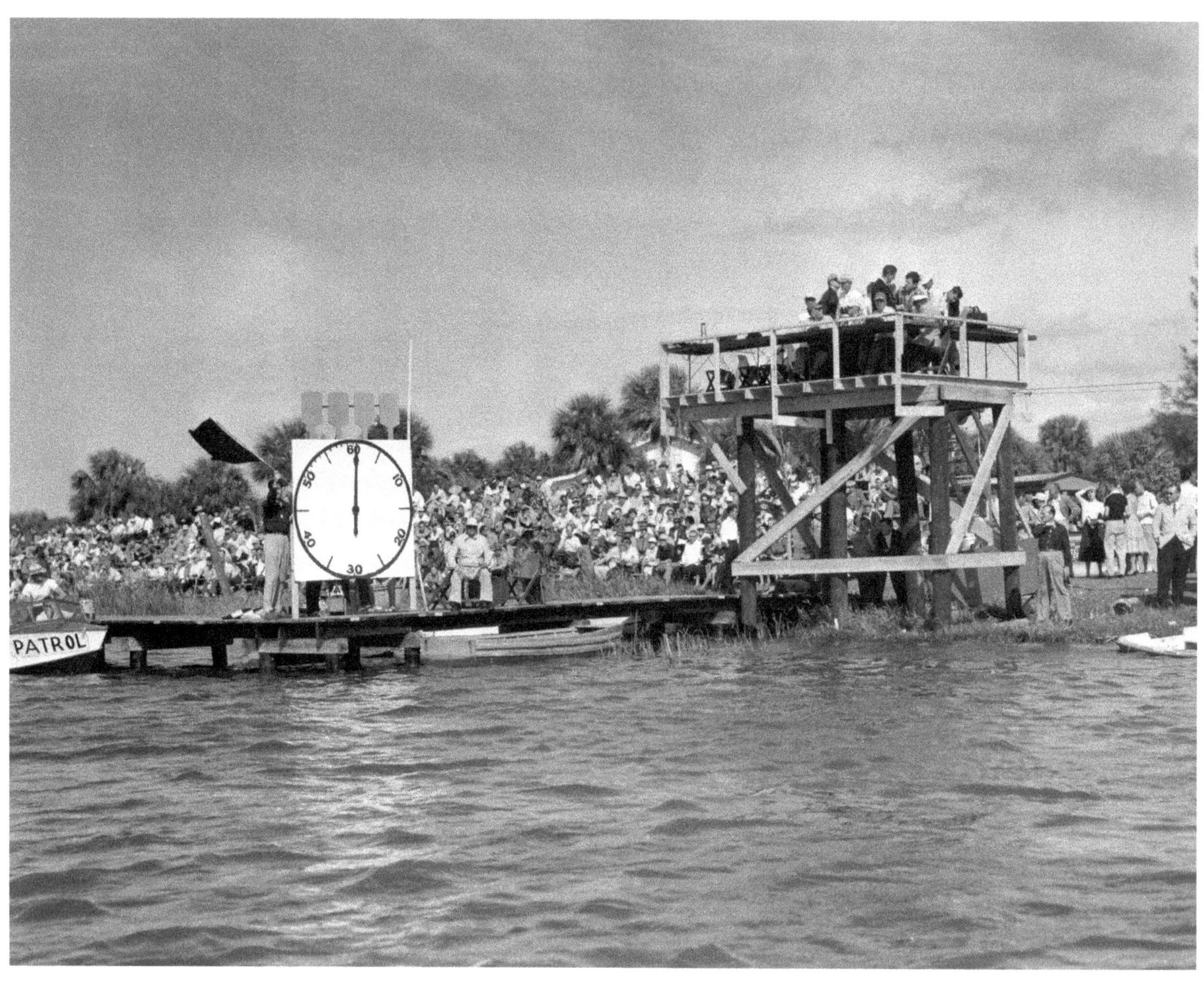

A flag is waved at the judges' stand for the 1955 Southland Sweepstakes Regatta held at the race course on Lake Maggiore. The race chairman controlled the race from the judges' stand. When all was ready, the signal was given to the dock manager to fire the cannon, raise the "five-minute" red flag, and start the clock.

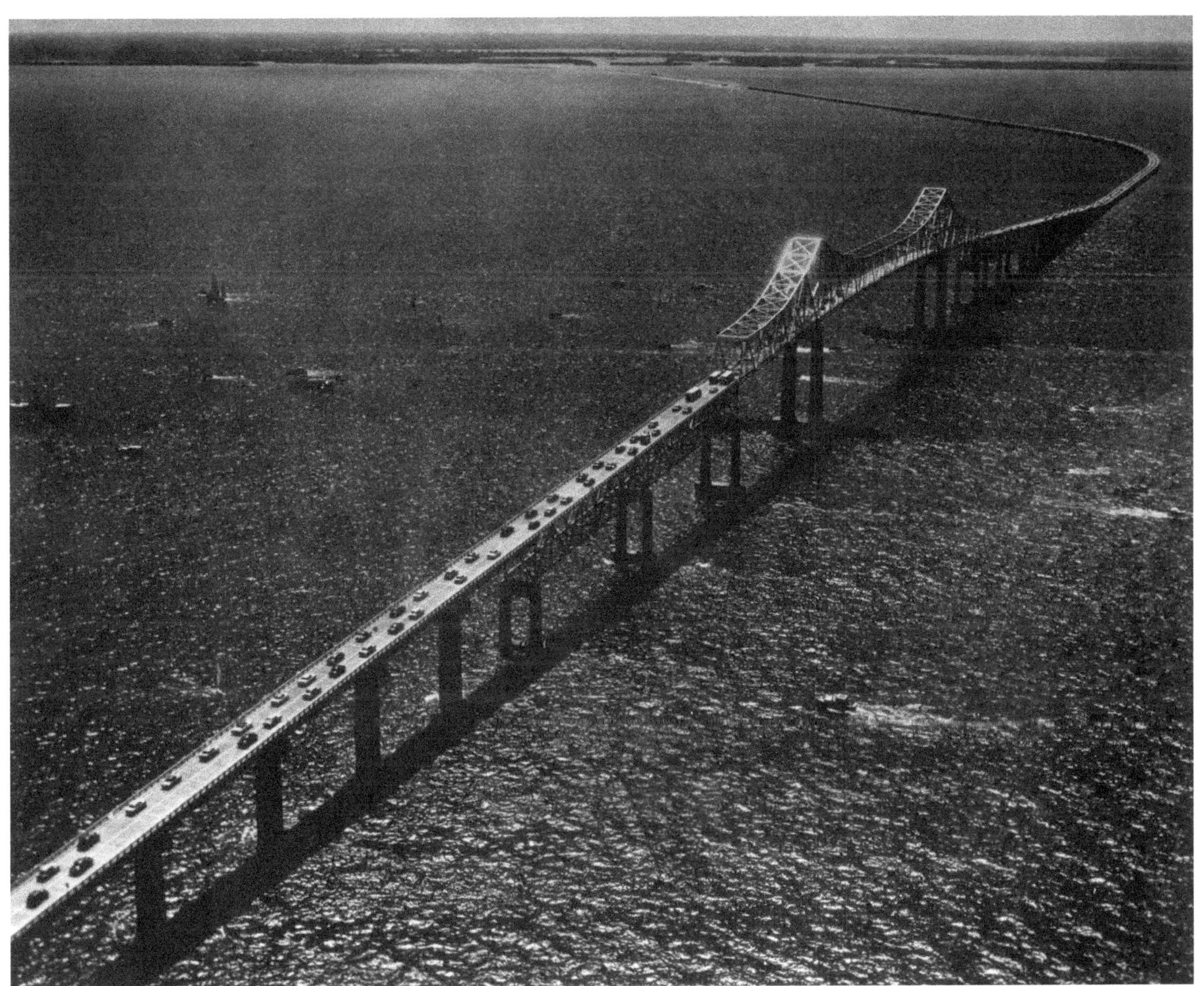

Construction started in 1950 on the original Sunshine Skyway Bridge, to replace the old Bea Line Ferry. It opened with a dedication ceremony on Labor Day 1954 and is shown here in 1955. A second span was completed in 1971 but was struck by the *Summit Venture* in 1980, taking 35 lives. A new Sunshine Parkway Bridge was dedicated February 7, 1987.

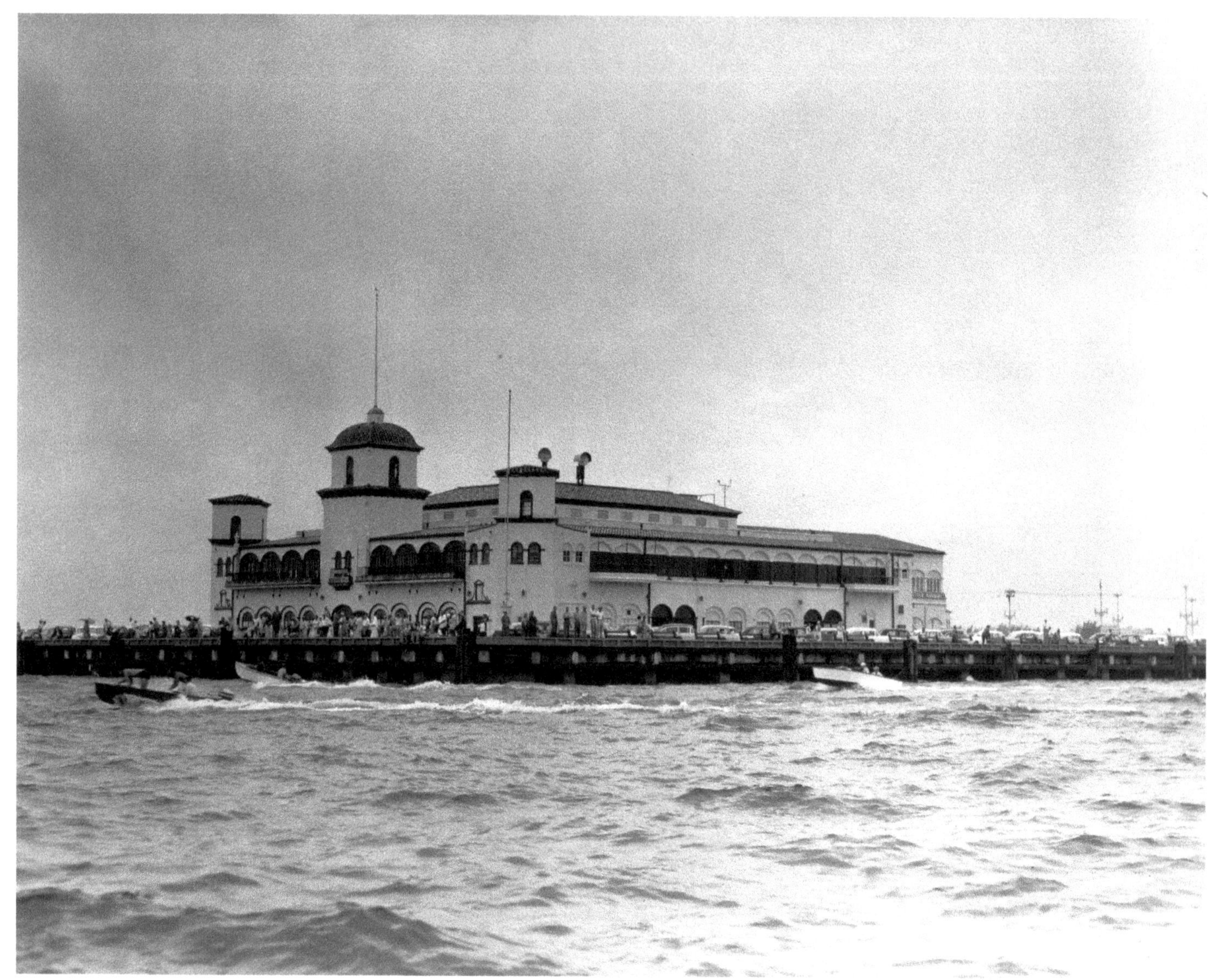

“Live, from the Million Dollar Pier . . .” The colorful history of the pier included its stint as a television studio. For two years, starting in 1953, St. Petersburg’s only TV station, the city-owned WSUN-TV, broadcast from the site. The studios of Channel 38 were located in a former trolley turnaround. This image shows the pier as it looked in 1956.

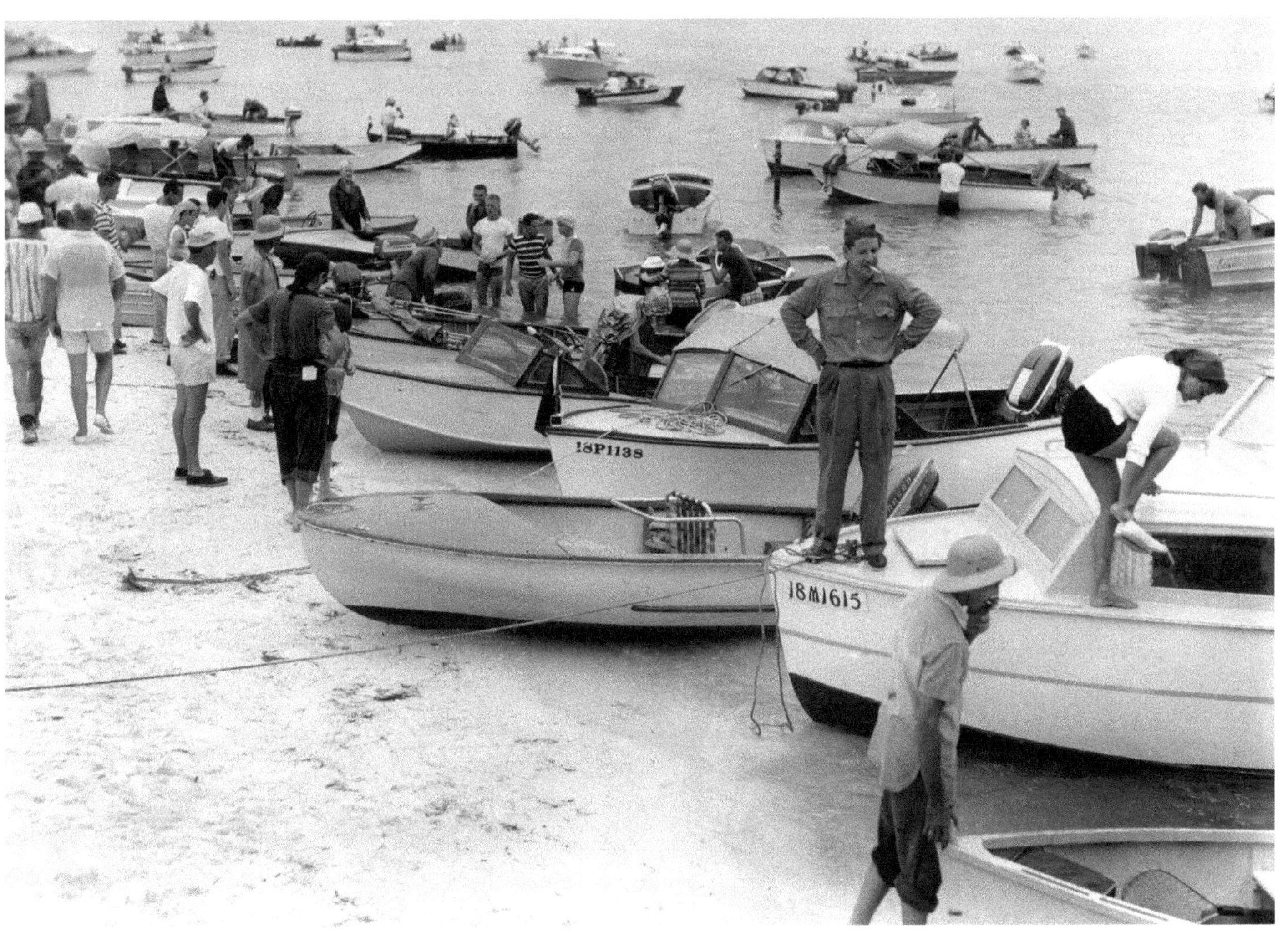

Boaters prepare to embark on a treasure hunt, equipped with pith helmets, khakis, and cigars. The suggested apparel for the Sunshine City: women should wear pedal pushers, shorts, and bathing suits; sports clothes for men; and for the children—let them go barefoot!

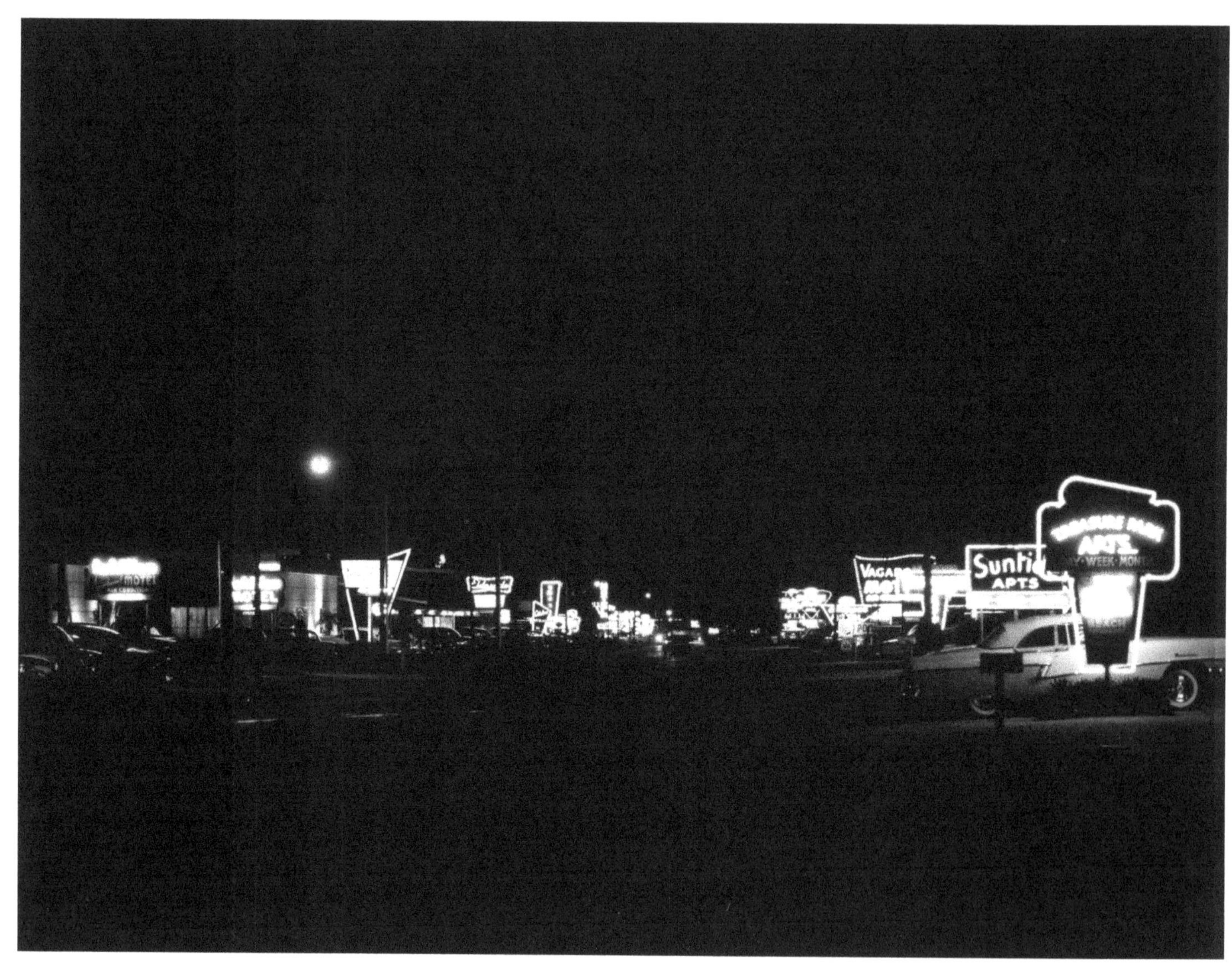

Neon signs glow at night on Gulf Boulevard in October 1958. By that time the old motor courts had transformed from isolated little cottages to a single multi-room structure illuminated by neon lights and referred to as the "motel." As families became more mobile and traveled the highways, motels began to compete with the elegant large hotels.

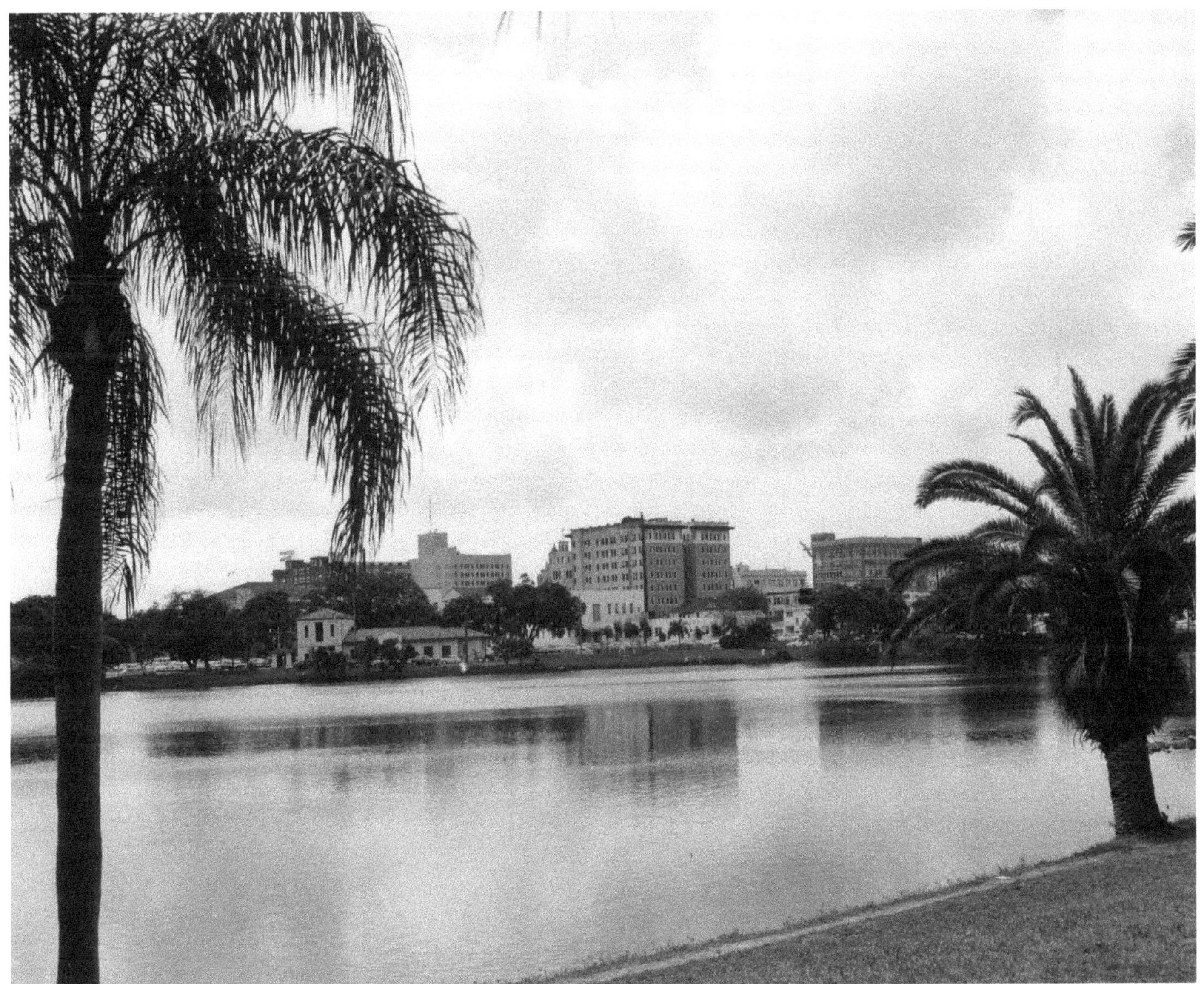

By the late fifties, St. Petersburg's first major industries had little impact on its skyline. Four aerospace industries had built plants in the outlying areas, adding more than four thousand jobs. In 1959, the city had a population of around 180,000, among which were 83,700 employees earning an average of $2,863 a year.

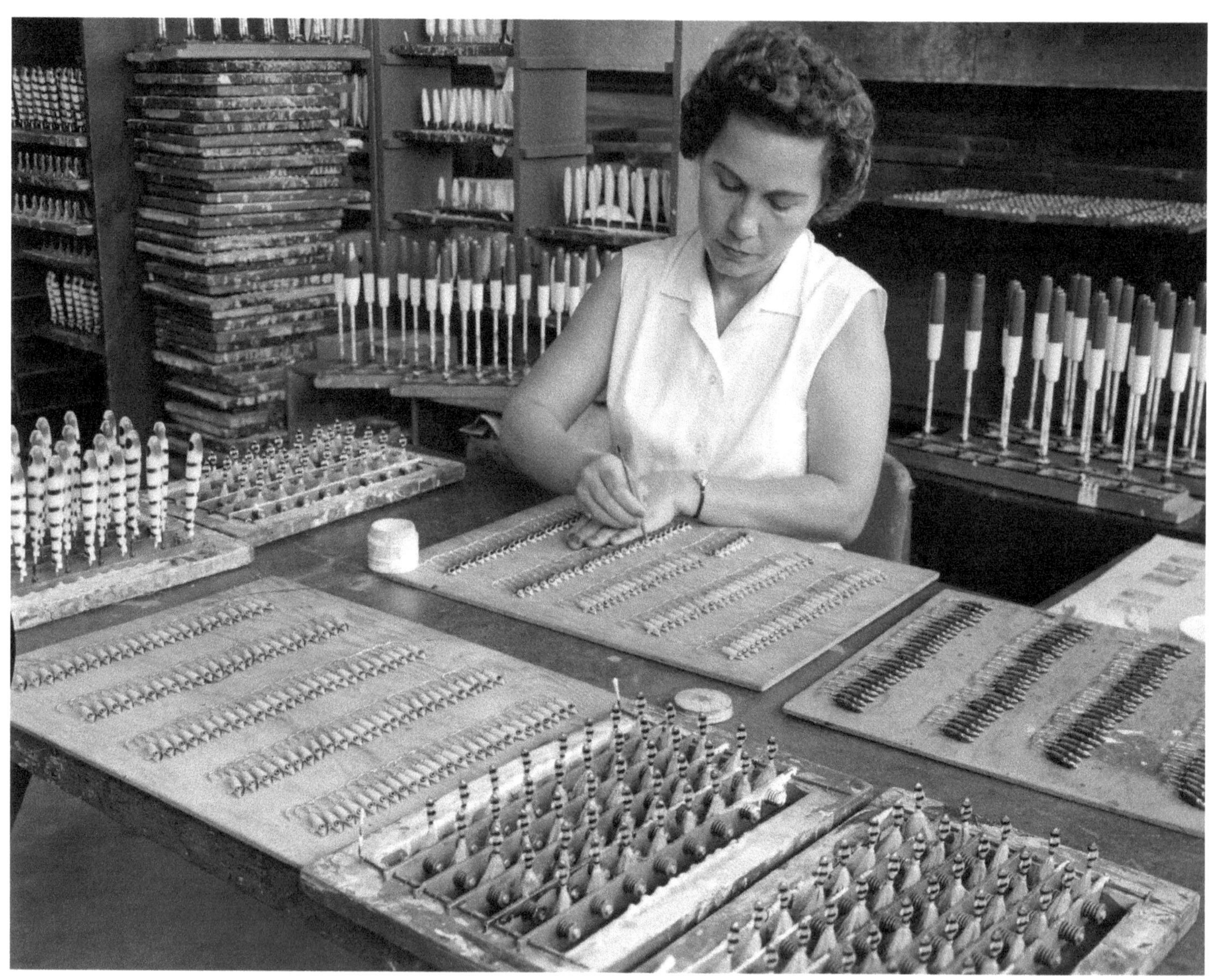

An employee handpaints jigs at the Florida Fishing Tackle manufacturing company. Founded by Jack Reynolds, the company made fishing lures from the late 1920s to the 1970s. The earliest Barracuda Brand lures had glass eyes.

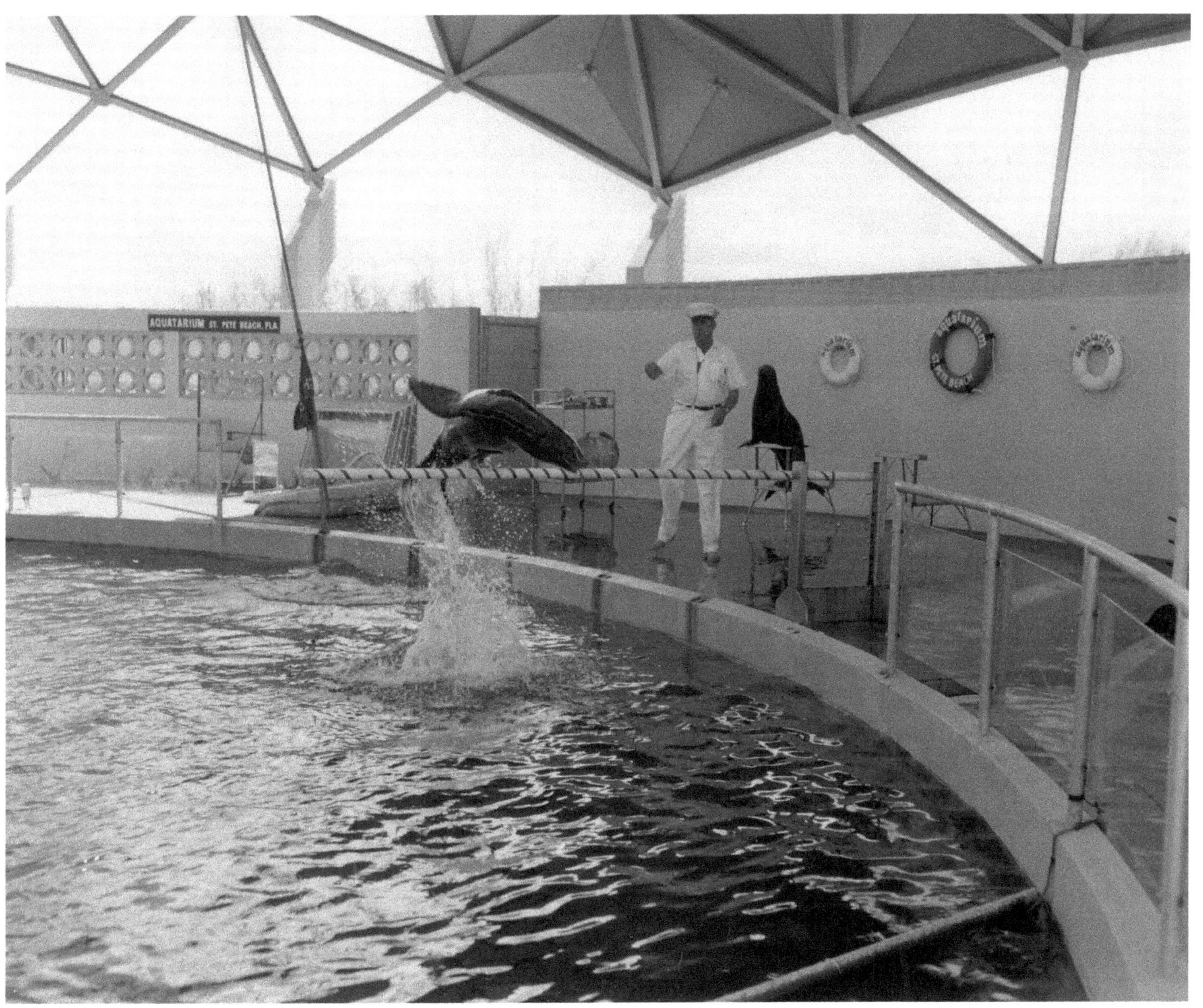

The Aquatarium, located on St. Petersburg Beach, opened in 1964 under the "Golden Dome," a 160-foot-tall golden geodesic dome. The attraction showcased trained porpoises, sea lions, and pilot whales. At the time it claimed to have the world's largest tank, holding more than 1.2 million gallons of seawater. Admission in 1964 was $2.20 for adults and $1.10 for children.

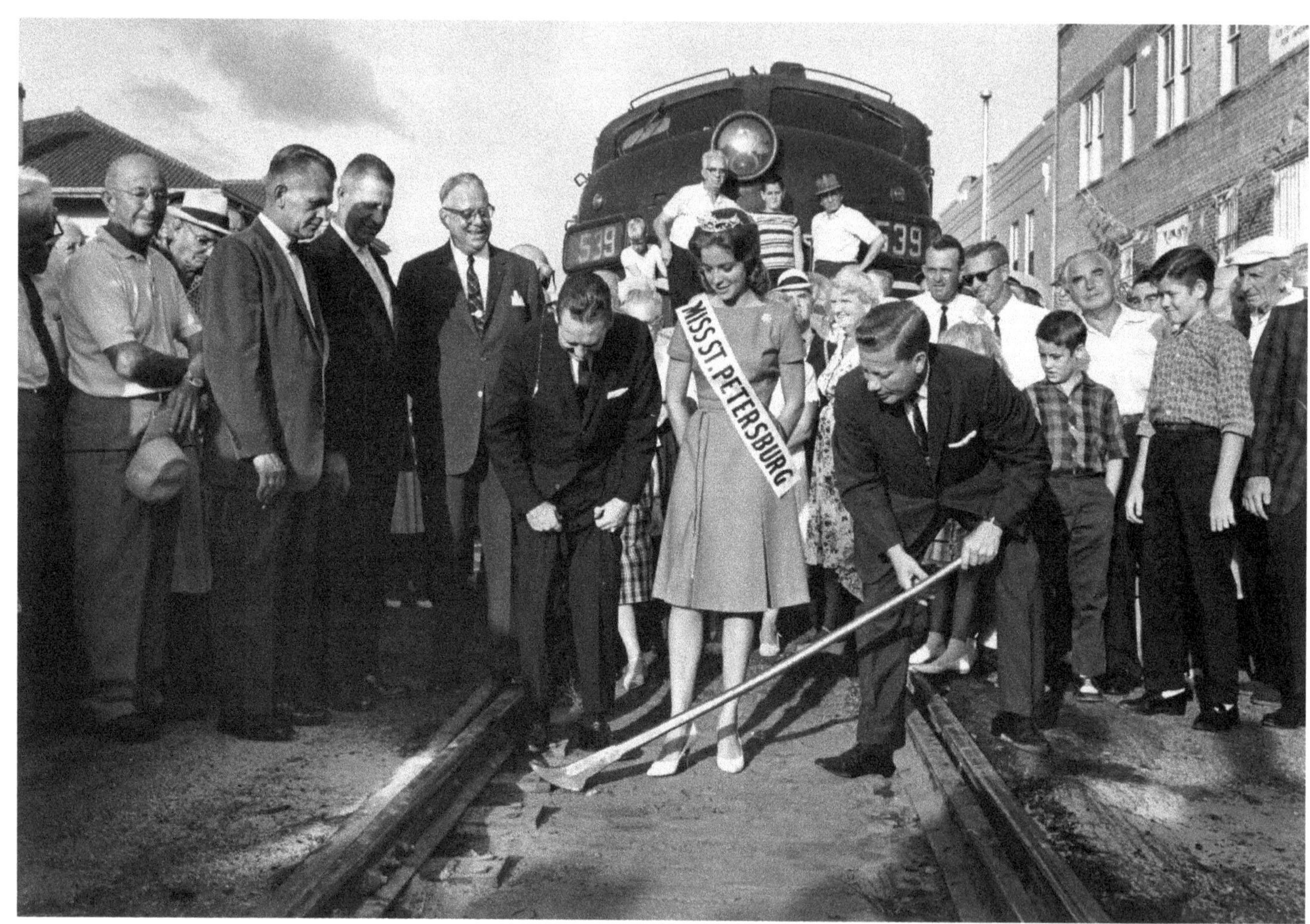

Although the railroads were instrumental in the founding of St. Petersburg, in the early 1960s the city pushed to remove the lines from downtown because the First Avenue track was hindering expansion. In this 1963 ceremony, the last train leaves downtown as Miss St. Petersburg, Diana Gregory, watches Mayor Herman Goldner pulling up a railroad tie.

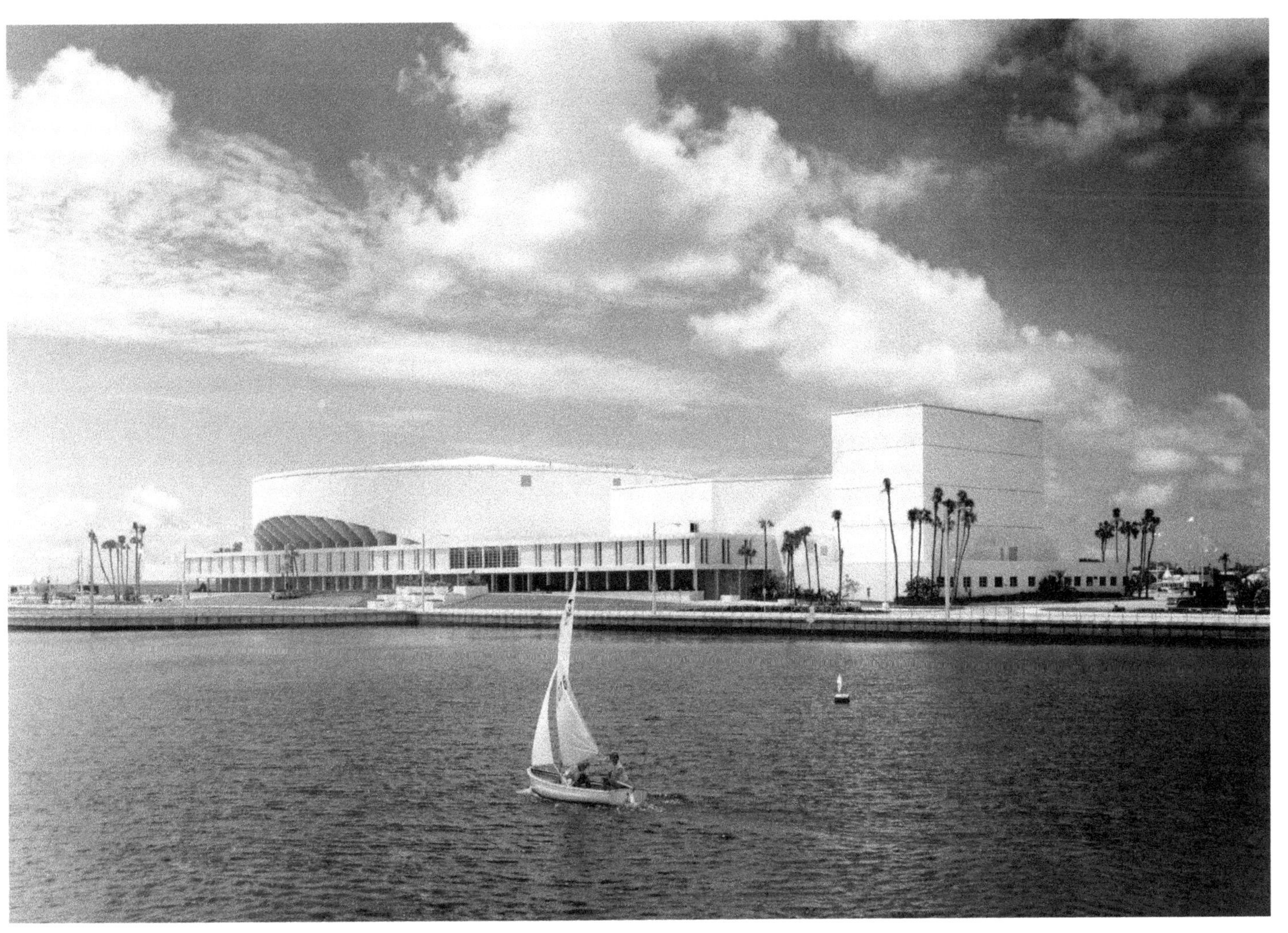

A sailboat glides past the new $5 million St. Petersburg Municipal Auditorium, opened in 1965. Named the Bayfront Center, its arena and theater offered the city a new venue for entertainment and cultural events, sometimes held concurrently. One evening, a group of spectators attended pro wrestling while another audience listened to the Florida Orchestra.

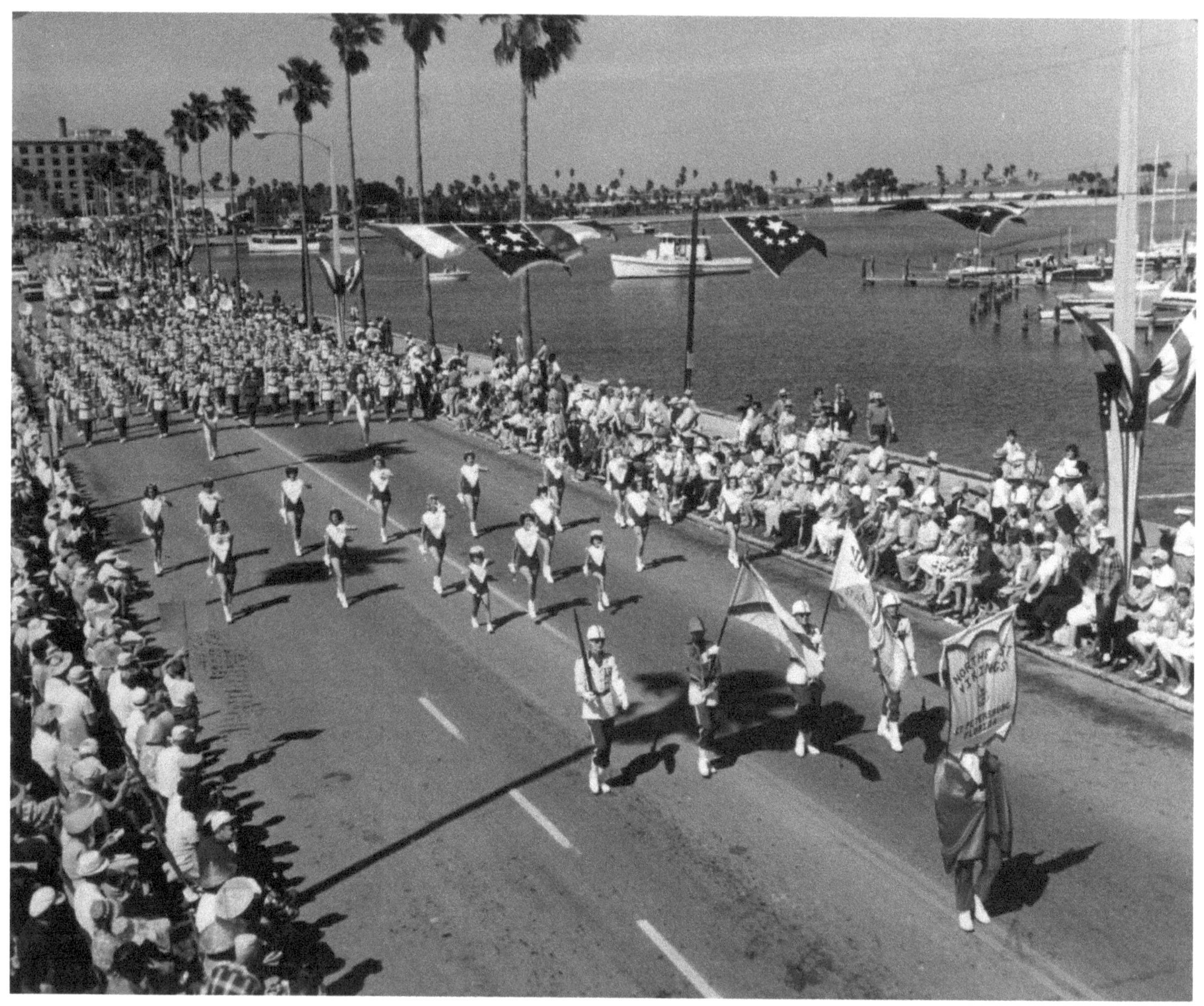

The Northeast High School band in the 1966 Festival of States parade. One of the city's oldest traditions, the festival has offered an assortment of events, including a circus, rodeo, fencing, water skiing, pro tennis, folksingers, opera, and square dancing.

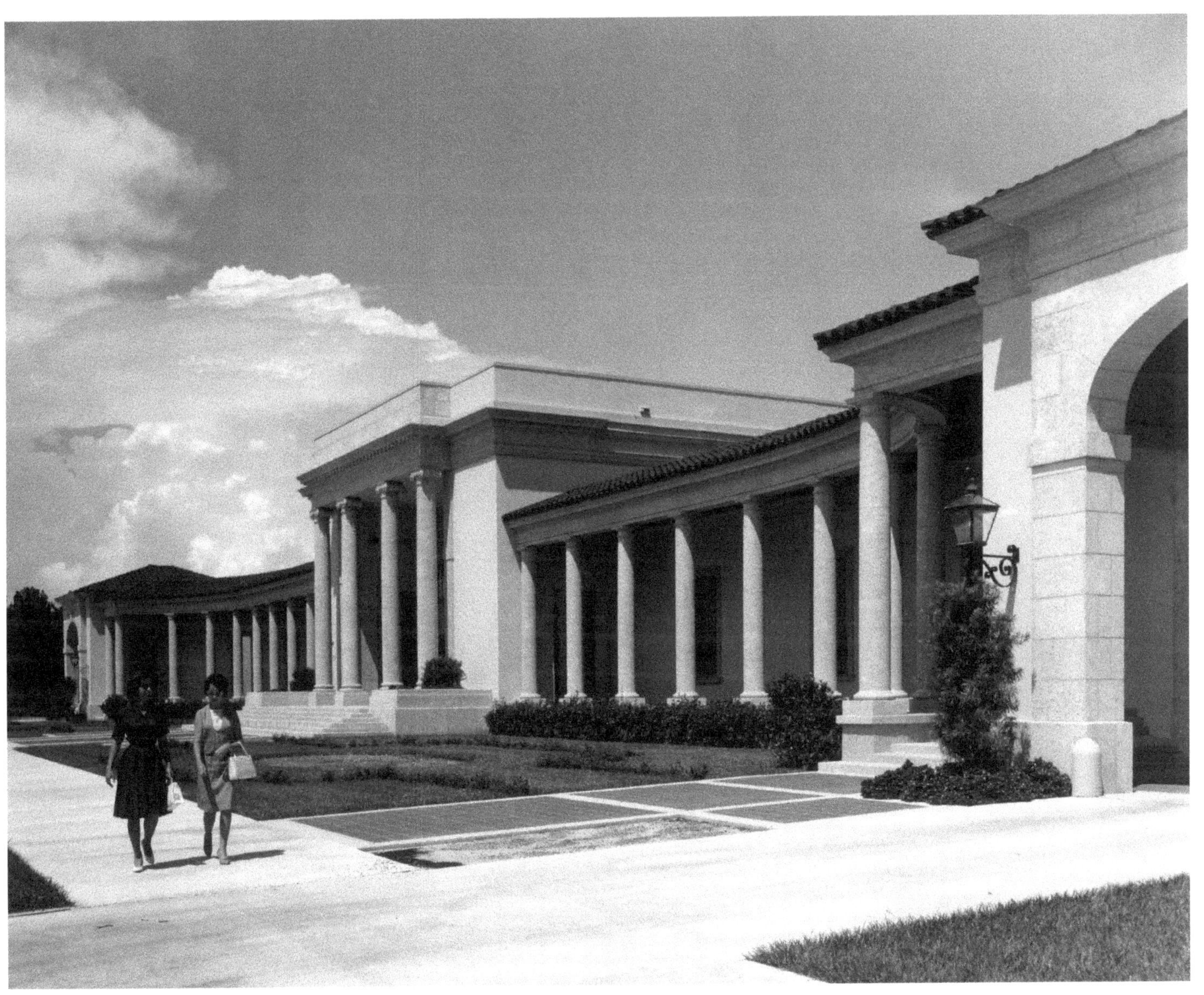

Visitors to the newly opened Museum of Fine Arts in 1966 were treated to George Bingham's scene of Daniel Boone, and works by Cezanne, Monet, O'Keefe, and Whistler. The impressive collection of more than 4,000 objects was made possible through the efforts of Margaret Acheson Stuart and housed in this elegant Palladian-style building in Waterfront Park.

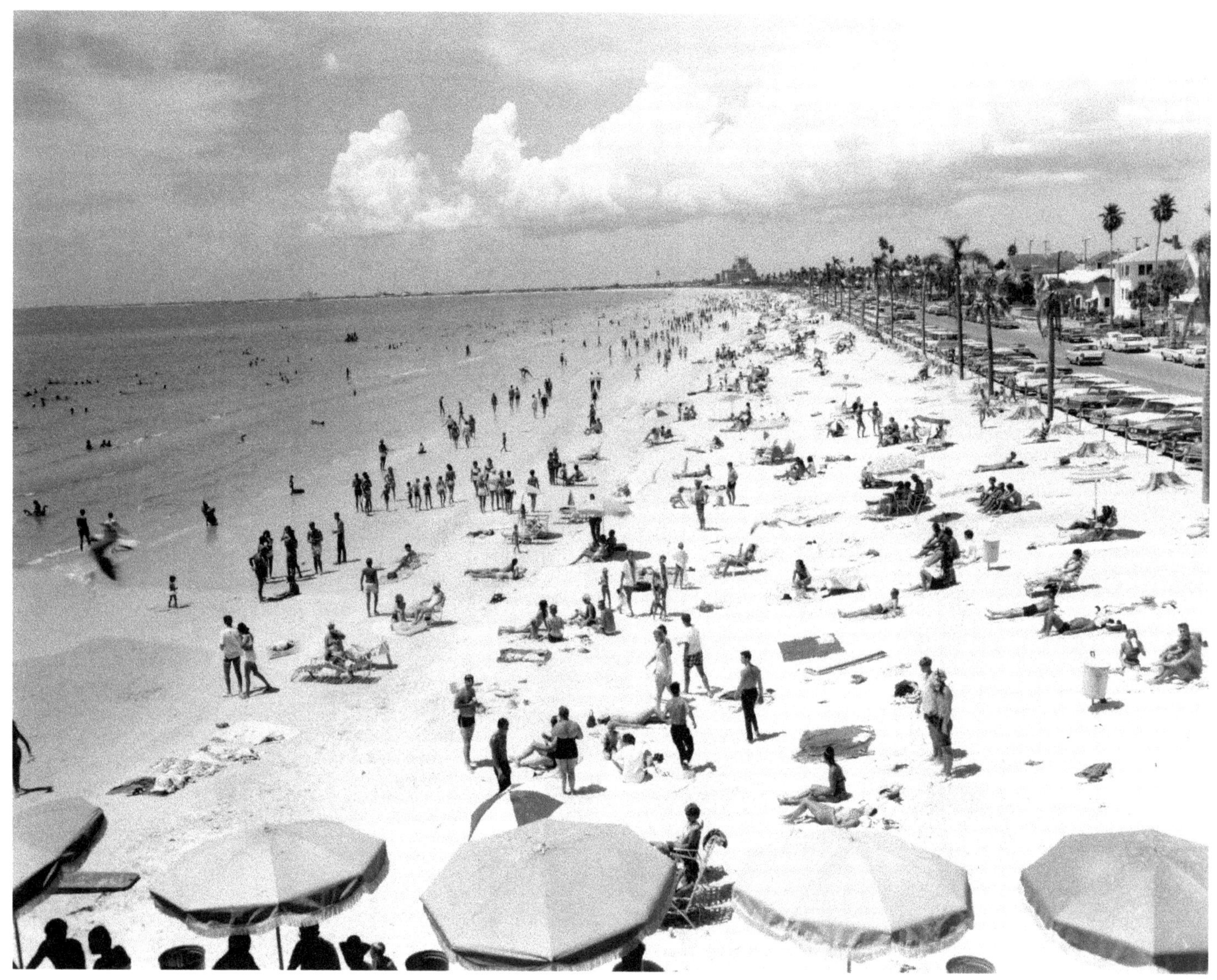

In 1950, the entire population of Long Key numbered only 3,293; by 1960 it had risen to nearly 20,000, prompting a push for consolidation. Despite heavy opposition the measure passed, by only five votes. On July 9, 1957, Belle Vista, Pass-A-Grille, Don CeSar Place, and "old" St. Petersburg Beach were consolidated to become the new St. Petersburg Beach.

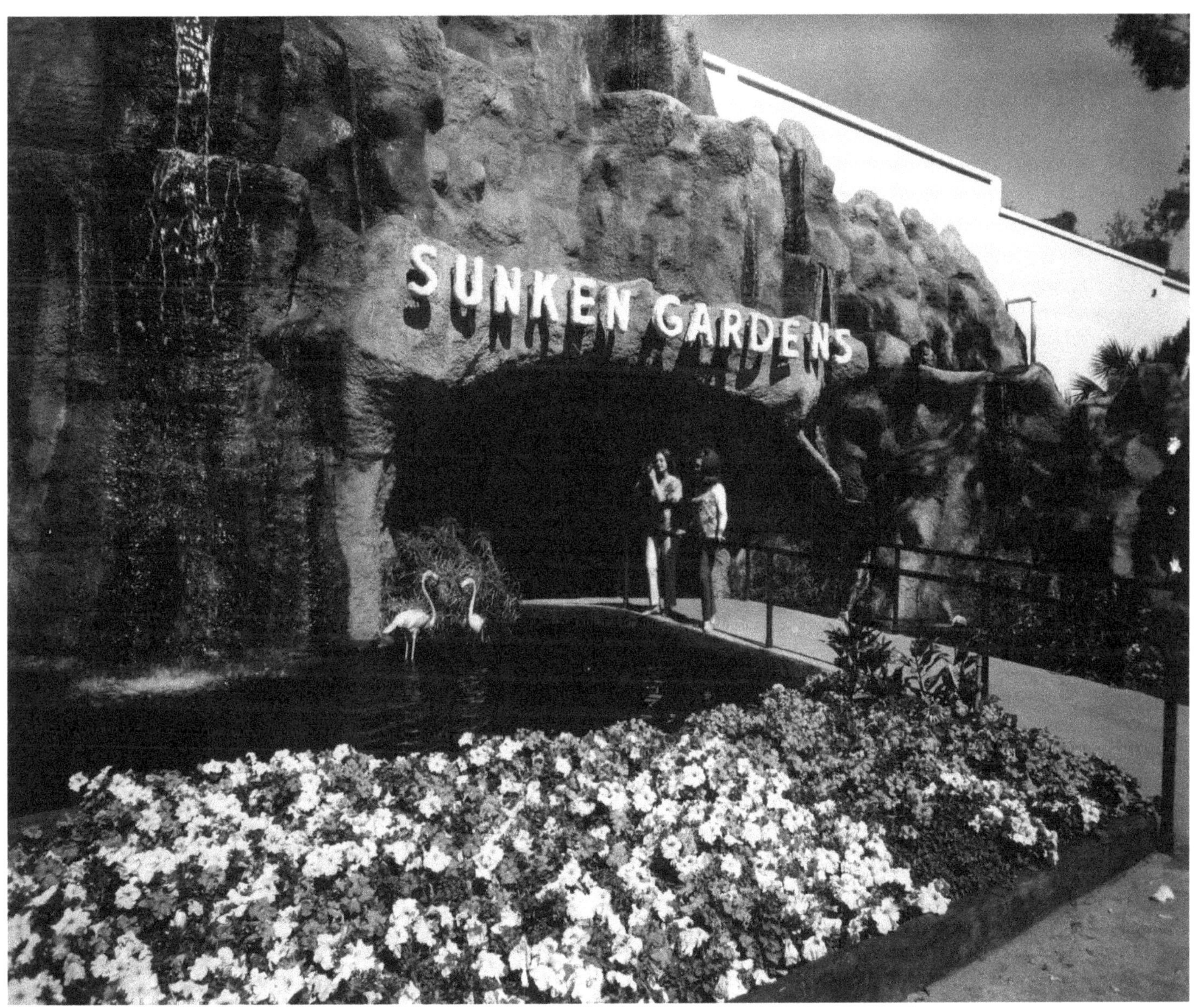

Exotic Sunken Gardens, the oldest commercial tourist attraction on Florida's west coast, was one of Florida's top ten tourist attractions in the 1960s, with 250,000 visitors annually. In 1903, George Turner, a plumber, started the botanical garden around the sinkhole and shallow pond on his property. Eventually, he started charging a nickel for tours.

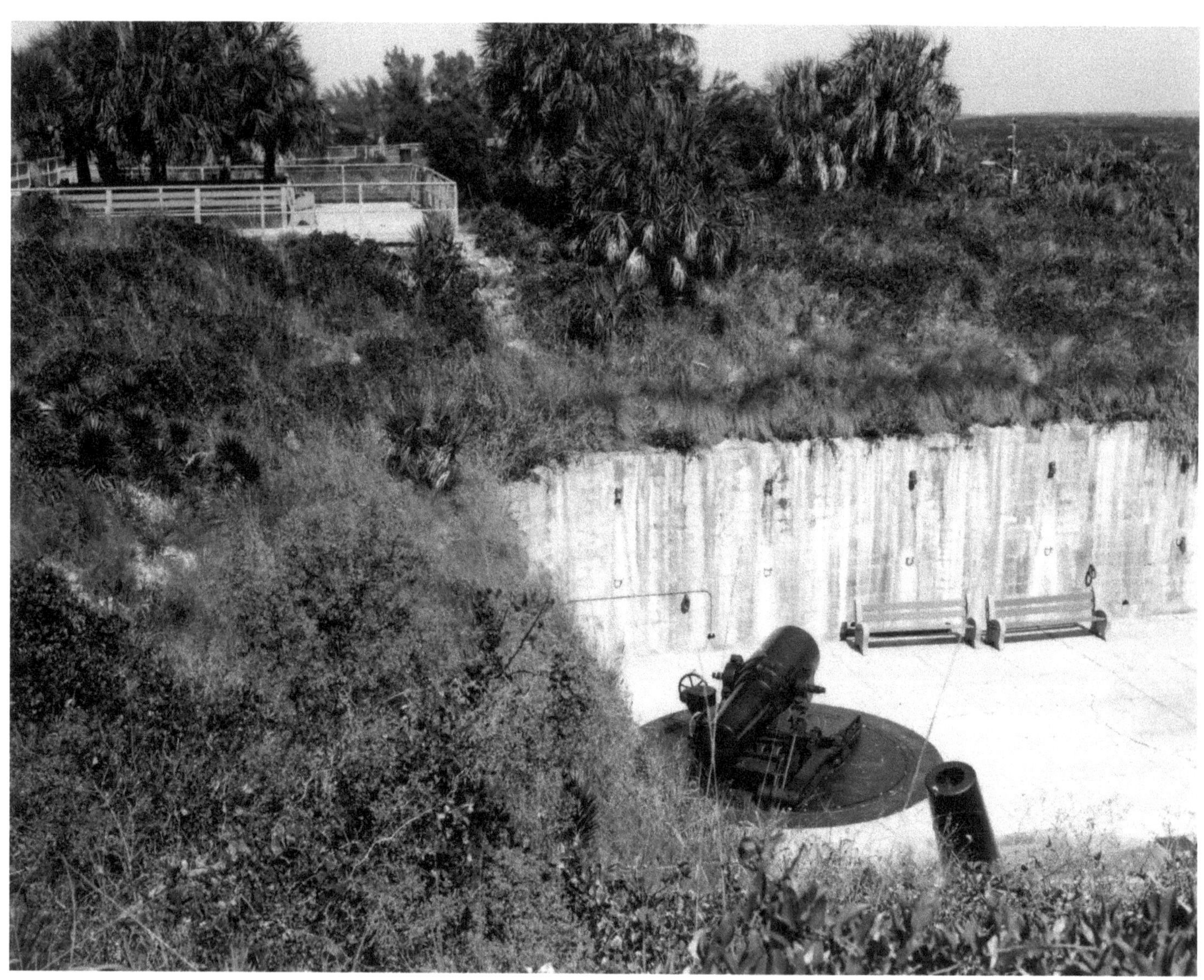

Operated by Pinellas County, Fort De Soto Park, dedicated in 1963, consists of five offshore keys. The island's rich history traces from the Tocobaga Indians and includes Spanish explorers, the Civil War, the Spanish-American War, and both World Wars. The fort's construction began in 1898. Armed with eight 12-inch mortars, the fort never saw combat.

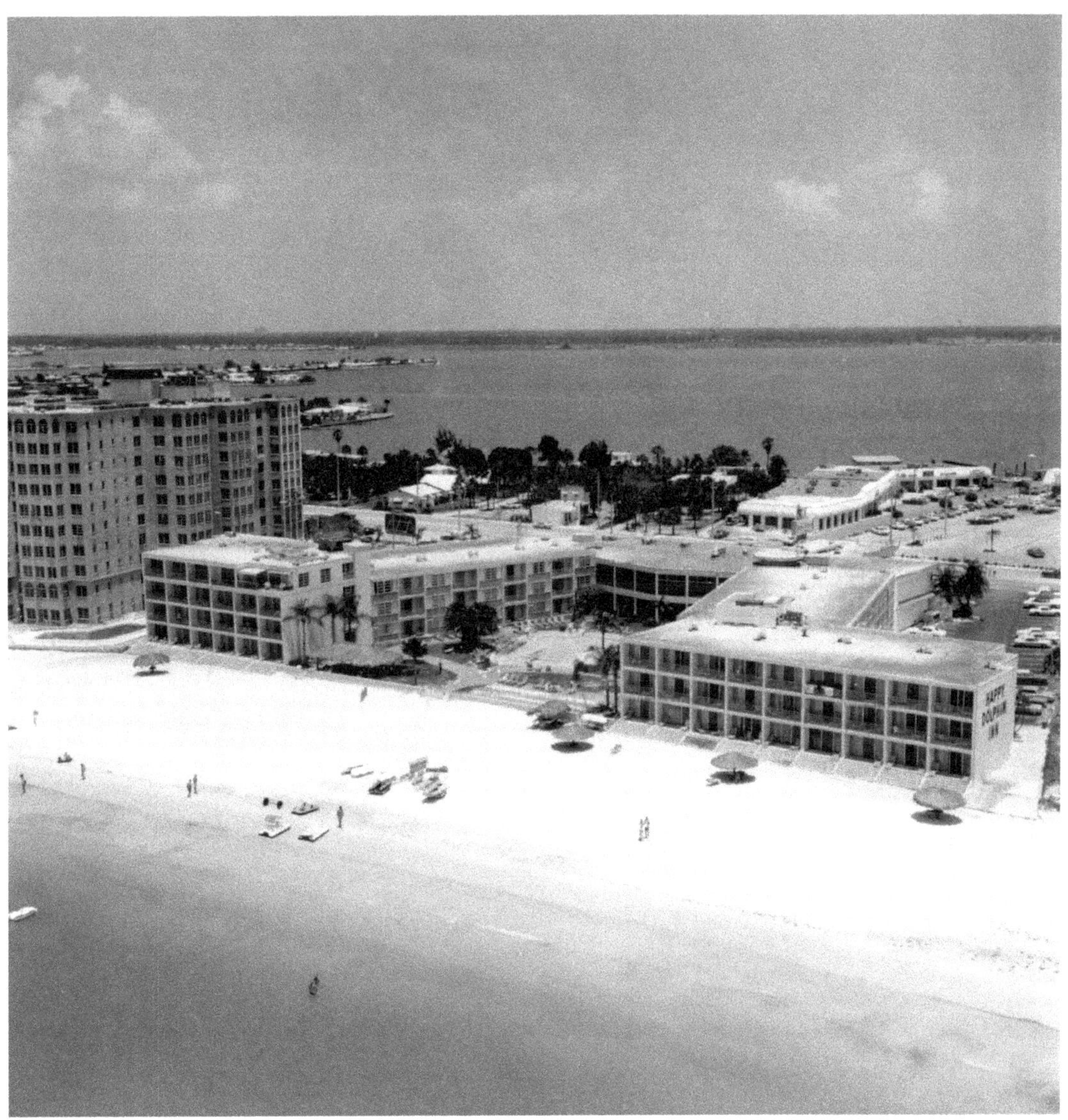

Fittingly, the very first Miami Dolphins team held their initial training camp at the Happy Dolphin Inn on St. Petersburg Beach in 1966. In the ocean lot across the street, the players used a makeshift practice field. One rookie recalled, "Sod right on the blowing sand, along with the gulls, and seashells, and bikinis that came with it." This is a view of the beach in 1972.

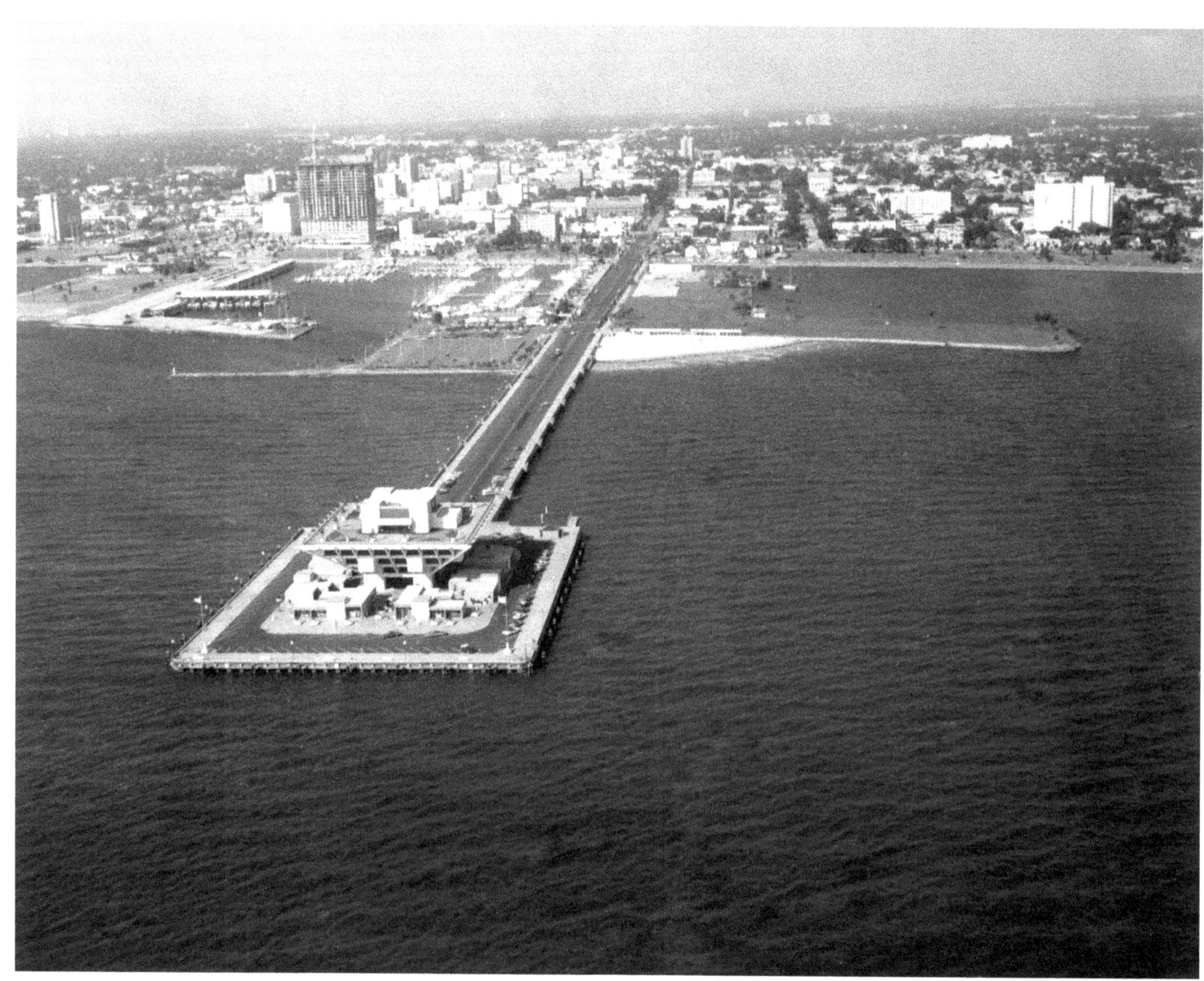

In 1973, the new landmark pier, with its distinctive inverted pyramid design, replaced the 40-year-old, Million Dollar Pier, which was demolished. Activities at the new pier are still a social focal point of the community, a tradition started with the first Orange Belt Railway pier in 1889.

Notes on the Photographs

These notes, listed by page number, attempt to include all aspects known of the photographs. Each of the photographs is identified by the page number, photograph's title or description, photographer and collection, archive, and call or box number when applicable. Although every attempt was made to collect all available data, in some cases complete data was unavailable due to the age and condition of some of the photographs and records.

II **Skyline**
Courtesy of St. Petersburg Museum of History
RC19753

VI **Type XIII Flying Boat**
Courtesy of St. Petersburg Museum of History
P00056

X **MGM Bounty**
Courtesy of St. Petersburg Museum of History
C672148

3 **General Store**
Courtesy of St. Petersburg Museum of History
P02174

4 **First Post Office**
Courtesy of St. Petersburg Museum of History
P05547

5 **Derailment**
Courtesy of St. Petersburg Museum of History
P00012

6 **Men with Bicycle**
State Archives of Florida
N047556

7 **Women's Relief Corps**
Courtesy of St. Petersburg Museum of History
P07382

8 **Turtles**
Courtesy of St. Petersburg Museum of History
P02176

9 **Detroit Hotel**
Courtesy of St. Petersburg Museum of History
P00920

10 **Sanford & St. Petersburg Railway Company**
State Archives of Florida
RC12940

11 **Sixth Avenue**
State Archives of Florida
203

12 **Bayfront from Orange Belt Railway**
State Archives of Florida
RC02302

13 **Lakeview House**
Courtesy of St. Petersburg Museum of History
P00288

14 **The Swale**
Courtesy of St. Petersburg Museum of History
P01203

15 **James G. Bradshaw's Drugstore**
Courtesy of St. Petersburg Museum of History
P00701

16 **Central Avenue**
Courtesy of St. Petersburg Museum of History
P00437

17 **Hubert and Walter Coleman**
State Archives of Florida
N047522

18 **Lake Weir**
Courtesy of St. Petersburg Museum of History
P04630

19 **Golf Course**
Courtesy of St. Petersburg Museum of History
P01122

20 **Schoolchildren**
Courtesy of St. Petersburg Museum of History
P01502

21 **Fair and Winter Exposition**
State Archives of Florida
RC05677

22 **Long Key**
Courtesy of St. Petersburg Museum of History
P05127

23 **Bird's Eye**
Courtesy of St. Petersburg Museum of History
RC07462

24 **Washington's Birthday Celebration**
Courtesy of St. Petersburg Museum of History
P00573

26 **Fife-and-Drum and Military Cadets**
Courtesy of St. Petersburg Museum of History
P01750

27 **1902 Classroom**
Courtesy of St. Petersburg Museum of History
P06991

28 **Syrup Shop**
Courtesy of St. Petersburg Museum of History
P00646

29 **Domestic Science and Manual Training School**
Courtesy of St. Petersburg Museum of History
P00215

30 **Orange Belt Railway and Pier**
State Archives of Florida
RC05681

31 **Effie Stone Rolfs**
State Archives of Florida
N048854

32 **First National Bank**
State Archives of Florida
RC19745

33 **Central Avenue Parade**
State Archives of Florida
PC3949

34 **Town's First Trolley**
Courtesy of St. Petersburg Museum of History
P01551

35 **Ox Cart**
State Archives of Florida
RC05678

36 **Detroit Hotel and Trolley**
Courtesy of St. Petersburg Museum of History
P00499

37 **Williams Park**
State Archives of Florida
N027011

38 **Park Day**
Courtesy of St. Petersburg Museum of History
P00241

39 **Shell Fence**
State Archives of Florida
PC4011

40 **Fire Station at First**
State Archives of Florida
N047520

41 **Young Hubert and Walter Coleman**
State Archives of Florida
N047532

42 **Foley and Fisher Real Estate**
Courtesy of St. Petersburg Museum of History
P01856

43 **Greeting**
Courtesy of St. Petersburg Museum of History
P00172

44 **Bottling Works**
Courtesy of St. Petersburg Museum of History
P03012

45 **Roads**
Courtesy of St. Petersburg Museum of History
P00766

46 **Marine Supply Store**
Courtesy of St. Petersburg Museum of History
P02539

47 **United Confederate Veterans**
Courtesy of St. Petersburg Museum of History
P00102

48 **Fountain of Youth**
Courtesy of St. Petersburg Museum of History
P01749

49 **Car**
State Archives of Florida
N040203

50 **Steamship Manatee**
State Archives of Florida
N040673

51 **Decorated Horse**
Courtesy of St. Petersburg Museum of History
P00248

52 **William "Alligator Man" Carpenter**
Courtesy of St. Petersburg Museum of History
P02322

53 **Automobile Town**
State Archives of Florida
PR09628

54 **Detroit Hotel**
Library of Congress
LC-USZ62-119761

56 **Students**
Courtesy of St. Petersburg Museum of History
P00300

57 **Crowd**
Courtesy of St. Petersburg Museum of History
P00322

58 **Fair and Tourist Week**
Courtesy of St. Petersburg Museum of History
P01323

59 **Benoist Type XIV Flying Boat**
State Archives of Florida
P00056

60 **Flight of Benoist**
Courtesy of St. Petersburg Museum of History
P00944

61 **St. Petersburg Police Department**
Courtesy of St. Petersburg Museum of History
P00784

62 **Browns-Phillies Baseball Game**
Courtesy of St. Petersburg Museum of History
P01363

63 **Levine Family**
State Archives of Florida
MS25825

64 **Ambulance**
State Archives of Florida
PR13536

65 **The Municipal Recreation Pier**
State Archives of Florida
N047900

66 **Soldiers**
State Archives of Florida
N047891

69 **Central Avenue**
State Archives of Florida
PC3952

70 **Biplane**
Courtesy of St. Petersburg Museum of History
P01184

71 **Bathers**
State Archives of Florida
N040025

72 **Rebuilding Pier**
State Archives of Florida
N040114

73 Million Dollar Pier
Courtesy of St. Petersburg Museum of History
P00905

74 Labor Workers
Courtesy of St. Petersburg Museum of History
P01382

75 Municipal Pier
State Archives of Florida
PC3914

76 Don CeSar Hotel
State Archives of Florida
PR08361

78 Florida Milk Company
Courtesy of St. Petersburg Museum of History
P01651

79 Coliseum Dance Hall
Courtesy of St. Petersburg Museum of History
P02179

80 Band Concert
State Archives of Florida
RC19754

81 Pass-A-Grille Casino
Courtesy of St. Petersburg Museum of History
P01515

82 Fifth Street
State Archives of Florida
RC09303

83 Roser Park
State Archives of Florida
N047886

84 Grocery Store
Courtesy of St. Petersburg Museum of History
P02830

85 Looking East Along Central Avenue
State Archives of Florida
RC00232

86 Pass-A-Grille Casino During Prohibition
Courtesy of St. Petersburg Museum of History
P00877

87 First National Bank
Courtesy of St. Petersburg Museum of History
P06191

88 Spa Beach
Courtesy of St. Petersburg Museum of History
P01403

89 Central Avenue
State Archives of Florida
PC3954

90 Million Dollar Pier
State Archives of Florida
RC06822

91 Playograph
Courtesy of St. Petersburg Museum of History
P01879

92 Jewelry Store
Leon Haliczer Jewelry Store
State Archives of Florida
MS25815

93 Chess-Checker-Domino Club
State Archives of Florida
RC11504

94 Festival of States Parade
State Archives of Florida
N040005

95 Festival of States Parade
State Archives of Florida
N040181

96 Central Avenue Decorated for Festival of States
State Archives of Florida
N047823

97 Fire Department
Courtesy of St. Petersburg Museum of History
P00508

98 Babe Ruth
Courtesy of St. Petersburg Museum of History
P03661

100 Bird's Eye
State Archives of Florida
RC11301

101 Looking South on 5th Street
State Archives of Florida
RC19743

102 The Vinoy
State Archives of Florida
PR09632

103 Dog Races
State Archives of Florida
PR01102

104 Trolley Line
Courtesy of St. Petersburg Museum of History
P02466

105 The Soreno Hotel
State Archives of Florida
RC09292

106 Bird's Eye
State Archives of Florida
PHA123

107 Fourth Street
State Archives of Florida
PHA209

108 Carl Sandburg
Courtesy of St. Petersburg Museum of History
1011

111 Snell Arcade
Courtesy of St. Petersburg Museum of History
P00377

112 Snell Arcade
Courtesy of St. Petersburg Museum of History
P01434

113 Eureka Filling Station
State Archives of Florida
N047547

114 David Rothblatt
State Archives of Florida
MS25738

115 Goodyear Blimp
Courtesy of St. Petersburg Museum of History
P2278

116 Boxing
Courtesy of St. Petersburg Museum of History
P00355

117 Spanish Bob's Nightclub
Courtesy of St. Petersburg Museum of History
P01435

118 Playground
Courtesy of St. Petersburg Museum of History
P01606

119 Crowded Sidewalk
State Archives of Florida
RC000121

120 Bank Run
State Archives of Florida
RC06538

121 Buster Keaton and Molly O'Day
Courtesy of St. Petersburg Museum of History
P2132

122 Million Dollar High School
State Archives of Florida
N040161

123 Day's Catch
Courtesy of St. Petersburg Museum of History
P01128

124 The Florida Military Academy
Courtesy of St. Petersburg Museum of History
P01207

125 First Baptist Church
Courtesy of St. Petersburg Museum of History
P00103

126 Fish
Courtesy of St. Petersburg Museum of History
P00396

127 Atlantic Coast Line Railroad
Courtesy of St. Petersburg Museum of History
P00253

128 Giant of an Airplane
State Archives of Florida
RC13100

129 Publicity Shot
Courtesy of St. Petersburg Museum of History
P00822

130 Famous Green Benches
State Archives of Florida
FR0794

132 Harrison's Hardware
Courtesy of St. Petersburg Museum of History
P02662

133 The Plaza Buildings
Courtesy of St. Petersburg Museum of History
P05357

134 Engine
Courtesy of St. Petersburg Museum of History
P01449

135 Cardinals
Courtesy of St. Petersburg Museum of History
P01888

136 Coca-Cola
State Archives of Florida
N040165

137 Aerial View of Downtown
Courtesy of St. Petersburg Museum of History
P00261

138 City from Whitted Airport
Courtesy of St. Petersburg Museum of History
P00029

139 Equitable Building
Courtesy of St. Petersburg Museum of History
P01818

140 Card Tournament at Mirror Lake Park
State Archives of Florida
N040118

141 Central Avenue
Courtesy of St. Petersburg Museum of History
P02618

142 National Airlines over the Everglades
State Archives of Florida
P04316

143 Southland Sweepstakes Regatta
Courtesy of St. Petersburg Museum of History
P00409

144 Sailboat Race
Courtesy of St. Petersburg Museum of History
P01351

145 Women's Club of Largo
Courtesy of St. Petersburg Museum of History
P2182

146 Boy Scout Troop
Courtesy of St. Petersburg Museum of History
P00824

149 Coliseum Dance
Courtesy of St. Petersburg Museum of History
P02211

150 Festival of States Parade
Courtesy of St. Petersburg Museum of History
P00235

151 Volunteer
State Archives of Florida
N044852

152 Women's Army Auxiliary Corps
Courtesy of St. Petersburg Museum of History
P01902

153 Army Air Corps Trainees
Courtesy of St. Petersburg Museum of History
P06019

154 Soldiers Training
Courtesy of St. Petersburg Museum of History
P01913

156 Women's Air Force Service
Courtesy of St. Petersburg Museum of History
P03137

157 Donkey Baseball
Courtesy of St. Petersburg Museum of History
P03137

158 War Bond Drive
Courtesy of St. Petersburg Museum of History
P03173

159 Coast Guard
Library of Congress
LC-USW33-026119-C

160 Lifeboat
Library of Congress
LC-USW33-026123-C

161 Hurricane Threat
Courtesy of St. Petersburg Museum of History
P02028

162 **Busy Intersection**
State Archives of Florida
C004126

163 **Green Benches**
State Archives of Florida
C004127

164 **Million Dollar Pier**
State Archives of Florida
C004131

165 **Umbrellas**
State Archives of Florida
C004983

166 **Vinoy Hotel**
State Archives of Florida
C004998

167 **Fifth Street**
State Archives of Florida
C008162

168 **Mirror Lake**
State Archives of Florida
C007958

169 **Sip from the Fountain of Youth**
State Archives of Florida
C008164

170 **Water Skiers**
State Archives of Florida
C007902

171 **St. Petersburg and Gulf Electric Railway**
State Archives of Florida
PR12588

172 **Shorecrest Outdoor School**
State Archives of Florida
C008245

173 **Beauty Contestants 1948**
State Archives of Florida
C008460

174 **Baseball Team on Beach**
State Archives of Florida
C009579

175 **St. Petersburg Children's Fishathon**
State Archives of Florida
C010349

176 **Mirror Lake Park Shuffleboard**
State Archives of Florida
C010904

177 **Eborn School of Dance Art**
State Archives of Florida
C009984

178 **Open-air Post Office**
State Archives of Florida
RC19759

179 **Central Street**
State Archives of Florida
RC13761

180 **St. Petersburg–to–Havana, Cuba**
State Archives of Florida
C017818

181 **Stetson Law School**
State Archives of Florida
C019758

182 **Johns Pass Bridge**
State Archives of Florida
PC3965

183 **Waiting at Sunshine Skyway Bridge**
State Archives of Florida
Rc15466

184 **1955 Southland Sweepstakes Regatta**
State Archives of Florida
C020583

185 **Sunshine Skyway**
State Archives of Florida
C022428

186 **Live from Million Dollar Pier**
State Archives of Florida
C023482

187 **Boaters**
State Archives of Florida
C023481

188 **Gulf Boulevard**
State Archives of Florida
C028735

189 **Skyline**
State Archives of Florida
C030052

190 **Lures**
State Archives of Florida
C036452

191 **The Aquatarium**
State Archives of Florida
C640255

192 **Removing Tracks**
State Archives of Florida
RC18258

193 **Sailboat and St. Petersburg Municipal Auditorium**
State Archives of Florida
C660696

194 **Festival of States Parade**
State Archives of Florida
C660106

195 **Museum of Fine Arts**
State Archives of Florida
C660685

196 **Beach**
State Archives of Florida
C660684

197 **Exotic Sunken Gardens**
State Archives of Florida
C671781

198 **Fort De Soto Park**
State Archives of Florida
C000823

199 **Happy Dolphin Inn**
State Archives of Florida
C679615

200 **Landmark Pier**
State Archives of Florida
C680822

Bibliography

Allyn, Rube. *Visitor's Guide to Attractions on the Florida Suncoast.* St. Petersburg: Great Outdoors, 1966.

Arsenault, Raymond. *St. Petersburg and the Florida Dream, 1888-1950.* Gainesville: University Press of Florida, 1996.

Atchley, J. F. *This Week in St. Petersburg.* Arcade City, Fla.: J. F. Atchley Pub., February 20, 1935.

Deese, A. Wynelle. *St. Petersburg, Florida: A Visual History.* Charleston, S.C.: History Press, 2006.

Fuller, Walter Pliny. *St. Petersburg and Its People.* St. Petersburg: Great Outdoors Pub. Co., 1972.

———. *This Was Florida's Boom.* St. Petersburg: Times Pub. Co., 1954.

Gould, Rita Slaght, and Diane Stewart Tonelli. *Pioneer St. Petersburg: Life in and Around 1888 "Out Near the Back of Beyond."* St. Petersburg: Page Creations, 1987.

Grismer, Karl H. *The Story of St. Petersburg: The History of Lower Pinellas Peninsula and the Sunshine City.* St. Petersburg: P. K. Smith, 1948.

Gulfport Historical Society. *Our Story of Gulfport, Florida.* Gulfport, Fla.: Gulfport Historical Society, 1985.

Hartzell, Scott Taylor. *St. Petersburg: An Oral History.* Voices of America. Charleston, S.C.: Arcadia Pub., 2002.

Hurley, Frank T. *Surf, Sand, and Post Card Sunsets: A History of Pass-a-Grille and the Gulf Beaches.* St. Petersburg Beach: Hurley, 1977.

Jackson, Page S. *An Informal History of St. Petersburg.* St. Petersburg: Great Outdoors Pub. Co., 1962.

Meade, Marion. *Buster Keaton: Cut to the Chase.* New York: HarperCollins, 1995.

Pass-a-Grille: A Patchwork Collection of Memories. Women's Fellowship of Pass-a-Grille Beach Community Church, 1981.

Pinellas County (Fla.) Dept. of Planning. *Historical Background of Pinellas County, Florida.* Clearwater, 1968.

St. Petersburg and Florida's Gulf Coast: Official Guide. St. Petersburg: Griffith Advertising Agency, 1935.

St. Petersburg, Florida: By the Gulf-Stream, in the Land of Health, Opportunity and Fulfilment. St. Petersburg Board of Trade, 1908.

St. Petersburg, Florida: The Sunshine City. St. Petersburg Board of Trade, 1912.

St. Petersburg, Florida: The Sunshine City. St. Petersburg: Chamber of Commerce, 1921.

St. Petersburg, Florida: The Sunshine City. St. Petersburg: Chamber of Commerce, 1928.

Seeing St. Petersburg: A Book of Information for Visitors: Tourist News Pub. Co., 1924.

Straub, William L. *History of Pinellas County, Florida, Narrative and Biographical.* St. Augustine, Fla.: Record Co., printers, 1929.

HISTORIC PHOTOS OF ST. PETERSBURG

Founded in the late nineteenth century as a railroad town, St. Petersburg quickly emerged as the "Sunshine City," a preferred west-coast destination for Americans seeking Florida's sun, sand, and surf.

The images collected in *Historic Photos of St. Petersburg* combine to form a remarkable portrait of this unique community. Among numerous subjects key to the city's past are an early Mirror Lake, the Detroit Hotel, the Million Dollar Pier, the Snell Arcade, shuffleboard courts, Whitted Airport, the Aquatarium, Festival of States parades, the Orange Belt Railway, Roser Park, and of course, the famous green benches.

In stunning black-and-white photography, this handsome coffee-table book details the historical growth of St. Petersburg from its early days up to recent times. Spanning two centuries and nearly 200 images, the book follows the building of this history-rich city, offering a compelling look into the past for any longtime resident and every history buff of St. Petersburg.

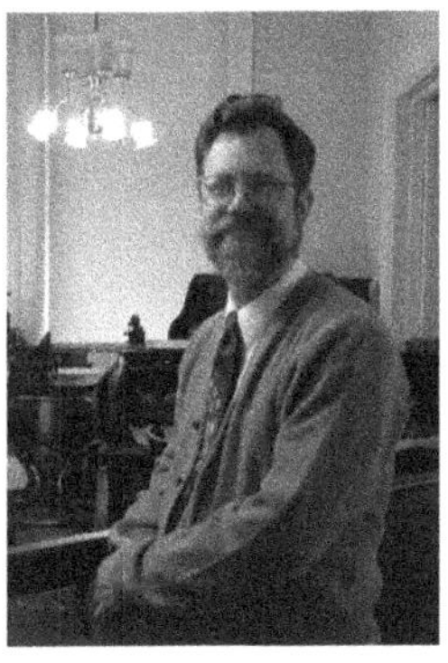

Andrew N. Edel, a retired twenty-year Air Force veteran from Jacksonville, Florida, spent his childhood in Tallahassee and north Florida. After retirement he enrolled in a Masters of Administration in Public History program at Florida State University. He has worked as independent research historian for museum exhibits: "San Marcos De Apalachee" for Florida State Parks, "The Florida Center of Political History & Governance" for the Florida Department of State, and "The Evolution of Justice in Florida" for the Supreme Court of Florida. Currently Edel holds three part-time positions—he is interpretive program specialist at the Historic Capitol Museum, Archivist of the Supreme Court of Florida, and a ranger and lighthouse historian at St. Marks National Wildlife Refuge—and is President of the Tallahassee Historical Society. Edel has also written *Historic Photos of Tallahassee,* also available from Turner Publishing.

WWW.TURNERPUBLISHING.COM

www.ingramcontent.com/pod-product-compliance
Lightning Source LLC
LaVergne TN
LVHW060613110826
845154LV00003B/81

* 9 7 8 1 6 8 3 3 6 9 9 9 8 *